THE SPANISH LANGUAGE

THE GREAT LANGUAGES

GENERAL EDITOR:

L. R. PALMER, M.A., D.PHIL., PH.D.
Professor of Comparative Philology in the University of Oxford

THE FRENCH LANGUAGE
By A. Ewert, M.A., Litt.D.

THE GERMAN LANGUAGE
By R. Priebsch, Ph.D. and W. E. Collinson, M.A., Ph.D.

THE SPANISH LANGUAGE, TOGETHER WITH PORTUGUESE,
CATALAN, BASQUE
By William F. Entwistle, M.A., Litt.D., Ll.D.

THE CHINESE LANGUAGE
By R. A. D. Forrest, M.A.

RUSSIAN AND SLAVONIC LANGUAGES
By William F. Entwistle M.A., Litt. D., and W. A. Morison, B.A., Ph.D.

THE LATIN LANGUAGE
By L. R. Palmer, M.A., D.Phil., Ph.D.

THE SANSKRIT LANGUAGE
By T. Burrow, M.A.

THE ROMANCE LANGUAGES
By W. D. Elcock, M.A., L.`es L., D. de L'U. Toulouse

THE ITALIAN LANGUAGE
By Bruno Migliorini, Dott. in Lettere
(abridged and re-cast by *T. G. Griffith, M.A., B.Litt.*)

In Preparation

THE ENGLISH LANGUAGE
By N. Davis, M.A.

THE GAELIC LANGUAGES
By Kenneth Jackson, M.A.

THE SCANDINAVIAN LANGUAGES
By Einar Haugen, M.A., Ph.D.

INDO-EUROPEAN LANGUAGES
By G. Bonfante, Ll.D.

THE HEBREW LANGUAGE
By G. R. Driver, M.A.

THE ANATOLIAN LANGUAGES
By R. A. Crossland, M.A.

THE GREEK LANGUAGE
By L. R. Palmer, M.A., D.Phil., Ph.D.

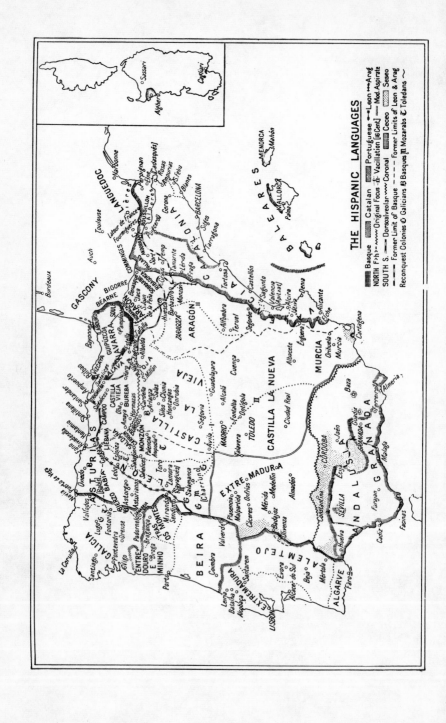

THE HISPANIC LANGUAGES

THE
SPANISH LANGUAGE

TOGETHER WITH

PORTUGUESE, CATALAN AND
BASQUE

by

WILLIAM J. ENTWISTLE, M.A.

FABER & FABER LIMITED

LONDON

*First published in 1936
by Faber and Faber Limited
24 Russell Square London W.C.1
Reprinted 1948 and 1951
Second edition 1962
Reprinted 1965 and 1969
Printed in Great Britain
by John Dickens and Co Limited, Northampton
All rights reserved*

SBN 571 06404 3

CONTENTS

MAPS

FOREWORD

Professor W. J. Entwistle died at Oxford in 1952, at the age of fifty-six. The second in order of his books, *The Spanish Language* was published in 1936; a quarter of a century later it remains unchallenged as the only competent and scholarly work on the subject to have been written in English.

These twenty-five years have nevertheless been a time of notable advance in Hispanic studies.

Writing in the early nineteen-thirties Entwistle was handicapped by the fact that much of the essential groundwork for a really comprehensive study of the Hispanic languages still remained to be done. There was no satisfactory etymological dictionary of Spanish and dialectal survey was confined to a few very limited areas. The former deficiency has now been superbly eliminated by Joan Corominas with the publication in four volumes of his *Diccionario crítico etimológico de la lengua castellana* (Berne, 1954-7), a pioneering work of the highest competence and fully Hispanic in scope. Almost simultaneously there appeared V. García de Diego's *Diccionario etimológico español e hispánico* (Madrid, 1954), less ambitious, lacking the critical element, but very serviceable. In the field of dialectology Entwistle had access to the Catalan explorations of A. Griera, including the four volumes of his linguistic atlas of Catalonia which appeared from 1923 to 1927 (a fifth, reaching the letter F, was published in 1939 before war brought the enterprise to an untimely end). There was no complete linguistic atlas of Spain, and this remains a much-felt need, though its absence has been partially compensated by an abundant growth of local monographs. Over the Aragonese dialect, to which Entwistle rightly attributes an important place in the history of Hispano-Romance, there had hung in the words of one scholar 'a conspiracy of silence'; yet even while Entwistle was wrestling with *The Spanish Language* at least four different dialectal explorers, unbeknown to one another, were perambulating the villages and hamlets of the Pyrenees, recording the last vestiges from surprised oldest inhabitants. A synthesis of the results obtained has been made more recently by Manuel Alvar (*El dialecto aragonés*, Madrid, 1953). For a knowledge of Leonese it is on the work of Menéndez Pidal that Entwistle was largely dependent; a full-scale study, of which sufficient has already been published to confirm its high quality, is being prepared at present by two former pupils of the Madrid school, Diego Catalán and Alvaro Galmés. For southern Spain there was little reliable information; here Manuel Alvar, physically translated from Saragossa to Granada, has undertaken a survey of Andalusia and promises an imminent linguistic atlas which could be a step towards an integrated linguistic atlas of Spain, conceived on a regional basis like the new French atlas. Two general studies of Spanish dialectology have meanwhile become available: V. García de Diego's *Manual de dialectología española* (Madrid, 1946) and the recent *Dialectología española* by A. Zamora Vicente (Madrid, 1960), which differs from the former in that it leaves aside Galician as belonging more properly to the Galician-Portuguese complex, and also Catalan, to concentrate more closely on what is historically Spanish.

In the medieval field, publication of twelfth- and thirteenth-century legal codes, the *Fueros*, particularly in the series of *Leges Hispanicae Medii Aevi* produced in Sweden under the direction of Gunnar Tilander, has considerably increased the volume of accessible early Spanish prose. No less worthy of remark is Tomás Navarro's collection of *Documentos lingüísticos de Aragón* (Syracuse, New York, 1957), a work originally intended as vol. ii of the *Documentos lingüísticos de España* (ed. Menéndez Pidal). An up-to-date anthology of linguistic texts intended for the use of students has recently been published in this country: *Textos lingüísticos del medioevo español*, by D. J. Gifford and F. W. Hodcroft, Oxford, 1959. For the history of Spanish pro-

nunciation there was available to Entwistle, though he does
not mention it, H. Gavel's *Essai sur l'évolution de la prononciation
du castillan depuis le XIVe. siècle* (Paris and Biarritz, 1920).
The late Amado Alonso has treated the same theme again,
from different view-points, in *De la pronunciación medieval a la
moderna en español* (Madrid, 1955). Tomás Navarro's *Pronunciación española*, several times re-edited, remains the
standard work for the modern tongue. Amado Alonso, his
unrelated namesake Dámaso Alonso, Rafael Lapesa and
many others have contributed studies of the linguistic usage
of later authors, though it is perhaps not entirely relevant
to dwell on these, since Entwistle's concern is with the
creation of Hispanic languages and their diffusion rather
than with subsequent literary manifestations.

Interest in Catalan, which perforce fell into abeyance for
a while, has been actively revived. We have a new and
fundamentally important *Gramática histórica catalana* by
A. Badía Margarit (Barcelona, 1951) and from J. Ruiz i
Calonja an *Història de la literatura catalana* (Barcelona, 1954).
For English-speaking students there is an introductory
Catalan Grammar, with a selection of extracts from Catalan
writers, by Joan Gili (2nd ed. Oxford, 1952).

Portuguese studies too have considerably expanded.
Manuel de Paiva Boléo founded in 1947 a *Revista Portuguesa
de Filologia*, of international range, and from his department
at the University of Coimbra come many pertinent contributions. In Portugal as in Spain, attention has turned to the
cultural and linguistic value of medieval legal texts; *A linguagem dos Foros de Castelo Rodrigo* by Luis F. Lindley Cintra
(Lisbon, 1959) contains a detailed examination of Leonese
and Galician-Portuguese in the thirteenth century. A
Brazilian scholar, Serafim da Silva Neto, has become known
during the past few years as a leading authority on Portuguese problems, with particular reference to his own country
(*Fontes do latim vulgar*, 3rd ed. 1956; *Manual de filologia
portuguesa*, 2nd ed. 1957; *História da língua portuguesa*, 1952-7;
etc., all from Rio de Janeiro).

Kurt Baldinger treats Peninsular development as a whole in *Die Herausbildung der Sprachräume auf der Pyrenäenhalbinsel* (Berlin, 1958), of which a translation into Spanish, *La formación de los dominios lingüísticos en la península ibérica*, is announced by the Editorial Gredos (Madrid). A critical bibliographical guide has been supplied by G. Rohlfs, under the title *Manual de filología hispánica* (Bogotá, 1957). In this wider field Yakov Malkiel has produced a number of studies primarily of a lexical character, both as separate monographs and in the review *Romance Philology* which he edits from the University of California. The *Bulletin of Hispanic Studies*, edited at Liverpool by A. E. Sloman, has raised its sights and become more representative of all Hispanic interests. And last not least, if we may use the favourite English expression of our foreign colleagues, the annual publication of the Modern Humanities Research Association, *The Year's Work in Modern Language Studies* (ed. W. H. Barber), of which in its present form Entwistle himself was the first editor and for long the guiding inspiration, grows ever richer in detail and may justly be claimed as indispensable for whoever would take a more than passing interest in the study of modern European languages.

For such a person, as these brief comments may have implied, the Hispanic world alone offers an *abîme de science*. It is an abyss of which Entwistle was almost painfully conscious. 'I suppose you do not feel, after each new book read, as full of shamed ignorance as I do', so he wrote in a letter addressed to me a few weeks before his death. In a relatively short span of life his 'shamed ignorance' was a goad which drove him to seek knowledge in many directions, to intellectual forays of which his various books preserve the record. *The Spanish Language*, the most intimately related to his activity as a teacher, is probably the one by which he will be best remembered.

Hampstead   W. D. Elcock
September, 1960

Note by the Editor

Professor W. D. Elcock prepared this Foreword shortly
before his death, and made minor corrections to the text,
so that Professor Entwistle's book could be reprinted. I have
shortened the Foreword and altered some of the revisions
in order to minimize disturbances to the text.

Oxford
March, 1962   L. R. Palmer

CHAPTER I

THE LANGUAGES OF THE SPANISH PENINSULA

The purpose of this book is to give an account of the Peninsular group of Great Languages. The epithet 'great' can have no purely linguistic meaning. To the philologist all languages are of equal interest; they all contribute to our knowledge of the great human fact of Language. What each has to display is not equally essential, since many belong to vast speech-families and so in the main repeat the same or similar phenomena. Outside these families there exist, however, some languages which are unique. They do not reiterate the experience of many others, but, in their independence, offer the student an unusual wealth of fresh facts. Such a language is Basque. For peers it does not admit the circumjacent Romance tongues, French and Spanish, which are comparatively recent immigrants into its neighbourhood. It is comparable, in its antiquity and originality, not even with Latin, but with primeval Indo-European and the ancestral stocks of the great speech-families. For these qualities Basque draws to itself the eyes of the most proficient and broad-minded students of language, who find in its structure alternative and original solutions for the problems of human expression. In respect of its uniqueness the Basque language merits the description 'great'.

Greatness, however, is not a philological quality, but social and historical. Richness of thought-content and ample diffusion, singly or in combination, confer prestige on a language. The speech of the Athenians in the day of Euripides and Plato, enriched with the thoughts and rhythms of Homer, the lyrists, the tragedians and the historians, was already more copious and beautiful than any tongue before or since, though it was confined within part of one peninsula and some adjacent islands. The conquests of Alexander made it also territorially great. With less cultural experience the language of imperial Rome exercised in its time, and increasingly exercises, a portentous territorial domination. Extensive and intensive greatness are not necessarily combined; the cases of Bantu and Swahili may be cited as proof. But in general, use over a wide area and by millions of speakers endows a language with depth and experience. Languages of rich thought-content tend to propagate themselves over the largest areas, and conversely they come to know, like the travelled Odysseus, 'the minds and cities of many men'. High social and cultural value expands the use of French and Italian wherever the decencies and loveliness of life are esteemed; English, Spanish and Portuguese are of enormous spatial and numerical importance. These languages do business on the oceans and converse with the ends of the earth, and by such intercourse they have been enriched with a marvellous booty of experience.

Such is the greatness, then, of the Peninsular languages. They are not philologically unique, like Basque, for they are but forms assumed by Latin in particular areas. Even within the Latin group, Spanish, Portuguese and Catalan show fewer ramifications and innovations than a restless tongue such as French. Theirs is a wealth of thought, art, and, above all, human experience. The genius of Cervantes and Camões, of an infinite number of playwrights, novelists, moralists, mystics, has entered into the innermost fibres of these tongues. In their expansive and colonizing urge and their contact with American, African and Asiatic races, Spanish and Portuguese are supreme among Romance Languages. But for the additions they made to the Latin-speaking world in the age of the great discoveries the frontiers of Romania would have shown a permanent contraction since Roman times. Summoning, before Canning, the New World to redress the balance of the Old, Spain and Portugal brought into being that equipoise of Latin and Germanic speech which is a characteristic mark of western civilization.

The expansion of Spanish and Portuguese was principally the work of the great discoverers who followed Columbus to America and Gama to Calicut. Their feats have sometimes been deemed fortuitous, particularly in the case of Spain, which was preoccupied, during the Middle Ages, with merely European interests. In the case of Portugal, the circum-navigation of Africa was a policy deliberately conceived in one great mind, that of Henry the Navigator, and obstinately followed for sixty years at great cost in life and treasure. Columbus, who was prone to exaggerate, perhaps, estimated in 1492 that half the population of the small kingdom had been used up on the African adventure. Gama's successful voyage and the thalassocracy set up by Almeida and Albuquerque are immediate consequences of a great idea courageously applied. Portugal had no Moors on its soil in the fifteenth century, and one of the Navigator's motives was to carry the war across the Straits, not by a frontal attack, but by encircling the rear of Islam. Spain, at that time, still had to reduce the Moslem remnant in Granada. Yet Spain had already extended overseas in a south-westerly direction by occupying the Canary Islands (1402 ff.), and could be expected to pursue an expansionist policy beyond the Straits. The Aragonese monarchs, who were also freed from Moorish complications on their own soil, extended their dominion over Sardinia, Sicily, Naples, Athens and the Morea in the fourteenth century, following a course of Mediterranean ambitions; and in consequence of their action Sicily and Naples maintained at least a family connection with Spain until the unification of Italy last century. We may take it therefore that expansion and colonization are not accidents, but characteristic marks of Spanish history. The experience gained in 'populating' devastated lands, won in the early Middle Ages from the Moors, gave the Hispanic peoples an aptitude for conquest and colonization in which their only modern rivals are the English. It is one of many resemblances between Britain and the Spanish Peninsula which constitute a just claim for mutual study and appreciation.

Determined by the circumstances of the age of great discoveries, the extension of Spanish and Portuguese over the globe corresponds closely with the world as known at the close of that period. The Portuguese extension is African and Asiatic, and as it was essentially maritime, it has made permanent settlements only in islands and ports—Cape Verde, Portuguese Guinea, Santo Tomé, Daman, Diu, Goa, Ceylon, Malacca, Macau, Ternate, Tidore and the Spice Islands. Landward territories like Angola and Moçambique are the result of capitalizing the vague coastal dominion of the earlier explorers under the influence of the nineteenth-century scramble for Africa. Early settlements in Brazil were also of the factory and insular type. Extension into the interior came partly as a result of a change of method in the eighteenth century, when colonization ceased to be conquest and exploitation, but rather occupation of the ground; partly also because the Amazonian forest converted eastern Brazil into a kind of vast island, immune on the land side from attack. The Portuguese penetrated to the edge of this area, to the line where began the Andine dominion of Spain. Spain occupied with her arms and her language the other half of South America, with the sickle of Antillian Islands (though losing many of the smaller ones to France and England in the eighteenth century); she occupied also Mexico and Central America, together with an undefined area to the north of the Río Grande—an area of conquistadors, missionaries, and sailors. Thus in New Mexico and Arizona there is still an area of Spanish speech, assaulted by the dominant English; but in former times the Spanish claim was thinly asserted over a much wider area. Florida was Spanish, together with some coast forts further north. Contracting towards the Mississippi delta, the indefinite frontier ran far enough northward to give Spanish names to a number of western States—Nevada, Texas, California, Oregon (?), to towns—San Francisco, Los Angeles, Santa Fe, Sacramento, rivers—Colorado, Grande, Verde, Brazos, mountains, islands and straits. The last-named extend as far as the Alaskan border.

Only Basque has shown no urge to expansion, but it displays the characteristic of tenacity, the prime condition on which colonies are retained; and in the fifteenth century Basque whalers established something like a thalassocracy in the waters of the Atlantic.

To estimate the number of persons speaking one or other of the Peninsular languages is not easy, and widely varying figures have been given. Census returns for American states are not always available, and it is uncertain how large a deduction is to be made for aborigines totally or partially unacquainted with the language of their rulers. To commence with the smallest, some 550,000 speakers have been attributed to Basque, of whom some 450,000 reside on Spanish soil. The number is decreasing as the territory contracts. Bilbao is a town that can no longer be deemed Basque-speaking, as it was sixty years ago, and the loss of speakers has been estimated at 70,000 in the same period. Catalan is spoken still in Roussillon, since the primitive frontier between France and the Peninsula followed the line of the Corbières, the northern fork of the Pyrenean chain. The language occupies all Catalonia and the Balearic Islands, the coastal half of Valencia, and the single town of Alghero in Sardinia. It was formerly in use in Cagliari, and in medieval times must have had a considerable official standing in the whole island and in Sicily. A total of 5,410,000 has been claimed for Catalan, which includes the 10,000 Algherese and some 100,000 who have emigrated to America and still use their native tongue as a means of private communication. In Roussillon, the use of Catalan runs concurrently with the official and cultural use of French; and from the Alberes southward educated men are to be deemed bilingually Spanish.

About sixteen and a half million Spanish subjects have Spanish for their mother-tongue. The remainder—Catalans, Galicians and Basques—use the language for official purposes, and comparatively few are to be reckoned wholly unacquainted with the dominant speech. Thus we may reckon as speakers of Spanish the 24,242,039 inhabitants of Spain

and the Canary Islands.[1] Spanish dependencies are found
on the Moroccan coast (especially Tetuan, Ceuta, Melilla,
Alhucemas) and in Río de Oro, Adrar, Ifni, Guinea, Annobon,
Corisco, the Great and Little Elobey. Almost a million persons live in these places, but they do not proportionately
augment the number of Spanish-speakers. On the other hand,
along the northern littoral of Africa and in the Balkans
(Salonica, Constantinople, Üsküb, Monastir, etc.) there are
still some 200,000 Jews who use ancient varieties of Castilian,
derived from the days before their expulsion in 1492. In the
Philippine Islands there is a Castilian literature in prose and
verse, and 660,000 persons claim a knowledge of the language,
though the use of English is rapidly growing. North of the
Mexican frontier there must be between 150,000 and 250,000
speakers of Spanish. The estimated total population of Mexico
and Central America is 22,663,672; of the Spanish-speaking
Antilles (Cuba, Dominican Republic, Puerto Rico), 6,555,000;
of the Caribbean and Andine states (Bolivia, Colombia,
Ecuador, Peru, Venezuela), 23,744,557; of Chile, 4,287,445;
of the Plate republics (Argentina, Paraguay, Uruguay),
14,918,900. While all these millions are ruled in Spanish,
they do not all know the language; and there are heavy
deductions to be made in Mexico, Guatemala, Ecuador,
Peru, Bolivia and Paraguay especially, before we can reach
the linguistic census. Roughly speaking, there are at least
85,000,000 persons who habitually speak Spanish as their
first or second tongue, and about 100,000,000 in its penumbra.
The figure is the highest for a Romance language, and most
directly comparable with the hundred and sixty millions who
use English.

The numerical strength of Portuguese is lower, but still
stands high among Romance languages. In Portugal, Madeira
and the Azores there are 6,825,883 persons, and in the
Galician provinces of Spain another 2,180,000. Portuguese
possessions include almost nine million souls, of whom six
and a half million are found in Angola and Moçambique.

[1] *The Statesman's Year Book* (London, Macmillan, 1935).

These latter provinces furnish probably 35,500 Portuguese speakers. Portuguese Asia contains 1,211,507, scattered in islands and ports, and there is some use made of the language in Ceylon. Brazil is estimated to include 43,323,660 inhabitants, subject to a very slight deduction for the Indians of the Amazon unfamiliar with the official tongue, and another for unassimilated immigrants. At least 53,000,000 persons speak Portuguese or a dialect of the same language, and sixty millions are governed through Portuguese.

Remembering that Portuguese and Spanish are closely related and mutually intelligible tongues, it is not unreasonable to claim that the Peninsular group of languages has power over 150,000,000 souls. It controls all South America (save the Guianas), Central America, most of the Antilles, and points along the African and southern Asiatic littoral. With English, Russian, Japanese and Chinese, Spanish makes a ring round the mighty Pacific; with English, Spanish and Portuguese are valid languages of intercourse on the southern Atlantic; and Portuguese occupies key-ports on the Indian Ocean. They are oceanic languages of continental magnitude.

This vast extension in area and population is mirrored in the enrichment and diversification of the languages. The first impressions of the newly found continents, their strange birds, beasts and customs, their rites and polity, were conveyed to Europe and the world through the Spanish and Portuguese languages; these tongues still contain what is, in many ways, the most accurate series of correspondences with the native terms. They have exercised, conversely, a powerful influence on the languages they encountered, mingling them, breaking down their forms, and augmenting their vocabulary. Many varieties of 'Creole' speech have arisen. The nett result of this linguistic experience is that when once we raise the eyes of our minds off the single continent of Europe, it is from Spanish and Portuguese, apart from our own tongue, that we have most to learn. Entirely congruent with Spanish experience is the fact that the first scientific catalogue of the languages of the world, that of

Hervás y Panduro, should have been the work of a Spanish scholar. Not only do the Peninsular languages reflect the conditions found in so vast a portion of the earth, but they contain evidence of experiments in colonization, transient states of society, and a cultural equilibrium which is rather coming into existence than already established. They contain, as it were, some sort of augury for the future.

The Peninsular group is determined not merely by philological considerations. Basque is philologically isolated, and Catalan has been deemed by a majority of experts to stand rather closer to Provençal than to Spanish. But the four languages have lived together for many centuries in a sharply defined area. They enjoy a kind of symbiosis. They offer similar solutions to the same linguistic problem, indicating a common mental attitude in their speakers. They have experienced the same influences under the same conditions, though each has also its own history. Despite the differences between the literary languages, no frontier line can be drawn between the three Romance tongues, which merge into each other over wide bands of country, except in their more recently conquered southern extensions. The instinct for the positive and concrete is as marked in Basque as in Castilian. The phonetic bases of all four languages present much agreement, as, for instance, the fricative values assigned to *b d g* and the general forward articulation. In other respects Spanish, Portuguese and Catalan offer nuances. If we consider Castilian as characterized by a regular alternation of vowels and consonants, then Portuguese appears as predominantly vocalic, and Catalan as predominantly consonantal; though this does not prevent Portuguese from possessing a rich consonantal, and Catalan a subtle vocalic, system. Fundamentally the same material is subjected to three differing rhythms. Romanization, the Moorish invasions, the great discoveries, humanism, Italian and French influences have left similar impressions on the three Romance tongues, so that their vocabularies largely coincide. Even Basque has experienced a romanization of its lexicon, and one of a generally Spanish complexion. There is a high common measure of agreement between the Peninsular languages, though there is no identity. Unity has never been achieved; only hegemony. Even the theocracy of the Philips brought no more than a single ruler of independent states. The centre of Peninsular balance has, however, always occupied the same area, though the precise point has shifted between Córdoba, León, Burgos and Toledo. There has thus been no doubt that the Castilian point of view is central, and others peripheral and divergent. Catalonia falls away from the Meseta to look towards the Mediterranean: it is related to Provence, reaches out hands to Italy, and aspires (or aspired) to Mediterranean empire and trade; but at the same time Catalonia remains indivisibly part of the Peninsula. The amphitheatre of Lisbon has the Atlantic for its stage: it sees English ships and the highway to India and Brazil. Navarre is a land of mountainous cup-depressions (*navas*); Galicia, of *rías* and valleys; Andalusia, of the Guadalquivir and Genil *vegas* and the coast lands that face Africa. All these divergent interests make for variety in Peninsular life, and therefore in Peninsular languages; but they have not always been equally prominent, and the unification of the whole area has more than once been within sight.

Language is the repository of man's experience. It contains a record of what is normal and of what has occurred but once. Were it possible fully to analyse the languages of our study, we should doubtless be able to present a portrait of the peoples more intimate and exact than that which we see in their literatures. But we should require a more precise psychological method than is at present at our disposal. It has been possible to cull from the Spanish language, for instance, evidence of realism, courtesy, stoicism, fancy, impulsiveness, etc. But a phenomenon like the 'courtly style' of the sixteenth and seventeenth centuries is itself complex. That *usted* 'you' was originally *vuestra merced* 'your worship' is certain, but its use was as much to exact a corresponding honorific as to show deference to another person; and it has lost all implications of 'courtliness' since the Golden Age, to become merely a symbol of formality. Indeed it has gone so far as to become familiar and suspect in some varieties of American Spanish, so that new devices have been adopted to indicate respect. Moreover, though *usted* represents an experience common to all Spaniards, at least in a given epoch, there are other words which must be deemed exceptional. To give meaning to the word *quijotismo* 'quixotry' required the divine accident of *Don Quijote* and Cervantes' genius, while by *quijotizar* 'to defy public opinion with the sang-froid of a Don Quixote' Sr Unamuno indicates hostility to the common norm. Yet more, the linguistic experience is not necessarily ethical; it may have its basis in plain fact. Thus there is a small, but definite, nautical element in American varieties of Spanish (e.g. *amarrar* for *atar*, 'to tie a hawser' becoming simply 'to tie'), which suggests colonists seeking, while still on shipboard, to adopt the colonial pose. So the qualitative interpretation of these languages is one which lies within the more ample historical account of their growth and the influences affecting their development; and it is on the historical statement, though in mere outline, that I wish to dwell. Such an account is often described as the 'external' history of the language, as opposed to the 'internal' history of its sounds, forms and constructions; but there is reason to reject the invidious adjective. The analyses of sounds, forms and constructions separately are partial studies which look forward to the history of the language as a whole. They are essential to the training of the philologist, but he should also not fail to strive towards the whole of which these studies are part. It is this whole which concerns the general reader and student of literature, who must strive to acquire a sense of phases of development in the speech and an appreciation of differences in its texture.

In view of these considerations this book imposes its own plan. A sketch is first attempted of the Peninsula before romanization so as to indicate the linguistic conditions encountered by the Romans. Basque survives from that epoch,

either as representing a widespread 'Iberian' speech or on
a narrower basis, and I describe Basque chiefly by its contacts
with the Romance languages, its successors. The latter are
forms taken by Latin in different portions of the Peninsula;
the primitive conditions are in no sense the foundation of
Spanish Romance, since they have no relevance except in so
far as adopted into the Latin of Spain. With an account of
Spanish Latinity the main theme of the book is proposed, and
suggestions are made as to possible causes of the later diversity
of languages. The earliest of these bifurcations is that which
drew apart Catalan and Ibero-Romance. Catalan therefore
occupies the fourth chapter, and is studied down to the present
day. The remaining chapters are devoted to Ibero-Romance
in its two leading forms: Spanish and Portuguese. As this
study is pivoted on Spanish, much of what is common to
both tongues, and even to both and Catalan, is described
under the rubric of Spanish. For instance, the strong Arabic
element in all three tongues is treated in association with the
Mozarabic dialect of Old Spanish. In three stages we follow
the rise of Castilian, so as to understand why Castilian, and
not Mozarabic or Leonese, has come to be standard Spanish,
though in the older periods Castilian was at variance with
common Hispanic speech-habits; we watch the standardization of this Castilian-Spanish under the influence of literature,
and its enrichment at various periods; and we note the effect
of the American adventure on the language, and the traffic
with European and aboriginal tongues. In two more chapters
we see how Portuguese-Galician bifurcated from the central
dialects at a relatively late date, how they themselves separated, and how Portuguese acquired a rich literature and
maintained its cultural independence; briefly we note also
what effects have been produced on Portuguese by the expansion of the language in Africa, Asia and Brazil. An
anthology which would fairly illustrate this diversity of
Hispanic languages and dialects would be more bulky than
the format of this book permits. It must be left to the reader's
initiative. No attempt is made to give the systematic account

of phonology and morphology which can be obtained in several excellent and well-known text-books, since this work treats only of those facts which have most historical significance; but a tabular summary of comparative phonology is appended, so as to serve for a first reference.

In writing this book I have sought to keep in mind the languages as they can now be heard. It is an account of modern Spanish, Portuguese and Catalan, and how these have come to be what they are. This is not a study of Vulgar Latin in the Peninsula, and nothing is to be gained by picking on medieval or hypothetical forms which would be unfamiliar to the reader, save when attempting the description of a particular period in past time; but on the other hand, I hope attention will be called to the amount of Old Spanish which may be found to-day in use by archaic dialects. This method brings as much of the subject as possible under a listener's personal observation, and should involve the least admixture of conjecture. Lastly, I have endeavoured to choose examples from the most obvious and fundamental elements of the Peninsular speeches, risking a charge of platitude. In constructing a history of the Peninsular languages the best evidence for conclusions is what is self-evident.

The reader is recommended to study the treatises of Sr Menéndez Pidal on subjects connected with Spanish philology, and particularly his *Manual de gramática histórica española* and *Orígenes del español* (Madrid, 1926), to which I am deeply indebted in this book. His article 'Filología (idiomas y dialectos españoles)' in *España* (Madrid, 1925) is the treatment of this subject which stands closest to that which I am attempting. Useful also are the articles in Gröber's *Grundriss der romanischen Philologie* (by Baist, Cornu, Saroïhandy, etc.), and the comparative sketch of the Peninsular languages in E. Bourciez, *Éléments de linguistique romane*. F. Hanssen's *Spanische Grammatik auf historischer Grundlage* (Halle, 1910; Spanish translation, 1913) contains syntax as well as phonology and morphology, and the same is true of Sr Menéndez Pidal's *Cantar de mío Cid*, I, ii: *Gramática* (Madrid, 1908). The standard inventory of modern Spanish idiom is R. J. Cuervo's revision of A. Bello's *Gramática castellana*. A number of suggestive details are discussed in R. Lenz, *La Oración y sus partes* (Madrid, 1925). Spanish has received an 'idealistic' analysis from E. Lerch in *Handbuch der Spanienkunde* (Frankfurt a.M. 1932). For Portuguese consult particularly J. Leite de Vasconcellos, *Opúsculos* (Coimbra, 1928 ff.), *Lições de Filologia Portuguesa* (Lisbon, 1926) and *Esquisse d'une dialectologie portugaise* (Paris, 1901), together with J. J. Nunes, *Gramática histórica portuguêsa* (Lisbon, 1919). For Catalan there is A. Griera's *Gramàtica històrica del català antic* (Barcelona, 1931) and W. Meyer-Lübke's *Das Katalanische* (Heidelberg, 1925). Useful also are A. Zauner's *Altspanisches Elementarbuch* and J. Huber's *Altportugiesisches Elementarbuch* (both from Heidelberg).

Texts illustrative of linguistic history may be seen in Menéndez Pidal's *Orígenes* and his *Documentos lingüísticos*, J. Leite de Vasconcellos's *Textos arcaicos* (Lisbon, 1923), J. D. M. Ford's *Old Spanish Readings*, and W. Giese's *Anthologie der geistigen Kultur auf der Pyrenäen-Halbinsel (Mittelalter)* (Hamburg, 1927).

The standpoint of this book resembles that of O. Jespersen's *Growth and Structure of the English Language* (8th ed. Leipzig, 1935) and W. von Wartburg's *Évolution et structure de la langue française* (Leipzig, 1934).

The current bibliography of linguistic studies referring to the Spanish Peninsula is to be found in the quarterly *Revista de Filología Española* and in the annual *Year's Work in Modern Language Studies*. These works may excuse me from attempting a formal bibliography.

I take this opportunity of thanking Professor González-Llubera, of Belfast, for his great kindness in reading the book in its first draft and suggesting improvements. I thank also my colleague Mr A. A. Rodrigues, Lecturer in Portuguese in the University of Oxford, for similar courtesies. Neither gentleman is responsible for any blemishes that may remain in the book. I desire also to tender my respectful homage and thanks to my distinguished master in these studies, Sr R. Menéndez Pidal, Litt.D. (Oxon.), who has generously permitted me to make use of his innumerable additions to Spanish philological science. He has discovered much of the truth, and we who write after him, if we would wish to speak the truth, cannot do otherwise than repeat his conclusions and demonstrations.

To my friend, Professor A. Ewert, I am indebted for courteously reading the proofs.

CHAPTER II

BEFORE THE ROMANS

When the legions of Scipio Africanus entered the Peninsula by its north-eastern extremity to add the Spains to the Roman dominion, they discovered the land in the power of many masters, several of whom were immigrants like themselves. A few Greek trading-ports descended the eastern coast, and were then continued by the more flourishing Phœnician factories of the far south. The Carthaginians had established an uneasy lordship over the whole south and centre of the Peninsula, and were in contact with the Celtiberian tribes, powerful when they acted together. These tribes, by their name, bore witness to the presence of Celts, who had been mentioned by Herodotus as early as the fifth century B.C. The second half of the word—'Iberians'—was of a more indefinite value: it meant at least 'persons dwelling near the mouth of the Iberus or Ebro', and at most 'the inhabitants of the Iberian peninsula'. An intermediate extension of the term designates an 'Iberian' racial bloc, surrounded by others still less perfectly known to science. Thus we hear of Tartessians, Lusitanians, Gallæci and Vaccæi, who may not have been 'Iberians'. One of these groups survives to this

---

The shortest introductions to Basque are H. Schuchardt, *Primitiæ linguæ Vasconum* (Halle, 1923) and J. van Eys, *The Basque Language* (London, 1883). A definitive grammar is H. Gavel's *Grammaire Basque*, I. *Phonétique, Parties du discours autres que le verbe* (Bayonne, 1929). There are many discussions of the Basque verb, mostly inventories, notably K. Bouda, *Das transitive und das intransitive Verbum des Baskischen* (Amsterdam, 1933). On pronunciation there is a useful article by T. Navarro Tomás, 'Pronunciación guipuzcoana', *Homenaje a Menéndez Pidal*. R. M. Azkue's *Dictionnaire Basque-espagnol-français* (Bilbao, 1905–1906) is the best complete lexicon. For further information consult the *Revue Internationale des Études Basques* and works by Schuchardt, Vinson, and Uhlenbeck.

day in its ancient emplacement and speaking its ancient language: the Basques. The Vascones of classical times have given their name to Biscay, the Basque Provinces and Gascony. Their frontiers have contracted, and their language has suffered from, or profited by, contact with the neighbouring Latin tongues; but it is essentially a survival from pre-classical antiquity. A description of the main features of Basque therefore will give us a platform for discussing the linguistic state of Spain before the Romans.

BASQUE

Basque is known as *Vascuence* to the Spaniards, but as *Euskera* to the Basques. There are seven independent provinces protected by the Pyrenean ranges, and as they have known no other unity than that of language, they are wont to call themselves by its name: *Euskalerri*, the people (*herri*) who speak *Euskera*. The unit of society is the 'house' (*etxe-a*), and millennia of isolation without literary or cultural control have split Basque into numerous dialects, which are not mutually intelligible, such as Biscayan, Guipúzcoan, Lower and Upper Navarrese, Labourdin and Souletin; with at least twenty-five subdialects, and local differences for each village and even for each generation of speakers. Under such circumstances only a summary description of the language can be effected here. It has been known adequately since the publication of Dechepare's poems in 1545 and Leizarraga's Basque New Testament in 1571; but we have medieval jottings by the traveller Arnold von Harff in the fifteenth century, the pilgrim guide to Compostela in the twelfth century, and the *Glosas Emilianenses* in the tenth (two verbs),[1] which show that the language was then substantially what it is now. Basque before the tenth century of our era is territory for conjecture.

The Basque accent differs from that of the Latin languages by being movable; it is transferred from one syllable to

[1] See R. Menéndez Pidal, *Orígenes del Español*, p. 492.

another according to the structure of the phrase and the requirements of emphasis. When a word is cited separately there tends to be an accentuation of the final syllable. In present-day practice speakers of Basque are influenced by the habits of their neighbours, and in the Spanish provinces there is a perceptible castilianization of the accentual scheme. At any rate, so malleable an accent constitutes no obstacle to the adoption of a foreign system.

The vowel system is very simple. There are only five vowels, as in Spanish, and they have much the same values. The vowels *e o* are not divided into an open and a closed series as in French, Italian, Catalan and Portuguese [e ɛ o ɔ], but they allow of considerable variation under the influence of neighbouring vowels and consonants. Thus *e* has a range almost from *i* to *a*, and seems rather more open in general than Castilian *e*. Middle vowels, so frequent in French, are absent from Basque apart from the *ü* of the Souletin dialect which is doubtless due to the influence of French and Provençal. There are no nasal vowels, but only a slight nasalization in the vicinity of *n m*.

The system of consonants agrees mainly with that of Spanish. The Basque *f* has attracted most attention. It is present in all dialects, but it nowhere appears indigenous. In many cases it is found in foreign words, and its presence has been held to be due to French or Spanish influence. Romance words in *f*, moreover, tend to be reproduced with a Basque *p*, as FILU 'thread' B. *piru*, which hints at an even greater aversion from *f* in past times. But there are a few words, particularly in French Basque, which are apparently indigenous and yet show *f*. All that can be asserted is that the acquisition of a foreign *f* is not of insuperable difficulty for Basques. *V* does not exist in Basque as a labiodental sound, the voiced equivalent of *f*, but is identified, as in Spanish, with *b*. Akin to *f* is the aspirate *h*. This is now wanting in Spanish Basque dialects, but occurs in French Basque, and is also frequently employed to denote an aspirated pronunciation of some other consonant, *p t k l n r*.

So we have equivalents like *erri herri* 'people', or conventional distinctions like *aur* 'child' *haur* 'this', and the Labourdin aspirations *ikhusi* 'see' *ethorri* 'come' *ekharri* 'bring'. It is probable that there was a weakly aspirated *h* in medieval Spanish Basque also, which accounts for such spellings in the thirteenth and fourteenth centuries as *Harriaga Harrigorría* from (*h*)*arri* 'stone'. There is no evidence that Basques treated *h* as the nearest equivalent for Latin F, though such a substitution is not inherently improbable.

The language shows reluctance to use initial voiceless *p t k*, with the result that *p* also is of infrequent occurrence. *K* is much used in suffixes, and it permutes also with *h* and may then disappear. In *b d g* Basque, like the three Peninsular Romance languages, recognizes two series of consonants: an occlusive order in absolute initial positions or after a nasal and some other consonants [b d g], and a fricative order in 'weak' positions [ƀ đ ǥ]. When final, as in Old Spanish and Catalan, they become unvoiced. There are many fricative and affricate consonants, all of which can be paralleled from the Peninsular Romances. The sibilants are three: a cacuminal *s* pronounced with the tip of the tongue on the gums [ś], a voiceless *z* with the tip of the tongue on the lower teeth [s], and the palatal *x* which has the value of English *sh* [š]. When the tongue makes a momentary contact before these sounds, they pass into the affricates *ts tz tx* [ŝ ŝ ĉ]. The last is represented by *ch* in Spanish borrowings, as *Echeverría* from *etxe* 'house' and *berri* 'new'. 'Impure' *s*, that is an initial *s* followed by a consonant, is not tolerated in Basque, but a vowel is prefixed, generally *e* as in Spanish but sometimes *i*: *esker* 'thanks', *ezker* (Soul. *ixker*) 'left' Sp. *izquierdo* Cat. *esquerre*. Similarly the language does not tolerate an initial *r*, but prefixes *a* or *e*: *Erramon* Sp. *Ramón*, *errege* REGE 'king'. An initial *r* is strongly vibrated, and this vibrant *r* (written *ŕ* or *rr*) generates a fugitive vowel, as it also does in the history of many words in Spanish, Portuguese and Catalan. There is also a weak fricative *r* [ɹ] in such words as *iri* 'city', *ur* 'water'. Weak *r* is not far distant from *l*, and

2

this explains the uncertainty as to which consonant is the original in the suffixes *la ra*. For *iri* ancient place-names show *ili*. The pronunciation of *j* depends on geography. The French provinces pronounce *j* as in French and Older Spanish [ž or ĵ], but in the Spanish provinces the modern Spanish [χ] is normal. [š] also occurs. Spanish Basque, like Spanish, rejects final *-m* in favour of *-n*.

There are one or two general features of Basque pronunciation. One is a facility for palatalizing consonants; not only *ñ l* as in Spanish *ñ ll*, but also *l d*. The effect is frequently that of a Spanish diminutive. Basque reduces double consonants to singles and resolves groups. Peculiarly Basque are the numerous metatheses of consonants, as *bage = gabe* 'without', and the interchange of consonants in accordance with tables of permutation, as *m b* in *mezpera* OSp. *viespera* VESPERE 'eve'.

Basque vocabulary bears witness to the tenacity with which its speakers have clung to the essentials of their language in the face of overwhelming pressure from highly civilized peoples. Such pressure was exerted even before Roman times by the Celts. The Celtic influence is debatable, but it is probable that their example helped the Basques to a better family organization (*andre* 'young woman' Celt. **andera* OIr. *ainder* OFr. *andier* MFr. *landier* Eng. *andiron*; possibly *aita* 'father' OIr. *athir* with Celtic loss of *p-* PATRE), and to name certain animals better known to the Celts ((*h*)*artz* 'bear' OIr. *art* W. *arth*; *ork*(*h*)*atz* 'roe' Celt. *iorkos* W. *iwrch*; *izoki* 'salmon' Asturian *esquin* OIr. *eó iach* W. *eog* ESOX). The Basques use the vigesimal system in reckoning: *ogei* 20 *berrogei* 40 = 2 × 20 *irurogei laurogei*. This is comparable with Fr. *quatre-vingts*, and may be of Celtic provenance. One of the oldest Basque verbs, *ekarri* 'bring', may be of Celtic origin, and so connected through CARRU CARRICARE with Eng. *carry*.

Though the Celtic element is small, the Latin and Romance influence is greater than in any other language that has maintained its independent character, such as German or Albanian, and it gives the Basque lexicon a markedly

Romance appearance. Almost all terms of administration, Christian rites and usages, thought and culture are drawn from the Latin reservoir. At the present day the invasion continues in the speech of younger Basques, who discard native terms for a foreign equivalent lightly adapted to Basque speech-habits. Striking instances of such changes are *seme* 'son' SEMEN, *gorputz* 'body' CORPUS, *boronte* 'forehead' FRONTE. Administrative terms of Latin origin are *lege* 'law' LEGE, *errege* 'king' REGE. Of ecclesiastical origin are *eliza* 'church' ECCLESIA Fr. *église*, *gurutz* 'cross' CRUCE, *aphezpiku* 'bishop' EPISCOPU, *pake bake* 'peace' PACE, *besta* 'festival' FESTA. Educational words are also ecclesiastical in inspiration: *eskola* 'school' SCHOLA, *liburu* 'book' LIBRU. Words denoting a high standard of social intercourse, trade and communications, stone and gypsum architecture, textiles, milling, blacksmith's work, agriculture and viniculture, fruits, domestic economy and cooking, etc., are generally of Latin or Romance provenance. The names of some most common animals are striking evidence of this indebtedness: *a(h)ate* 'duck' ANATE, *antzar* 'goose' ANSERE, *asto* 'ass' ASINU, *zamaɹi* 'horse' (larger than the Basque breed *zaldi*) SAGMARIU. All abstract terms are foreign to Basque: *zentsu* 'meaning' SENSU, *borondate* 'will' VOLUNTATE, *gauza* 'thing' CAUSA, *arima* 'soul' ANIMA, *asturu* 'luck' ASTRU, *zeru* 'heaven' CAELU.

The Latin element in Basque resembles Spanish or Provençal rather than French, but is notable for its archaic character. Between vowels *p t k* are conserved, as in the valleys of Upper Aragón, and unaccented vowels do not suffer apocope as in the Romance languages: *aphezpiku* EPISCOPU Fr. *évêque* Sp. *obispo* Ptg. *bispo* Cat. *bisbe* 'bishop'. The Latinisms of Basque are also drawn from an old stratum of the language, which has shown little power to survive into Romance: *atxeter* 'doctor' ARCHIATER, as well as *mediku miriku* MEDICU, *seme* 'son' SEMEN, *opus* 'physical effort' OPUS.[1]

[1] See especially G. Rohlfs, 'Baskische Kultur im Spiegel des lateinischen Lehnwortes', *Voretzsch-Festschrift* (Halle, 1927).

When we turn from the sounds and words of Basque to the forms taken by the words in preparation for the sentence, we are arrested by the extraordinary appearance of the Basque verb, and in particular by its 'passivity'. It cannot be said yet to have yielded to analysis. Humboldt alleged that there were 216 Basque conjugations, and Schuchardt amassed 50,000 verbal forms in search of a solution; but the work of inventory still goes on. There is substantial agreement on the principle of verbal 'passivity', which was formulated by Schuchardt thus: if *aitak maitatua da* can only be translated 'he is loved by the father', then *aitak maitatzen du* is not 'the father loves him' but 'he is loved by the father'. He admitted that, though the present tenses are purely passive, the imperfect is partly passive and partly active, and further that there remain problems puzzling to any theorist. Accepting the same restrictions as to the imperfect, the theory of verbal passivity implies that the arrangement of parts in a Basque verb and of relevant words outside the verb corresponds to the passive construction in Indo-European languages; that is, it rests, ultimately, on equivalence in translation. Thus, to simplify, *dut* 'it is-had by-me' consists of *d-* 'it', *-u-* the verb proper and *-t* 'by me'. But the Indo-European passive is a device for ringing the changes on the Indo-European active. Instead of the normal order Subject–Verb–Object, we make the Object take the Subject's place, and express the Subject adverbially by means of a preposition and noun. Hence the Indo-European passive depends on the active and is highly unstable. It has suffered constant re-modelling, as in Latin, Romance, Slavonic, German and Scandinavian, in each of which it has been rebuilt out of the active with a suffix, or out of a participle with an auxiliary (prefixed or suffixed). But there is no such opposition of active and passive in Basque, but only the one voice, which denotes the verbal activity. *Dut* is translated 'it is-had by-me', but also '*lo teng-o*', where *lo* is third personal and *-o* first personal; thus it is also equivalent in form to a Spanish active. What is gained by the theory of passivity is chiefly the elimination

of the terms 'subject' and 'object', which are quite misleading
in dealing with Basque. A verbal activity affects a Patient
and proceeds from an Agent, and the Basque order is Patient–
Verb–Agent in the verbal paradigm. We are referring here
to the pronominal elements that enter into the verbal form.
The sentence may contain nouns indicating the Patient and
Agent, and these do not necessarily adopt the same order
around the verb that is taken by the pronominal elements.
Apart from Patient and Agent, one other relation of importance is that of the Recipient, corresponding to our dative.
The Recipient may also appear as a personal pronominal
element in conjugation.

What has been said above refers to the transitive verb, in
which an activity passes from one party to another. In the
intransitive verb, the activity or state proceeds from or affects
only one party, and it is not relevant to enquire whether this
party be Patient or Agent, sufferer or cause. In 'I live' 'I'
do not cause the living, unless by a grammatical convention;
in 'I run' 'I' cause the running, but 'I' alone am put in
motion by the running. One does not know, therefore,
whether the subject of an intransitive verb be Patient or
Agent until one compares with the grammatical forms of the
transitive verb. One then discovers that in Indo-European
languages, the pronominal elements in the intransitive verb
correspond with those of the Agent in the transitive; but in
Basque, with those of the Patient. To *dut* corresponds *doa*
'he goes'.

Thus the Basque verb has only one voice, and the subject
is the Patient. Other persons in the action, if any, are the
Agent and Recipient. These are represented by pronominal
elements which make up the conjugation of the verb. In
Indo-European languages generally the Agent forms part of
the verbal form (e.g. Sp. *tienes*, where -*s* indicates the second
person singular), but the Patient is grammatically separate
(e.g. *lo tienes*, where *lo* indicates the third person singular),
though enclitic and thus brought under one accent with the
verb. There is some tendency to repeat an object by means

of a pronoun associated with the verb, e.g. Sp. *todo lo puede*
'he can do everything' (where *lo* merely repeats *todo*). This
must be done in Basque. As for the Recipient, his attitude
to the main activity varies. He may receive it directly, or be
interested in it (ethic dative), or merely be supposed to have
an interest. This usage leads to the 'familiar' constructions
in Basque and elsewhere. An interlocutor is supposed to have
a controlling interest in all that a speaker says. So in German
'ich habe es dir gesehen' 'I have seen it (by your leave)',
'gestern gehe ich dir in den Wald' 'yesterday I went (by
your favour) into the wood'. The dative Recipient is represented by an infixed -(*k*)*i*-, of which the *k* is liable to disappear. The ethic Recipient is given by infixed -*ki*- for a man,
or -*n*- for a woman (probably from *ña na*, shortened forms
of *doña* 'lady'). Thus, with third person singular Patient *d*-,
we have

Intrans.   3 *doa* 'he goes'
Trans.   1 *dut* 2 *duk* 3 *du* 4 *dugu* 5 *duzu* 6 *dute* 'I, thou, etc. have him'

And varying the Patient we get

Intrans.   1 *noa* 2 (*h*)*oa* 3 *doa* 4 *goaz* 5 *zoaz* 6 *doaz* 'I, thou, etc., go'

while the transitive forms have the thirty-six permutations
of Patients *n*- (*h*)- (from *k*) - *g*- *z*- *d*- with Agents -*t* -*k* - -*gu*
-*zu*-. To these we must add the Recipient and Ethic forms,
and allow for the insertion of vowels of support, the elision
of consonants, plural -*z*- and -*te*, and the modification of
vowels in hiatus, including the stem-vowels of the verb itself.
Hence from *euki* 'have' we get *dot jon dabe diłue*, etc., which
bear no obvious relation to the original stem.

The conjugation of the imperfect tenses stands apart from
this explanation, since it is normally 'active'. The Patient
is not expressed in the verb, and the Agent is prefixed.
A final -*n* is a characteristic of this tense.

Trans.   *nekarren hekarren ekarren gekarren zekarren ekarren* 'I bore, etc.'
Intrans.   *nioan   hioan*   etc.   'I went, etc.'

Moods are indicated by particles, usually suffixed. The

negative is *ez-*, as *da* 'it is' *ezta* 'it is not'; hypothesis *ba-*, as *ni eroriko banintz* 'if I fell'; potentiality *-ke*; gerund, indirect speech *-la*; cause *-lako*; imperative third person singular *b-*. The suffix *-n* gives to a whole clause the nature of an adjective qualifying a noun, and this is the means of representing relative sentences. The clause thus made adjectival is capable of taking the further suffix *-a* 'the'. Thus the *Paternoster* opens: *aita gurea, zeruetan zaudena*, which might be rendered 'Our Father, thou the being in Heaven', and so 'which art'. This use of the definite article to make noun-clauses out of relatives is also a feature of Spanish: *el que compra* = *el comprador* 'the one-who-buys', 'the buyer'. Suffixes and prefixes are also used to make up the various infinite forms of the verb: past participles in *-i -n -tu*, which may have a prefixed *e- i-* (*izan* 'been' *ikusi* 'seen' *artu* 'taken'); gerund in *-t(z)e* (*ibiltze* 'walking'); adjectival *-ko*.

Actually the intricacies of Basque conjugation affect only a small group of ancient verbs, generally called 'auxiliaries'. Some of these are employed with gerunds and participles to conjugate all remaining verbs. Thus *ikusi* 'seen' has: present *ikusten dut* 'I see it', *ikusi dut* 'I have seen it', *ikusiko dut* 'I shall see it'. The system is attested for the tenth century by the *Glosas Emilianenses*, and is thus as old as our earliest evidence. A striking resemblance between Basque and the Peninsular Romance tongues is the wealth of auxiliaries and quasi-auxiliaries, and especially the two each for 'to be' and 'to have'. Subtle refinements of time and mode of action characterize all these languages, and an important rôle is assigned to auxiliaries which imply motion.

When contrasted with the verb the Basque noun is simple. In principle the word does not vary, but adds suffixes to indicate relations with the verb and other nouns. In practice, however, these suffixes are not all on the same footing. Some are long and readily detached, as *bage* (*gabe*) 'without' or *gana* 'toward'. Others have no independent meaning or existence, and it is not certain that they ever possessed one. These are the most common, and can be arranged as a declensional

scheme, which varies slightly in accordance with the final
sound of the stem. So for the village of Licq:

Inert (Patient)	*Ligi*	Adjectival	*Ligiko* 'of'
Agent	*Ligik* 'by'	Locative	*Ligin* 'in'
Recipient	*Ligiri* 'to'	Aditive	*Ligira(t)* 'to, toward'
Instrument	*Ligiz* 'with, by'	Abitive	*Ligitik* 'from'
Sociative	*Ligirekin* 'along with'	Partitive	*Ligirik*
Possessive	*Ligiren* 'of'		

The plural signs are -*k* and also -*eta*- as an infix in certain
oblique cases. The origin of -*eta*- is apparently the Latin
collective suffix in ROBURETU Sp. *robledo* 'oak-wood', and so
'oaks' as compared with *roble* 'oak'. A relic of an old
demonstrative -*a* is used as a suffixed definite article (as in
Scandinavian languages and Rumanian).

Of these cases, only the first three correspond with the
verbal conjugation, the remainder being either adverbial or
(in the possessive and adjectival) adjectivally·attached to
nouns. The Patient of a verbal activity is properly described
as inert, and there is even in Indo-European a tendency to
prefer in this capacity inert and lifeless objects. Hence it is
that the Indo-European neuters exist primarily in the accusative case, and merely lend that case for the uses of the nominative. On the other hand, the notion of Agent is cognate with
that of personality, and involves in Basque and Indo-European
a modification of the noun-stem: in Basque by -*k*, in Indo-
European generally by -*s*. There is thus no essential difference
between the Basque Agent-case and the Indo-European
nominative; just as the suffixed sign of the Agent in Basque
verbs corresponds with the suffixed subject-pronominal element in the Greek or Latin verbs.

Where words are grouped, suffixes are applied only to one
member of the group, as *aita gurea* 'our Father' (-*a* 'the').
The adjective thus has no special declension, and offers only
the peculiarity of eschewing the 'comparison of inferiority'.
To say that 'A is less than B' is merely the negative way of
putting 'B is more than A'. The pragmatic Basque tempera-
ment prefers the positive affirmation in such cases.

Particles often belong to the oldest strata of a language. They include numerals, pronouns, some adverbs and conjunctions. The cardinal numbers are

1 bat	7 zazpi	20 (h)ogei	Ordinals: 1st len(en)go
2 bi(ga)	8 zortzi	21 (h)ogei eta bat	2nd bigarren
3 (h)iru(r)	9 bederatzi	30 ogei ta amar	and so on in -garren
4 lau(r)	10 (h)amar	40 berrogei	
5 bost, bortz	11 (h)amaika	60 irurogei	
6 sei	12 (h)amabi	80 laurogei	
		100 e(h)un	
		1000 mila	

One notices the vigesimal arrangement. *Bat* has a plural *batzu* 'some', Sp. *unos*. *Lenengo* is from *len* 'before' with the adjectival suffix *-ko*.

The personal pronouns are 1 *ni* 2 *(h)i* 4 *gu* 5 *zu*, with possessives in *-re*. The third personal possessive is *bere*, and forms a reflexive *bere burua* 'his head' 'himself'. The third personal pronouns in the singular and plural are drawn from the demonstratives, which distinguish, as in Spanish and the other Peninsular languages, three degrees of distance from the speakers: 'this by me' *on* Sp. *este*, 'that by you' *ori* Sp. *ese*, 'that away from both of us' *ar-* Sp. *aquel*. There are no relative pronouns, as that idiom is turned by the verb and *-n* as already noted. The interrogatives are *nor* 'who?' *zen* 'who? which?' *zer* 'what?'

There are primitive adverbs like *(h)an* 'there' *(h)emen* 'here', but the greater number of adverbs are nouns in the locative case, as *aitzinean* 'in the front' 'before'. *Ba* affirms 'yes', and also serves as a verbal prefix of intensity; *ez-* 'not' is a verbal prefix. *Eta ta* 'and', *ala edo* 'or'. Generally the office of our conjunctions is performed by verbal prefixes and suffixes, as already described.

BASQUE AND IBERIAN

The Basques have occupied their present sites from time immemorial, but their territory was formerly more extensive. The last sixty years have seen a widening of the bilingual

belt on the Spanish side, a castilianization of the principal
towns, and an estimated loss of 70,000 speakers. The present
southern and eastern frontiers pass through Salinas, north
of Estella and Tafalla, and thence north-eastward to the
Pic d'Anie. Beyond this frontier, however there are numerous
Basque village-names, such as *Ulliberri Echaberri Baigorri
Iriberri Benagorri* (containing *iri* 'town', *etxe* 'house', *bai*
'river', *berri* 'new', *gorri* 'red'), which indicate a frontier
running from west to east *south* of Estella and Tafalla, and
then turning abruptly northward toward the Pic d'Anie. To
the east of the line thus established, around Navascués and
Lumbier, there is a district traditionally labelled *Romançado*,
which indicates a still earlier romanization. In it the vowels
ĕ ŏ of Basque place-names do not persist, as in the Estella-
Tafalla area, but give diphthongs *ie ia ue ua*; that is to say,
the romanization must have taken place here while the
processes which give diphthongs in the Spanish dialects were
still active. The area extends eastwards of the *Romançado* as
far as the Catalan frontier, and we have *Javier* (a form of
etxe berri) *Lumbier* (*irum berri* 'new town') *Ligüerre Lascuarre*
(*gorri* 'red'), *Aragüés* (*ara-otz* 'cold plain'), as well as hybrids
like *Montiberri Paternuy Aquilué* (MONTE PATERNA AQUILA plus
berri oi). This evidence extends the earliest known frontier
eastward from Tafalla to Ejea, and thence just north of
Huesca by a loop which touches the Isuela; another larger
loop carries the line north of Barbastro and Graus, whence
it descends towards Tamarite, and at last takes a north-
easterly direction to Tremp and the valley of the Noguera
Pallaresa. In this way we know that the Basque area included all the foothills of the western and central Pyrenees
until well within the Vulgar Latin period. The frontier was
determined by the thrust of Roman civilization along the
great military road leading to the Upper Ebro valley, passing
through Lérida, near Barbastro, Huesca and Zaragoza,
whence it ascended the right bank as far as Logroño, before
branching off to the west. In the area affected by this road
the traces of Basque are much slighter.

Along the northern frontier Basque has been stationary at
Bayonne since the twelfth century, but must formerly have
extended up to Bordeaux. Here again it was a road which
carried the Roman influence, that from Narbonne to Toulouse
and Bordeaux.

In the south the pilgrims' guide to Compostela fixed the
Montes de Oca as the limit of Navarrese territory in the
twelfth century, but that was presumably a political rather
than a linguistic estimate. The linguistic frontier doubtless
lay to the north of the Ebro, though there may have been a
bilingual belt of considerable depth. In the tenth century
Basque was not normal at the monastery of San Millán de la
Cogolla, but the insertion of a couple of Basque glosses in
the *Glosas Emilianenses* hints that the language was understood
by some of the monks. The province of Álava, now quite
Spanish in speech, is otherwise conspicuously Basque in its
characteristics.

Towards the west the Basques, astride the Cantabrian
mountains, were in contact with the Cantabrians, who were
the ancestors of Old Castilians. The political and social connection between these tribes was close, both in resistance to
the Roman conquerors and in opposition to the Visigoths.
It was against the Basques and Cantabrians that King
Rodrigo was campaigning when he heard the news of Târiq's
invasion in 711. Ethnically, Basques and Cantabrians seem
to have been connected, and in point of language we shall
have reason to attribute to the Cantabro-Basques the substitution of *h* for F, which is characteristic of Spanish.

Thus far we may proceed with assurance; but the identification of Basque with 'Iberian' is a matter of conjecture. The
most helpful evidence is that of classical place-names and
some of more recent times, but these have gone through
phonetic developments which are imperfectly known, and
classical authorities are notoriously lax in rendering 'bar-
barous' names. Wherever an etymology is not self-evident,
there is a risk of error through our ignorance of all Basque
before 1545, and of any other language which may have been

used in the Spanish Peninsula. There are, however, a number of persuasive etymologies. *Araduey* in León is evidently 'the land of plains' (*ara* 'plain', *-toi* 'the place where anything is found'). The suffixes *-otz* 'cold' and *-oi* 'tendency, propensity' give Sp. *-ues -uas* and *-ue -uy -oy* over a wide area, though these suffixes have unfortunately no great individuality. Place-names show frequently the element *iri ili uri uli* 'town', as in *Iria Flavia* (Galicia) *Iliberris* (*Elvira*, Granada, and *Elne*, Roussillon). In Roussillon there is considerable use made of *ur* 'water'. Such names indicate knowledge of a Basque-like language over most of the Peninsula, though one cannot exclude the possibility of borrowing. On the other hand there are, particularly in Lusitania and Baetica, names of a non-Basque type, such as *Baetis Baetulo Ulisipo Scallabis Saetabis Asido*, etc. The name *Ilerda* (*Lérida* Cat. *Lleida*) is probably to be interpreted *il-erda* 'foreign town' (cf. *erdera* 'foreign speech' as opposed to *euskera*), and so bears witness to racial mixture. Hybrid names occur: Basque-Celtic *Medu-briga* 'lead town'; Latin-Basque *Pompaelo* 'Pompey's town', *Graccuris* 'Gracchus' town', *Iria Flavia* 'the Flavian town'.

Iberian inscriptions have been preserved, but few are of any length. They have been transcribed with fair probabilities of accuracy, but they have not been interpreted. In the Alcoy lead-tablet, which is the longest prose text, we notice the absence of *f*, initial *r* and 'impure' *s*: a simple vowel system and freedom from consonantal groups; prefixes *i- b- ba- da-*; suffixes *-la -ra -k -ik -n -i*; *iri* 'town' *gara* 'height' *ildu* 'furrow' *kide* 'companion'; a general disyllabic basis for the roots. Inscriptions on coins conform to strict formulæ, and so offer a basis for inferences as to Iberian declension. Basque may be treated as declensional and so parallel to Latin: *alaba alabai* FILIA FILIAI 'daughter, to a daughter'. Thus we establish further equations of the type *Laiešcen* = *Laietanorum*, *Urkskn* = *Urcitanorum*, and deduce a genitive plural in *-cen*. On this plan Schuchardt reconstructed the Iberian declension:

	Iberian			Basque	
Case	Singular	Plural		Singular	Plural
Inert	—	c		—	k
Agent	c	?		k	kek
Recipient	i e	ce(a)i		i	ki
Instrument	š s	ciš		z	kez
Possessive	n m	cen		n	ken
Adjectival	co	—		ko	—

Such comparisons would be quite convincing had they stood the test of translation; despite them the relics of the Iberian language remain uninterpreted.

Archæology does not throw a sure light upon these problems, since it is faced with others of equal difficulty. Instead of assuming a homogeneous mass of inhabitants before the known invasions, we should rather believe the Peninsular populations swollen by fresh waves, in ancient times as in modern, some of African, and some of European origin. History shows an ebb and flow of European Celts, African Carthaginians, European Romans and Germans, African Moors; and so we must conceive of prehistory also. Indigenous elements were probably the Cantabro-Basques, but it is supposed that the Iberians were invaders from Africa, racially akin to the Kabyle tribes of the Riff, who thrust north into the centre and east of the Peninsula, and hedged the Cantabro-Basques within their mountains. It is possible that their rule was strengthened by the formation of 'towns' (*iri*), as that of the later Celts who mingled with the Iberians was by similar works (-*briga*); and if so, the method and the name may have been borrowed by non-Iberians also. As for the remaining inhabitants of the Peninsula, some authorities see in them Ligurians from Genoa and Provence, while others maintain that the Ligurians did not reach Roussillon. It seems only logical to suppose that the Iberians also encountered a racial mixture, of unknown ingredients. From the archæological point of view, it would seem most probable that the Basques were not Iberians in race; but race and language are independent, and the Basque language may not be indigenous.

Speculation as to the origin of the language has taken two main directions: some aver that Basque resembles North African languages, others prefer the Caucasus. It is even held that these hypotheses are not mutually exclusive. Now, though language is independent of race, it does not migrate except with its speakers; and of the two suggestions, the North African presents fewest physical improbabilities. It is also the one which looks most probable on the proofs offered. The Basque verb does not enter into such a comparison, but tends to be discounted as less original in fact than in appearance. We have seen that extremely complex forms are built up by the association of pronominal fractions in a verb, for instance, *draukat*. But we have also seen that our own languages group these elements under one accent, and that their separation is merely a grammatical convention. We might conjugate Sp. *lo tengo* as *loténgo lotiénes lotiéne lotenémos*, etc., and similarly for *la los las te os* and the other pronouns. This would produce a conjugation of great apparent complexity. If, further, colloquial abbreviations were left unrestricted, we should write *hy't'm* for Dutch *hebt gij het hem*, and *yufseenm* for 'you have seen them'. The nominal suffixes are not easily paralleled, and in consequence we can say that this argument is borne entirely upon the vocabulary. Schuchardt produced an imposing list of 105 words fundamental in the Basque lexicon which have, or seem to have, parallels in Berber, Copto-Egyptian, Nubian, African Semitic, Cushite, Nilotic and Sudanese. They include the numerals 2 3 5 6 7, primitive verbs like *joan* 'go' *eman* 'give' *artu* 'take' *egin* 'do' *etorri* 'come', adjectives like *on* 'good' *berri* 'new' *otz* 'cold' *andi* 'big', particles like *bage* 'without' *nor* 'who?', and the names of fundamental things like 'sun' 'moon' 'man' 'woman' 'town' 'people' 'name' 'bread' 'meat' and parts of the body. For the Caucasus claims have been made on *gu* 'we' and *zu* 'ye', but the resemblances are harder to see. Unfortunately, a recent writer has shown that these methods would prove German to be an African or Caucasian language! Their degree of probability is very low, amounting to little more, in the African thesis, than an intelligent guess.

Classical writers and inscriptions supply a store of words listed as peculiar to the Spains. Some of these are certainly, some probably, Celtic, and the remainder are not very often to be explained by Basque. Hübner cites

acnua amma aparia apitascus arapennis arrugiæ asturco bacca balluca balsa balux barca cælia cætra cantabrum cantus celdo corrugus cuscolium dureta gangadia gurdus iduma inula lancea lausia pala palacurna palaga paramus reburrus saliunca salpuga sarna segutilum talutatium tasconium urium viriæ.

To sum up: Iberian may have been a language of North African origin. In its vocabulary and structure it probably resembled Basque closely, but the gap of a millennium between its documents and the earliest Basque texts prevents an accurate identification; it was used over a wide area of the central and eastern Peninsula, and contributed at least place-names to the west and south.

The literature concerning Basque origins is vast. Among the most serviceable contributions on the linguistic side are W. von Humboldt, *Prüfung der Untersuchungen über die Urbewohner Hispaniens* (Berlin, 1821); H. Schuchardt, 'Die iberische Deklination', *Sitzungsberichte der kais. Akademie der Wissenschaften in Wien, Phil.-Hist. Kl.* clvii, 2, and 'Baskisch-hamitische Wortvergleichungen', *Revue Internationale des Études Basques*, vii; R. Lafon, 'Basque et langues kartvèles', *Revue Internationale des Études Basques*, xxiv (the Caucasian case); R. Menéndez Pidal, 'Las vocales ibéricas ẹ ọ en los nombres toponímicos', *Revista de Filología Española*, v; E. Hübner, *Monumenta Linguæ Ibericæ* (Berlin, 1893).

The following texts may assist the reader to form a clearer conception of Basque and Iberian:

The Alcoy lead-tablet (as read by M. Gómez Moreno, *Homenaje a Menéndez Pidal*, Madrid, 1925):

Irike or'ti garokan dadula bask/buistiner' bagarok sssxc turlbai/lura legusegik baserokeiunbaida/urke basbidirbar'tin irike baser/okar' tebind belagasikaur isbin/ai asgandis tagisgarok binike/bin salir' kidei gaibigait.
Ar'nai/sakarisker.
Iunstir' salir'g basirtir sabadi/dar bir'inar gurs boistingisdid/sesgersduran sesdirgadedin/seraikala naltinge bidudedin ildu/niraenai bekor sebagediran.

Untranslated. Apparently Basque features mentioned on p. 28.

From the *Liber Quartus S. Jacobi Apostoli*, cap. vii:

Barbara enim lingua penitus habentur. Deum vocant *urcia*; dei genitricem *andrea Maria*; panem *orgui*; vinum *ardum*; carnem *aragui*; piscem *araign*; domum *echea*; dominum domus *iaona*; dominam *andrea*; ecclesiam *elicera*; presbyterum *belaterra*, quod interpretatur pulchra terra; triticum *gari*; aquam *uric*; regem *ereguia*; sanctum Jacobum *iaona domne iacue.*

> *ortzi* 'thunder, thunder-cloud, God, sky', replaced by *Jaungoiko* (from *jaun*) 'the Lord'. *belaterra* OBLATORE? The other words are still usual.

The *Paternoster* (Guipúzcoa):

> Aita gurea, zeruetan zaudena; santifikatua izan bedi zure izena; betor gugana zure erreinua; egin bedi zure borondatea zeruan bezela lurrean ere. Emaiguzu gaur gure eguneroko ogia; barka zazkiguzu gure zorrak, guk geren zordunai barkatzen diegun bezela; ez gaitzazu utzi tentazioan erortzen baizikan libra gaitzazu gaitzetik. Amen.

> Latin and Romance: *zeru* CAELU 'heaven', *santifikatu* 'blessed', *erreinu*, Sp. *reino* 'kingdom', *borondate* 'will', *barka(tzen)* PARCERE 'pardon'. *tentazio* 'temptation', *libra* 'free', *-eta-* plural sign.

Analysis of the *Paternoster*:

> *aita* 'father', Celtic origin? *gu* 'we', *gure* 'our', *-a* 'the'. *zeruetan*, *-eta-* plural sign, *-n* locative, 'in heaven'. *zaudena*, *z-de* 2 Pl. for 2 S., verb *egon* 'be', *-n* relative, *-a* 'the', 'You who are'. *santifikatua* 'hallowed', *-a* 'the'. *izan* 'be'. *bedi*, *b-* 3 S. imperative, verb *edin* 'may'. *izen* 'name', *-a* 'the'. *betor*, *b-* 3 S. imperative, verb *etorri* 'come'. *gugana*, *gu* 'we, us', *-gana* 'towards', 'to us'. *zure*, *zu* 'you', *-re* possessive, 'your'. *erreinua*, *-a* 'the', added only to the second member of a group (so *zure*, but *gurea* above), 'the kingdom'. *egin* 'done'. *bedi* 'let it be', as above. *zure* 'your'. *borondatea* 'the will'. *zeruan*, *-a-* 'the', *-n* locative, 'in the heaven'. *bezela* 'as'. *lurrean*, *lur* 'earth', *-a-* 'the', *-n* locative, 'in the earth'. *ere* 'also'. *emaiguzu*, verb *eman* 'give', *-zu* 2 Pl. for 2 S. imperative, *(k)i-gu-* 'to us' dative. *gaur* 'to-day'. *gure* 'our'. *eguneroko*, *egun* 'day', *-ero-* adjectival suffix, *-ko* adjectival, 'daily'. *ogia*, *-a* 'the', 'the bread'. *barka* 'pardon'. *zazkiguzu*, *izan* 'be', *-ki-gu-* 'to us' recipient, *-z-zu* 'you' agent. *gure* 'our'. *zorrak*, *zor* 'debt', *-a-* 'the', *-k* plural inert. *guk* 'we', *-k* agent. *geren* 'our'. *zordunai*, *zordun* 'debtor', *-a-* 'the', *-k-* (elided for euphony) plural, *-i* recipient, 'to the debtors'. *barkatzen*, *barka-tze* gerund, *-n* locative, literally 'in the pardoning'. *diegun*, *d-* 'them' 3 Pl. patient, *-(k)i-* 'to them' recipient, verb *euki egin* 'have', *-gu* 'we' agent, 'we pardon them to them', *-n* subordinating particle with *bezela*. *bezela* 'as'. *ez* 'not'. *gaitzazu*, *g-tz* 'us' inert, verb *euki, egin* 'have, do', *-zu* 'you' agent, 2 Pl. for 2 S. subjunctive. *utzi* 'leave, abandon', 'leave us not'.

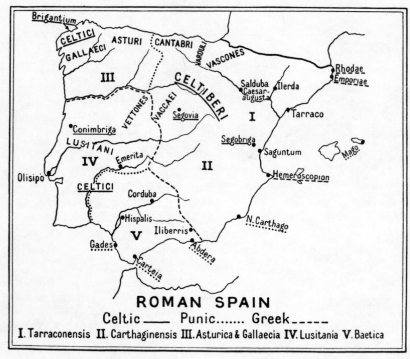

Racial distribution in Roman Spain

tentazioan, *-a-* 'the', *-n* locative, 'in the temptation'. *erortzen, erori* 'fall', *-tze* gerundial suffix, *-n* locative, 'in the falling', 'to fall'. *baizikan* 'but'. *libra gaitzazu* 'make us free'. *gaitzetik, gaitz* 'evil', *-tik* 'away from' origin.

BASCO-IBERIAN AND PENINSULAR ROMANCE

Spanish vocabulary shows elements in common with Basque and (so far as we know it) Iberian. It is not always certain which language is the debtor, since Spanish Romance has propagated in Basque not only a large body of Latinisms, but also sqme probable Celticisms of ancient date; while other elements may belong to unknown tongues. Nor is it possible sharply to mark off what Spanish owes to Iberian, from its more recent indebtedness to Basque. Beyond this traffic in vocabulary it is a fact that Iberian constituted, with some Celtic, Greek and Punic elements, the substratum of Spanish Latin, and its influence in shaping Spanish Romance has been variously computed. The 'substratum-theorist' would hold that the Latin of Spain was modified in important particulars by the peculiar speech-habits of the Iberians, and so inevitably differed from the Gallic type of Latin spoken in France; others hold that the speech-habits of a substratum have little or no effect on the language they learn. The linguistic deficiencies of the first generation of speakers (supposing it is possible to conceive of anything so abstract as a generation) are corrected by the second; for children are wont to acquire languages to perfection. As the proof or disproof of these contentions depends on the evidence of loanwords, we may settle the simpler question first.

The best-attested Peninsular word of ancient date is *páramo* 'bare plateau', which occurs on a Leonese inscription (*CIL*, ii, 2660: QUOS VICIT IN PARAMI AEQUORE). The term is not Basque, and is possibly not Iberian. It may belong specifically to the language of the Vaccæi or Vettones who inhabited the high plains. On the other hand *nava* 'plain among mountains' is not attested by ancient authors, but is universal in Peninsular Romance; it is the Basque *naba*, and, as a characteristic of Basque scenery, it gives the name *Navarra*. *Vega* 'wooded ground by a river', Sp. *vega* Ptg. *veiga*, is the Basque *ibaiko* 'riverine', and was borrowed early enough to suffer the same changes as Lat. -AI- > *e*. BALSA 'pond', B. *balsa*, occurs as the name of a Lusitanian city. BALLUX and PALACRA 'nugget' are attested by Pliny the Elder and may both be Iberian; Sp. *baluz palacra(na)* Cat. *palacra*. ARRUGIAE 'channels used in mining' may be connected with Sp. *arroyo* Ptg. *arróio* 'rivulet', and with the place-names *Requejo Requena*. SARNA 'itch' is found in Basque, as well as the other Peninsular languages, but it may be Celtic; and similarly CANTUS 'dressed ashlar', which Quintilian says was Spanish or African (Basque *kanto(in)* 'corner, angle'). The majority of loan-words are definitely Basque, and later than the romanization. A conspicuous group is in -*rro* -*rra*; B. *ezker* 'left' Sp. *izquierda* Ptg. *esquerda* Cat. *esquerra*; B. *bei* 'cow' *zekor* 'bullock' Sp. *becerro* Ptg. *bezerro*; B. *txakur* 'whelp' Sp. Ptg. *cachorro*; B. *pizar* 'fragment' Sp. *pizarra* Ptg. *piçarra* Cat. *pissarra* 'slate'; B. *bizar* 'beard' Sp. Ptg. *bizarro* 'gallant' (whence our *bizarre*, through French depreciation); B. *gisuarri* 'limestone' Sp. *guijarro* 'pebble'. Gk. *kithara* + B. -*arra* gives Sp. *guitarra* 'guitar'. *Abarca* 'rustic shoe or sandal' is attested in the *Codex Compostellanus* (twelfth century) and yields a nickname to the Navarrese king Sancho *Abarca*; *ardite* 'coin of little value' is from B. *ardit*. Berceo uses *çatico* 'piece of bread', B. *zati*. *Urraca* 'magpie', used also as a proper name, is probably of Basque origin. With Sp. Ptg. *zorra* 'fox, vixen' compare B. *zugur* 'prudent, clever'. Some knowledge of Basque extended as far as Portugal in the fourteenth century, as may be seen in the *Livro de Linhagens*, cap. ix: '*Arguriega*, que tanto quer dizer por seu linguagem de vasconço como pedras vermelhas*' ('Arguriega means in Basque red stones').

Basques have originated or popularized a number of Christian names and surnames. Such are *Ximena Jimena Jiménez Eiximeniç* (obsolete *Ximeno*), *Sancho Sancha Sánchez, Íñigo, Ignacio* (after Loyola), *Xavier Javier* (after St Francis Xavier, B. *etxe-berri* 'new house'), *Echeverría, Mendizábal* 'broad hill', *Zumalacárregui* 'place of willows', *Arteaga* 'place

of holm oaks', *Madariaga* 'place of pears', *Lizárraga* 'place of
ash-trees', *Jáuregui* 'palace', *Irigoyen* 'upper city', etc. As for
place-names, apart from those cited as evidence of the former
extension of Iberian, Basque names are seen to be with-
drawing before Roman equivalents from the earliest historical
times. Thus CAESARAUGUSTA (*Zaragoza*) has ousted *Salduba*
(*zaldi* 'horse' or *saldo* 'troop'), AUGUSTA AUSCIORUM (*Auch*)
stands on an older *Eliberris*, *Granada* has displaced *Elvira*
ILIBERRIS. Doublets occur in the Basque country itself. What
is *Pamplona* 'Pompey's town' to Romance-speakers, is *Iruña*
'the good town' to the Basques; and similarly *Burguete* =
Auritze, *Valcarlos* = *Lusaide*, *Bonloc* = *Lecuine*, all on the 'French
Way' to Compostela. In some cases the doublet is due to
translation: *Roncesvalles* = *Orreaga* 'place of junipers', *Villa-
nueva* = *Iriberri* 'new town'.

The traffic in loan-words between Basco-Iberian and
Romance is thus seen to be slight, but ancient. It is very far
from remodelling the Latin vocabulary of Spain. The claims
for a considerable influence as a substratum are based, in
consequence, mainly on phonology. In one case, at least,
Basque or Iberian has modified the pronunciation of all
Spain, namely the elimination of F and then of aspirated *h*:
FABULARE *hablar* 'speak'. This point will be discussed more
fully when we treat of the expansion of Castilian against the
other Spanish vernaculars, for the phenomenon is, in Spanish,
strictly Castilian. The change does not take place at all in
Portuguese or Catalan, nor did it occur in the Mozarabic,
Leonese or Aragonese dialects of the older language, which
occupied the whole Peninsula south of the Duero, west of the
Pisuerga, and east of the Montes de Oca. Even within the
small remaining fragment, as we shall see, the *h* was an
immigrant in Burgos. It belonged originally to Cantabria,
the strip of hilly land hard up against the Basque border.
Hence this development, so characteristic of modern literary
Spanish, did not occur in the whole area occupied by the
Iberian tribes who learned Latin, and should rather be
described as Basque. It is only to be deemed Iberian, if the

Cantabrians retained their Iberian language until a late date, and their Latin patois was not corrected by education. We cannot be certain, however, that they did not simply borrow this pronunciation from their neighbours, the Basques, since our evidence peters out in the tenth century. Two suggestions are advanced to explain the phenomenon. One relies on the aspiration of initials in Basque (particularly French Basque) which gives forms like *ethorri ekharri ikhusi*. As applied to *f*, which is already an aspirate, this aspiration would cause the labiodental element to disappear: *Felipe Hfelippo Helizes*. Alternatively, it is asserted that *f* is not a Basque sound, and that the nearest equivalent was *h*. Adult speakers, imitating Latin and Romance F, would pronounce *h*. The premiss is not absolutely secure, and the substitution made for *f* in later times was not *h* but *p*. However, the coincidence of Gascon dialects (Gasc. *hilh* 'son', Sp. *hijo* FILIU) with Castilian in this matter, and the great rarity of *f* in Basque, makes the thesis highly probable. Iberian inscriptions show no *f*.

In other respects, we note that the effect of a substratum is not to change the acquired language in any way, but to exercise some influence in the choice of alternatives. Basque, for instance, does not tolerate either 'impure' *s* or initial *r*. In the former case it chanced to concur with a change taking place in all Romance, as far as Italy, and Sp. *espíritu espada* Ptg. *espirito espada* Cat. *esperit espasa* agree with Fr. *esprit épée* It. (*i*)*spirito* (*i*)*spada*, as well as with Basque usage; but the Basque prejudice against *r*-, finding no support in Romance, does not influence Spanish, apart from one or two loan-words: Sp. *rey* B. *errege*. Basque palatalizes *n l t d*. This may have helped to confirm the Sp. Cat. palatalization of LL NN, but it does not spread further. Here again, however, there may be some trace of Basque phonetics in Castilian alone, for Cast. *fecho hecho* FACTU, as against Ptg. *feito* Cat. *fet*, probably reposes on a stage **feiło*, with a palatalized *t*.

Apart from these doubtful details, those who study both Spanish and Basque become aware of a subtle correspondence between the two, all the more persuasive when it can hardly be set down in formulæ. There is, as it were, a common mental outlook in the two languages. They eschew the negative and are forthright and concrete. What imagination they have is exercised on things rather than ideas; they refine on circumstances of action, such as time and person in the verb, and prefer only one voice; they are rich in auxiliaries, which are rather felt than logically distinguished. Basque is turned into Spanish much more readily than into any other language. In pronunciation there is a common basis of enunciation. It is not that Basque has imposed conditions upon those who learned Latin in Spain; but rather that Latin, which presented alternative possibilities of treatment and development sufficient to give all the diversities of Romania, was subjected to the same mental control that had given Basque its special qualities.

CELTIC AND PENINSULAR ROMANCE

The Celtic invaders of the Spanish Peninsula brought this region within the orbit of vast European movements, and drew closer its links with Gaul. Raids may have occurred as early as the ninth century B.C., in Catalonia, but the principal thrust seems to have occurred two hundred years later, in the seventh century. Then the Turmogidi, Berones, Pelendones, Arevaci, Lusones, Belli and Dittani pushed rapidly through the Landes and the mountainous regions of Guipúzcoa and Álava, and effected a lodgment on the heights at the headwaters of the Duero and Tagus, overlooking the Ebro valley from the west. In this region the invaders retained their tribal organization and names, but they mingled with the natives to form the nation of the Celtiberians, who were masters of the central meseta. It is not clear that they were numerous, or formed more than a military aristocracy soon diluted with indigenous blood. They maintained themselves in fortresses (*-briga -dunum*), sometimes connected with a memory of victory (*sego-* in place-names). Their chiefs' names were of a Celtic type (*Istodatios, Karaunios, Moenicaptus*

'slave of the Main river-god', *Boudica*), but these have not
survived in Romance. They implanted their own customs
as to duelling, religion, etc., but employed the local language
for their coins, inscriptions and practical purposes. It would
appear that the Celtic language was in disuse when the
Romans arrived.

The lines of the Duero and Tagus mark the further advance
of these peoples, whom Herodotus reports in the fifth century
as established about the Pillars of Hercules and Cape St
Vincent. Lines of posts in *-briga* follow the rivers, and in
Portugal there are many settlements in strong positions between the streams, notably *Coimbra* CONIMBRIGA. In the
north-west some Celts reached the sea, and established themselves near *Betanzos* BRIGANTIUM. They were the CELTICI of the
Nerium Promontory. The Galicians, however (GALLAECI Gk.
Kallaïkoi), were probably not Celts, despite the temptation
to connect their name with that of the *Galati* or Gauls; and
it is doubtful whether the *Artabri* or *Arotrebæ* of the same
region had any connection with the Celtic tribe of the
Atrebates. In the far south-west, the Guadiana led them away
from the Tagus valley to become the CELTICI of the Lusitanian
region (S. Portugal). The term 'Iberian' is not found with
these names, but we have no reason for supposing that this
connotes greater racial purity. The original tribal organization does not seem to have survived the westerly migration.
The Guadalquivir basin was in the hands of the comparatively civilized Turduli and Turdetani, who halted the
invaders on the line of the Sierra Morena; but they seem
to have possessed mines at Cazlona, and to have owned
Cartima, near Málaga. The whole Levantine coast and
Catalonia was clear of Celts, but SEGOBRIGA *Segorbe*, at the
end of the Idubedan chain, overlooked Saguntum and brought
the invaders within a few miles of the Mediterranean. Cut
off from Gaul, and from reinforcements, by the Basques and
Catalan Iberians, they do not seem to have received fresh
drafts; and their system of alliances, while it extended their
sphere of influence, was probably too fluctuating to con-

stitute, as D'Arbois de Jubainville has it, the 'Celtic Empire of Spain'.

The record of their achievements is written in the names of their forts. The older nomenclature of rivers and mountains is not Celtic, with the exception of the *Deva* (our *Dee*) in Guipúzcoa. The DURIUS *Duero* might be Celtic, but is more likely to be connected with the *Adur* and other rivers of Basco-Iberian name. The element most frequently encountered is *briga* 'eminence', which answers to the Basco-Iberian *iri ili*. It occurs as a first element in BRIGANTIUM (*Betanzos*), BRIGAECIUM in León and BRIGANTIA (*Bragança*). As a second element, it is found associated with *Amalo- Ara- Arco- Cala- Ceto- Cottæo- Deo- Meidu- Meri- Miro- Nerto- Nemeto- Sego- Tala- Tongo- Turo-*. The list is increased in classical geographers by attributions to the Celtic tribes of towns evidently non-Celtic in name, as *Acinippo Arunda* (Ronda) *Asta Salpensa*, which all lay between Ronda and Sevilla. Many of the names are manifestly hybrid, such as *Mundobriga Amalobriga*. The termination *-briga*, like our *-chesters* and *-villes*, was capable of migrating beyond the range of the people to whose language it belonged; and the general impression produced by the Spanish place-names is that of survivors from a lost tongue. The alternative term *-dunum* is rare on Spanish soil, though frequent in France. *Besalú* from BESALDUNUM is a case in point, and parallel to the French *Bezaudun*. *Sego-* 'victory' appears in SEGISAMO (*Sasamón*) *Segovia Segorbe* SEGONTIA (*Sigüenza*). *Deobriga* and *Deobrigula* recall the name of the 'divine' *Deva*, and *Vindeleia* and *Contrebia*, in the heart of Celtiberian territory, are evidently Celtic.

The language brought into Spain by the invaders was presumably that of Gaul, which is fairly well known from inscriptions. Of dialect variations we find recorded ARAPENNIS OSp. *arapende* for AREPENNIS Fr. *arpent* (a measure of land), VIRIAE for VIRIOLAE 'bracelet', and *-brigula* alongside *-briga*. The first of these might arise out of contamination with B. *ara* 'plain', but St Isidore suggests a cross with ARARE 'plough' ('ab arando scilicet'). Only one word of proved Celtic origin is peculiar to the Peninsula: Gal. Ptg. *tona* 'rind' Welsh *ton* Ir. *tonn.* Doubtful are Sp. *manteca* Ptg. *manteiga* 'lard, butter', Sp. *berro* 'watercress' Welsh *berwr* Fr. *berle* (from Lat. BERULA Gaul. **berura*), Sp. Ptg. *parra* 'vine-leaves', which has been claimed for Germanic. With the exception of *tona* and *arapende*, therefore, we have no evidence of direct contact between the Celtic of Spain and the later Peninsular languages. The Celtic element is thus but part of the Latin taught to Spain, largely under the influence of Gallic innovations. These innovations have various dates, according as they affected Old Latin, Classical Latin, Vulgar Latin, Western Romance, and even the Gallo-Iberian bloc. An ancient loan-word is CARRU Sp. Ptg. *carro* 'vehicle' Rum. *car* It. *carro* Fr. *char.* Imperial and Vulgar Latin knew such words as BRACAE Sp. Ptg. *bragas* Cat. *bragues* 'breeches' Rum. *îmbrăcá* 'to dress' It. *brache* Fr. *brayes.* Western Romance (i.e. excluding Rumanian) has such terms as Sp. Ptg. *brío* 'mettle', Sp. *camino* Ptg. *caminho* Cat. *camí* 'road', Sp. Ptg. Cat. *legua* 'league'. It is rare for the Peninsula to possess a Celticism in common with France but not with northern Italy, though there are such: *berro* 'watercress', Sp. *alosa* Fr. *alose* 'shad'.

Under these circumstances it is superfluous to discuss the Celts as an element of the substratum which (according to the well-known hypothesis) remodelled the Latin of Spain. The Celts exercised their influence in Gaul, and only the consequences of that action reached Spain. Spain and Portugal, in any case, offer only one of the alleged Celtic characteristics in phonology, namely the change from -CT- to -*it*- Cast. -*ch*-. The development may have taken its origin equally well in Italic dialects, and we find it not completely effected in southern Spain as late as the twelfth century A.D., when all contact with Celts had been lost for about a millennium.

The quality of the borrowings, however, gives an interesting sidelight on the changes wrought by the Celts in European life and habits. The greater number of Gaulish words recorded by ancient authors are names of plants which were alien to the Mediterranean: as BETULLA Sp. *abedul* 'birch'. Next to these are the names of animals, tame or wild. CABALLU Sp. *caballo* Ptg. *cavalo* Cat. *cavall* 'horse', CATTU Sp. Ptg. *gato* Cat. *gat* 'cat' (which may be of African origin), PARAVEREDU Sp. *palafrén* 'palfrey' (a French loan-word), ALAUDA Fr. *alouette* Prov. *alauza* Cat. *alosa calandria* OSp. *aloa calandria* (by contamination, MSp. *alondra*) 'lark'. Sp. Ptg. *bico* Cat. *bec* 'beak' is one of the words referring to parts of the body; but OSp. *camba* Cat. *cama* 'leg', though claimed for a Celtic CAMBA or GAMBA, may be derived from Gk. *kampé* 'bending, joint'. Lat. PĔRNA 'ham' gave, humorously, the Ibero-Romance term for 'leg' Sp. *pierna* Ptg. *perna*, and kept its original meaning only in *pernil*; Sp. *jamón* 'ham' is a later borrowing from French *jambon*. The Celtic house impressed the Latins by its crudity: CAPANNA Sp. *cabaña* Ptg. Cat. *cabana* 'hut'. Of the foodstuffs, beer and its manufacture attracted attention: CEREVISIA Sp. *cerveza* Ptg. *cerveja* Cat. *cervesa* 'beer'. There were also names of clothing among the loan-words: *bragas* 'breeches', SAGU Sp. *sayo* Ptg. *saio* 'smock'. Two important measures were the 'rood' OSp. *arapende* and the 'league' Sp. *legua* Cat. *llegua* Ptg. *légoa* LEUCA. TARATRU Sp. *taladro* Ptg. *trado* Cat. *taladre* 'auger', and LANCEA Sp. *lanza* Ptg. *lança* Cat. *llança* 'lance', are Celtic tools in peace and war.

Taken in general these words resēmble those Spanish and Portuguese later borrowed from the American Indians. They describe a new region of flora and fauna by way of augmenting the nature-knowledge of the Mediterranean conquerors. Otherwise they betray a culture below that of the invaders, and so requiring indigenous names, but with some devices of peculiar effectiveness, in clothing, vehicles and tools.

Consult G. Dottin, *La Langue Gauloise* (Paris, 1920), and the articles of H. d'Arbois de Jubainville and J. Leite de Vasconcellos in *Revue Celtique*, xiv, xv, xxxiii, as well as the relevant parts of Hübner's *Monumenta linguæ ibericæ* and the *Grundriss der romanischen Philologie*.

PHŒNICIANS AND CARTHAGINIANS

Sidonians traded at Tarshish or Tartessos in the ivory, apes and peacocks of Morocco, the tin of the Cassiterides, and the gold, silver and lead of Spain. So rich was the country in comparison with the needs of antiquity, that the myth of Pyrene associated the Pyrenees primarily with gold, and Stesichorus speaks of the 'silver-rooted' Guadalquivir. The site of Tarshish remains a subject of controversy. About 1100 B.C. it became necessary to move the Sidonian factory to the more defensible position of Cádiz. This venerable city has been refashioned for successive generations of inhabitants so that it is singularly devoid of antiquities. Similarly the name has received an imprint from each of a long succession of masters. The Punic *Gadir* or *Aggadir* 'wall, enclosure, fortified place' appears in the Moroccan *Agadir*. To the Greeks the place was known as *Gádeira*, with which we compare the Biblical *Gadara*. The Romans altered the termination: *Gades*. The Arabs transliterated this word with *q-*, doubtless in its ancient value, still extant in Egypt, of [g]: *Qâdis*. The pronunciation [k] supervened, and the Arabic vowels persisted, giving the Spanish *Cádiz*.

Tyre succeeded to Sidon as the commercial centre of the old world, but when Tyre fell before the Persian armies, Carthage took over the mandate for the Punic colonies in the western Mediterranean (*Mainaca Abdara Carteia*, etc.). She introduced a new spirit of empire. A 'New Carthage' arose as the capital of Hamilcar Barca's dominions, from which Hannibal marched against Rome: *Cartagena*. Scipio's invasion of Spain in 207 B.C. was the first move in the ruin of Carthage, whose Spanish empire vanished leaving scarcely a trace. The names of Punic towns remained, notably *Cádiz* and CARTEIA (*qereth* 'city'), which later became *Algeciras* 'the (green) island'. *Cartagena*, *Mahón* (PORTUS MAGONIS, after Hamilcar's third son), are specifically Carthaginian; but BARCINO *Barcelona* should probably be deemed Iberian (like RUSCINO *Roussillon*), and not associated with the Barcidæ.

Two common nouns have come down to Peninsular Romance, not directly, but because of their adoption by Latin: MAPPA Sp. Ptg. Cat. *mapa* 'map', and MAGALIA OSp. *nagüela* 'hutment' (cf. Hebrew *mágôr* 'temporary dwelling, inn'), which also gives Sp. *mallada majada* Ptg. *malha malhada* Cat. *mallada* 'sheepfold'. The name HISPANIA has been connected with a root SPAN, and the Hebr. *sáphan* 'hide, conceal', in the sense of the 'hidden, remote land'. The alphabets used in Iberian inscriptions are indebted to Punic models more often than to Greek.

THE GREEKS

The Greek element in the Peninsular languages is, apart from a couple of place-names, merely part of their Latin inheritance. Greek traders and colonists appeared early on the Levantine coast of Spain, working coastwise from Marseilles, or making the direct crossing from Cumæ by the Balearic island-bridge to Hemeroscopion. The periplus of the Peninsula was achieved under Pytheas, but the Phœnicians, in alliance with the Etruscans, inflicted a crushing defeat on the Massiliots at Alalia (Aleria) in Corsica, in 537 B.C. The Greeks were excluded from the commerce of the Straits and the Atlantic, and their Spanish establishments were at RHODE (*Rosas*) and EMPORION 'the mart' (*Ampurias*). *Hemeroskopion* has become *Denia*. It was the Greek traders and geographers who determined the form given to Peninsular place-names in the classical period, and who generalized the terms *Iberia* and *Iberi*, from the more restricted meaning of 'dwellers beside the Ebro'. The Greek alphabet was used in some native inscriptions, such as that of Alcoy.

Greek has served Latin, as Chinese has served Japanese, for a reservoir of cultured terms in all its epochs; and in consequence, the Greek element in the Peninsular languages shows an elaborate stratification. We may distinguish five principal layers. The oldest loan-words in Latin are of pre-classical date, and use only native Latin vowels and consonants. Thus Gk. υ (*y*) φ χ θ are represented by Latin *u p c t*, and *c g* frequently interchange: *porphyra* PURPURA OSp. *porpola* Aljamiado *polbra* Cat. *porpra* 'purple'; *kybernán* GUBERNARE Sp. Ptg. Cat. *gobernar governar* 'govern'; *thýmon* TUMU Sp. *tomillo* 'thyme'; *kólaphos* *COLPU OSp. *colpe* Cat. *cop* MSp. Ptg. *golpe* 'blow', a word which has lost its -*u* through French mediation; *kréte* CRETA Sp. Ptg. Cat. *greda* 'chalk'. Very much larger was the second stratum of Greek loan-words in Classical Latin. They were more abstract and cultural, and they were transliterated by the aid of fresh alphabetical signs (*x y z ph ch th*) designed to represent the Greek sounds. These give Peninsular *x i z f c t*, though the Latin orthography persisted in Portugal until 1911, and is still to be met with in Brazil and in private use. Hence CYMA Sp. Ptg. *cima* Cat. *cim* 'peak' (preclassical CUMAE), GYPSU Sp. *yeso* Ptg. *gesso* Cat. *guix* 'gypsum', ÓRPHANU Sp. *huérfano* Ptg. *orfão* Cat. *orfe* 'orphan', SCHŎLA Sp. *escuela* Ptg. Cat. *escola* 'school'.

The third stratum of Hellenisms corresponds to the late Latin and Romance periods, and contains chiefly ecclesiastical terms characterized by 'iotacism', i.e. by the single value [i] for the vowels and diphthongs *ē i y ei oi yi*. The history of *ekklēsía*, a younger term for church than the Roman BASILICA Ptg. *Baselgas* (place-name), is complex in the Peninsula. The iotacism appears in Fr. *église*. Spanish has *iglesia* and formerly *elguesia* (twelfth century) and *elglesia* (1212), Ptg. *igreja*, Cat. (*e*)*sgleya església*. *Apothḗkē* 'store' gives the Classical Latin APOTHECA, whence OSp. *abdega* Ptg. *adega* and Sp. *bodega* 'wine-cellar'; but the Byzantine form is represented by Sp. Ptg. *botica* Cat. *botiga* 'shop', words which are also semi-learned. Characteristic words of this series are Sp. *obispo* Ptg. *bispo* Cat. *bisbe* 'bishop', *ángel* 'angel', *blasfemar* 'curse, blaspheme', *bautizar* 'baptize', etc., together with the suffix -*izar*, equivalent to Gk. -*izeîn*. *Katà*, in *katà pénte* 'each five, groups of five', has the value of 'each', and so *cada uno* 'each one' OSp. *cadaguno* Ptg. *cada hum* Cat. *cadascú*, and formations like *quiskataqui uamne* 'each man' (*Glosas Emilianenses*) and *cadalguno*. OSp. *maguer* 'despite the fact that' probably renders the Gk. *makárie* 'but, my dear sir!' (in a tone of mild protest).

More specialized to the Peninsula are those Greek words which have been borrowed through the Arabic. They are generally Byzantine, and replace or run concurrently with other previous borrowings. Samples are *Almagest*, Ptolemy's *Megíste Syntáxis* with the Ar. *al-* 'the', *atramuz* 'lupin' (*thérmos*), *adarme* 'dirhem' (*drachmé*). The fifth and last Greek current is that of pseudo-Greek scientific and technical terms which have an international vogue: *monarquía drama mecánica crisis telégrafo*, etc. Modernist poets have been given to coining Greek neologisms to diversify their style and to give a dactylic rhythm to the verse: e.g. Rubén Darío's *liróforo* 'lyrebearer'.

The Classical Greek accent was musical; that of Modern Greek, Latin and Romance an accent of stress. In the process of conversion from one system to another, the pitch accent has sometimes been made into a stress accent, sometimes ignored in favour of Latin accentual rules. Thus we have *golpe Estéban* according to the Greek accent, but *huérfano escuela cuerda cada* for *orphanós scholé chordé katá*. *Káthedra* 'seat' gives the latinized Sp. *cadera* 'hip', and the learned *cátedra* 'professorial chair'. Greek *-eia* corresponds with Lat. -ĬA -*ia*, but also resembles -ĬA -*ia*; and from this confusion arises, particularly in vulgar pronunciation. For instance, Sp. Ptg. *academia* 'academy' is accented in Spanish on the *e*, but in Portuguese on the *i*. Spanish writes *período océano* but pronounces [perjóđo oθeáno]. The Baroque tendency to adopt trisyllabic endings also causes confusion in accents, and that not merely in Greek words. Thus for Calderón's *hipogrifo violento*, modern taste tends to prefer *hipógrifo*; for Alfonso el Sabio's *cantigas*, *cántigas*; and there are many vulgarisms of the type *intérvalo méndigo Itúrbide*.

CHAPTER III

THE LATIN OF SPAIN

When lovely Venus, moved to protect the Portuguese people for their pristine Roman virtues (as Camões tells us), thought of the language, she took it, with slight corruption, for Latin—

> com pouca corrupção crê que é a latina.

In Spain also, Nebrija composed the first of modern European grammars, his *Gramática de la Lengua Castellana* (1492), on the lines of, and as it were a gloss on, his Latin grammar. These testimonies bear witness to the essential Latinity of the three Peninsular Romances. Latin is their sole basis. It is only by adoption into Spanish-Latin that the influence of the Iberian and Celtic tongues comes into play, and that only to the slight extent already described. It is true that the problem of substrata occupies much of the space devoted to linguistic research; but that is a measure not of their basic importance, but of the remoteness and difficulty of the allegations, leading to intricate, and proportionately insecure, arguments. In contrast therewith, the Latinity of Spanish, Portuguese and Catalan is self-evident, and for that reason receives normally the less attention.

Latin, we repeat, is the basis of the three Peninsular Romance tongues; specifically the Latin talked in Spain, either as a uniform speech or with local variations. Something may be known of its divergences from standard Classical Latin by studying the monuments engraved during the first centuries of our era, or by collecting stray notices from Pliny, St Isidore and other ancient encyclopædists; though the interpretation of this evidence is not without obscurity. In particular it is remarkable that many of the most striking characteristics

of the surviving languages—characteristics which go back
through all medieval documents—are not recorded on monuments and in the Classical authors. It is possible that these
authorities may have been already widely separated from
current Spanish Latin, for even masons cut their inscriptions
as grammatically as they knew how; or it may have been
that a linguistic landslide took place in the dark period
between the exhaustion of Classical scholarship in the sixth
century and the emergence of the first vernacular documents
in the tenth. The new languages emerge, each in its own
character, each handling in a distinctive fashion the Latinity
at the disposal of them all, having assimilated not only the
Iberian, Celtic and early Greek elements, but those of
Byzantium and of the Germanic dialects, and marked by
tides of phonetic change which are least noticeable in the
West, and more numerous and violent in the East as we
approach the great centre of innovation in Gaul. The Frankish
character of many German loan-words, and the Gallo-
Roman form adopted for others of Latin or Greek origin
(e.g. *tapete* and *tapiz*), are additional witnesses to the importance of this Trans-Pyrenean focus of linguistic change.
Even some of the earliest Arabic loan-words come within
the Romance period before the final determination of the
separate vernaculars, and so help to characterize the Latin
of Spain.

Latin, however, is not merely the basis of Spanish, Portuguese and Catalan, but has continued to live with these
languages in a sort of symbiosis. The language of the law,
of the church, and of the schools, it has continued to be
available, in forms more and more precise and classical, for
comparison with the vernaculars, to halt a process of change,
to reverse the process by adopting an older form, to supply
a fresh word by a table of recognized equivalences, or to
reintroduce an old word which had been discarded or
forgotten by fashion. Hence the wealth of 'learned' and
'half-learned' words which occupies the greater part of the
dictionaries. The former are, apart from some simple altera-

4

tions, recognizably the Latin word: Sp. *espíritu* (Ptg. *espirito*)
SPIRITU 'spirit', Sp. Ptg. *tribu* TRIBU 'tribe' have merely discarded the Latin case endings, while *espíritu* has modified the
initial SP-. SAECULU 'century', however, gives the 'learned'
Ptg. *século*, but in Sp. the 'half-learned' *siglo* (OSp. *sieglo*,
for which the popular form would have been **sejo* in Castilian, cf. OCULU *ojo*). The sense of FIDE 'faith' is not kept
in mind in the Sp. *a la he*, an exclamation, which has an
unimpeded phonetic evolution; but the Latin word has maintained the *f-* in Sp. *fe*, which has enjoyed otherwise an
entirely popular development. Similarly, FIDELIS Sp. *fiel*
'faithful', but FEL Sp. *hiel* 'gall'; FESTA *fiesta* 'festival', but
INFESTU *enhiesto* 'steep'. Examples of retrogression, due to
the symbiosis of Latin with the vernacular, are PRINCIPE
OSp. *princepe*, MSp. *príncipe* 'prince', DIGNU *dino* (in the
seventeenth century), MSp. *digno*. *Acto* and *auto* are both
'learned' words, derived from ACTU at different times, and
now used in different senses. The terms 'learned' and 'half-
learned', with their Spanish equivalents *cultismos* and *semi-
cultismos*, need not be given too rarified a sense. To coin a
'learned' word is within the power of any moderately alert
speaker of the language, and the conventions that rule are at
all times widely known, though not in each century the same.
Suffixes play an important part in such formations; as *-ado*
-ATU, *-able* *-ABILE*, *-idad* *-ITATE*, *-izar* (for verbs), etc.

While reserving for a later paragraph the discussion in
detail of phases of Spanish Latinity, we may here note the
recurrence at intervals of the Classical ideal, and the impulse
it gives *per contra* to the development of the vernacular. The
monumental work of St Isidore, in the sixth century, is an
effort of this kind; and in the ninth, St Eulogius and Alvarus
of Córdoba display as much anxiety to tighten up the rules
of composition in Latin as to purify the faith. In León, however, Latin was led along a path of compromise by those who
drew up legal documents as late as the tenth century. They
felt the need of being understood, and minimized the difference
between Latin and Leonese by voicing *-p- -t- -k- -f-* in

cingidur (CINGITUR) *accebi* (ACCEPI), etc., omitting -*g*- in
reliosis (RELIGIOSIS), vocalizing -*l*- cons. in *autairo* (ALTARIU),
changing the timbre of unaccented vowels in *ribolo* (RIVULU),
etc. A great wave of Classical influence from Cluny in the
eleventh century put an end to this compromise, and the
so-called Monk of Silos (*c.* 1109), with his propensity for
Vergilian hexametrical rhythms, is a relatively 'correct'
author. He and those like him, notably Archbishop Rodrigo
Ximénez de Rada of Toledo in the thirteenth century,
initiated in Spain the period of scholastic Latin, and set up
a standard too exacting for popular entertainment or general
instruction. To diffuse more widely general notions of history
and science Castilian prose came into existence under the
pen of Alfonso the Wise, and the beginnings of Portuguese
prose followed a generation later. To the insistence on a
scholastic standard in Latin corresponds, therefore, a great
advance in the use of the vernacular. The vernacular borrowed from its rival such vocabulary as it required, and it
borrowed also for the sake of eloquence. In the fifteenth
century the latter type of borrowing—both vocabulary and
syntax—became intense in the works of the Marquis of
Santillana, Enrique de Villena and the court of Juan II,
and reached a state of congestion in the aureate manner of
the poet Juan de Mena, who practised all the tricks and
inversions of Classical grammarians. A new standard of
Latin composition entered in the sixteenth century with the
Humanists. Cicero was the model, and Erasmus and Vives
represented the height of feasible attainment. Purity of style
could be maintained, Francisco de las Brozas averred, only
by the disuse of Latin for vulgar purposes; and in consequence
many departments of literature (notably theology and philosophy) were thrown open to the vernacular. This is the Age
of Gold for the Spanish and Portuguese literatures. They
expand to their full limits of thought and action; while Latin
is reserved for the school-dramas and bucolics of the Jesuits
or the technical erudition of theologians. It is an age of
neologisms borrowed from Classical Latin, generally with

Italian precedents, at first under the need for words to fit the new concepts, but later as an adornment; and again there is in the latinizing of the vernacular a moment of crisis, which is termed *gongorismo* or *culteranismo*. The Latin of Spanish schools has not surpassed the level reached by the Jesuit teachers of the seventeenth and eighteenth centuries, but in other parts of Europe a still more exacting standard has been set up which rejects even the compromises of Vives and Erasmus; and this Latinity has accentuated again the distance between the vernacular and the 'dead' languages, and has given rise to a more strictly classical standard in loan-words. The period is marked by the rise and authority of the Academies, and by academical 'reforms' of spelling, such as the reinsertion of *-g-* in *digno*, the value [ks] for *x* and its restoration for the older *-s-* as in *examen* 'examination', the retention of *c* in *luctuoso* 'grievous' (but *luto* 'grief, mourning'), and the host of cosmopolitan neologisms formed on conventional patterns from Greek elements.

Two tendencies are at work throughout this history of the relation between the vernaculars and Latin. On the one hand, there is the desire to use Latin as the national and international medium for the commerce of ideas, with a necessary measure of compromise with current vernacular vocabulary and linguistic habits; on the other hand, the indignation of scholars against such vulgarisms has caused them to erect afresh the classical standard. To do so is to sacrifice the many to the few. With each classicizing reform Latin has become less generally serviceable, and the vernacular has flowed in to fill the void; but the latter has at the same time suffered such discipline as has greatly increased its resemblance to its rival.

THE TESTIMONY OF INSCRIPTIONS AND CLASSICAL AUTHORS

The inscriptions of Spain from the first to the eighth century have been examined with a view to throwing light on the phonetic changes which presumably took place within that period. They offer the guarantees of precise dating and location, together with the certainty of being still in their original form, unmutilated by the scribal tradition which diminishes the authority of written documents. But they have proved surprisingly uninstructive. The masons of Bætica, in particular, show few local peculiarities, and may have been foreigners in some instances. It is only in Lusitania that vulgarisms are numerous. These vulgarisms are typically those of all Romania rather than Spain in particular, and not infrequently run contrary to later Peninsular speech-habits. Thus AUNCOLO (AVUNCULO) 'uncle' is related to Fr. Cat. *oncle*, but not to Spanish *tío*, which does not appear on the inscriptions (Isidore reports *thius* as a Græcism); SERORI (SORORI) is related to OFr. *seror* but not to Sp. *hermana*; 'impure' *s* has for prefix *i* rather than *e*, being the Italian rather than the Spanish usage, as in ISCOLASTICUS; the closing of Ě before R (TIRRA, PUIR, for TERRA, PUER) is at variance with the open vowel in Portuguese and Catalan and the diphthong in Spanish; INTERANNIENSIS (-*nn*- for -*mn*-) corresponds to the Spanish treatment (*sueño*, *suenno*, SOMNU 'sleep'), but INTERAMICO (-*m*- for -*mn*-) answers to the French (*sommeil*); NEPOTA appears for NEPTIS, but it is not a Spanish or Portuguese word, though it continues in Catalan as *neboda* 'niece', Prov. *neboda*, Venetian *neboda*, Rum. *nepoată*. No light is thrown on the characteristic Spanish development F > *h*, nor on the evolution of the group -CT-. The inscriptions bear witness to several common Romance changes, not as verified but as possible, in their variations of orthography, such as the simplification of unaccented vowels, the Romance values of old diphthongs, etc. They are notable for their 'betacism' (confusion of *b* and *v*), but this phenomenon is different from the equivalence of *b* and *v* in Spanish, Catalan and North Portuguese, and possibly starts from words like BIBIT VIVIT VOBIS BOVIS which provoke assimilation and dissimilation. Epenthetic vowels take their timbre, as in Basque, from neighbouring vowels rather than from neighbouring consonants as in French and Italian; and intervocal -P- -T- -K- are frequently voiced (IMUDAVIT for IMMUTAVIT, SAGERDOTES for SACERDOTES), though it is doubtful whether we should connect these forms with the voicing of intervocal voiceless occlusives in Portuguese and Spanish (other than Aragonese). Among interesting forms recorded are ALIS (for ALIUS) cf. OSp. *al* 'something else', PARAMUS Sp. *páramo*, TAM MAGNUS Sp. *tamaño* 'so big, size', CABALLUS 'horse', MANCIPIUS Sp. *mancebo* Cat. *macip* 'youth' (for MANCIPIUM), SOCRA Sp. *suegra* Ptg. Cat. *sogra* 'mother-in-law' (for SOCRUS), LAUSIA Sp. *losa* 'flagstone', COLLACTEUS Sp. *collazo* 'farm-hand', NATUS in the sense of 'child', NATALES in the sense of 'ancestry', MULIER replacing UXOR 'wife' as in all Romance languages, SUPERUM Sp. *sobre* as an adverb tending towards a preposition (QUIBUS SUPERUM PONITUR CAMERA), ALTARIUM a new singular from ALTARIA and source of Sp. *otero* 'hillock'.

Pliny, Columella, Pomponius Mela and St Isidore have preserved words popularly used in Spain, but naturally have no cause to indicate changes of pronunciation or syntax. These words are frequently technical terms: the names of plants or animals or of processes in mining. Most of them have left no trace in Romance. The testimony of St Isidore of Sevilla, in the sixth century, is the fullest and the most instructive. He quotes THIUS, from which derive Sp. Ptg. *tío* It. *zio*, as a Græcism, ANTENATUS Sp. *alnado* 'stepchild', CAPANNA Sp. *cabaña* 'hut', CATENATUM Sp. *candado* 'bolt', CATTUS Sp. *gato* 'cat', BURGUS cf. Burgos, CAMISIA Sp. *camisa* 'shirt', ARGENTEUS in the sense of 'white', SYMPHONIA as a musical instrument (Sp. *zampoña*), MALLEOLUS Sp. *majuelo* Cat. *mallol* 'new vine, white hawthorn', MANTUM Sp. *manto* 'cloak', MERENDARE Sp. *merendar* 'to lunch', PLAGIA Sp. *playa* 'beach', SAIO Sp. *sayón* 'executioner', SARNA

Sp. *sarna* 'itch', SERRALIA or SARRALIA Sp. *cerraja* 'common sow-thistle', etc. His vocabulary contains a few Iberian terms, more Celtiberian or Celtic, a considerable number of German terms (ARMILAUSA, BLAVUS 'blue', BURGUS, FLASCA, HOSA, MEDUS, SAIO, etc.), and others of doubtful provenance.

Cf. A. Carnoy, *Le Latin d'Espagne d'après les inscriptions* (2nd ed. Brussels, 1906), J. Sofer, *Lateinisches und Romanisches aus den 'Etymologiæ' des Isidorus von Sevilla* (Göttingen, 1930).

RELATION TO THE REST OF ROMANIA

Owing to the inconclusiveness and insufficiency of the monumental and literary record, it is from the Peninsular vernaculars themselves that we must enquire what was the special character of their Latinity, and how they developed their inheritance. In the first place our attention is called to a number of developments which the Peninsular languages share with those of Gaul, but which are quite absent in Rumanian. With regard to these criteria the northern dialects of Italy, occupying the site of the classical Gallia Cisalpina, are found to be in agreement with French and Provençal; whereas those of southern Italy, occupying Magna Græcia and the adjacent territories, show frequent affinities with Rumanian and with the Latin element in Albanian. Standard Italian, based on the Tuscan dialect, has vacillated between Eastern and Western Romance, and may be termed Central.

Spanish, Portuguese and Catalan agree with French and Provençal in the strong preference shown for a penultimate stress accent, though antepenultimates are more frequent the farther we go west in the Peninsula. Thus Western Romance comes to possess a notably trochaic rhythm (subject to further modification in the case of French), whereas Italian and Rumanian are rich in dactyls. Thus HÓMINES gives Ptg. *homens* Sp. *hombres* (OSp. *omnes*) Cat. *homes* Fr. *hommes* (with an *e* formerly pronounced); but It. *uòmini* Rum. *oameni*. As applied to declension, Western Romance has eliminated the type PECTUS PECTORA (with antepenultimate accent in the

plural); Eastern Romance has notably extended its use. The
plural of TEMPUS 'time' is thus Ptg. *tempos* Sp. *tiempos* Cat.
temps Rum. *timpurĭ*: of LATUS 'side' Ptg. Sp. *lados* OCat. *lats*
Rum. *lăturĭ*. In Western Romance -P- -T- -K- between vowels,
or between a vowel and -R-, became voiced (*b d g*), and
were then subjected to various changes amounting sometimes
to elimination; in Eastern Romance these voiceless occlusives remain; Italian vacillates. Thus

	Ptg.	Sp.	Cat.	Prov.	Fr.	It.	Rum.
RIPA	*riba*	*riba*	*riba*	*riba*	*rive*	*ripa, riva*	*rîpă*
VITA	*vida*	*vida*	*vida*	*vida*	*vie*	*vita*	*vită*
PATRE	*padre, pai*	*padre*	*pare*	*paire*	*père*	*padre*	—
PETRA	*pedra*	*piedra*	*pedra*	*peira*	*pierre*	*pietra*	*piatră*
PACAT	*paga*	*paga*	*paga*	*paga*	*paie*	*paga*	*pacă*
FOCU	*fogo*	*fuego*	*foc*[1]	*fuec*[1]	*feu*	*fuoco*	*foc*

In the West the -s of Latin accusative and nominative plurals
has been retained, while in Italian and the East it has been
lost. Spanish and Portuguese have used only the accusative
forms of the plural, whereas Provençal and Old French preserved both the nominative and the accusative in the singular
and plural. So we have

	Ptg. Sp.	Cat.	OFr.	MFr.	It.	Rum.
MURI	—	*mur*	—		*muri, mura*	*muri*
MUROS	*muros*	*murs*	*murs*	*murs*	—	—
CAPRAE	—	—	—		*capre*	*capre*
CAPRAS	*cabras*	*cabres*	*chievres*	*chèvres*	—	—

In the verbal flexion, apart from the retention of FIERI by
Rumanian and its use to form the passive (as against ESSE
in the West and Italy), the Eastern languages form the new
Romance future as one of 'volition' (VELLE), as *voĭŭ cantà*
'I shall sing' ('I wish to sing'), while the West and Italian
use the future of 'necessity' (HABEO), as Ptg. *cantarei* Sp.
cantaré Cat. *cantaré* Prov. *cantarai* Fr. *chanterai* It. *cantarò*. The
idea of necessity or compulsion still remains in the formula
Ptg. *hei-de cantar* Sp. *he de cantar* 'I have to sing', 'I must
sing'. The differences in vocabulary between the Eastern
and Western varieties of Romance are very numerous, owing

[1] -c from -g when the latter became final by loss of -o.

to the long seclusion of the Rumanians, cut off from the Adriatic by a ring of southern Slavonic tribes. The most conspicuous sign of this separate development is the presence of Germanic words in the West and Slavonic in the East; but the total want of Germanic in the East or Slavonic in the West. In this matter Italian is part and parcel of Western Romance, showing Eastern characteristics only in the greater number of its Hellenisms. Thus we have *WERRA 'war' Sp. Cat. Prov. *guerra* Fr. *guerre* It. *guerra*; but Rum. *razboĭŭ*, cf. Russ. *razboĭ*.

This essential cohesion of the Western half of Romania appears also in certain characteristics of Peninsular Romance which are not shared by the Castilian dialects. In comparatively recent times—after the eleventh century—Castilian has imposed itself as the literary and official speech of the central region; Castilian has, in fact, become 'Spanish'. It is an innovating dialect amid others that are more conservative, and the evidence of the other dialects of Spanish, taken with that of Portuguese and Catalan, shows Peninsular Romance as standing closer to Western Romance and to the general tendencies of Romania than does Castilian-Spanish. It is highly characteristic of Castilian-Spanish, as of Gascon, to have made initial F- an aspirate *h* and then to have silenced this letter; but in Catalan, Portuguese, Leonese, Aragonese and Mozarabic the F- remains:

> FACTU 'done' gives Cast. *hecho*, but Ptg. Leon. *feito* Arag. *feto fet* Cat. *fet* Fr. *fait* It. *fatto*.
> FABULARE 'talk' gives Cast. *hablar*, but Ptg. *falar* Fr. *fabler* OIt. *favolare*.

In Castilian-Spanish initial J- and Ġ- (i.e. before E or I) disappear, but it is elsewhere retained:

> JANUARIU (JEN-) 'January' gives Cast. *enero*, but Ptg. *janeiro* Moz. *yenair* Cat. *gener* Fr. *janvier* It. *gennaio*.

In Romance -CL- -LI-, medial, have given a palatal [λ], rendered *ll gl* or *lh*; in Castilian-Spanish this palatal has

suffered a further development to [ž] and later [χ], written *j*.
Thus

> FILIA 'daughter' gives Cast. *hija*, but Ptg. *filha* Leon. Arag. *filla*
> Cat. *filla* Fr. *fille* It. *figlia*.
> MULIERE 'woman' gives Cast. *mujer*, but Ptg. *molher* Leon. Arag. *muller*
> Cat. *muller* OFr. *moillier* It. *moglie*.
> OCULU 'eye' gives Cast. *ojo*, but Ptg. *olho* Moz. *welyo* Cat. *ull* OFr. *œil*,
> but It. *occhio*.

The group -CT- has suffered various transformations: in
Rumanian to *pt*, in Italian to *tt*. In the other Western
languages it has evolved as far as the stage *it*, but has been
carried further by Castilian to [ĉ] *ch*: as LACTE 'milk' Cast.
leche, but Ptg. Moz. Leon. Arag. *leite* Cat. *llet* Fr. *lait*. In
the evolution of the diphthongs from accented Ĕ and Ŏ,
though the various Western languages have not equally par-
ticipated and Portuguese not at all, the changes were carried
through, when they took place, with a measure of common
consent; and in the case where these vowels occurred before
a palatal, Castilian-Spanish again conceals the general tendencies of the Spanish dialects. ŎCULU, cited above, illustrates
this fact. Castilian does not diphthongize in this case; but
a diphthong is found in Mozarabic, Leonese and Aragonese,
in French, in Provençal *uelh* and Cat. *ull*, which conserves
in its *u* for Ŏ the trace of a former diphthong. The development of Ĕ Ŏ + palatal into a diphthong is the widest spread
of such diphthongs, and was general in the Spanish dialects
and in Catalan, but did not reach to Portugal, Galicia or
Cantabria, the ancient home of Castilian. The emergence
of these diphthongs in other cases (not shared by Catalan
and Provençal, nor by Portuguese) unites all the Spanish
dialects.

There are some instances of agreement between the Peninsula and Eastern Romance which have been argued to imply
an original contact between the two. The lost Latin of
Africa, the latinity of Sicily and Calabria, and the now lost
Romance of Dalmatia doubtless bridged the distance be-

tween Spain and the Balkans. Hence we note the agreement
in the metaphor used for discovery:

AFFLARE 'to sniff out' (of a hound?)   Ptg. *achar* Rum. *a aflá*
*FAFLARE (imitative)   Sp. *fallar, hallar,*

but *TROPARE 'to invent phrases' (school word) Cat. *trobar*
Fr. *trouver,* whence It. *trovare.* Similarly, the metaphor used
for arrival or departure was in Spain and Rumania PLICARE
'fold, tie up', but in France *AD-RIPA-RE 'come to the bank'.
Rum. *plecà* 'go away' (originally 'fold up a tent'), Sp. *llegar*
Ptg. *chegar* 'arrive' (originally 'tie up the ship to the bank');
Fr. *arriver* (whence It. *arrivare*) 'arrive' (originally 'come to
the bank'). Similarly Spain and Rumania have preferred
RIVU 'river' to FLUMEN or FLUVIU: Sp. Ptg. *río* Rum. *rîŭ;*
but Fr. *fleuve* It. *fiume.* They use PASSERE 'sparrow' in the
general sense of 'bird': Ptg. *páxaro,* Sp. *pájaro* Rum. *pasere;*
but Cat. *ocell* Fr. *oiseau* It. *uccello* from AVICELLU. For PULCHRU
'beautiful' they prefer FORMOSU to BELLU: Ptg. *formoso* Sp.
hermoso Rum. *frumos;* but Fr. *beau, bel* It. *bello.* REU 'defendant'
has been extended in Spanish and Portuguese to mean
'criminal' *(reo),* and further in Rumanian to mean 'bad'
(răŭ). QUEM has persisted in Ptg. *quem* Sp. *quien* Rum. *cine.*
but not to the north of the Pyrenees; and Spanish and
Rumanian make use of demonstratives compounded with
*ACCU- in preference to ECCE: Ptg. Sp. *aquí* Cat. Rum. *aci*
'here'. Coincidences of this kind do not suffice to divide
Romania into northern and southern Romance languages,
as has been alleged. They bear additional evidence to what is
otherwise quite plain, namely, that the most active centre of
innovations in Romania was Gaul, where French is found in
the eleventh-century *Chanson de Roland* further removed from
its parent Latin than Spanish is at the present day. Northern
and Central Italian lay more open to French influence (e.g.
trovare, arrivare) than the Peninsula, and some innovations
did not establish themselves in Spanish and Portuguese;
these testify to an older stage of spoken Latin, shared by
Rumanian also. The obliteration of African Latin by the

Vandals and Moslems prevents the formulation of any sure statement as to the dialectal peculiarities of that region.

Within Western Latin, that of Spain and Portugal forms a close group with certain characteristic differences from French, Provençal and even Catalan. The final vowels in Ibero-Romance are *a e o*; in the Asturias there is also a trace of *u* in the declension of masculine nouns S. *u* Pl. *os* or in *dixo* (*dijo* 'he said') but *xudíu* (*judío* 'Jew'). The Romance of Gaul preserves only final *a* (in French as *e* 'mute'), and when *e* appears it is only as a vowel of support for a difficult consonant group. So Cast. *hija hijo infante* contrasts with Cat. *filla fill infant* Fr. *fille fils enfant*. Spanish and Portuguese agree in conserving a declension in the accusative case only: *muro*, *muros*. Gallo-Romance distinguished a nominative and an oblique case in both numbers and declined in OFr. Nom. S. *murs* Obl. S. *mur* Nom. Pl. *mur* Obl. Pl. *murs*. A few sporadic nominatives and genitives are found in Spanish and Portuguese. DEUS 'God' gives Ptg. *Deus* Sp. *Dios*, through the influence of the liturgy; but Jewish-Spanish *El Dio* from DEUM. *Carlos, Oliveros, Montesinos, Marcos* are due to clerical influence, supported in some instances by memory of the French nominative in *-s*. The genitive is found in VENERIS (DIES) Sp. *viernes* 'Friday' JOVIS (DIES) Sp. *jueves* 'Thursday' MARTIS (DIES) Sp. *martes* 'Tuesday', while *lunes* (LUNAE) *miércoles* (MERCURII) are analogical formations. The patronymic ending *-ez* is best explained as due to analogical influence. The model was the names in -ACI (RODERICUS DIDACI, *Dídaz*, *Díaz*). A parallel ending -ICI would have given rise to *-ez* (Fernández as if from *Fernandici*, FERNANDI). In the relative pronoun the nominative *qui* persisted as well as the accusative *quem*, and in the personal pronoun the nominative accusative dative all survived, Sp. *yo me mi*, Ptg. *eu me mim*. But these are merely relics of declensional cases; there were no systematic distinctions as in Gallo-Romance. Gallo-Romance developed mixed vowels (*ü, œ*) which are not found in Ibero-Romance, nor in Catalan. In the Peninsula the seven Vulgar Latin tonic vowels persisted in Ptg. Cat. *a ɛ e i o ǫ u*, and in

Spanish ę ǫ developed further into the diphthongs *ie ue*. The
system of pronunciation is basically the same in all the Peninsular languages, despite superinduced differences. In the
treatment of the verb Ibero-Romance reduced the number
of 'strong' perfects and past participles much more drastically
than Gallo-Romance, Catalan occupying a middle position
in this respect; and Ibero-Romance made no use in conjugation of inceptive forms (-ESCERE), used in Gallo-Romance
and Catalan to regularize the accent in the *-ir* conjugation:
Sp. *floréce florecémos*, Prov. *florís florém*, Cat. *floréix florím*.
A notable archaism of Ibero-Romance has been the retention of the pluperfect in -RA, which has in Portuguese
regularly, and in Spanish occasionally, the pluperfect sense.
Rumanian also has preserved the pluperfect idea, but has
used for it the Latin pluperfect subjunctive. In Gallo-
Romance this tense was preserved only by Provençal, and
only for the conditional, as also in Catalan. Ibero-Romance
is marked, naturally, by the presence of Iberian and Basque
words, though these are few in number, and often difficult
of demonstration.

The correspondence between Portuguese and the older
dialects of Spanish, such as Mozarabic, is so close that the
language appears in general archaic beside Castilian. Innovations are few. Portuguese has endeavoured to eliminate *-l-*
between vowels (CAELU Ptg. *céu* Sp. *cielo* 'heaven, sky'), and
-n-, OLISIPONE *Lisboa*, BONA Ptg. *boa* Sp. *buena*. The process
of denasalization is not everywhere complete, and is frequently encountered in the intermediate stage at which the
nasal consonant has disappeared but the preceding vowel
has suffered nasalization, as LANA *lã* 'wool'. In other instances the vowel had combined with the lost *m* to give
a nasal diphthong: TAM BENE *tambem* [tẽ̯u̯bẽi̯] Sp. *también* 'also'.
The sources of these nasal vowels and the grade of their
nasality differ from those of the French nasals. Portuguese
has developed the faculty of conjugating its infinitive to
indicate person (the 'personal' infinitive) in cases where
Spanish uses the nominative of a personal pronoun with the

infinitive; and it has made more use of TENERE Ptg. *ter* as the auxiliary of perfect tenses. It was from the side of Portugal (from Galicia or León) that there came the initial impetus to modify PL- CL- FL-; and the Portuguese *ch* (*chama* from CLAMAT 'he calls' or FLAMMA 'flame', *chaga* from PLAGA 'wound') has carried the process some stages further than Sp. *llama llaga*. While there is no need to suppose that the Portuguese-Galician and Spanish languages were ever identical, each being descended in an equally direct line from spoken Latin, it is evident that they were originally distinguished only by minimal points of difference.

Catalan is very different from Portuguese and literary Spanish, and its precise situation in Romania has been, and continues, to be a matter of dispute. Some philologists hold that it belongs essentially to Ibero-Romance, chiefly on the ground of the very easy transition from Spanish to Catalan through the Aragonese dialects of the two Nogueras. In that region, to the north of Tamarite and Binéfar, the characteristics of Spanish in the Aragonese patois transform themselves gradually into the characteristics of Catalan. On the contrary, the cleft between the Catalan of Roussillon and the Provençal of Languedoc is abrupt, and has always held to the same frontier, so far as evidence survives. This frontier is determined by the northern branch of the Pyrenees—the Corbières—which protected the medieval frontier, and probably coincided with ancient ethnic divisions. The present line of division follows the southern range, the Alberes. If, however, standard Catalan, standard Spanish and Provençal be arranged in parallel columns, then the occasional agreement of Catalan with Spanish is overbalanced by the proportion of its coincidences with Provençal. Such a method, however, may prove fallacious. We have seen, for instance, that Castilian-Spanish does not represent the consensus of Spanish dialects, and that for comparison with Catalan the Aragonese dialect would be a more adequate criterion: on the other hand, Provençal is so wanting in unity that to describe forms as 'Provençal' is arbitrary. It is, however clear that the evidence of common-sense must be accepted and the palpable similarity of a Catalan to a Provençal text, for instance in the Catalan and Languedocian versions of the Viscount of Roda's voyage to the Purgatory of St Patrick, must be duly recognized; while at the same time we must admit that the transition from Spanish to Catalan is effected without interruption in the Pyrenean region. The latter does not prove Catalan to be a branch of the Ibero-Romance family any more than the similar band-frontier between French and Italian cancels the difference between those two great languages. The term 'language', indeed, in this acceptation is not exclusively a philological expression. It involves cultural elements. A 'language' has a cultural centre, often a literature, at least some middle point whence influences radiate. A dialect also has its dialectal centre, and the difference between language and dialect is one of degree. There is greater independence in a 'language'; it looks towards some veritable capital. Such a capital Catalan has had since the tenth century in Barcelona, and even in earlier times the Marca Hispanica possessed a certain self-determination. The clear-cut frontier by the Corbières proves that Catalan is a trans-Pyrenean language, and not a dialect of Provençal, however close the two speeches may otherwise stand; the possession of a separate culture and a linguistic centre in the Peninsula, supported by the existence of a band-frontier in Aragon and by the sum total of its differences, cuts off Catalan from Ibero-Romance strictly so called, and shows it to be an independent language of a type approximating to Provençal.

The differences of the three languages may be appreciated from the following *Paternosters*:

Catalan: Pare nostre, qui estau en lo cel: sia santificat lo vostre sant nom; vinga a nosaltres lo vostre sant regne; faça's, Senyor, la vostra voluntat, aixì en la terra com se fa en lo cel.

Lo nostre pa de cada dia donau-nos, Senyor, en lo dia d'avui; i perdonau-nos les nostres culpes, aixì com nosaltres perdonam a nostres deutors; i no permetau que nosaltres caigam en la temptació, ans deslliurau-nos de qualsevol mal. Amén.

Spanish: Padre nuestro que estás en los cielos, santificado sea tu nombre. Venga tu reino. Sea hecha tu voluntad, como en el cielo, así también en la tierra.

Danos hoy nuestro pan cotidiano, y perdónanos nuestras deudas, como también nosotros perdonamos a nuestros deudores. Y no nos metas en tentación, mas líbranos del mal: porque tuyo es el reino, y el poder, y la gloria, por todos los siglos. Amén.

Portuguese: Padre-nosso, que estais nos céus, santificado seja o vosso nome; venha a nós o vosso reino, seja feita a vossa vontade, assim na terra como no céu.

O pão nosso de cada dia dai-nos hoje. Perdoai-nos, Senhor, as nossas dívidas, assim como nós perdoamos aos nossos devedores. Não nos deixeis, Senhor, cair em tentação, mas livrai-nos de todo o mal. Amen.

CHARACTERISTICS OF IBERO-ROMANCE

The Romance of the centre and west of the Peninsula is marked by certain characteristics, in which Catalan shares to a much slighter degree. It is remarkably conservative and traditional. These notes are most evident in Portuguese, which has, in many of its particulars, an air of being an archaic condition of Spanish. Innovations have occurred, but at all epochs there has been resistance to neologisms, which have tended to be restricted to the names of things, and so to pass out of the language with the disuse of the thing they imply; or else neologisms have been adjectives confined to specific strata of the language, like poetry or science. The chief centre of novelty in Romania was in Gaul, and frequently the Peninsula owes its innovations to French precedent. The Frankish form taken by many Germanic loan-words is evidence of this. At the same time Peninsular Romance shows a profound instinct for simplification and rationalization. In this respect Castilian is the most characteristic form: diphthongs have become monophthongs, consonant-groups have been simplified, the noun has shed its declensions and the verb its 'strong' conjugations more completely than in other parts of Romania. Transitional forms, it is true, have arisen which were more complicated than their Latin originals. Elimination of unaccented vowels has left new clumps of consonants, but these have been for the most part ironed smooth again by the genius of the language for simplification. On the other hand, there is a sense of realism and liveliness in the handling of the linguistic material. The verbal paradigm has remained for the sake of expressing in subtle detail all the concomitant circumstances of an activity or state—mood, time, person. Numerous auxiliaries augment the possible moods and tenses. The choice between alternative words and the rich store of diminutives allow the speaker's emotion to play over his whole discourse. Thus the manner of handling common Latin material is what chiefly gives their special character to Spanish, Portuguese and Catalan.

There are interesting archaisms in the latinity of Spain. Traces of pre-classical Latin occur, which may be due to the early subjection of Valencia and Andalusia by Scipio's legions. The adjective CUIUS -A -UM Sp. *cuyo* Ptg. *cujo* 'whose' does not occur in Catalan or French (cf. Vergil, *Ecl.* iii, 1: 'Dic mihi, Damœta, cuium pecus? an Melibœi?'); cŏva (CLat. cava) Sp. *cueva* Ptg. *cova* 'cave' and VOCARE (CLat. vacare) Sp. *bogar* Ptg. *vogar* 'row' do not show participation in a change which occurred in Latin itself. Possibly FACE (CLat. FAC) Sp. *haz* Ptg. *faz* 'do' may be an archaism. In the *Poema de mio Cid* (c. 1140) the classical CRAS 'to-morrow' still survived, alongside *mañana*, which is now only used. All three languages retain SEMPER Sp. *siempre* Ptg. *sempre* Cat. *sempre* 'always', though Catalan has also *tots temps*, a new formation like the French *toujours* OCat. *tots jorns*. The classical RES REM are found: Cat. *no. . .res* 'nothing at all', Sem Tob's *sabelo toda res* 'all things know that', OSp. OPtg. Cat. *ren* 'thing'. But CAUSA is the normal word employed: Sp. Cat. *cosa* Ptg. *cousa* 'thing', cf. Fr. *chose*.

Besides specimens of archaic and Classical Latin retained after they had fallen elsewhere, it has been claimed that the Peninsula shows traces of Italic dialects other than Latin. The name of the city chosen by Sertorius as the capital of an independent Spain, OSCA *Huesca*, suggests the name of the Oscans of southern Italy. It happens, also, that this district is the focus of certain peculiarities of pronunciation which run parallel with those of southern Italy as known in classical and modern times. Thus when we compare

	Ptg.	Leon.	Cast.	Arag.	Cat.	Fr.
PALUMBA, COLUMBA 'dove'	pomba	palomba	paloma	paloma	coloma	palombe
LOMBU 'loin'	lombo	lombo	lomo	lomo	llom	lombes

we find Aragonese the centre of a special treatment of -MB-, which recalls the misspelling COMMURERE for COMBURERE on an inscription at Ostia, and the development of COLUMBULA in Neapolitan *kolommrę*. So AMBO gave in OCast. *amos* 'both', of which the modern *ambos* is a latinization. Similarly the treatment of -ND- in UNDA Cat. Arag. *ona* 'wave', which does not extend to Castilian, resembles the QUANDO *quannu* 'when' of southern Italy and the equation between OPER-ANDAM and Oscan UPSANNAM. More restricted still is the reduction of -LD- to *l*. These circumstances have suggested the possibility of an Oscan colonization of this region, modifying the latinity of Spain. But there is as yet no direct evidence of such a colony, and a spontaneous development is by no means impossible. We have, indeed, our *plummer* for 'plumber', vulgar *Lunnon* for 'London' and *chillun* (Negroid) for 'children', without Oscan intervention; and the same may have been true of Aragón and Catalonia.

Nouns of relationship show remarkable changes in the Peninsula, and especially in its centre and west. There has been a general shifting of meaning, and some substitution. 'Father' and 'mother' remain, but in Portuguese affectionate nursery forms are also current, especially for 'mother': *pai mãe*. UXOR disappears, and MULIERE serves for 'wife' as well as 'woman'. FRATRE and SORORE were ousted by GERMANU -A 'brother', 'sister', in all three languages: Sp. *hermano -a* Ptg. *irmão -ã* Cat. *germà -ana*. Similarly in all three NEPOS, NEPTIS (NEPOTA on an inscription) shifted from the sense 'nephew' 'niece' to that of 'grandchild': Sp. *nieto -a* Ptg. *neto -a* Cat. *nét -a*. This left an empty category. Spanish and

Portuguese used for the purpose *sobrino -a* 'nephew' 'niece', but Catalan *nebot neboda*. Thus SOBRINU and CONSOBRINU were unsuited to express the idea 'cousin' in Spanish and Portuguese (Cat. *cosí -ina* Fr. *cousin -e*), and PRIMU (HERMANU) or CONGERMANU were employed: Sp. *primo (hermano)* OSp. *cormano*. This was the simpler, since PRIMUS did not serve as an ordinal number, where it had yielded to PRIMARIU. 'Uncle' 'aunt' were named by what St Isidore reports as a græcism, THIU -A, perhaps with affectionate good-humour: Sp. Ptg. *tío tía* (cf. It. *zio zia*), but Cat. *oncle tia* Fr. *oncle tante*.

Certain domestic objects are liable to change nomenclature, often for humorous and deprecatory reasons. This refers to parts of the body, the serviceable animals, and the house and house-work. For 'heart', COR OSp. *cuer* Cat. *cor* has given way to *CORATIONE Sp. *corazón* Ptg. *coração*. For 'head', CAPU(T) survives in Cat. *cap*, but in Sp. Ptg. *cabo* 'cape, end, corporal' Sp. *cabe* 'near' it survives in transferred and metaphorical senses only. The deprecatory *CAPITTIA has been preferred (OSp. Ptg. *cabeça* MSp. *cabeza*), but these languages have not indulged in humorous metaphor like French and Italian, which use TESTA 'potsherd' It. *testa* Fr. *tête*, from which the OSp. *testa* is a loan-word used in literature. ROSTRU 'beak' has been, as it were, ennobled to mean 'face': Sp. *rostro* Ptg. *rosto*; BARBA 'beard' has extended its domain to include not only 'chin' (*barbilla* Fr. *menton*) but also the 'heavy father' of plays, though it has not gone so far as to supplant the general terms for 'man' 'husband', like Rum. *bărbat*. The 'eye' remains OCULU Sp. *ojo* Ptg. *olho* Cat. *ull*; but the 'ear' is the 'little ear', AURICULA Sp. *oreja* Ptg. *orelha* Cat. *orella* Fr. *oreille*. As for the limbs, the 'right' arm and hand are indicated by DEXTERA and DIRECTA; the 'left' is ill-omened and more liable to change. LAEVU does not survive; SINISTRU persisted as Sp. *siniestro* Ptg. *sestro* Cat. *sinistre*, but it has been avoided in general use by the employment of a Basque loan-word B. *ezker* Sp. *izquierdo* Ptg. *esquerdo* Cat. *esquerre*. For 'leg' the humorous equivalent 'ham' has been employed: PERNA Sp. *pierna* Ptg. *perna*. Catalan, like French, has preferred Gk. *kampé* CAMBA GAMBA (if this be not Celtic) Cat. *cama* Fr. *jambe*.

The domestic animals affected are the horse, dog, cat, bee, and cattle. For 'mare' EQUA persisted in Peninsular Romance (Sp. *yegua* Ptg. *egua* Cat. *euga*) since the word had not suffered serious phonetic loss like OFr. *ive*, for which MFr. substitutes JUMENTU *jument*. The 'horse', however, encouraged distinctions. In general use EQUU gave place to the popular CABALLU Sp. *caballo* Ptg. *cavalo* Cat. *cavall*. Where horses are bred, as in Spanish America, the use of *caballo* is rare, but some more specific reference to the animal, for instance its colour, is customary. For 'mule' as well as MULA there came into use MASCULU Sp. *macho*. A general word for cattle was adopted after the Moslem irruption: Ar. *rá's* 'head' Sp. Ptg. *res* 'head of cattle'; but the Germanic *ganar* 'win', applied particularly to cattle-lifting and cattle-breeding, gave Sp. *ganado* Ptg. *gado* 'herd'. OVE 'sheep' gave way to OVICULA Sp. *oveja* Ptg. *ovelha* Cat. *ovella*, with a new Spanish masculine *carnero* 'ram'. Similarly APE 'bee' was replaced by APICULA Sp. *abeja* Ptg. *abelha* Cat. *abella*. The motive may have been a desire to avoid a monosyllable, though AVE 'bird' has survived alongside PASSERE Sp. *pájaro* Ptg. *pássaro* and AVICELLU Cat. *ocell*, at least for poetical purposes. FELI 'cat' was replaced by CATTU, of uncertain origin: Sp. Ptg. *gato* Cat. *gat*. For 'dog' CANE remained in Sp. *can* Ptg. *cão* Cat. *cà*, but has yielded for general purposes in Spanish to *perro*.

In the house we notice the disappearance of DOMU, which survives only in the compounds Sp. *mayordomo* Ptg. *mordomo* Cat. *majordom* 'steward, superintendent'. Otherwise it has given way to CASA Sp. Ptg. Cat. *casa*, and the latter has further tended to become an enclitic (*cas ca*) in vulgar Spanish, in the sense of 'at the house of': *ca cura* 'at the priest's house'. The tendency has not been carried through, as in Fr. *chez*, so as to require the creation of yet another term for house. Fr. *maison*, when borrowed, took the sense of 'inn' Sp. *mesón*. The 'estate' round the house consisted of tasks that had to be performed, FACIENDA Sp. *hacienda*

Ptg. *fazenda*; and from that beginning we have *hacienda* meaning 'estate' 'house on the estate' 'farm', and also 'national estate, exchequer'. These 'things to be done' implied, for men, agriculture; hence the specialization of LABORARE to farm-work in *labrar labranza labrador*. For women, however, *labor* is 'needle-work'. As to the things of the house, Sp. Ptg. *cama* 'bed' is more usual than LECTU Sp. *lecho* Ptg. *leito*, which Catalan and French prefer: Cat. *llit* Fr. *lit*. The 'door' appears as OSTIU *uço* (in the *Poema de mio Cid*), but otherwise is PORTA Sp. *puerta* Ptg. Cat. *porta*. The idea of 'window' is more variable. Spanish prefers *ventana* 'wind-hole', since in hot countries air is more welcome than light, and Portuguese has *janela* 'little door'; but FENESTRA gave OSp. *hiniestra* Ptg. *fresta* Cat. *finestra*. The words for 'road' are numerous: Ptg. *rua* Cast. *calle* Cat. *carrer*, as well as *camino calzada carretera*, etc.

The Peninsula preferred to retain DIES 'day' in the form DIA Sp. Ptg. Cat. *dia*. Catalan also has DIURNU *jorn*, for literary purposes (cf. Fr. *jour* It. *giorno*). For POMA 'apple' Cat. *poma* Fr. *pomme*, the name of a specific brand was preferred: POMA MATTIANA Sp. *manzana* Ptg. *maçã*. To express the idea 'small' the word PARVU was deemed inadequate, though it survives in Ptg. *parvo* 'simpleton', and as a learned word in Spanish. A root *PIK or *PIT may have seemed sound-symbolic of the idea, and led to the *PICCUINNU of Sp. *pequeño* Ptg. *pequeno*, as well as the *PETTITTUS of Fr. Prov. Cat. *petit*.

The labour of selection occurred also among well-known verbs, and helped still further to characterize the Peninsular lexicon, and particularly that of Ibero-Romance. For 'wish' VELLE disappeared, *VOLERE gave Fr. *vouloir* Cat. *voler*, but is found in Spanish only in fixed phrases of the old language such as OSp. *si vuel que*. In Ibero-Romance its place was taken by QUAERERE 'seek' Sp. Ptg. *querer*, which also acquired the sense of 'love' and that of immediate futurity: *Tan malo está don Tristán que a Dios quiere dar el alma* 'Sir Tristram is so ill that he is on the point of giving his soul to God.' 'To

take' is Sp. Ptg. *tomar*, Fr. Cat. *p(r)endre* from PREHENDERE.
'To look at' is 'to take with the eyes' CAPTARE OCULIS OSp.
catar, and then 'to wonder at' MIRARI MSp. *mirar*. Though
EDERE 'to eat' is lost, COMEDERE survives on Spanish soil as
Sp. Ptg. *comer*; Cat. *menjar* Fr. *manger* is from MANDUCARE
'to masticate', which has given Sp. *manjares* 'victuals'.
OCCIDERE 'kill' remains in OCat. *occir*; Sp. Ptg. *matar* is a
generalization of MACTARE 'to slay a victim', perhaps due
to the semantic influence of Ar. *mâta* 'he has died'. In
addition to DICERE Sp. *decir* Ptg. *dizer* Cat. *dir* 'to say', Ibero-
Romance has preferred FABULARE to the Gallo-Romance
PARABOLARE in the sense 'to speak': Sp. *hablar* Ptg. *falar*,
Fr. *parler* Cat. *parlar*. A depreciative meaning is associated
with the borrowed term: Sp. *parlar* 'to chatter' Fr. *hâbler* 'to
brag'. IRE 'to go' was eked out in its paradigm by VADERE
and AMBITARE, and in the past tenses by the stem FU-. 'To
find' is in Ibero-Romance 'to breathe on sniff out (a
rabbit?)' AFFLARE Sp. *hallar* Ptg. *achar*; but in Gallo-Romance
'to invent tropes' *TROPARE Fr. *trouver* Cat. *trobar*. The latter
was used in Spain and Portugal of poetical invention: *trobar*
'to make verses', *trobas* 'songs, verses'. *Trobador* 'poet' displaced at court the older *juglar*, and was itself ousted in the
early fifteenth century by the Italianate *poeta*, as implying
a higher conception of art.

ILLE has given the article to all the Peninsular languages,
but in the notarial documents of the early Middle Ages we
find IPSE used undemonstratively, like an article. In the
Catalan area its use was considerable, and rivalled that of
ILLE, and in the Balearic Islands it has gained the upper hand.
A demonstrative was obtained from ILLE by using the demonstrative prefix *ACCU- (preferred in the Peninsula to the
ECCE, ECCU- of French and Italian): *aquel* 'that'. Peninsular
Romance maintains with precision the three spatial indications of Latin HIC ISTE ILLE ('this by me' 'that by you' 'that
by someone else'). HIC, however, disappeared, save in *aquí*
*ACCU-HIC 'here by me', and set phrases like *agora* HAC HORA
'now' *hogaño* HOC ANNO 'this year' *pero* PER HOC 'but'. The

place of HIC was taken by ISTE; that of ISTE by IPSE; and the series came to run *este ese aquel*, with the variants *aqueste aquese* in old and classical Spanish (Cat. *aquest aqueix aquell*). The same personal relations were imported into adverbs of place 'in which' (*aquí ahí allí*), and less perfectly into place 'towards which' (*acá...allá*). Among other particles we may instance TAM MAGNU Sp. *tamaño* Ptg. *tamanho* 'size'; PER PRO merged into a single preposition Sp. Ptg. *por* (Cat. *per* OPtg. *per* and *por*), and from this the creation of *pora para*. The system of conjunctions and prepositions in Peninsular Romance is simple. They are rarely combined in pairs, and never in longer groups, like It. *acciochè* 'to the end that'. As the sign of the comparative all three languages use MAGIS Sp. *más* Ptg. *mais* Cat. *més* 'more' (PLUS Fr. *plus* It. *più*). Old Portuguese had *chus*, and medieval Catalan preferred *pus*.

In dealing with the forms of words inherited from Latin (declensions and conjugations) the Peninsular languages display simplifying and rationalizing tendencies. Indication of number is reduced to a common formula S. - Pl. (*e*)*s*. This was easier since the neuter declensions had been distributed among the other two genders, the singular to the masculine (which became the common gender in consequence), and the plurals in -A to the collective feminine: LIGNU LIGNA Sp. *leño* 'faggot' *leña* 'wood'. Declensions of the type TEMPUS, TEMPORA disappeared: Sp. *tiempo*(*s*). In a few cases this neuter singular was construed as a plural: OSp. *huebos* OPUS Sp. *pechos* PECTUS Cat. *temps* TEMPUS. At the same time the case-system was reduced to the accusative alone: -*o* -*os* -*a* -*as*. Traces of the nominative occur in DEUS Sp. *Dios* Ptg. *Deus* (but Jewish *el Dio* DEUM) 'God', Ptg. *demo*, *Marcos Carlos Oliveros*, etc. A vocative occurs in OSp. *Santiague* SANCTE JACOBE, and genitives in the days of the week JOVIS Sp. *jueves* MARTIS Sp. *martes* VENERIS Sp. *viernes* (and so *lunes miércoles* from LUNAE MERCURII + -*es*). Relics of the ablative are *hogaño* 'this year', *agora* 'now'.

The verbal paradigm was much simplified. Almost all 'strong' past participles have disappeared, save for *visto dicho hecho* 'seen' 'said' 'done'. A few survive as adjectives: *bienquisto* 'well-liked', but *querido* (past participle of *querer*). Of the regular past participles, those in -UTU played a part in medieval Spanish, but have been restricted since to adjectival use. The future participle in -URU, the present in -NTE and the gerundives have also been eliminated, to the sole profit of the gerund -NDO. They remain only among adjectives: *futuro amante tremebundo* 'future' 'loving' 'frightful'. 'Strong' preterites have also been vastly reduced, in contrast with their survival in French and Italian, and the forms even of 'irregular' verbs are surprisingly regular. The conjugation in -ĔRE disappeared in Spanish and Portuguese, to the profit of -ĒRE, and the latter tended to pass into -IRE. The paradigms in *-er -ir* show only half a dozen divergent forms. The passive was lost, as in all Romance; but Spanish and Portuguese have shown particular reluctance to readmit the passive, preferring to give the reflexive forms in *se* an extended use covering both middle and passive purposes. The future and conditional tenses are compounds of the infinitive + HABEO. Spanish and Portuguese, however, have retained the Latin pluperfect indicative, in both indicative and conditional senses.

On the other hand, a great development of auxiliaries has vastly increased the subtlety of the verb. 'To have' and 'to be' have each two forms: HABERE TENERE, ESSE (SEDERE) STARE, to which the Portuguese add *ficar*. For each of these auxiliaries there are synonyms: Sp. *quedar llevar resultar venir* etc., and even *amanecer anochecer* 'to break (of day)' 'to fall (of night)', which give such odd results as *amaneció muerto* 'he dawned dead', 'he was dead at dawn'. Verbs of motion are used freely as auxiliaries, as *voy a decir* 'I am about to say'; but OSp. *fué a dar* Cat. *va donar* are preterites. *Acabar de* is 'to have just done'; *volver a* OSp. *tornar a* 'to do again'.

CAUSES OF THE DIFFERENTIATION OF THE PENINSULAR LANGUAGES

Ingenious theories have arisen to account for the changes which occur everywhere in human speech, and no one of them can be deemed wholly to cover the facts. The sources of disintegration are doubtless many, and their mode of operation complex. The phenomena to be explained are so numerous, but the changes which we can personally witness are so few, that we can scarcely avoid generalizing on a basis of insufficient experience. The emergence of differences within the Peninsula has been variously explained, and usually on the basis of a formula too simple for the facts. We shall consider all these partial causes as contributory, though in unsettled proportions, to the total effect.

The most abstract and general cause to be alleged is the effect of time and space. In course of time human speech acquires new characteristics, no matter what effort is made to keep it constant; and over wide areas a language begins to vary. But the effect of time and space is not mathematically constant. Education may counteract dispersion by maintaining a standard and restoring 'correct' forms. Thus the Spanish of America, after showing signs of diverging from European Spanish and setting up a new speech-family in the New World, now appears to be converging on the standard tongue, thanks to the educative influence of grammars, education, literature and travel. What causes diversity in the Peninsula in respect of space is the fact that it is seamed with mountain ranges which break up its surface into regions and *patrias chicas*; these are self-centred and, huddling each round its nucleus, they offer facilities for local divergences whenever other circumstances permit. Similarly, the languages have remained almost constant over considerable periods of time, so that, for instance, to read a thirteenth-century work in Spanish does not require a special grammatical training; but there are other epochs in which change works rapidly, as in the sixteenth century.

That change is due to imperfect imitation of an older generation by a younger has been averred. The alleged reason is too abstract. Generations are not marked off in this rigid fashion, but exist coetaneously. Many an uncle has a nephew of his own age. It is not certain that imitation is imperfect, nor that change is an imperfection. On the contrary, we make deliberate changes with some idea of betterment. In time of war there is a rapid coining of new words or borrowing of loan-words thanks to rapid and violent successions of new experiences. Such were the Hindustani terms that gained some vogue in English during the late War, and the Italian military terms that invaded Spanish during the Golden Age. Indeed, one notices that it is the languages which have the most active intellectual background (English, French, Chinese) that show the most rapid changes—evidence that phonetic alteration is not solely due to imperfection.

The substratum-theory of change is similarly insufficient to account for the facts and is excessively abstract. In this case it is supposed that when a nation or tribe acquires a new language—and specifically when the Iberians acquired Latin—they learn it with the imperfect articulation of adults, and perpetuate old prejudices of pronunciation, vocabulary and syntax, in the new medium. From what has gone before, it will be apparent to the reader that we are unable to say with certainty what were the linguistic prejudices of an Iberian, nor can we be definite as to the proportion of Iberians among the total population of the Peninsula. The same is true of the Celts, for even those of Gaul are not adequately known. The substratum-theory has flourished abundantly where the substratum is virtually unknown. In the Spanish of America we have plenty of evidence as to the kind of Spanish implanted and the preferences of many different substrata; but we shall see that their influence is restricted, diminishing, and less effective than that of an external language like French. The notion is too abstract: a tribe does not go to school *en bloc* but as individuals, of different ages and at different times. The errors of adult speakers are not

those of younger learners, nor are they maintained longer than the duration of the speaker's unawareness of error. Both old and young are subjected to the pressure of education, seeking to impose the normal standards. Only under special circumstances will tribal prejudices be permitted to survive. Communication with the centres of the acquired culture may be severed or difficult, the influence of education neutralized through poverty or barbarism, or some peculiarity may, through military or feudal prestige, become a shibboleth. Any or all of these conditions may have combined with Basque origin to supplant in Cantabria the Latin F; Castilian prestige carried the Cantabrian h over all the Spanish-speaking world.

The tribal boundaries may have a secondary importance for language when they have perpetuated themselves in later organization. Though imperfectly recognized by the Romans, there is not infrequently an agreement between the tribal frontier, the *diœcesis* and *provincia*, and the medieval bishoprics, which maintains old units. Each such division has its capital or nucleus, and the latter operates the more powerfully in conservation and innovation the longer it stands undisturbed. Hence the importance of bishoprics in determining varieties of Romance: that of Elne which maintained the frontier of Catalan in Roussillon against Narbonne, or that of Astorga which is the bulwark of western Leonese, and thanks to inclusion in it the Portuguese town of Miranda do Douro is Spanish-speaking. The frontiers of kingdoms are often due to more arbitrary causes, and fail to coincide with linguistic boundaries.

That the circumstances of romanization must have exerted a powerful formative influence on the later languages is certain, but hard to make precise in detail. We have so little knowledge of those circumstances, nor do we see the changes actually taking place. The roads of the Empire played their part. They carried speakers of Latin from town to town, imposed some measure of Latinity on the travelling community, and so laid down a band of Latin speech. Thus the great road from Tarragona to the Ebro, via Lérida and Huesca, is a main cause of the romanization of Aragón, and drove Basque into the hills. The dates of the arrival and of the departure of the legions were both, doubtless, significant. Thanks to their very early arrival in Spain (207 B.C.) they probably implanted in Spanish Latin those Plautine words (CUIUS COVA VOCARE, etc.) which were not carried to Gaul by Cæsar. Remoteness from Rome, and a certain cultural semi-independence in Bætica prevented their being obliterated when the fashion changed at the capital. But the early arrival of the legions explains only a tiny fraction of Spanish Latinity. The language as a whole was the *koiné* of the Empire, and of date much later than Scipio Africanus. As for the departure of the legions, this broke up the formal unity of the Empire in the fifth century, and made communication more difficult. Isolation set in for the ancestors of the Rumanians and the Sardinians. But in Spain the break-up of the Empire was less felt. The Visigothic kings aped the style of regents for the Empire. They had extensive interests in France, and family connections with northern Italy. A Visigothic king defended civilization against Attila at Châlons. The Spanish church kept up the Roman connection with especial fervour, as a protest against the Arianism of their rulers; and traders continued to move internationally. Isolation set in for Spain only with the Arab-Berber conquest of A.D. 711, which enclosed the Christians of the south (Mozarabs) within a Moslem state at war with Christendom, and so led to the stagnation of Southern Romance. It reduced the north to beggary and fragmentary resistance, loosened cultural control, and confided the survival of Christianity to a number of petty nuclei.

It has been supposed that the incoming Romans brought not always the standard Latin of literary circles. Some were doubtless Oscans or Umbrians. The name of *Huesca* (OSCA) and its prominence as a quondam capital of Spain tempts the theory that in Huesca there was a focus of Oscan colonization. The linguistic evidence (solution of MB as *m*, ND as *n*, etc.)

has already been mentioned; but the premisses of this argument are insecure. Again, it has been ingeniously suggested that Catalonia was a peaceful province, like Narbonese Gaul, especially suited for the settlement of discharged legionaries. These *coloni* would bring with them the debased Latin of the camps, and consequently the Latin of Catalonia would contain within it more seeds of change than that of Spain. Spanish and Portuguese Latin, on the other hand, may have been acquired primarily under the influence of the great rhetorical schools of Bætica. This Latin was PINGUIS 'ornate' in the opinion of some Italians, but with the Senecas and Lucan it set a new fashion in the capital. It was the medium of an urban aristocracy who may have lived as a small minority among non-Latin rustics and plebeians for an unspecified period of the duration of the Empire. The Cantabrians, at least, were only pacified under Augustus, but not actually subdued by either Rome or the later Visigoths; and they may have preserved their linguistic independence also. When at last the Spanish masses were romanized, therefore, the Latin they learned would still have the grammatical structure and conservative vocabulary of the schoolmasters. In a similar fashion, the Spanish of America is most conservative where it is the speech of an aristocratic minority living among non-Spanish masses, as in Mexico and Peru; it is most altered where it is a general tongue, as in Chile and the Argentine.

The conditions of the Reconquest further advanced the disintegration of the Peninsular tongues. Catalan does not owe its existence to the Carolingian Marca Hispanica, in the sense of being a Gallo-Romance dialect that has been implanted in the Peninsula. South of the Corbières, it was still Peninsular, and its peculiarities may go back to the sixth century in essentials. But the fact that independence in the north-east was due to French influence, undoubtedly accentuated all that Catalan had in common with Provençal and Languedocian, just as the final severance of the connection in 1213 led on to an accentuation of Peninsular elements.

Similarly the oscillation of the northern centre of gravity, from Santiago and Oviedo to Castile, gave prestige now to one, now to another, form of Northern Spanish. The innovations affecting PL- CL- FL- spread as far as Castile under the early hegemony of León, but those affecting -L- -N- between vowels affected only Portuguese as well as Galician. When the later change was commenced, Castile was already beginning to impose Castilian dialectalisms on eastern León. The Moorish rush failed to dislodge the inhabitants of the north, with the result that a continuous linguistic band runs from Galicia to Catalonia under the shadow of the mountains. There we find only band-frontiers, where one speech slowly takes on the characteristics of another. But territory that had to be reconquered from the Moors and settled, after devastation, from the north (*poblar*) has much more precise linguistic features, and is definitely either Galician-Portuguese or Leonese-Castilian-Aragonese or Catalan. From the Duero and from Tamarite southwards, therefore, the various criteria of division gather together in the form of line-frontiers, with no intermediate dialects.

The history of the separate states has induced further modifications in their languages, and deepened their differences. The great changes wrought in Spanish in the sixteenth century were forwarded by the importance of the Castilian capitals for Spain, but in Portugal the older common Peninsular phonetics continued. Portuguese and Spanish in the New World acquire further differences in their lexicon by borrowing from different aboriginal tribes. The style of Camões in Portugal and those of Cervantes and Calderón have established for the two kindred languages slightly different standards of elegance. In respect of the most recent technical borrowings, the Brazilian or the Argentine has not always obtained the article and its name from the same source as the Portuguese or the Spaniard. Liability to vary persists, but it is under the control of tradition, corrected by education, and rejected in favour of the *koiné* by commerce and communication. Where these corrections were lacking,

as in the days of Moslem domination, the tendency to innovate worked with little to check it, and linguistic landslides
broke up the unity of Ibero-Romance.

See especially H. Meier, *Beiträge zur sprachlichen Gliederung der Pyrenäen-
halbinsel* (Hamburg, 1930).

THE GERMANIC ELEMENT IN PENINSULAR ROMANCE

Of the Germanic tribes one of the earliest to be set in movement, and the most glorious in its achievements, was that
of the Goths, the western branch of which—the Visigoths—
began to interfere in Spain from the year A.D. 412, under
Ataulf, Alaric's successor. Their power was centred in Provence, while the Peninsula was under the disorderly control
of the Swabians, Alans and Vandals who had poured over
the frontier in the year A.D. 407. They were western Germans,
whereas the Goths were easterners; their leader was a certain
Radagaisus. The Vandals pressed on into the rich lands of
the Bætis valley, and then took ship for Africa. There they
devastated the Roman provinces of Mauritania, Tingitana
and Africa, and, under Gaiseric, took Rome itself; but their
power was weakened by Justinian's generals and obliterated
by the Berbers and Arabs in the seventh century. The Alans
played little part in the building up of modern Spain. The
Swabians concentrated in the north-west, and were there
subjected to the increasing pressure of the Visigothic power,
to be subdued by the long and bitter war from A.D. 456–470.
Apart from these invaders, German influence had long been
exerted through the important camps maintained on the
Rhine and Danube frontiers, and through the Germans en-
rolled in the legions.

Traces of the invaders are not numerous. The Vandals are
probably remembered by the name of the province of Anda-
lucía, the *Al-Andalus* of the Moslem historians. The loss of
initial *w-* is perplexing, as the sound and letter exist in
Arabic. Dozy suggested that the Vandals embarked for

Africa at Tarifa, which may have been known for a time as
PORTUS WANDALORUM on their account, until it was renamed
in honour of the invader Ṭarîfa (A.D. 710): from Tarifa the
name spread over the adjacent lands until it came to replace
the ancient BÆTICA. *Andalíes*, near Huesca, may also com-
memorate the Vandals. The name of the Alans remains in
Puerto del Alano (Huesca), *Villalán* (Valladolid), and perhaps
Catalonia (Goth-Alan-ia). The name of the Swabians is met
often in the north-west, where also we find the name of the
Goths and even of the Romans in place-names. This circumstance suggests that we have not to do with the Swabian
kingdom of the fifth century so much as with the period of intensive colonization in the eighth, caused by the displacement
of the Germans from the south and centre. So *Suevos* occurs
four times in Coruña, *Suegos* in Lugo, *Puerto de Sueve* in
Oviedo; and the element *Sab-*, *Sav-* or *Jab-* is found in *Agro
de Savili*, *Sabín*, *Sabegode*, *Villasabariego*, *Jabariz*, *Jabalde*, *Saboy*,
etc. Such names run parallel in Galicia, north Portugal and
the north-west generally, with GOTHI GOTHA GOTHONES, etc.,
in village names like *Goda*, *La Goda* (near Barcelona), *Gudín*,
Gude, *Godos*, *Gotones*. Sometimes the name of the chief who
established the community is preserved, and we hear of
Baldus, Bertrand, Aiza, Andulf, Adalsind, Nandus and others:
Villabalde (Lugo), *Vilabertran* (Gerona), *Villeza* (León),
Castro Adalsindo (Lérida), *Casaldoufe* (Viana do Castelo),
Casanande (Coruña). Purely Germanic names are not common, e.g. those in *-ing* so frequent in England and south-
west France: *Soenga(s)* in north Portugal depends on Suninga,
with the termination already romanized; *Villa Albarenga* also
occurs. Generally the names show Latin common nouns, as
villa, *casa*, Latin case endings as *Casale Andulfi Casaldoufe*,
VILLA IN CAMPOS GOTORUM *Villatoro*; or Romance cases as
VILLA DE *AGIZA *Villeza*, *Casal da dos Godeis*, or Romance derivatives as *Godinho*, *Godinhaços*. They therefore do not indicate
a lively interest in the German dialects, but rather that the
memory of caste outlived the language. Gothic customs remained the mark of the military caste as late as the *Poema*

del Cid (1140) and even later, while the name persisted in such phrases as *sangre de los godos, alcurnia goda* as the equivalents for our 'Norman blood', and in the ironical *los godos* applied by the American revolutionaries to the royalist troops in 1810–26.

Common nouns bearing dialectal marks are rare. Gal. *lobio* 'low vine', Gal. *laverca* 'lark', and OPtg. *trigar* 'hasten' are given as survivals of Swabian *laubja, *lâwerka, *thrīhan. Gothic possessed but three vowels (*a i u*), but this system of vocalization is not characteristic of Germanic words in the Peninsular languages, apart from personal names: *Ramiro* RANIMIRUS, *Fernando* FRĬTHUNANDUS, *Elvira* GAILIVIRÔ, *Fruela Gondomil* (-MIR 'more'), *Gondómar* (-MARH 'horse'), *Alfonso* ILDIFUNSUS, etc. (in which the *e* and *o* vowels are Romanic). With these names there came into Spanish the Gothic suffix *-ila*, and the declension in *-n*: *Cintila, Cintillán*. Spanish names of men are, in fact, either Gothic or names of saints; those of women normally in modern times invocations of the Virgin. The Gothic legal code contains a few Gothic terms: a *gardingus* (a high domestic officer in the palace), an *astualdus* (given as a gloss for the same), a *comes scanciarum* 'escanciador', and a *thiufadus* or 'millenarius, commander of a thousand' (showing a confusion between *thusundi-* and *thiu-* 'slave'). The terminology of the Laws, however, is markedly Latin.

Generally speaking the Germanic element in the Peninsular languages consists either of German words older than the dialectal divisions in Germany, which had been borrowed by the camps and traders of the Empire, or else technical terms of war and chivalry borrowed from the French, and with Frankish features. War takes a prominent place in this vocabulary: *guerra* 'war' and its derivatives; *Burgos Burgo de Osma* 'small city', with the masculine gender of Gk. *pýrgos* 'tower'; *tregua* 'truce'; *yelmo* 'helm'; *espuela* 'spur', *espolon(ada)* 'spur', 'spurring, raid'; *banda* 'band'; *robar* 'sack, rob'; *rapar* 'shave, plunder'. OSp. Ptg. *elmo* represents the Gothic *hilms*, while MSp. *yelmo* corresponds to Fr. *hiaume* Frankish *hĕlm* (*ę* from Ĭ, but *ę, ie* from Ĕ); in Spanish the Frankish form has driven out the Visigothic, which remains in Portuguese. A legal term is the Sp. Ptg. *lastar* 'pay'. Ptg. *estala* 'stable, stall', Sp. Ptg. Cat. *estaca* 'stake', and possibly Sp. Ptg. Cat. *parra* 'vine' (if it be not Basque nor Celtic), describe the humble Germanic house in contrast with Roman architecture; and Sp. *rueca*, Ptg. Cat. *roca* 'distaff, rock' and Sp. *huesa* OPtg. *osa* 'hose' allude to its handicrafts. Sp. *rueca* implies an open ǫ, but **rukka* would give a closed ǫ (Sp. **roca*). On the other hand Vulgar Latin **rŏcca* 'rock' gives Sp. *roca* where we should expect **rueca*. It is probable, then, that **rukka* and **rŏcca* interfered with each other's development.

Affective words indicating shades of appreciation are also prominent in the Germanic element of Spanish and its sister-languages. Sp. Ptg. *bramar* 'bawl'; Sp. *orgullo*, Ptg. *orgulho*, Cat. *orgull* 'pride' derive from the Frankish **orgóli*; OSp. *fonta* (*Cid*) 'shame, dishonour' represents by *f-* the French initial aspirate of *honte* Frankish *haunitha*; in addition to the Lat. TRADITIONE Sp. *traición* 'treason (as such)' need was felt for a word connoting its reproach, **at-leweins*, Ptg. *aleive*, **at-lēweis*, Sp. *aleve* 'treacherous' (whence *alevoso*, *alevosía*). Similarly the word Sp. Ptg. *rico*, Cat. *ric* 'wealthy' belongs to the order of chivalrous ideas, and has been borrowed through Prov. *ric*. In the line of the *Cid*

> creçiendo ua en riqueza myo Çid el de Biuar
> 'my Cid was growing richer',

the context refers not merely to his booty, but also to his followers; and in Don Juan Manuel's *Conde Lucanor* wealth is considered as the means of rewarding and holding together a body of adherents, and so of resisting aggression or taking up the offensive against one's rivals. Words of colour are subject to change as the speaker seeks to express the shades more precisely. Sp. *blanco* Ptg. *branco* 'white', *bruno* (from It. *bruno*, and this from Fr. *brun*), *blondo*, Cat. *blau* 'blue', are of this order.

Gothic has supplied the suffix *-ila* and the declension *-a -ane*, as OSp. *Wamba Wambán*. Other suffixes are *-engo*, as *abadengo* 'abbatial', *realengo* 'royal patrimony'; *-aldo* in *heraldo* 'herald' (*faraute* being obtained from French); *-ardo* in *gallardo* 'high-spirited', *bastardo* 'bastard'. The common noun *guisa* 'way, wise', employed with feminine adjectives, e.g. *fiera guisa*, rivalled the use of *mente* (*fiera mientre*) in medieval Spanish as a means for expressing adverbs of manner. The alternative has been rejected in classical and modern Spanish and Portuguese, and the word survives in *guisar* 'cook'. There has been no syntactical influence of German on Spanish, Portuguese or Catalan. Cases of coincidence between Latin and Germanic forms are Sp. Ptg. Cat. *gastar* from Lat. VASTARE with the initial of *wost*-; Sp. *compañón*, Cat. *companyó*, OPtg. *companhão*, and kindred words, springs from CUM - PANE modelled on *ga-hlaibs* 'companion, sharer of bread'. Another such social term is Sp. (*a*)*gasajar*, Ptg. *agasalhar* 'welcome, entertain', Goth. *gasalha*. Sp. *avispa* 'wasp' from Lat. VESPA does not show the influence of Ger. *wespa* as in Fr. *guêpe*.

See especially G. Sachs, *Die germanischen Ortsnamen in Spanien und Portugal* (Jena, 1932) and E. Gamillscheg, 'Historia lingüística de los visigodos', *Rev. Fil. Esp.* xix, as well as more generally his *Romania Germanica* (Berlin, 1934).

CHAPTER IV

CATALAN

On developing into Romance, the Latin spoken in the Spanish Peninsula shows two principal fissures, which mark off from Spanish the Catalan and Portuguese languages. The deeper of these clefts is that which separates Catalan from Spanish by characteristics which are mostly held in common between the latter and Portuguese; and thus the question arises whether this language can be considered a part of Iberian Romance. It shows a marked resemblance to the dialects of Provence and Languedoc, so that speakers are still mutually intelligible; and during the first two centuries of Catalan literature *lemosí*, an adaptation of Provençal, served as the dialect of poetry. Three views have been held by scholars: that Catalan is a form of Gallo-Romance—a prolongation of Provençal; that Catalan is a form of Ibero-Romance; and that Catalan is an independent language.

For the term 'language' it is scarcely possible to offer a purely philological definition. A language is the expression of a community which enjoys a culture with some pretension to permanence. Even a dialect is wont to show a geographical centre of radiation and to be associated with some social organism; but a dialect is, at the same time, in evident dependence on some greater linguistic centre. The characteristic mark of a language is its equipoise with reference to a cultural centre; and when this test is applied, Catalan is evidently a language. Its capital is Barcelona. At Barcelona, during the Middle Ages, kings of Aragón who were counts of Barcelona established their chanceries and ruled over a Mediterranean empire; they regulated the national speech, which became also the mouthpiece of an interesting literature, both in prose and verse. This literature, and the society which it expressed, stood apart from both Provence and

Castile, and has qualities not to be found in either of its neighbours. Even when eclipsed in the sixteenth century, the language continued as the mother-tongue of Catalans and as the vehicle of religious instruction. Barcelona was always a provincial, and sometimes a rebel, capital. The literature of Catalonia revived in the nineteenth century, at first to express regional, then later national and autonomous, aspirations. On social and historical grounds there can be no doubt that Catalan is an independent language, a sister to Spanish, Provençal or Italian.

CATALAN AND ITS NEIGHBOURS

To compare this speech with its neighbours two methods have been employed: a comparison of the languages as wholes, and a study of conditions at the linguistic frontier. Both methods are instructive. The former gives total resemblance and difference as judged at the linguistic centre; the latter tells us what is the nature of their separation.

When Catalan is compared with Spanish and Provençal, however, it is necessary to proceed with caution. Neither medieval nor modern Provençal has been so unified as to permit comparison with literary Catalan, and it is necessary to make sure that a term cited as Provençal is widely used in Provence and also belongs to a date corresponding to the Catalan to which it is compared. Besides, Provençal does not stand alone to represent Gallo-Romance, and the evidence of French must be invoked, before we can so classify Catalan. For instance, Catalan and Provençal differ from Spanish in that tonic Ĕ ŏ remain monophthongs, as PEDE Cat. *peu* Prov. *pe* 'foot', MOLA Cat. Prov. *mola* 'molar', for which Spanish has *pie muela*. But here French has *pied meule* and Portuguese *pé mó*. It follows that the treatment of these short vowels is not one of the *differentiæ* between Gallo- and Ibero-Romance. Within the Peninsula, on the other hand, we shall have reason to note that Castilian, which has become the literary language, differs in many important respects from the ancient Spanish *koiné*, and is to that extent not capable of representing Ibero-Romance. Nothing so characterizes modern Spanish as the development of F to *h*, so that we may oppose Sp. *hormiga* Cat. Prov. *formiga* 'ant'. But the Spanish *koiné* employed *f*, which is still to be found in western Leonese and in Aragonese, as well as in Portuguese and Galician; so that for comparison with Catalan we should use not *hormiga* but OSp. *formiga*. This *koiné* is represented to some extent by non-Castilian forms which continue to be used in medieval documents, but more often it must be discovered by comparing Leonese, Aragonese and the relics of the Mozarabic dialect of Al-Andalus; and when it is used for comparison with Catalan, the differences become fewer between the two languages. It is essential to remember also that the *koiné* was never systematized by a literary tradition, and consequently to pay due attention to Aragonese variants on the common pattern. When this is done, we find that Spanish glides through Aragonese almost imperceptibly into western Catalan. On the side of Provence, the Gascon dialect also demands notice, since it is a neighbour of Catalan and is actually spoken on Spanish soil, in the Vall d'Aran in the vicinity of Viella. In this region, to recur to the treatment of F, we find *urmiga* 'ant', not Prov. *formiga*.

If we compare Spanish with Catalan we are at once aware of a difference in the form and accentuation of words. Catalan is more abrupt. Both languages share the strong tendency of Western Romance to eliminate unaccented vowels which fall between one accented syllable and another, but Catalan has carried through the change more thoroughly than Castilian, and in this respect coincides with the tendencies of French and Provençal. It still retains, however, a considerable number of proparoxytones like *llàgrima rònega mànega* 'tear' 'rough' 'sleeve'; and in certain cases, where a final -*o* has been lost, we find trochees like *espàrrec orfe cànem* 'asparagus' 'orphan' 'hemp' which correspond with the Sp. *espárrago huérfano cáñamo*. In this insistence on trochaic rhythm Catalan forms a bridge from Gaul, the focus of this tendency, to the west; Spanish admits more trisyllabic endings, and Portuguese still more. Catalan goes further, however, and converts many trochees into iambs by the loss of final unaccented vowels other than *a*. In this respect it agrees entirely with Provençal, and more remotely with French, which conserves the memory of -*a* in the form of 'mute' -*e*; Catalan, Provençal and French eliminate final -*e* -*o*, apart from using a 'mute' -*e* as a vowel of support to difficult final groups of consonants. Spanish preserves all three vowels; -A Sp. *piedra* Cat. *pedra* Prov. *peira* Fr. *pierre* 'stone'; -E Sp. *siete* Cat. Prov. *set* Fr. *sept* 'seven'; -O Sp. *ocho* Cat. *vuit* Prov. *uech* Fr. *huit* 'eight'; -E Sp. *padre*, retained as vowel of support to group -*dr*- > -*ir*- -*r*- in Cat. *pare* Prov. *paire* Fr. *père* 'father'. Thanks to the final -*a* and the vowel of support -*e*, Catalan combines trochaic and iambic rhythm, whereas French is characteristically iambic and Spanish characteristically trochaic. Catalan stands closer to the French languages in its forms, but represents a transition, which continues through the Spanish dialects. In Aragonese the final -*e* is as often lost as retained, e.g. the adverb is always formed in -*ment*; and in Castilian -*l* -*n* -*r* -*d* -*s* -*z* stand regularly as finals, with the loss of the original -*e*: *sal ten dar dad cortés paz*. In old Castilian this vowel was more frequently lost, notably after fricatives; as *nuef noch Lop* for *nueve noche Lope*. The vowel was restored as a result of the reaction which set in in the thirteenth century, supported by the plural forms of nouns (-*es*) and the vowels preserved by the verbal paradigm (e.g. 3 Pl. *tienen*, which helped to restore *tiene* from *tien*). The loss or conservation of -*e* is thus less notable than the retention by Spanish of -*o*. This is much more regular; but occasionally -*o* is lost in Aragonese (*fei* as well as *feito feto* Sp. *hecho* FACTU), and the ancient Mozarabic dialect showed a distinct tendency to drop this final vowel (*Montiel Pascual* = *Vascuel Sanchol Royol Reberter*). Once again Portuguese is more conservative than Spanish, as witness *parede* Sp. *pared* 'wall', *dai* (from *dade*) Sp. *dad* 'give', and the fugitive *e* that can be heard after the -*r* of Portuguese infinitives. We may speak therefore once again of a tendency towards a certain change, with France as its centre of radiation, which loses force gradually in passing across the Spanish peninsula, in the sequence Catalan-Aragonese-(Castilian) Spanish-Leonese-Portuguese. Unlike either Spanish or Provençal, Catalan forms the plural of nouns in *-a* by *-es*, and similarly the verb *-a -en*: *casa cases ama amen*. This formation occurs in the Asturias of Oviedo and at points in western León.

The accented vowels have suffered some characteristic changes. The most notable fact is that Catalan does not agree with Provençal and French in developing u to [y]: LUNA Fr. *lune* Prov. *luna* [y], Cat. *lluna* [u], Sp. *luna* Ptg. *lua*. This distinction is sharply effected on the linguistic frontier in Roussillon, where it coincides equally abruptly with a number of other criteria which distinguish Catalan from Provençal. In respect of this phenomenon the Peninsular frontier unquestionably lies near the Corbières, north of Perpignan, where the political boundary ran during the Middle Ages. No such sharp division results, as we have seen, from the treatment of accented ĕ ŏ. In this case Catalan and Provençal agree in resisting the diphthong save before a palatal: ŏCTO Cat. *vuit* Prov. *uech* 'eight', NŏCTE Cat. *nit* Prov. *nuech* 'night', PĕCTUS Cat. *pits* Prov. *pieitz* 'breast'. It will be seen that the Cat. *i* in these cases is reduced from a triphthong *-iei-*. All other cases show the monophthongs *e o*: Cat. *pedra pont mola ben*, etc. The kinship of Catalan and Provençal is clear at this point, but inferences as to Romance grouping are more difficult to make. French is a language which diphthongizes: *pierre bien meule huit nuit poitrine*, but *pont sept*; and Portuguese has none of these diphthongs: *pedra bem mó oito noite peito ponte sete*. In Spanish the diphthong occurred in all cases, apart from a centre of resistance in Granada and Lusitania, where the simple vowels were preferred. In Castilian the vowels did not form diphthongs before palatals: *noche tenga poyo* Leon. Arag. *nueite tienga pueyo*. Thus it is not possible to use the treatment of these vowels to characterize either Gallo-Romance or Ibero-Romance, nor to treat the Castilian development as equivalent to that of all Spanish. The only affirmation that arises, apart from the association of Catalan and Provençal, is that these regions lie at the heart of a vast area which diphthongizes ĕ ŏ before a palatal, including France and most of Spain, together with northern Italy. On the periphery of this movement lie Cantabria (the home of Castilian, against the Basque border), Galicia, Portugal, Lusitania and Granada. As for the treatment of AU in CAUSA Prov. *cauza* (Fr. *chose*) Cat. *cosa* Sp. *cosa* Ptg. *cousa* 'thing', and of AI (e.g. in AREA *aira*) in Prov. *eira* Cat. Sp. *era* Ptg. *eira*, we notice a decided tendency of Catalan and eastern Spanish (including Castilian) to simplify these diphthongs, but a slower development both in Provence and in western Spain (León, Mozarabic territories, Galicia, Portugal).

In the same way the Catalan consonant system shows leanings towards Provençal solutions without involving a break away from the tradition of Peninsular Romance. A number of divergences have been provoked by the special development of Castilian among the Spanish dialects, so that Cat. *formiga gener vuit faixa ull fill filla* merely adopt solutions for F- J- -CT- -SCI- -C'L- -LI- which are found in most of Romania and in the consensus of Spanish dialects, though different from Cast. *hormiga enero ocho Hacinas ojo hijo hija*. An instance of resemblance to the other Peninsular languages and dissidence from Provençal is the pronunciation of *b d g* in 'weak' positions, i.e. not at the beginning of a breath-group nor protected by a preceding *n* (or *l* for *d*). In such cases Provençal pronounces occlusive consonants [b d g], but Catalan and all other Peninsular speeches use a series of fricatives [ƀ đ ǥ] that closely resemble the occlusives and pass into them in emphatic enunciation. There is, however, a much greater use of the occlusives in Catalan, and the fricatives may be modern. In the treatment of -NN- and -LL- Catalan resembles the Spanish dialects of the Ibero-Romance group, in palatalizing the nasal [ɲ] and lateral [λ]: DAMNU *dannu* Cat. *dany* 'injury' ANNU *any* 'year' CABALLU *cavall* 'horse' as Sp. *daño año caballo*. Prov. *dan an* and Ptg. *dano ano* are not palatalized; while -LL- gives Prov. *l ll* Ptg. *l*: Prov. *estela sella* Ptg. *estrêla sela*. In some cases the correspondence is restricted to some considerable portion of the Spanish area. Those which affect Aragonese and eastern Spanish are naturally the most interesting. -ND- -MB- assimilate to *n m* in Cat. *ona coloma* UNDA COLUMBA 'dove' 'wave'. Aragonese possesses both these features, and has spread -MB- *m* as far as Castilian and standard Spanish (*paloma lomo*), so that *mb* only commences with Leonese (*palomba*), whence it continues through Galicia and Portugal (*pomba*), Prov. *onda palomba*. In this instance Catalan shares in an innovation of eastern Spain, like the prompt reduction of AI to *e* which also characterizes Catalan with Aragonese; in treating of initial PL- CL- FL-, which remain *pl- cl- fl-* in these regions, Catalan has shared with Mozarabic and Aragonese resistance to a change which radiated out from the north-west (Galicia and León), and which affects Castilian: *llama llamar llaga* from FLAMMA CLAMARE PLAGA.

Initial *ll-* occurs in Catalan by palatalization of L-, as LUNA *lluna* 'moon'. This word and others like it have led to a false inference that Catalan once possessed the Gallo-Romance *ü*, and that the development of *lluna* ran through a stage *lüna*, identical with Provençal. This inference cannot be maintained in view of the fact that *ll-* occurs with all vowels, and not only with *u*, as *llarg* 'wide' from LARGU. Prov. *lüna* Sp. *luna* Ptg. *lua* all show *l-* as against the Catalan *ll-*; but for all that the phenomenon is not uniquely Catalan. It occurs regularly in the Asturian dialects, and there is evidence of the change having occurred also in Al-Andalus, where *yengua* from LINGUA implies an intermediate stage *llengua*. The palatalizing of initial *l-* is thus seen to be a feature recurring sporadically in all Peninsular Romance. ALTERU gives *altre* 'other' in Catalan, with a velar [ł]; in Provençal it is *autre*, with [u̯]; in Portuguese *outro*, originally and in north Portuguese [ou̯], but now pronounced [o] in south Portuguese [ǫ́trŭ]; in Spanish it is *otro*. Thus Catalan occupies here the most ancient stage of a development which ends in Sp. *otro* in Ibero-Romance and Fr. *autre* [ọtR] in Gallo-Romance. The retardation of this change occurs in many Spanish words that have remained with *-lt-* like *salto alto*, etc. Similarly in MULTU Cat. *molt* [mɔlt] Prov. *mout* 'much', Catalan is conservative compared with Provençal; but Ibero-Romance has palatalized this L instead of velarizing it, Ptg. Leon. *muito* Sp. *mucho* (from *muiǒ*). Medial -TR- in PATRE 'father' gives Cat *r* Sp. *dr* Prov. *ir, pare padre paire*. In this instance Catalan differs from both Spanish and Provençal, but perhaps more from Provençal. In vulgar Spanish *pare mare* are found by the elimination of the weak fricative [đ] in *padre*, as also in OSp. *Pero = Pedro*, so that it is probable the Catalan form has arisen in the same way, without passing through *ir* as Prov. *paire* Fr. *père*. Final *r* is silent in eastern Catalan and Provençal, but also in Aragonese and Andaluz, though retained in Spanish (Castilian and Leonese) and in Portuguese. Cat. *muller mullers* [muλé muλés], Arag. *mullé mullés*, but Sp. *mujer mujeres*.

There are a few features which are more particularly Catalan, such as the treatment of intervocalic -ć- -D-, and of final -ć -D -B and -N. VICINU AUDIRE give Cat. *veí oír* as against Prov. *vezí auzir* 'neighbour' 'hear'. The Spanish equivalents are *z-* in *vecino* (OSp. *vezino*) *oír*; so that only the silencing of -ć- pertains exclusively to Catalonia, while both criteria mark off Catalan from Provençal. BREVE CRUCE PEDE all lead to *-u* in Cat. *breu creu peu* 'short' 'cross' 'foot'. Sp. *breve* is due to the retention of the final vowel, lost in Catalan, but in Aragonese we encounter *breu*, as also in Provençal. The criterion thus does not distinguish Catalan from all the Spanish dialects. *Creu peu*, however, are clearly marked off from Sp. *cruz pie* Prov. *crutz pe*. In the twelfth century PLACET FECIT CRUCE were represented by Cat. *platz fet crod* 'pleases' 'did' 'cross', which show that the evolution to *-u* was not then complete, and the criterion of -ć > *-u* is relatively modern. The development from -D to *-u* is an ancient characteristic of Catalan. As for final -N, Provençal and Catalan agree in eliminating the nasal (BENE *bé* 'well' BONU *bo* 'good' PANE *pa* 'bread'), which is retained by all Spanish dialects; but they disagree in the plural, where Catalan restores the nasal (*bens bons pans*).

If we consider the forms of words, we find the same similarity between Provençal and Catalan as appears from the sounds as well as the same impossibility of establishing a clear frontier against Spanish dialects. The loss of final vowels leads to a considerable resemblance in the paradigms between Provençal and Catalan; but in 2 Pl. -TIS -*t's* gives Prov. -*tz* Cat. -*u* (*tenetz teniu*). This -*u* is relatively modern in Catalan, and in the older language ran concurrently with -*ts*; but the latter also extended into the Spanish area in Aragon, where we still have *tenez*. It is characteristic of Catalan to have retained the Latin third conjugation in -ĔRE, which remains in Gallo-Romance, but has been submerged in the second by the Ibero-Romance tongues (Cat. *conèixer* Sp. *conocér* Ptg. *conhecér* COGNOSCĔRE 'know'); it also resembles French and Provençal in making use of the inceptive suffix -ESC- to conjugate verbs in -*ir* so that the accent always falls on the termination (*serveixo -eixes -eix -im -iu -eixen* 'serve'). In Ibero-Romance this termination loses its inceptive sense, but serves to form new verbs in -*ecer* (*amanecer rejuvenecer florecer*, etc.). Catalan uses past participles in -UTU (*crescut tingut*) as freely as French and Provençal; in medieval Spanish these also existed, but disappeared during the medieval period in favour of -ITU (*crecido tenido*). Catalan builds its past participles on the preterite stem of the verb, but Spanish on the present (Cat. *tenir tinguí tingut, haver haguí hagut*, Sp. *tener tenido, haber habido*). The practice extends over the frontier into Aragonese, where we find *tuvido supido*, etc. from *tener saber* via *tuve supe*.

Among the pronouns the use of *jo tu* 'I' 'thou' as disjunctives after a preposition is also customary in Aragonese, where the 3 Pl. possessive is, as in Catalan, from ILLORUM Arag. *lur-es* Cat. *llur-s* 'their' (Sp. *a mí, a ti; su-s*). The use of *qui* 'who' as a nominative was widespread in Old Spanish, and continues in Aragonese, where we also find the feminine of *cual* as *cuala*, cf. Cat. *quina*. Catalan has developed a rich series of reinforced negatives (*no...pas punt mica gota gens gaire res cosa cap*, etc.); the same impetus was felt in medieval Spanish, but has been repressed. The comparative was formed by OCat. *pus*, which has now yielded to *més* (*lo pus bell catalanesc del mon* 'the finest Catalan in the world'). Though French and Provençal have derived their particle from PLUS and Spanish and Portuguese from MAGIS, the former was not unknown to Ibero-Romance, as witnessed by OPtg. *chus*. A conspicuous Ibero-Romance feature of Catalan is the absence of declension, in opposition to the two-case system of Old French and Provençal.

In respect of vocabulary there is a more decided approximation of Catalan to the other Peninsular languages; naturally so, as the vocabulary has arisen out of common experiences in organization and history. The similarity between Catalan and Provençal forms is so great that it is not possible to distinguish at all times whether a word is native or foreign; and there is in any case a very heavy dose of French and Provençal in Catalan. The Provençal contribution is at its highest in the medieval rhyming dictionaries composed to aid Catalan poets: *causen cresén ausir auçir tesaur lays*, etc. Castilianisms are frequent in the modern speech, and enter the language at a very early stage; they are quite numerous in the chronicle of James the Conqueror which stands at the head of the great Catalan histories. The resemblance to the Peninsular languages, however, is not due merely to this kind of borrowing, but to intrinsic similarity arising out of identical experience: the presence of Iberian words, and of the same kinds of Celtic and Germanic elements, the abundant Arabisms, and a general parallelism between Spanish and Catalan loan-words taken from Latin at recent dates.

The study of the characteristics of these neighbouring tongues has also been made on the frontiers between them, viz. that between Catalan and Provençal in Roussillon, and

that between Catalan and Aragonese Spanish in Ribagorza.
The principal mark of distinction between Catalan and
Provençal is certainly the treatment of Lat. ū, MURU Prov.
mür Cat. mur 'wall', and this phenomenon is found to coincide precisely in area with a number of other differences,
so as to form a deeply drawn frontier:

Prov.   mür fröit pieitz febrier uech fuelha paire peira auzir genre onda vezi
        tenetz car causa auca pretz detz patz crutz pe
Cat.   mur fruit pits febrer vuit fulla pare pedra oír gendre ona vei
        teniu carn cosa oca preu deu pau creu peu

The line of demarcation for all these features alike starts
from the Andorran border just north of L'Hospitalet, and
proceeds eastwards so as to pass between Querigut and
Fourmiguères to just south of Latour de France, significantly
so called; it then trends north-eastward to the massif of
Perillou, and then south-eastward to bisect the Étang de
Leucate, or de Salses. The same frontier marks the northern
extension of a number of very common Catalan words, such
as *ben cabells trencar ganivet mantega aviat carnicer ballar dona dia
casa sabater esmorzar cara metge germana hortolà nou sempre*, etc.

On the Spanish side the situation is quite different. A line-
frontier does not begin to appear until we reach the plain
of La Litera, clear of the hills, between Tamarite and Binéfar.
From this point of union many of the principal criteria
distinguishing Spanish from Catalan unite and cross the
Ebro, and then descend through the medieval kingdom of
Valencia so that the hills are held by Spanish and the coastal
plain by Catalan, until they reach the sea along the River
Vinalapó, which flows through Elche in Murcia. La Litera
was the scene of hot contests in the great days of the Reconquest, and has been depopulated by the expulsion of the
Moriscos. It is evident that the frontier from Tamarite
southward is the product of reconquest and resettlement,
during the twelfth century and early thirteenth for the most
part. To the north of Tamarite we find no such frontier.
Aragonese features gradually diminish and Catalan gradually
increase over a range of 40 or 50 miles. In the intervening

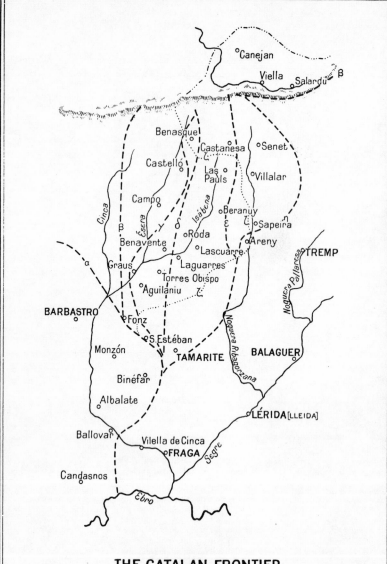

THE CATALAN FRONTIER

CRITERIA: α h,f β ʟ->[λ] y ιε,ε δ uε,o ɛ -[s]--[z]-ʑ,-as,-es ŋ [č],[ǰ]

(Rev. Fil. Esp. iii)

territory it is impossible to say whether a given township
speaks Aragonese or Catalan, especially since Aragonese
itself represents, when compared with other Spanish dialects,
an approximation to Catalan. The political units involved
here are primitive Aragón, the county of Ribagorza (with
an ecclesiastical centre at Roda), and the county of Pallars;
the first and last speak unmixed languages, but Ribagorza
is debated ground. Until the tenth century the counts of
Ribagorza cultivated the alliance of the Catalan counts of
Pallars; but after that date Ribagorza was merged with the
kingdom of Aragón. On the Aragonese side the River Cinca,
which falls into the Segre near the Ebro, and the town of
Barbastro, are the main Aragonese defences; on the Catalan
side, the Noguera Pallaresa and Segre, with Tremp, Balaguer
and Lérida, supports Catalan tendencies. The middle ground
is occupied by the upper valley of the Noguera Ribagorzana
and the valleys of the Isábena and Ésera. In this region each
linguistic phenomenon has its own frontier, but a few of the
more significant may be cited here.

The Castilian change of F to *h* has taken place in the
Barbastro region, and forms a frontier-line running between
Monzón and Fonz, Binéfar and Tamarite, Albalate and
Fraga. As, however, this development is not characteristic
of Aragonese, there is no frontier in this respect between
Catalan and the dialects of Upper Aragón to the north of
Barbastro. The first such frontier is met in the opposition
of *luna* : *lluna*, on a line running between the Cinca and
Ésera, and descending to Fonz. On the Ésera, Benasque,
Castellón, Campo and Graus all show *ll*. The central line
of division is traced by the diphthongization of ŏ and ĕ. Here
the middle course of the Ésera (Campo and Castellón) and
Fonz have both diphthongs (*ue ie*), and in addition Benasque,
Benavente, Torres and Aguilaniu have the diphthong *ie*, giving
a line which separates the valleys of the Ésera and Isábena.
The easternmost lines are those marked by the unvoicing
of sibilants in the sixteenth century. By this process OSp. *-s-*
[z] became [s], and *j* [ž] became [š]. In the case of JUNIPERU,

7

JUVENEM, etc., Aragonese has developed [ĉ] from the affricate pronunciation of OSp. *j* [ĵ], which occurred as an alternative. The frontiers referred to are thus those between the values [s] and [z] for the *s* of *casa rosa camisa*, etc., and [ĉ] and [ž] for *chinebro ginebre, choben jove*, etc. They separate after leaving the Vall d'Aran and the Pyrenees to run on either side of the upper Noguera Ribagorzana, which is crossed in a westerly trend by [ĉ] : [ž] between Sopeira and Areny. Thereafter they join together and trend south-west to Tamarite, which belongs in these respects to Aragonese (*joven* > *choben* ECCLESIA *lazlesyo*). Other lines wander over these to make a complicated pattern: for instance, the antithesis of the plurals of *-a* nouns (*casas* : *cases*) commences at Benasque on the sources of the Ésera, trends eastward to the Noguera Ribagorzana and follows its west bank from opposite Villalar to Sopeira, crossing the stream for a while at Areny, and then trending as sharply westward in the direction of Fonz, short of which it turns south-eastward towards the junction of linguistic frontiers between Binéfar and Tamarite. These criteria make up together an appreciable frontier, since their total effect is considerably to change the nature of the language, from Spanish to Catalan; but they do not constitute a bundle nor make an abrupt cut like that which occurs in Roussillon.

On Catalan and its relation with other Romance languages consult W. Meyer-Lübke, *Das Katalanische* (Heidelberg, 1925), A. Alonso, 'La subagrupación románica del catalán', *Rev. Fil. Esp.* xiii, A. Griera, 'Castellà—català—castellà', *Zeitschrift für rom. Phil.* xlv, P. Fouché, 'Études de philologie hispanique', *Rev. Hist.* lxxvii, K. Salow, *Sprachgeographische Untersuchungen über den östlichen Teil des katalanisch-languedokischen Grenzgebietes* (Hamburg, 1912), J. Hadwiger, 'Sprachgrenzen und Grenzmundarten des Valencianischen', *Zeitschrift für rom. Phil.* xxix.

For the sake of simplicity I have made the comparison of the three languages on the basis of phonology and morphology alone. Naturally, they can be compared in respect of vocabulary, word-formation or syntax also, and the resemblance of Catalan to Provençal would be striking.

CATALAN ORIGINS AND EXPANSION

The foregoing evidence makes it clear that between Roussillon and Languedoc lies a linguistic frontier which has not been transgressed. Roussillon, therefore, takes its language from some centre lying to the south of that line, such as Ruscino the Roman colony, or Elne the seat of a medieval bishopric, or Perpignan the administrative capital. The line is marked by the northern range of the Pyrenees at its eastern extremity, which leaves the central line of mountains in Andorra, and trends east-north-east behind the line of the Corbières. The linguistic frontier runs, not along this crest, but rather along the southern slopes. It is supported at last by the massif of Perillou, and then descends to the sea through the middle of the obstacle offered by the lagoon of Salses. This frontier separated Gaul from Iberia in ancient times; the Cerretani occupied Cerdagne and the Sordones, with settlements at Illiberis on the Tech and Ruscino on the Tet, extended as far as Salses in Roussillon; both peoples were of Iberian stock, pure or mixed. There appears to have been some infiltration of Celtic tribes into this region, but under the Romans it was marked off from the territory of the colony Narbo Martius, and the division corresponds almost precisely with that between the bishoprics of Narbonne and Elne (Vingrau belongs to Narbonne, but belonged to Elne until 1359). The frontier held good for the kingdom of Aragón or the satellite kingdom of Majorca during the Middle Ages, and it was only in 1659 that the French border was advanced across Roussillon to the line of the Alberes, the southern terminus of the Pyrenees. For purposes of our investigation, therefore, we must suppose that Spain extends to the Corbières; Catalan, geographically, is one of the Peninsular languages.

This region formed part of the Spanish March under the Carolingian emperors, and received the fugitive *Hispani* driven northward by the Moorish invasion. Who they were is doubtful, and it is equally difficult to determine the *loca erema* where they were established. The latter appear to have included districts as far south as Gerona and Barcelona. It is inadmissible to suppose that the north-east of Spain was abandoned by its inhabitants and resettled by Franks from the Empire; but the inclusion of the region within the Marches undoubtedly contributed to the association of Catalonia with Provence, as it laid the basis for Catalan intervention in the affairs of southern France until 1213 (Muret). The common interests of Provence and Catalonia were embodied in the Visigothic dominions of Ataulf and his successors, before the acquisition of the rest of Spain, and there were doubtless under the Roman Empire close commercial and colonial relations between Narbonensis and Tarraconensis, which may have received in common a considerable influx of discharged legionaries.

On the side of Spain, we have to admit the continuous presence of the Catalan dialects alongside the Aragonese, as made evident by the zone of gentle transition in Ribagorza. This gradual passage from one speech to another makes Catalan part of a linguistic band along the Pyrenees and Cantabrian mountains; in all this stretch there is no brusque frontier, but a series of transitions by which we pass through Aragonese, Castilian and Asturo-Leonese, until we reach Galician. This does not, however, prove the identity of Catalan with the Spanish group of dialects any more than a similar transition between French and Italian proves the identity of those two languages. On the contrary, the sum total of the changes wrought on the Ribagorzan band-frontier places Catalan rather nearer to Provençal than to Spanish. We have only evidence for the permanent existence of Catalan in the valleys running southward from the Pyrenees. How far south the dialect reached cannot be determined with absolute certainty. It is clear that at Valencia a Mozarabic dialect ruled in which ĕ ŏ became *ie ue* or *ua*, and in the Baleares final *-o* was preserved until after the Christian Reconquest. But also *Tarragona* and *Barcelona* (TARRACONE BARCINONE) show Mozarabic intervention by their final -a, so that for the eighth century we have to exclude some of the principal Catalan cities. In the west the primitive frontier doubtless descended to Tamarite, where the lines join together as Catalan and Aragonese advanced with the Reconquest at the expense of the older Mozarabic. Barbastro and Lérida were Mozarabic cities. The primitive seat of Catalan is thus restricted to the hill-country in the north of the province and the land between the two ranges of the Pyrenees.

The counts of Barcelona gradually ceased to acknowledge their dependence on the Frankish Empire, though still described by the Moors and Christians of Spain as Franks. An early frontier *contra Ispaniam* was established on the Llobregat, which flows past Barcelona, or more exactly in the Penedès district, where Castellví de la Marca and Sant Vicenç de Calders are given as frontier posts in the eleventh century. This line divided Old from New Catalonia, and slightly less advanced is the present linguistic frontier between eastern and western Catalan. Eastern Catalan has for capitals Perpignan (Perpinyà), Vich, Gerona (Girona) and Barcelona; the principal centres of western Catalan are Urgell, Lérida (Lleida) and Tarragona, of which Lérida was the educational, and Tarragona the ecclesiastical, capital of all Catalonia. Eastern Catalan tends to open its *e* sounds; atonic *a e* become either [ə] or [ɐ] according to circumstances, and atonic *o* becomes [u]. Western Catalan distinguishes clearly *a* and *e*. This form of the language is of considerable importance, since the earliest documents, the *Homilies d' Organyà*, come from the west. The dialectal difference was observed by Pujades, the author of the *Crònica universal del Principat de Catalunya* (1609). There are several subdialects of each group. The eastern dialects include the Catalan of Roussillon, and notably the provençalized speech of Capcir, Ampurdanese (where the article *es sa* appears at Salat), and Barcelonese. The region of Tarragona may be considered transitional. In it *b v* are distinguished, though confused in Tarragona city, and at Reus the western features are pronounced. The western dialects include the Catalan of Andorra, Pallars, parts of Ribagorza, the Catalan lexical elements in the Gascon of the Vall d'Aran, and the speech of Tortosa, which forms the transition between Catalan and Valencian.

South of the Ebro an important military frontier occurred at Burriana, south of Castellón de la Plana. It was here that the Cid established his advanced base against Valencia (1094), so as to have his back to Catalonia, whence he might draw friendly support; and it was from Burriana that the final reduction of Valencia was effected by James the Conqueror in 1238. The Catalan advance pressed on to Alicante, and in 1263–66 James was master of all Murcia, which, however, he restored to Castile. Concerning Orihuela, Elche, Guadamar, Alicante, Cartagena and Murcia city Muntaner says that the inhabitants were true Catalans and spoke perfect Catalan. The language, however, has retired to the north-eastern frontier of the province, where it rests at Elche and along the Vinalapó River. To the north of Elche and Alicante Catalan occupies not the whole of the provinces of Valencia and Castellón, but only the coastal plain. The high ground was settled by Aragonese colonists, whose dialect has given way to the invading Castilian. The type of Catalan imported was the western, and suffers local modification in the three regions of Castellón, Valencia (the modern *apitxat* dialect) and Alicante.

Eastern Catalan extended oversea. It first occupied the Baleares in 1229, giving rise to *mallorquí*. In the Baleares there is confusion between tonic *a* and *e*, as in the Majorcan *Grail* manuscript (*aqast crau* etc. for *aquest creu*) and still more the atonics (*sanyor avangelis pravare* for *senyor evangelis prevere*). Here also we find the archaic article from IPSE *es sa*, which struggled for mastery against ILLE *lo la* in all Catalonia before 1200. This article is petrified in place- and personal-names like *Sacasa Descoll*, and is still found on the mainland at Salat, as well as in Provence and Sardinia. *Mallorquí* has played a considerable part in the reconstruction of literary Catalan during the nineteenth century.

Farther into the Mediterranean the kings of Aragón extended their dominion over Sardinia, Sicily, Naples, and indirectly for a period over the Morea. This led to no linguistic conquests save in Sardinia. The inhabitants of Cagliari were expelled from their city by Pere del Punyalet, and replaced by Catalan colonists; and the official use of the language persisted into the sixteenth century, when it had yielded to Castilian in the mainland. Spanish, in fact, did not displace Catalan in the island; but the rivalry of languages undermined both, so as to facilitate the ultimate triumph of Italian. At this day Catalan has contracted to the single township of Alghero, where it is spoken by some 12,280 people in an archaic form, attesting its arrested development. The colony took the name of *Barceloneta*; established in 1355, it was kept as a preserve of Catalans and Aragonese, while in 1478 the immigration of foreigners, even of Corsicans and Sardinians, was absolutely prohibited. *Alguerés* has suffered little from Spanish or Italian, but is much influenced in lexicon and syntax by the neighbouring Sardinian.

On Alghero and *alguerés* see H. Kuen, 'El dialecto de Alguer', *Anuari de l'Oficina Romànica*, v ff.

MEDIEVAL LITERARY CATALAN

The development of Catalan through the medieval period includes a number of phonetic changes, the product of conflict within the dialects, and an effort towards its emancipation from Provençal and stabilization as a cultural speech. The *Homilies d'Organyà* give us the measure of the twelfth-century language before the emergence of the great literary documents, and can be called the standard of reference for pre-literary Catalan. In this early period the article *es sa* from IPSE appears frequently. It occurs sometimes in the documents of the thirteenth century, which are mostly of legal origin; more frequent are *el lo la les los*. In the fourteenth it has disappeared. Up to the thirteenth century also, the final -*n* continues to appear in documents: *cordoan* 'shoe-

maker' (MCat. *sabater*), *pan* 'bread', *raon* 'reason', *son* 'sound'.
The fourteenth century carried through another pair of
changes: initial *l-* was palatalized to *ll-* in such words as
lletra 'letter' *lladre* 'thief' *dilluns* 'Monday' *llegir* 'read'; and
certain finals in [ŝ] were vocalized into [u]. Final -*ċ* gave
creu veu plau feu for pre-literary *crod crou vots vou platz fet*,
involving simultaneously a change in the *o* before -*u*. This
is most important in the 2 Pl. of verbs, which, about the
middle of the fourteenth century, changes from -*ts* to -*u*.
Forms in *u* appear before 1400: *haveu rebeu guardeu* as well as
siats avisats; and between then and 1450 they become dominant: *sou voleu sperau vullau teniu*, etc., but still we find sporadically *havets certificats hoiats*. The change may have been
forwarded by a desire to distinguish the masculine plural past
participle from the finite verb: *fets guardats* 'made' 'kept'
from *feu guardeu* 'you make' 'you keep'. The endings -*ats*
-*ets* are still found at Benasque on the frontier with Aragonese,
and at Peralta, Fonz, Graus we have the east Aragonese -*z*
in *cantaz portaz*. It was in the fifteenth century that final -*r*
became silent in words accentuated on the last syllable and
in all infinitives. The -*r* remains in the official orthography,
but does not always serve to keep hiatus.

In the first instance the *langue d'oc* served Catalonia as a
literary language. Catalans took up the art of the troubadour
somewhat later than their neighbours in southern France,
and with a more didactic manner. They experienced, however, some difficulty in keeping out of their verses the peculiarities of their own tongue, and to aid them there were
composed those early Provençal grammars by Ramon Vidal
and Jofre Foixa, which are introductions to the technique
of society verses. Standardized supposedly on the dialect of
Limoges, though really more like that of Toulouse, this conventional tongue became known as *lemosí*; and it was the
principal endeavour of the national literature to throw off
the encumbrance of *lemosí*. That this was effected, Catalans
owe to the tireless energy of Ramon Lull and to the four
great chroniclers of the fourteenth century. Lull began as

a troubadour, but with his conversion he turned his back on
literary artifice and aimed at sincerity, alike of language and
thought. His poems are still marked by the tradition in
which he had first worked, for the association of Catalan and
Provençal was too intimate to be dissolved at once; but his
great prose works are models of *pla catalanesc*. When Lull laid
down his life, in 1315, the four great chronicles commenced.
The third and liveliest chronicler, Ramon Muntaner, was
an enthusiastic partisan of the national language, though he
still adopted a provençalized idiom for his verses. He rarely
names the language without some adjective of superlative
commendation such as *lo pus bell catalanesc del mon* 'the loveliest
Catalan in the world'. The chronicle of Pere del Punyalet
is the fourth specimen of this developing language; but the
king did more for it through his chancery. In his time
practically all documents were drawn up in the vernacular,
and constant usage determined the literary idiom. His
epistolary genius covered all aspects of Catalan life. At the
same time he was a magnificent parliamentary orator, whose
harangues remained as models of convincing eloquence.
Other great orators—Cardinal Margarit, Martí l'Humà,
St Vicent Ferrer—contributed to fix in the memory of all
men the accepted pattern of cultured expression in Catalan.
The crucial moment was expressed in the career of Bernat
Metge, whose first work (the *Llibre de Fortuna e Prudència*,
1381) still employs a provençalized idiom; his second (a
translation of Petrarca's *Griseldis*, 1388) is Catalan, but
medieval in complexion; while his third (*Lo Somni*, 1398)
is touched with humanism and is the purest model of Catalan
prose (cf. A. Par, *Sintaxi catalana*, Halle, 1923).

With the close of Metge's career the interest shifts to
Valencia. The House of Barcelona came to an end and the
accession of the Castilian prince Fernando de Antequera in
1412 gave lustre to the Aragonese portion of the kingdom,
hitherto somewhat repressed. Fernando's successor, Alfonso
the Magnanimous, transferred his seat of government to Naples,
where the *Cancionero de Stúñiga* (1458) shows Catalan as no

more than the equal of Aragonese in court favour. The great writers of the fifteenth century are all Valencians. The two poets, Jordi de Sant Jordi and Auzias March, writing in evident dependence on Arnaut Daniel and the more philosophical *troubadours*, are provençalizers in language, as is also the *Diccionari de rims*. In richness of language and thought Catalan reached its zenith with March. The best representative of the novel, Joan Martorell, wrote his *Tirant lo Blanc* (1490) in *vulgar valenciana*, and the same is true of Jaume Roig's *Llibre de les Dones*. Thus when the crowns of Castile and Aragón were united in 1474, and Catalan felt the brunt of the Castilian literary and cultural invasion, the language had already lost the strong political and cultural support given it by the House of Barcelona.

THE REVIVAL OF CATALAN
AND VALENCIAN

We have already noted that with the House of Trastamara there came a considerable diminution of cultural activity in Catalan at the capital; with the union of the crowns the native language became more and more local, and Spanish was the means of appeal to a wider audience, or of transacting national business. The sixteenth century saw Catalan still in use for topographical and antiquarian works, but in the seventeenth even this employment tended to cease. The language survived in the countryside as a *patois*, and its highest use was by the clergy, obeying the rule to preach always in the vernacular of their parishioners. In the great towns a bilingual population arose, with Catalan for its maternal and familiar tongue, but Spanish for literature and administration. Inevitably Spanish came to exert an influence on the local language, which it had already begun to infect as early as the fourteenth century. The 1 Sg. present indicative of verbs acquired an *-o*: *porto perdo dormo serveixo* for *port perd dorm servesc*. The pronoun of polite address Sp. *usted* gives Cat. *vosté*, which has colloquial sanction. The revived language has naturally reacted against flagrant castilianisms, but those which arrive from the bilingual training of educated men contribute to the enrichment of the language. The americanisms of the sixteenth century are current in Catalan as in Spanish, and the latinisms acquired for the service of literature require only to be catalanized for general use. This is not so much a debt to Castilian as evidence of a common cultural heritage; but it emphasizes the lexical similarity of the languages, especially in the Catalan of the newspapers. Other changes came over the language that are not due to Castilian. The present subjunctive tends to prefer forms in -*i*: *porti perdi dormi serveixi* for *port perda dorma servesca*. Imperfects in -*iva* do not appear in modern literary Catalan. Alternative forms in the preterite are simplified towards a single pattern for strong verbs: out of *paregué parech*, *plagué plach*, there remain only *paregué plagué*. The masculine article is *el els*, displacing *lo los*.

The rebuilding of Catalan has been the work of the nineteenth century, and has been accomplished in various stages which correspond to the clearness of vision among men of letters. The initial date is offered by Pau Ballot's grammar of the language, issued in 1814, which, although no more than a conversation-grammar, contained a fervent eulogy of the language. Torres Amat, cataloguing the medieval monuments, showed that Catalan had been more than a *patois* in the Middle Ages. The strong current of cosmopolitanism felt in the Age of Reason was now ebbing, and both antiquarian interest and the budding Romanticism stressed the importance of local inspiration. But as Catalan had only a local range, the generation of Cabanyes and Piferrer sought to give Catalan colour to works contributed to Spanish literature; drawing on vernacular songs and traditions, but transmuting them so far as possible into the language of culture. Their effort failed; it could not overcome the inner inconsistency of the two languages, and neither pleased Hermosilla and the Madrid critics nor adequately expressed the local truth. In 1833 Aribau launched his ode *A ma pàtria* which, as well as evoking unforgettable landscapes from Catalonia, gave expression to a sense of filial piety towards the language:

> *En llemosí sonà lo meu primer vagit,*
> *quan del mugró matern la dolça llet bevia,*
> *en llemosí al Senyor pregava cada dia,*
> *i càntics llemosins somiava cada nit.*

'It was in *lemosí* that my first cry was made, drinking the sweet milk at my mother's breast; in *lemosí* did I pray to God every day, and every night I dreamt of songs in *lemosí*.'

Aribau did not himself follow up this line, but devoted himself to literary scholarship in Spanish. The credit for all but the proclamation goes to Rubió and the generation of neo-troubadours, who set themselves to repeat the conditions of the Provençal lyric in Catalonia, and in 1859 established the Floral Games of Barcelona. The revival gained momentum, but was suffering from a basic misconception. Catalan in the Middle Ages was not *lemosí* but *pla catalanesc*, and it was necessary to repeat its emancipation from Provençal. This took the form of discovering what real Catalan was: Milà i Fontanals revealed the ancient literature with unmatched scholarship; Marian Aguiló covered the country in search of popular songs, recorded their words, and brought a foison of expressions from his native Majorca; and Jacinto Verdaguer, a country priest and true poet, divined the genius of the language. By 1880 the process of recatalanization was complete: what chiefly remained to determine was the extent to which this language might be employed. Maragall, Carner and others showed that it was capable of very varied styles in lyrical verse; Guimerà used it for dramas, orations and letters; Prat de la Riba built on it a political creed of Catalan nationalism; and the Institute of Catalan Studies used it for scientific prose. With the autonomous régime that accompanied the Republic, Catalan entered into dyarchy with Castilian in Catalonia.

The share taken by Majorcans in recreating the literary tongue has been most important. In collections of *rondalles* they preserve their local peculiarities, but for literary pur-

poses standard literary Catalan, as defined by Pompeu Fabra
and the Institute, suffices. The case of Valencia is different.
The language has separated from the pattern of Barcelona,
and the region had always enjoyed a certain local independence. As derived from western Catalan the *lengua
valenciana* distinguishes unaccented *a* from *e*, whereas Catalan
treats them indifferently; these vowels retain their timbre, as
also does unaccented *o* (which is dulled to *u* in Catalan).
Outside the city *b* is bilabial and *v* labiodental; Valencian
grammarians advise keeping this distinction, which is abandoned by their colleagues in Barcelona. The city employs
further the *apitxat* enunciation, i.e. it shares to some extent
the tendency of Spanish to transform voiced sibilants into
the unvoiced series: the consonants affected are -*s*- *tz j tj*,
Cat. [z ż ž ĵ]. They become [s ŝ ĉ ĉ] and then correspond
with -*ss*- *ts x* (initial or after consonant) *tx*: *casa* [kása]
dotze (dóŝe] *juny* [ĉuɲ] *pitjor* [piĉór] *xop* [ĉop] *arxiu* [arĉíu)
calaix [kalaiš]. The confusion arising from this change affects
the rhymes of Valencian poets, so as to make some of them
inadmissible in Barcelona; but grammarians attempt to en-
force the orthographical pronunciation, and the educated
speech tends toward the Catalan standard, with vacillation.
In the same way the literary revival of Valencian, which
began with Teodor Llorente, has followed a separate evolution, and it has not generated nationalist aspirations in
Valencia.

On Valencian consult T. Navarro Tomás y M. Sanchis Guarner,
'Análisis fonético del valenciano literario', *Rev. Fil. Esp.* xxi. Since the
above was written A. Griera has commenced publication of an
encyclopædic *Tresor de la llengua*, vols. i, ii (Barcelona, 1935).

CHAPTER V

THE RISE OF CASTILIAN

The Moslem invasion in 711 broke up the Visigothic unity of Spain, and placed the whole south and centre under the control of an alien culture. Two foci of resistance were recognized as menacing their rule: *Jalîkîya* or Galicia and *Al-Afranj*, the Franks or Catalans. There were also the *Baškuneš*, who had not submitted to Goth or Frank. *Jalîkîya* covered the whole north of Spain, and in the course of the centuries the main strength of the Christian resistance shifted gradually southward and eastward, from Galicia and the Asturias de Oviedo to León, from León to Old Castile, and from Old Castile ultimately to Toledo and the Tagus (1085). This record is mirrored in the language, where it is associated with the rise of Castilian to hegemony, until Castilian and Spanish become synonymous terms, supported on chancery tradition and a flourishing vernacular literature (twelfth and thirteenth centuries). The period opens with a state of linguistic unity, pregnant with change, which we may term the Visigothic platform. Doubtless linguistic change was accomplished more slowly than the dynastic, and during the eighth century there must have been, apart from the Catalan area, considerable uniformity of language. The southern and central Spaniards did not, as was once supposed, surrender their Romance tongue. It was the language of the marketplace, of all women and of unofficial intercourse; while Arabic was limited to administration, literature and high-class families claiming Arabian descent. In short, the relations between Romance and Arabic in Al-Andalus must have strongly resembled those existing between Guaraní and Castilian in the Paraguayan republic. This Spanish of the south, or Mozarabic, inherited the Visigothic capitals and great cities, continuing the Visigothic development of spoken Latin;

but it remained in a backwater, deeply indebted to Arabic for its vocabulary and shut off from the flow of change, so as to present a profoundly archaic appearance.

The modern language formed itself in the north and followed the fortunes of the Reconquest. At first it is seen under the tutelage of León, where *magni reges* and *imperatores* endeavoured to restore the image of the Visigothic monarchy with the aid of Galicians and the Mozarabs lying between the Duero and Tagus. Their language maintains an uneasy compromise between the conservatism of their Galician subjects and the inventiveness of the Castilians, between the Latin inheritance and the Arabic debt incurred by the Mozarabs. The savage razzias of Al-Manṣûr bi'llâh at the end of the tenth century broke the power of the Leonese emperors, leaving Castile relatively unhurt.

In Castile a radically innovating, native type of language was developing, which carried to their logical conclusions the changes already commenced in the era of unity. Based on the intense national sentiment of Old Castilians, this speech spread with the power of the sovereign counts, invading eastern León and pressing southward and south-westward into the borders of the Lusitanian province. The great epic poems of the eleventh and twelfth centuries accustomed all Spaniards to hear this accent, and to deem it suitable for narrative and other literary uses; until in the thirteenth century Toledo fell not to León but to Castile, and Castilian, with some compromises, became the language of the chanceries of Spain and of its great prose literature. Traces of the other dialects continue to appear in literary documents to bewray the authors' origins, but they are always compromise forms of Castilian. This is even true of Aragonese works. The kingdom of Aragón sheltered to some extent the local dialect, which was accepted by the chancery of Aragón and for literary works of considerable magnitude. But these also show castilianisms, some more some less, together with Catalan elements, presaging the extinction of literary Aragonese in the sixteenth century. On the other side, Castilian cut off Leonese from Toledo and from southern Extremadura, whence it descended along the whole Spanish front into Andalusia, giving rise to the modern Andaluz.

Above the Mozarabic substratum, therefore, and between its Leonese and Aragonese rivals, Castilian has thrust a fan-shaped wedge of innovations, which has caused standard modern Spanish to differ considerably from the consensus of the Spanish dialects. Where Leonese, Aragonese and Mozarabic agree in any phenomenon, it is thus possible to refer the feature to the language at the moment before the disruption, and to infer what was common form in Spanish at the close of the Visigothic era. But as well as innovations, Castilian has carried forward certain elements which it shares with Leonese against Aragonese, or Aragonese against Leonese; and in these cases the tendency is further prolonged to the east or west so as to include Catalan or Galician-Portuguese respectively. Through this evidence we become aware of the tendencies favouring a division of Spanish Romance before the rise of the dialects as such; and particularly we learn to know two masses which intersect in the Cantabrian area whence Castilian has arisen, the north-west pivoting on Galicia and León, and the north-east pivoting on Catalonia and Aragón. These masses are outlying portions of the Roman provinces of Asturica and Tarraconensis; a third Roman province, Lusitania, is more dimly in evidence, owing to its conservatism.

The changes common to all Western Romance languages, and which it is the function of the student of Vulgar Latin to investigate, had taken place before the disruption of the Spanish dialects; but not quite equably over the whole area. Except, perhaps, in the Asturias and the old Riojan glosses, where there are traces of final -u, the Latin final vowels had been reduced to three: *a e o*. In Catalonia, however, this tendency had gone so far as to eliminate the two latter; and in the north-eastern dialects the final -*e* was threatened with extinction. In Old Castilian it was dropped in the singular, but was retained in the plural -*es*; whence it has been restored to the singular since the twelfth century (*noch noches* becoming *noche noches*). After final *l m n r d j s x z* the *-e* is still lacking in the singular and present in the plural. Accented ĕ and ŏ tended to become diphthongs in a northern and central area, embracing the Asturias, León, Castile, Aragón, Toledo, generally Andalusia, Valencia and the Baleares. Galician-Portuguese had no share in this tendency; Catalan, like Provençal, only in the neighbourhood of a palatalized consonant (ŏc'lu Cat. *ull*, nŏcte Cat. *nit*, lĕctu Cat. *llit* Prov. *uelh nuech liech*). Castilian dissented from common Spanish practice precisely where ĕ ŏ were in contact with a palatal (*ojo noche lecho*). Lusitania did not at all favour the diphthong, and combined this conservative attitude with the retention of intertonic vowels in such names as *Mérida* emĕrita and *Mértola*. In Bætica, also, and especially in Granada, the diphthongs were resisted. Over the whole Peninsula the suffixes -ariu -eriu -oriu -asiu suffered metathesis into *-airo -eiro -oiro -eiso*, as the basis for further separate developments in Spanish, Portuguese and Catalan. In the north-east (Catalonia and Aragón) there was a tendency to reduce the diphthongs ai au to simple vowels; and Cantabria probably had no f.

Among the consonantal changes, we note that the tendency to voice the voiceless occlusives -p- -t- -k- between vowels and in weak positions is characteristically north-western. It is marked in Galician-Portuguese and in Leonese, where *-b- -d- -g-* were introduced even into Latin documents (e.g. *cingidur* for cingitur); and it extends as far as Castilian, where there are instances of vacillation in the oldest language. In Old Aragonese and in Mozarabic intervocal *-p- -t- -k-* are still frequent, especially in the suffixes -atu -ata (e.g. Moz. *boyaṭa* 'herd', ninth century), and they intrude in place of Latin voiced stops (e.g. Moz. *Qórṭuba* cŏrduba). The whole Peninsula possessed also the cacuminal pronunciation of *s* [ś], quite distinct from that of *ç*, formed by raising the point of the tongue to the alveoli. It sounded to the Arabs like *sh* [š], and they transcribe it with *shîn*, using *sîn* as the equi-

8

valent of *ç* [š]. The loss of this pronunciation in Andalusia and southern (standard) Portuguese is a later development. The *ç* (Lat. c before front vowels) developed in the Peninsular languages in common as far as to be produced in the front of the mouth, either as an affricate [ŝ] or as a fricative [s]; and similarly *j* (Lat. J Dǀ G before front vowels) shows a common development as far as the middle palate, where it is the affricate [ĵ] or the fricative [j], transcribed by the Arabic *jîm*. The further development of both these sounds is peculiar to Castilian, and marks the change over from the medieval to the modern form of that language. The group -CT- lingers in Mozarabic as -ḥt-, but elsewhere the Spanish dialects agree with Portuguese, Catalan and Western Romance to carry the evolution as far as -*it*-, from which point the Castilian -*ch*- is a further extension of the palatalizing process. All the Peninsular languages agree, again with the concurrence of Western Romance, to represent the groups -CL- and -LI- by palatal *l* [λ]; and in the central and eastern languages (Spanish and Catalan, but not Galician-Portuguese) the doubled consonants -LL- and -NN- were pronounced with such increased tension of the tongue against the roof of the mouth, as to turn them into palatals. At the beginning of words L- showed sporadic tendencies to palatalize, *ll*-, even before the disruption of the linguistic unity; a circumstance that accounts for its presence in the Asturias and Catalonia, and to some extent in the Mozarabic territory, but not in Castilian nor in Galician-Portuguese. Definitely northwestern was the tendency to palatalize the L in the initial groups PL- CL- FL-. These changes do not descend to the Mozarabic of the south, but they reach as far east as Aragón, where forms like *pll*- are found concurrently with *pl*-, etc., the latter supported not only by Latin but by Catalan. In Castilian the palatal *ll* has succeeded in eliminating the initial *p c f* (PLAGA *llaga*, CLAMAT *llama*, FLAMMA *llama*); while in Leonese and Galician-Portuguese a more complicated play of phonetic changes has given [ŝ] [ĉ] and [š] (Ptg. *chaga chama chama*). At the end of a syllable Latin L had universally a velar timbre, still attached to it in Portuguese and Catalan, though not in Spanish. This velar [ł] approximated on *u*, and led to the formation of diphthongs in *au* from *al* + consonant.

Among other forces which we must suppose to have been operating before the languages separated were those which simplified the declensions and conjugations. Catalan shares with Spanish and Portuguese the distinction of having reduced the Latin declension to the accusative singular and plural alone; and in this respect it differs pointedly from French and Provençal. It shows also a strong tendency to rationalize the verbal paradigm by eliminating 'irregular' past participles; but Catalan does this on the basis of the preterite stem (*venir vinguí vingut*), while Spanish and Portuguese start from the present stem (Sp. *venir vine venido*). Catalan does not share in the tendency to reduce the number of conjugations, which marks Spanish and Portuguese in all their dialects, and which must therefore be referred to the pre-dialectal state. The elimination of the third conjugation -ĔRE by identification with -ĒRE was then, doubtless, complete, and the further tendency to transfer verbs in -*er* to -*ir* had been initiated, especially for the Spanish dialects.

MOZARABIC DIALECTS

The Moorish invasion of 711 flowed over the Peninsula too swiftly to allow of large displacements of population. A minute force of twelve thousand Berbers destroyed the hosts of King Roderick and captured the great cities of Sevilla, Córdoba, Orihuela and Toledo, before the Moorish generalissimo Mûsâ ibn Nuṣair so much as set foot in the country. The first attempt at settlement occurred much later, when the contingents from Damascus and Kinnesrin were established in Granada; and even then the invaders left alone the towns, swayed by their innate passion for tent and country life. It is true that a certain number of Goths, either as being closely identified with the late régime or through love of liberty, fled northward, and settled in village colonies in Galicia and the Asturias; but the majority even of the ruling caste remained on their estates in the south. Roderick's widow married Mûsâ's son, and it appears that enough Rodriguists remained in Córdoba to form a faction. The sons of Witiza, on the other hand, had sided with the invaders in order to retain their 3000 estates, and their chief, Ardabast, became Count of Córdoba and one of the most powerful men in the emirate. The daughters of that house married into the Arab nobility. In Murcia Theodomir surrendered to the invaders on condition of retaining the province, and in Zaragoza, Badajoz and Toledo subsequent history lies largely in the hands of Spanish renegades. As for the Hispano-Romans, they had no reason to be discontented with the change of rulers. The long Arian controversy had bred in them a sense of antagonism to the Goths, in addition to the natural contempt of Roman for German. They constituted the population of the great towns, and in the country there was plenty of room for both possessors and invaders. They had their own bishops (the *çaet almatran*), and proselytism was against the interest of the state, as it exempted the convert from the capitation tax; they were ruled by their own laws and counts; and they enjoyed the use of their own language.

The establishment of the supremacy of Arabian culture did not go entirely unchallenged, and in the period of a hundred years between about 850 and 932 a sort of second Moorish conquest was effected. The emirate, founded in blood by 'Abd-al-Raḥmân I and upheld by Ḥakam I, descended to sovereigns who loved art and ostentation more than power, and the tide of sedition steadily rose. The first protest that concerns our theme, however, was religious and cultural. It is the movement known as that of the Cordobese martyrs, limited to the capital city, and championed by St Eulogius and Alvarus of Córdoba. The story is well known. A certain Flora, deemed a Moslem because her father was one, but actually a Christian, was denounced to the cadi by a fanatical brother. The only legal penalty was death. The

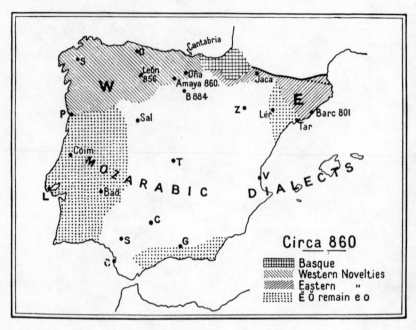

Peninsular Romance after the Visigothic era

cadi did all in his power to have the charge withdrawn and turn a blind eye on her technical apostasy; but the inhuman brother persisted. Flora suffered martyrdom for her faith, and was supported in her steadfastness by St Eulogius. From this event, St Eulogius drew the conclusion that martyrdom was meritorious in itself, that it should be provoked as a proof of faith. There was an orgy of zealots who rushed out to blaspheme the Prophet, despite the efforts of the bishop of Córdoba to dissuade them and those of the cadis to ignore the provocation. But the sequence of suicides brought the reform to a standstill by slaying its most devoted adherents, until at length Eulogius himself provoked and suffered the martyrdom he had urged on others.

In the ruin of religious zeal was involved the ruin of an attempted Latin Renaissance, ultimately dependent on that effected in the Carolingian courts. The prestige of Latin had fallen very low in the south. Many Christians could pronounce on the niceties of Arabic style, but were incapable of writing a Latin letter. 'Heu, proh dolor! Linguam suam nesciunt christiani', exclaims Alvarus. It is not that the Christians had lost contact with their own proto-Spanish tongue, as older philologists supposed. It is rather that, with the foundering of official and cultural Latin, a gap had been established between the current *latini* or '*ajami* (as the Arabic authors call it) and the classical standard. Between the vernacular and 'latinum obscurum' there had established itself for ecclesiastical purposes a 'latinum circa romancium' (first named in the thirteenth century by Virgil of Córdoba, but corresponding to an older state of affairs), necessarily an unstable dialect of compromise. Alvarus attacks this gibberish in his opponents as well as their heresies. He seeks to restore the purer and more ancient Latin tradition, and St Eulogius travelled as far as the Pyrenees to obtain suitable models. A Church should be zealous for its sacred language. The suicide of the zealots decided the Latin question by elimination. There remained only the Spanish vernacular and the cultural use of Arabic. The former was of no service for literature, though doubtless the vehicle of lyrics and oral tales, and the very Canons of the Church were turned into Arabic in 1049 to guarantee their preservation.

The vernacular remained unimpaired, and it had a second chance with the revolt of the renegades in the later years of the ninth century. In the long and disastrous reign of the emir 'Abd-Allâh (888–912) the capital was surrounded by concentric rings of rebels, the most powerful of whom were renegades like Ibn Marwân of Badajoz. On the 15th April, 891, the daring *caudillo* Ibn Hafsûn advanced to the castle of Polei (Aguilar), almost within sight of the city, and forced the sultan to fight. The Cordobese approached with so little heart that the Spanish leader exclaimed 'Now we've got that herd', using the word *boyaṭa*. But the event falsified his expectations. He was signally defeated, and hurled back on his stronghold of Bobastro, where he contrived to defend himself during the remainder of his life. He was further weakened by his return to the Christian faith, which act lost him the confidence of the renegades. Though he died in 917, the insurrection in the Serranía de Ronda was not extinguished entirely until his daughter Argentea (a Christian with a Spanish name) was captured and executed in 932.

What followed was a period of entire subjection to the central Moslem authority and to Arabian culture. The Arabs by race gained nothing from the re-establishment of order. On the contrary, the Arab aristocracy was systematically decimated; the state rested on the support of mercenaries, both northern Spaniards and Slavs. Its prestige became more and more identified with military success until, under Al-Manṣûr, such triumphs were sought without any attempt at political consolidation, raids and victories being the sole end of political action. The Christian princes were tributaries at the courts of 'Abd-al-Raḥmân III, Ḥakam II and Hishâm II, and were there made and unmade; their daughters entered the caliphal harems. But in the intervals of defeat the Christian north grew in strength and population, and made ready for the great advance of the eleventh century.

The brilliant Moslem capital began to give scope for literature. Ḥakam II collected an enormous library of 400,000
volumes, the contents of which he himself mastered during
the long years of his heir-apparency. He inspired great
historians like Ibn Ḥayyân, and traditionalists like Al-
Khushanî (Aljoxaní). Schools of philosophy began to appear,
though they were severely discouraged by Al-Manṣûr, who
wished to curry favour with the orthodox. Arabian literature
still lacked the brilliance it attained in the petty courts of
the early eleventh century, but it had already achieved a
decided superiority over its Latin rival.

But the Spanish vernacular continued unimpaired. It was
the language of all women. To enable a woman to plead her
case in the courts of the capital an obliging cadi conducted
the proceedings in *latinî*. For the harems of the wealthy, and
of the caliph himself, Christian slave-women were preferred,
and particularly those from Jalîkîya (Galicia, León and
Castile). The practice continued down to the fall of Granada
in the person of the famous sultana Doña Isabel de Solís.
The caliphs and the entire upper classes were bilingual, with
Spanish for their mother-tongue. We hear that they were
able to cap verses with Spanish rhymes, and the *Diwân* of
Ibn Quzmân (d. 1160) employs Spanish tags, as well as
verse-forms (the *zejel* and *muwaššaha*) admittedly borrowed
in the time of the first caliph by Muqaddam of Cabra from
Romance models. Arabic was an official speech, but those
who were not officials did not trouble to acquire it. Under
'Abd-al-Raḥmân II the father of the powerful eunuch Naṣr
could speak nothing but Romance. Arabic was the language
of the Coran and of religion; but the Romance-speaking
Yenair (Januarius) of Córdoba was so famous for his virtue
and orthodoxy that his testimony was accepted without
question as equivalent to a legal document. It was officially
decided that, in the case of an ascetic, ignorance of Arabic
was not a bar to sanctity. Persons of purely Christian extrac-
tion were candidates for office, and Christian names are frequently recorded (*Vicente, Comes* ben *Antonián*, Ibn *Montiel*,

etc.), both among the populace of the capital and as pet-names in the royal family (*Sanchol, Royol*, Cast. *Sanchuelo, Rojuelo*). The Spanish Moslem populace vigorously opposed the introduction of the turban and of silk, and Ibn Khaldûn remarks on their identity in features, manners and dress with the Galicians of the north.

Our knowledge of the language they used depends on chance anecdotes, like those preserved in Al-Khushanî's History of the Judges of Córdoba, where we encounter some instructive stories and the names of Romance persons; the names of places are preserved in the geographers, particularly Al-Idrîsî, while Ibn Jubair gives his dates according to both calendars, Moslem and Christian. The writers of popular Arabic lyrics, the *zejels* and *muwaššaḥas*, adopted Romance principles of verse and quote words from the vernacular. These are frequent in Ibn Quzmân's *Diwân* (his name is the Spanish *Guzmán*), as the line in his 82nd poem

> albâ albâ êš ḍa luǧ anûna ḍîyeh
> Alba, alba es de luz en un día.

Further, the mediciners and botanists who went out into the country to gather their simples, found themselves in places where Arabic was unknown, and so required to know the Spanish name for the plant, and in some cases the local name where dialect variations occurred; hence the preserva-tion of plant-names in botanical treatises like that of Ibn al-Baiṭar. Finally there are formal glossaries: a Leiden glossary from the eleventh century edited by Seybold, and a Valencian of the thirteenth. Our knowledge of the Arabic of Spain is chiefly drawn from the *Vocabulista in aravigo* of Fray Pedro de Alcalá (1505), which reflects both its pecu-liarities of pronunciation and its indebtedness to the circum-ambient Romance. The dialect he transcribes is that of Granada, and shows many features of late evolution.

The wars of the tenth and early eleventh centuries were waged between Spaniards, divided by culture and allegiance, but without extremes of religious bigotry. The Castilian victory and conquest of Toledo in 1085 forced on the south a painful choice between race and religion. They might have settled down under the hegemony of the petty kings of Sevilla, as tributaries to Alfonso VI; but the latter's cruelty and rapacity, and the discourses of the fanatical elements in the south, caused the Moors to call over from Africa hordes of Berber allies. These allies, the Almorávides, checked the Christian advance and threw Castile on to the defensive; but they were still more effective in suppressing the liberties of southern Spaniards, whether Moslem or Christian. The Christian Mozarabs found their position especially unhappy, as they were suspected of intrigues. It was on their support that the Cid based his tenure of Valencia (1094–99), and they emigrated in a body from that city in 1101, leaving it stripped and empty to the Berber generals. The war took on a more intensely religious aspect. Even the Jews were suspected by the succeeding Almohad (*Al-Muwahhid*) dynasty. Their great school at Lucena was broken up in 1146, and they transferred their studies to Toledo, Barcelona and Languedoc, to the benefit of the Christian scientists. In 1126 a Mozarab revolt in Granada, supported by Alfonso the Battler of Aragón, misfired, and 10,000 of them followed the Aragonese army in its retreat. At length St Ferdinand led the combined Leonese and Castilian armies into the Guadalquivir valley, capturing Córdoba (1236) and Sevilla (1248). Alfonso X reached the sea at Cádiz in 1264, and all hope of a Moorish revenge was ended by the great Christian victory of the Río Salado in 1340.

As a result of these triumphs the Moorish power was restricted to the vassal-state of Granada, where it took on a more religious and Arabian colour. But even in this quintessence of Arabian civilization it is recorded that out of 200,000 original inhabitants, only 500 were not the sons or grandsons of Christians. Bilingual persons existed, *moros latinados*, and traded on their knowledge so far as to give the word *ladino* the connotation of 'sly'. There are traces in Spanish ballads of specifically Moorish sentiments. Meanwhile the presence of large bodies of Mozarabs in the northern kingdoms profoundly modified Spanish culture, and the dialect itself survived in notarial documents even after the rise of Castilian literature. Such documents are especially frequent at Toledo.

As the Reconquest advanced southwards the dialects of the conquerors—Portuguese, Castilian and Catalan—flowed over the ground occupied by the ancient Mozarabic in sharply defined spheres of influence (*conquistas*). Clear linguistic frontiers replace the blurred transitions characteristic of lands which have had an uninterrupted development. It is thus at the point where the band-frontiers abruptly harden into lines that we are able to plot the original limits of Mozarabic, assisted also by what we know of their population in the early Middle Ages. Southern Portugal, we note, did not speak Portuguese (*Mértola* has -*l*- between vowels contrary to Portuguese norms). Lisbon, contrary to Portuguese usage, has -*n*- between vowels in OSp. *Lisbona* Fr. *Lisbonne* Eng. *Lisbon*, as in Ar. *Al-Ašbûna*; Coimbra is Froissart's *Conimbre*. Both cities were important for their Mozarabic population, and the latter was repeopled by a Mozarab, Count Sisnando. Both have been accommodated in later times to Portuguese (Sp. *Lisboa* is from the Portuguese; Ayala *c.* 1407 writes *Lisbona*, but *Coimbra*). On the other hand *Gaia* at the mouth of the Duero is the ancient *Cale*, whence *Portugal* (PORTUS CALE), and belongs to the Galician-Portuguese area. The Mozarabic frontier thus commenced in the west at the mouth of the Duero, which it followed inland so as to assign to Mozarabic the important cities of Salamanca, Zamora (re-walled by a Mozarab), and Toledo or *Ṭulaiṭula*. Alcalá de Henares, Guadalajara and Calatayud were Moorish bulwarks against Castile. Zaragoza or *Saraqusṭa* belonged also to the Mozarabic region, which reached the sea on the frontier between Valencia and Catalonia; and further embraced the Balearic islands. A point fixed by the change from band-frontier to line in the east is at Tamarite. Valencia was the home of the Banu Montiel (MONTĔLLU), who show the Spanish diphthong, and of the personage called Ibn Pascual

(*Ibn Baškuwâl*) who should rather be known as *Ibn Vascuel* ('little Basque', with the diphthong -*ue*- of the Spanish diminutive ending). The *Repartiment de Mallorca* is notable for names in -*o* (Spanish, therefore, not Catalan) at the moment of that island's pacification. Final vowels, however, except -*a*, are very frequently dropped in our authorities for Mozarabic. This may have been due to the influence of Arabic upon the orthography, since these words are recorded by authors accustomed to masculine nouns terminating in a consonant; and it probably influenced speech also. Thus we have vacillations: *mayo, bênâțo = penado* 'grieved', *bâdhu = vado* 'ford', *mâ rikêri = me requiere* 'he loves me', and *Montiel, Yenair, Bizent = Vicente, mars = marzo* 'March'. The geographer Ibn Jubair, writing in July 1187, is instructive, since he was a native of Valencia between the Cid's withdrawal and the campaigns of James the Conqueror. He uses Roman dates to correct the Hejira reckoning, and omits the final -*o* (e.g. *mars* 'March'), while using the diphthong in -*ai*- or -*ei*- which it is characteristic of Catalan to have early reduced to -*e*- -*o*-: thus *yenair* Cat. *gener* 'January', *febrair* Cat. *febrer* 'February'.

In this vast area there were local variations. Our authorities tell us of some differences of vocabulary in the northeastern frontier. In Zaragoza the 'speedwell' was *bentrónica*, but in the Levante *bentónica*. In Valencia the caper was *táparaš*, not *alcaparras*; at Córdoba a kind of cloak was known as *borocán*. These and one or two more words owe their preservation mainly to the botanists in search of simples, but they do not throw light on the major differences of the Mozarabic dialects. They must be inferred from place-names, particularly those which use the diminutive suffixes -ĔLLU and -ŎLA. In the whole central and eastern region these terminations tend to diphthongize, though with exceptions, whereas on the south coast and in the Sierra Nevada they remain monophthongs (e.g. *Ferreirola*), and the same is generally true of Portugal in the Alemtejo, Algarve and lower Guadiana valley. We find, in this way, that there were specially conservative dialects in the west and south.

Accented ĕ and ŏ remain *e* and *o* in conservative parts of
the country or under special influences of tradition (such as
those affecting the name of an important city); but generally
speaking they give diphthongs in all circumstances. These
diphthongs are not fixed as to quality, but vacillate as *ia*
whence also *a*) *ie* from ĕ and *wa we* from ŏ. ĕ gives *massanélla*
'chamomile' in Córdoba, *Lopel* as diminutive from *Lope*, *ben*
BĔNE, *rikêri*=*requiere* in Córdoba *c.* 1160, *Mérida* EMĔRITA;
also *šaḥamialla* (doubtful) as well as *šaḥamiella* 'truffle';
Cazalla and *Castalla* CASTĔLLA; *Ibn Qardiel*, *ešpatiella* 'corn-
flag', *ajetiella* Sp. *acedilla* 'wood-sorrel', etc. The forms in
-*ia*- are not easily demonstrable, as Arabic does not effectively distinguish between *a* and *e*, though our authors
frequently use *â* to indicate *e* in Spanish, as this was the
Moghrebî pronunciation of *â*. Place-names in -ĔLLU give
-*iel* in Valencia, Zaragoza, La Mancha, Murcia and the
Guadalquivir valley, but -*el* in Portugal and Granada-Málaga
(*Maurel Moradel*). In the case of accented ŏ there is very
considerable resistance to the diphthong, which, however,
was normal in the same regions as those indicated for ĕ:
Orihuela in Murcia, *Teruel Cuenca Caracuey* on the upper
Guadiana, *Huelva* ŏNOBA; but it is not found in the Algarve,
nor in Granada (*Ferreirola*, *Albuñol*), and in Córdoba there
was sporadic resistance. Ibn Quzmân of Córdoba (*c.* 1160)
writes *bún bono* for *bueno*, and nicknames were *Sanchol* (*Sanchuelo*) *Royol* (*Rojuelo* 'ruddy, Rufus'). On the other hand
Valencia seems to have favoured the diphthong: *Vascuel*,
Mauchuel. Whether *we* or *wa* is intended in any given case
can hardly be determined from Arabic spellings, and vacillations between them and *o* are very frequent: *puerco porco*
'pig', *laḥtairuela laitarola* Cat. *lleterola*, the name of a plant
with milky sap. The diphthong was not prevented by the
neighbourhood of a palatal, as in Castilian: *Caracuey* -ŏɪ,
welyo negro ŏCULU NIGRU Cast. *ojo negro*, the name given to a
kind of nettle.

In respect of the unaccented vowels, the most remarkable
feature of Mozarabic is the facility wherewith final -*e* and -*o*

are lost, apparently under the influence of Arabic prejudices. Ibn Quzmân keeps the final vowel in *katîbu = ca(p)tivo* 'prisoner', *waštâṭo = gastado* 'wasted', *roṭonṭo = redondo* 'round', *mâ rikêri = me requiere* 'loves me', *dunuχti = de noche* 'by night'; but he drops it in *bún = bueno* 'good', *baštiṭ = bastido* 'well set up', *ešt = este* 'this', *masqúl = masculo*, etc. It is wanting in the names of months and in many place-names.

As for the diphthongs AI AU, they remained as diphthongs. The quality of the former cannot be decided from Arabic spellings, but Pedro de Alcalá shows that it was still occasionally *ai* after the fall of Granada. Doubtless *ei* also occurs, as in Ibn Quzmân's *atarey ataré* 'I shall bind', and in the place-name in Granada *Ferreirola*. For *ou* the Arabic script does offer means of discrimination, and it is clear that both forms persisted in the south as late as the fall of Granada. Thus Sp. *losa* 'flag-stone' is *lauša* in the thirteenth-century vocabulary, and *Laujar* as a place-name. At Valencia there were the *Banu Mauchuel*, but at Sevilla in the tenth century the *Banu Mourgâṭ* MAURECATU. It is in the stage *ei ou* that Mozarabic strikingly resembles Galician-Portuguese, to which it stands in a relationship of greater archaism. *ei* is still a diphthong in standard Portuguese, but *ou* is either a close vowel [ǫ] or has suffered dissimilation to *oi*: *cousa coisa*, *ouro oiro* Sp. *cosa oro*. Mozarabic examples are: AI *pandair = pandero* 'tambourine', *šemtair = sendero* 'path', *baika baiga bega = vega*, *lahtaira* 'yellow bed-straw', and the place names *Poqueira*, *Junqueiro*, etc.; AU, as above. The ending -AGINE gives -*ain* in Mozarabic, where Castilian has -*én*: *plantain* Cast. *llantén* 'plantain'.

In its treatment of consonants also the Mozarabic dialect was highly conservative. It had no share in the northwestern change of initial PL- CL- FL- to palatals, which took place in Galician, Portuguese, Leonese, Castilian, and to a slight extent also in Aragonese. In this respect it agrees with Catalan: PLANTAGINE Moz. *plantain* Cat. *plantatge*. Like all the Peninsular languages and dialects other than Castilian, Mozarabic preserved initial J- ġ-: JANUARIU Moz. *yenair* Cast.

enero 'January' Cat. *gener* Ptg. *janeiro*. The phonetic value was [j], reflected in the place-names Yunquera and Tayunquera, but also occasionally [ĵ], affricate voiced palatal, as Junquera (MSp. pronunciation [χ], Ast. [š], Gal. [š], Cat. Ptg. [ž]). L- initial was sporadically palatalized in the south as in other parts of the Peninsula (west Leonese and the Bable dialects of Asturian, eastern Aragonese and Catalan). So the 'bugloss' is given by Ibn Kholkhol as *yengua buba* LINGUA BUBULA (*y*- from *ll*- from L-). F survived, as in all Romania save Castile and Gascony: *furn Buriel* 'Burriel's oven' at Córdoba, Cast. *horno*.

The most important among the medial sounds is the consonant-group -CT-, which shows remarkable archaisms in Mozarabic. The general resolution of this group is, as in all Western Romance but Castilian, -*it*-: *leiteĵinos* ModArag. *lechecinos* 'sow-thistle', *leitúqas* Cast. *lechugas* 'lettuces', *leiterola*, all from LACTE-. At the other end of this scale we have the Latin -CT- preserved in Ibn Jubair's *oktúbar* 'October', which Pedro de Alcalá writes *ogtubar*, possibly to represent that the C was not completely occlusive, as it is not in Modern Spanish. This voiceless velar fricative passed into a laryngeal aspirate as *ḥ* in Al-Kazwînî's *truḥta* 'trout' TRUCTA, or χ in Ibn Quzmân's *dunuχti* Cast. *de noche* 'by night', and Ibn Kholkhol's *laχtaira*=*cuajaleche* 'yellow bed-straw', and in *laχtairuela*, equivalent to *leiterola*. Thus Mozarabic contained simultaneously all the stages through which this change has been operated in Romance, commencing with the failure to pronounce the C as completely occlusive, and ending in the palatal semi-vowel. Medial -CL- and -LI- develop into -*ll*- [λ] in Mozarabic, as in Romance of the West, and thence into -*y*- or even [ž]. So ŏCULU gives *welyo* 'eye', *follar* Cast. *hojaldre* 'puff-paste', *konelyo* 'rabbit'. This is the pronunciation used by Toledan Mozarabs in the thirteenth century: *fillo mulleres* Cast. *hijo mujeres*. But *konĵair* 'dog used in hunting rabbits' shows [ĵ] derived from [j], and that from [λ], as in Modern Argentine; and *Dar-al-viejo* is due to popular etymology for *Dar-al-belyo* where the [λ] had passed to [ž] and so resembled the pronunciation of Cast. *j*. In PACE AUGUSTI *Badajoz* we have the stage **baśayóś*, with dissimilation of the two [ś]; in Ptg. *Badalhouce* and Moz. *Baṭalyús* the [λ] is a hyper-correction of *y*. The opposition between Castilian and Mozarabic usage in this matter was felt by the author of the *Poema del Cid*, a Mozarab of the Medinaceli region, when he wrote *Gujera* for *Cullera*, and *Castejón* for *Castellón*.

Mozarabic agrees with the eastern dialects of the Peninsula, against the north-western bloc, by preserving many voiceless occlusives between vowels. The participial ending -ATU is given regularly as -*aṭo*, and other instances as *Garnáṭa* or *Agarnáṭa* for Granada, *ṭoṭo* for *todo* 'all', *boyaṭa* 'herd' = *manada de bueyes*, *roṭonṭo* for *redondo* 'round'. Sometimes this voiceless consonant was restored by ultra-correction, as *Qórṭuba* CŎR-DUBA. The voiced forms were also known, as AQUA *agua*, AQUILA *águila* (with *ghain*). On the other hand, -F- showed a strong tendency to pass into a voiced fricative represented by *u*: *prouiciscor* PROFICISCOR, *reuocilo* REFOCILO, in the Latin of Mozarabic notaries, together with ultra-corrections like *referendus* for REVERENDUS.

The sibilants included [ĵ ž], spelled with *jîm*, a cacuminal *s*, and *ç z*. The *jîm* of Arabic corresponds with the Hebrew *gimel*, and was at first used to represent *g*. Thus Galicia was *Jalîkîya*, and the Tagus *Tájo* or *Têjo*. In the latter case the Latin G has been replaced by the Arabic *j*. The cacuminal [ś] and its corresponding voiced sound seemed to Arabian ears to be palatals of the nature of [š ž], and it is by *shîn* that they are represented. Italian *s* was not of this nature in Sicily, and so Ibn Jubair writes *Ṣiqilîya* and *Sarqûsa* for Sicily and Syracuse with *s*, but *śetember* for September (cf. his *Śaflûdî* for Cefalu, indicating the palatal, but not the affrication). In such words as Sp. *jabón* OSp. *xabón* SAPONE 'soap', the palatal is due to Arabic interference with the Spanish *s*, and similarly the *ch* of *albérchigo* PERSICU 'peach'. The *ç z* sounds were opposed to the cacuminal *s* as being sibilants pronounced with the tip of the tongue directed, not towards the gums or fore-palate, but behind the lower teeth. In this way they

9

resembled an *s* or *z*, and were written with *sîn* or *zâi* according as they were voiceless or voiced: *mars = marzo* 'March', *Bizent* in Al-Khushanî for *Vicente* (not *Jacinto* as Dozy supposed). If the forepart of the tongue happens to touch momentarily the teeth in the pronunciation of this *s*, an affricate results of the nature of *ts dz* [ŝ ẑ], representable by the Arabic *jîm*. So, in Ibn Quzmân, *bîj = pez* PISCE, *lūj = luz* LUCE. In this way the Mozarabic dialect was able to transform Latin ST into *ts* and *ç*: CAESARAUGUSTA Ar. *Saraqûsṭa* OSp. *Çaragoça*, ASTIGI Sp. *Écija*. P existed in Mozarabic Spanish, but had no place in the Arabic alphabet, where it could only be represented by *b*, or medially by *bb* to mark the unvoicing; hence, doubtless through official influence, the *b* in *Beja*, *Badajoz* PACE- and *albérchigo* PERSICU. *Beja* also represents the Moghrebî pronunciation [e] of long *á*, commonly employed to denote an accented *a* of Romance.

The Mozarabic dialect persisted in Toledo among the inhabitants of the six Mozarabic parishes throughout the twelfth and thirteenth centuries, where local forms still appear in conflict with the prevailing Castilian usages of the chancery, and ejaculatory formulæ of respect are added to the names of persons and places as they are mentioned in the documents. But the later history of the dialect is still somewhat obscure. There was indubitably a measure of substitution. The Andalusians speak now a dialect of Castilian, the Valencians of Catalan, the inhabitants of Algarve of Portuguese, the Moriscos of Aragonese until their expulsion. Was Mozarabic eliminated because it was generally like an archaic and out-of-date version of each victorious dialect? Was there a compromise, and if so how was it effected? What, in particular, does Andaluz owe to Mozarabic, if anything? The answer to such questions must be delayed until Andaluz is adequately surveyed. In the Toledo region, however, it is notable that literary Spanish is not identical with Old Castilian, but has effected some compromise with Leonese. Such a compromise would also be a compromise with Mozarabic, and the great influence of persons of this class in the literary circles of Alfonso the Wise and Don Juan Manuel suggests that they may have been instrumental in shaping standard literary Spanish.

SPANISH ARABIC

The Arabic language current in Al-Andalus resembled most intimately that of western Africa to-day, and particularly Morocco; but it contained features which forbid its identification with surviving dialects. As described by Pedro de Alcalá in 1505, the Granadine dialect is much more modern than that which gave to Spanish its numerous loan-words. This is especially noticeable in the *imâla*, the process by which *â* has passed to *i*. Pedro de Alcalá reports the final stage, but the evidence of the loan-words points to an intermediate *e*, and there are many cases of *a*. It is noteworthy that Ar. *th dh* continued to have the pronunciations [θ ð], though represented in the loan-words by *t d*. The smooth breathing was non-existent in Al-Andalus, and the rough breathing *'ain* tended to pass into an *h* or *a* or to disappear. As the *s* of Arabic was dorsoalveolar [s] it was deemed equivalent to Sp. *ç*, but never to Sp. *s* [ś] which was rendered by Ar. *š*.

The conquest occurred in the first century of the Hejira, and the language brought by the victors contained some archaic features, which later disappeared. Especially is this noted of the letter *jîm*. Listed as a guttural by Arabian phoneticians and corresponding to Heb. *gimel*, this letter had at first the value [g], and as such was used to transcribe place-names: GALLAECIA *Jalikîya*, TAGU Sp. *Tajo* Ptg. *Tejo*, PACE *Bâjja* etc. Later the *jîm* became an affricate or fricative palatal [ĵ ž], and the equivalent of Sp. *g* was *ghain*. In some cases this new value has been forced on the Spanish word, as in *Tajo Beja*, but in others it has been ineffectual, as in *Galicia*. Another primitive pronunciation was the value [g] given to *qâf*. This also appears principally in place-names: GADES *Qâdis* CAESARAUGUSTA *Saraqusṭa*. The later value was a velar [k], and the different results in Sp. *Cádiz Zaragoza* show that the change sometimes, but not always, affected the indigenous term. The language was equally archaic in respect of the emphatic letters *ḍâd* and *ṭâ*. For the former, the large application of the tongue to the fore-palate caused native phoneticians to describe the sound as escaping over the molars, and so of a lateral nature. It was a *d* with some of the characteristics of an *l*, and consequently was represented in Romance by *ld*: Ar. *al-qâḍî* Sp. *alcalde* 'judge, mayor'. For the latter, the emphatic pronunciation involved constriction of the larynx and consequently partial vibration of the vocal chord; it was a voiceless *t*, but partially resembled *d*. Thus it stood for the *d* of Romance words (*Córdoba* Ar. *Qórṭuba, roṭonṭo = redondo*) without necessarily implying that these sounds were unvoiced; at the same time it was preferred to represent Romance *t*, as the emphatic utterance constituted a sort of acclimatization of the foreign word.

In the case of the aspirate gutturals, the change to be noted is one which occurs in Romance. In the early centuries there was only *k* available, indicating the guttural nature of these sounds, but not the aspiration. Hence some place-names and common nouns represent the Arabic aspirate gutturals by *c*. Later, from the eleventh century, and still more from the end of the twelfth, the spread of the Castilian aspirate *h*, and its correspondence with the *f* of the other dialects, caused the Arabic aspirates to be rendered by *f* in Portuguese and Catalan and by *f h* in Castilian.

On the Arabic of Spain consult A. Steiger, *Contribución a la fonética del hispano-árabe y de los arabismos en el ibero-románico y el siciliano* (Madrid, 1932), who revises the conclusions of Dozy et Engelmann, *Glossaire des mots espagnols et portugais, dérivés de l'arabe* (2nd ed. Leiden, 1869).

THE ARABIC ELEMENT IN SPANISH

It was the business of the Mozarabs, these Spanish-speaking Christians under Moslem rule, to make easy the passage into Spanish of a considerable Arabic vocabulary. They required for their own use, and adapted to Romance norms, a large number of terms dealing with administration and the organization of society, commerce and industry, partly to indicate things new to, or best developed in, Al-Andalus, and partly because the administrative tongue was Arabic. What they borrowed were the names of things; there is only the slightest trace of Arabic in Spanish syntax, and no community of spirit. As an effective contribution to word-formation we note only the suffix -*i*; *jabalí* 'boar', *Alfonsí*, etc. The phonetic bases of the tongues also were quite distinct, and it is in the substitution of sounds required for the Romance adaptations that the bilingual Mozarabs must have exerted their influence. Bilingual Moslems (*moros latinados*) may have helped, and still more the Jews. The latter have transmitted little of their own language to Spanish and its sisters; merely such liturgical terms as have become international, like *Tora, Talmud, Gehena, taled* (a ceremonial head-covering), and, in Greek translation, *filacteria* 'phylactery'. Apart from the liturgy and the poetry used therein, the Spanish Jews supported the culture and prestige of Arabic, and wrote important philosophical works which were only subsequently rendered into Hebrew. When expelled from the Moorish territories in the twelfth century, they carried with them, it is true, a Hebrew culture which gave Spain a notable series of achievements in that tongue during the Middle Ages and Renaissance, but they were employed primarily in translating for schoolmen the philosophy of the Arabians, or in practising such professions as medicine, on the basis of Græco-Arabian treatises. The Jews, therefore, must be included among the supporters and translators of Arabic, but they had neither the numbers nor the good repute to authorize the passage of Arabic words into Spanish, Portuguese and Catalan. This was the work of Mozarabs.

The task of adaptation included the treatment of Arabic finals, the rendering of difficult consonants, and the solution of consonant-groups repugnant to Romance. In respect of finals, only nouns come into consideration, as the verbs bor-

rowed have purely Romance terminations. Nunation was
not in practice in the colloquial, and so leaves no trace in
Spanish borrowings. The feminine normally ended in -a,
which offered an easy analogy with Spanish feminines in -a.
A tendency to regard towns as feminine caused several in -e
to pass, through Mozarabic and Arabic mediation, into -a:
BARCINONE *Baršalúna Barcelona*, ASTIGI *Istiji Écija*, OLISIPONE
Al-Ašbúna Lisboa, HISPALI *Išbilîya Sevilla*, ILIBERRI *Ilbîra Elvira*
(near Granada). In TOLETU *Toledo* the Arabic doublet
Ṭulaiṭula has exerted no influence. SCIPIONE *Chipiona* owes
the initial and final to this interference. The feminine ending
was, however, actually in -at, and the *t* may make its presence
felt in compounds, as *qalʻat Ayyûb* 'Job's castle' *Calatayud*.

Arabic masculine nouns commonly end in consonants,
many of which are inadmissible in Romance. In this respect
the work of adaptation was carried out very thoroughly, and
sound-substitution was normal. Either, for the obnoxious consonant there was substituted one current in Ibero-Romance
(*Ayyûb -ayud*; *al-ʻaqrâb* 'scorpion' Sp. *alacrán* Ptg. *alacram
alacrão*), or an additional -e smoothed away the difficulty
(*al-χayyâṭ* 'tailor' OSp. *alfayate* Ptg. *alfaiate*; *al-duff* 'tambourine' Sp. Ptg. *adufe*). An -o occurs in *albérchigo* 'peach'
Ar. *al-firsiq* PERSICU, which is really a Romance word; and
in Sp. *alhóndiga* OCat. *alfóndech* 'granary' Ptg. *alfândega*
'custom-house', Ar. *al-fundaq* 'inn', and other similar instances, there has been a change of gender. Masculine nouns
have normally 'broken' plurals, that is, their vowels are
changed to indicate plurality. The Romance borrowings
may be made from either the singular or the plural, e.g.
adarme 'drachma' from the plural *al-darâhim*, not the singular
al-dirham.

In medieval loan-words it was customary to take over the
article *al-* as part of the word, assimilated to the initial when
assimilated in Arabic (*t th d dh s š z l n r*). The article is
not used when a noun stands before another in a genitive
relation: *qalʻat Ayyûb* 'the castle of Job' (not *al-qalʻa*). This
so-called construct case is represented in Spanish: *Calatayud*

OSp. *zavazoke* Ar. *ṣâḥib al-sûq* 'market superintendent', OSp. *zalmedina* Ar. *ṣâḥib al-medîna* 'intendant of the city', etc.

Within the word there also occurred sounds and combinations ungrateful to Romance ears. An *l* added to *d* had the effect of rendering the lateral element of emphatic *ḍ*, as well as making the pronunciation of *d* necessarily occlusive: Sp. *aldea* Ptg. *aldeia* Cat. *aldea* Ar. *al-ḍaiʻa* (pron. *aḍ-ḍ-*) 'village', Sp. Ptg. *alcalde* Ar. *al-qâḍî* 'city-magistrate, mayor'. The numerous aspirate gutturals of Arabic presented a further difficulty, and were variously represented by gutturals (*c g*), aspirates (*h f*), or ignored. It is particularly to be noted that no contact occurred between the modern Castilian guttural aspirate *jota* and interdental *zeta* and the Arabic sounds of the same value. The former were never represented by *j*, and the latter only by *t* in medieval Spanish, Portuguese and Catalan. The Arabic *shîn* [š] corresponded to the Sp. Ptg. Cat. *x*, and to cacuminal *s*; with the result that some instances of Latin s were transformed into *x* through Arabic interference. Arabic *jîm* [ĵ ž] corresponded sufficiently to the Romance *j*.

Groups of consonants are especially frequent in the Western Arabic to which that of Al-Andalus belonged. The accented vowels are stressed, and the unaccented vowels dwindle into 'fugitive' sounds. These sounds become full vowels in Romance loan-words, but are not always those of the original Arabic. Thus *-quivir* in *Guadalquivir* is Ar. *kabîr* 'big', Moghrebî *kbîr*. In other cases the group belongs to all Arabic: *qaṣr* 'castle' gives Sp. *alcázar* Ptg. *alcáçar* and *alcácer(e)*; *Ibn* became *Aben* 'son' (in patronymics). Initially consonant-groups do not occur in standard Arabic, and those of Romance are represented in Arabic script with an initial *alif* (*Al-Afranj* 'the Franks') or with an intrusive vowel (*Garnâṭa* Granada).

If we make a representative list of arabisms in Spanish and its sister languages, we note that the words are almost always names of objects or institutions connected with a certain stage of culture. Intimate intercourse of the two languages, which lived together for 800 years, is rare. Sp. *he* in *hete* 'here you have...', *he aquí* (OSp. *afe fe ahe he e*) is the Ar. *hâ* (pron. *he* in Al-Andalus), which is used in the same way with pronouns and simple adverbs of place: *hâka*, *hâhunâka*. The *a-* prefix, when it occurs, is probably due to analogy with the *a-* of other demonstratives: *aquí*, *acá*, *aquel*, etc. *Yâ* 'oh' (vocative) appears in the epic language: *ya Cid*. In Morisco works it occurs as *ye* also: *Ye Saad*; *ye mi Alá* 'oh my God'. *Hamihala*, in the twelfth-century *Auto de los Reyes Magos*, is an unexplained interjection, perhaps introducing the word *Allâh*, though some have taken it for a proper name, accompanied by the exclamation 'ha'. In *ojalá* OSp. Ptg. *oxalá* we find the Ar. *wa šâ' Allâh* 'if God will, would that'. Ar. *hatta* 'until' gives Ptg. *até*, *té* OSp. *fata*; under the influence of *FACIA Sp. *facia hacia* 'towards' it became the MSp. *hasta*, medieval *fasta*. There were also a handful of verbs, as *alifar* 'polish' *ahorrar* 'save'.

The Moorish organization was most striking for novelty and effectiveness in warfare. In place of the heavy-armed line of knights they employed light cavalry, who broke the line by pretending to retreat and then suddenly rallying against their pursuers—the method *al-karr w-al-farr*, retreat and rally. Hence the Moorish king in a ballad shouts *alcarria*, *moros*, *alcarria*. The Moorish rear (*zaga* Ar. *sâqa*) was as important as the Christian van (*delantero*); according to Fernão Lopes the Earl of Cambridge's expedition of 1381 introduced a new system of tactics, together with the new terms *avanguarda* and *retaguarda*. The Moorish campaign was a razzia (Sp. Ptg. *algara* Ar. *al-ġâra*); it was conducted amid uproar (Sp. Ptg. *algarada* OCat. *algarrada* Ar. *al-'arrāda*) at the moment of an attack, accentuated by drums and shrill trumpets (*atambores*, *añafiles* Ar. *al-nafîr*), preceded by a muster (*alarde* Ar. *al-'ard*), and led by *adalides* (Ar. *al-dalîl*). There were horsemen (*alférez* Ar. *al-fâris*) and skirmishers (Cat. *almogàver* Ar. *al-muġâwar*), and among their accoutrements one notes the scimitar (*alfanje* Ar. *al-χanjar*), targe (*adarga* Ar. *al-darqa*) and saddle-bag (*alforja* Ar. *al-χurj*). The organization of the Moorish fortresses was also important; the *alcázares* (Ar. *al-qaṣr*) and *alcazabas* (Ar. *al-qaṣaba*), commanded by their *alcaides* (Ar. *al-qâid*), and protected by their battlements (*almenas* and *adarves* Ar. *al-man' al-darb*). Against reprisals the Moors depended on their look-outs (*atalayas* Ar. *al-ṭalâ'iḥ* 'scouts' plural), and their detached castles (*Alcalá* in place-names, Ar. *al-qal'a*). A complicated quasi-monastic organiza-tion for war is revealed by such words as OSp. *arrobda*, *Arrábita*, *Almorávides* (Ar. *murâbiṭûna*), etc., which furnished models to the Christian orders of Calatrava, Alcántara, etc.

The head of the state for war and peace was the caliph, emir, or *Miramamolín* (Ar. *amîr al-mu'minîn* 'commander of the Faithful'), who relied on his vizier (*alguacil* Ar. *al-wazîr*). The city magistrate was the *alcalde* (Ar. *al-qâḍî* 'judge'), and there were those who superintended various depart-ments of activity, like the *zalmedina* (Ar. *ṣâḥib al-madîna* 'ruler of the city'), an official who continued in Aragonese ad-ministration, *zavazoke* (Ar. *ṣâḥib al-sûq* 'ruler of the market'), *almojarife* 'inspector, collector of the royal dues' (Ar. *al-mušrif*), *almotacén* 'inspector of weights and measures' (Ar. *al-muḥtasib*). The market-place (*zoco* in the Toledan *Zocodover* Ar. *sûq al-dawwâr* 'village market'), the customs-house (*aduana* Ar. *al-dîwân*, which gives also the modern *diván*), the arsenal (*dársena* Ar. *dâr ṣan'a al-baḥr* 'house of marine works'), the store-house (*almacén* 'shop' Ar. *al-maχzan*), were important aids to administration, which required a more elaborate classification of communities into cities (*Medina* in place-names), suburbs (*arrabal* Ar. *al-rabad*), villages (*aldea* Ar. *al-ḍai'a*, *aduar* Ar. *al-dawwâr*), districts (Ar. *balad* in *Vélez-Málaga*, *al-ḥauz* in *Alfoz de Lara*).

An accurate scale of weights and measures, and a money standard facilitated the heavy commerce of the southern cities. Dry measures were especially useful: *quintales*, *arrobas*, *almudes*, *cahices*, *fanegas*, *maquilas*. The carat (*quilate* Ar. *qîrâṭ*) measured gold and precious stones; the *adarme* and *azumbre*, liquids. The coinage of the Almorávides (*maravedí*) long served as the basis of northern coinage. The classification of city tradesmen showed that division of labour had gone far. There were the tailors (Ar. *al-χayyâṭ* OSp. Ptg. *alfaiate*), potters (*alfarero* Ar. *al-faxxâr*), pack-saddlers (*albardero* from *albarda* Ar. *al-barda'a* 'saddle'), farriers (*albeitar* Ar. *al-baiṭar*), barbers (OPtg. *alfageme* Ar. *al-ḥajjâm* 'cupper, barber'), carpenters (*albañil* Ar. *al-bannî*) and architects (*alarife* Ar. *al-'arîf*). The elegance and comfort of Moorish houses were striking. They were of sun-dried bricks (*adobe* Ar. *al-ṭûb*), often adorned with bluish ornamented tiles (*azulejos*, from *azul* 'blue' Ar. *lázuward* 'lapis lazuli'), with terraces for coolness (*azotea* Ar. *al-suṭaiḥa*), with convenient alcoves (*alcoba* Ar. *al-qubba*) and porticos (*zaguán* Ar. *saṭwân*), and made sanitary by culverts (*alcantarilla*). The minstrel class gave to Spanish a remarkable list of instruments, whether Arabic or Greek Arabicized, sufficient to constitute half the medieval orchestra: the lute, rebec, canon, dulcimer, drum, kettledrum, trumpet, etc.

The state rested on agriculture, and the agriculture on the water-supply. Water was conserved and used with a skill that has since fallen into decay; the Valencian Huerta is an indication of the once blooming condition of all Al-Andalus. There were names for various kinds of supply: the *albufera* or *albuera* 'lagoon' (Ar. *al-buḥair*), the *alberca* (Ar. *al-birka*) 'pool', the *aljibe aljube* 'well' (Ar. *al-jubb*). Water was gathered by weirs with sluices (*azuda* Ar. *al-sudd*) and raised to higher levels with water-wheels (*noria* Ar. *nâ'ûra*). Rice (*arroz* Ar. *al-ruzz*) and oil (*aceite* Ar. *al-zait*), together with the olive (*aceituna* Ar. *al-zaitûn*), were staple crops of the south, as were also the orange (*naranja* Ar. *nâranj*), the apricot (*albaricoque* Ar. *al-barqûq*) and the peach (*albérchigo*). One notes also salt-wort (*acelga* Ar. *al-silq*), the carob bean (*algarroba* Ar. *al-xarruba*) and the lupin (*atramuz* Ar. *al-tarmus*). The names of these much-wandered plants are not always pure Arabic. *Albaricoque* and *albérchigo* are from the Latin; *atramuz* and *acelga* from the Greek; *albérchigo* PERSICU means the 'Persian fruit', and Persian is the origin of *naranja* and *algarroba*. Spanish Arabic was more important as a carrier than as an originator of refinement.

This position as mediator is evident in the important scientific contributions made by Arabic to Europe. In the sphere of mathematics, arithmetic was long known as *algorismo* from the great mathematician *Al-Khwarismî*; and together with 'Arabian' numerals (really an ancient Indian alphabet), came the cypher (*cifra* Ar. *şifr*) which made rapid calculation possible. Similarly, *algebra* was theirs (*al-jabr*), together with its basic symbol *x* (Ar. *šai*, Sp. *xei* = 'thing'). In the mixed science and pseudoscience of astronomy and astrology, there are numerous Arabic terms (like *zenith, nadir, theodolite*) which are international in range. Many of the more brilliant stars are, for the same reason, called by Arabic names, while the most prominent remain Latin together with the constellations. Beside Sirius, Capella, Arcturus, etc., we have in all European languages *Aldebaran, Algol, Betelgeuse, Alkor, Atair, Rigel, Deneb, Akrab*, etc.

The Spanish map has been, to a considerable extent, re-named in Arabic. Ar. *Wâdî* 'river' appears in *Guadalquivir* 'the big river' (Ar. *kabîr*), *Guadiana* 'the Anas river', *Guadalete* 'the river Lethe', *Guadalajara* 'the river of the stony place' (*al-ḥajjâra*), *Guadalaviar* 'the white river' (*al-abyad*), *Guadarrama* 'the river of sand' (*al-ramla*), etc. ACCI gave *Iš*, and then *Wâdî-Iš Guadix*. The name of Guadalajara city was, for Arabic geographers, *Medînat al-dâḥiya* 'the frontier town'. This word Ar. *medîna* 'town' is also frequent: *Medinaceli* (*Sâlim* 'of Selim'), *Medina Sidonia, Medina del Campo*. Other names have a military significance, as *Alcalá* (Ar. *qalʿa* 'castle, fort'); Ar. *ʿisn* 'castle' (rare) in *Iznalloz*. *Gibraltar* and *Gibralfaro* have *jabal* 'hill' ('Ṭâriq's hill', 'lighthouse hill'). The *Albufera* of Valencia is based on *al-buḥair* 'the lagoon', and *Algeciras* on *al-jazîrat al-χaḍrâ* 'the green island', substituted for the ancient name *Carteya*. The famous Roman bridge over the Tagus gives rise to *Alcántara* 'the bridge', *Valencia de Alcántara*; and the word is connected with other bridges and aqueducts. These names are especially frequent in the region of Granada, with its *Alhambra* (*al-ḥamrâ* 'the red', fem.) *Generalife* (*janna(t) al-ʿarîf* 'the architect's garden'), etc. The Granadine *Vivarrambla* means 'gate of the sandy way' (*Bâb al-ramla*), and Barcelona's *Ramblas* have the same word. The Toledan *Puerta de Visagra* is twice named, since *vi-* means *puerta*. Ar. *Bāb* 'gate' was pronounced with imāla [bīb].

This Arabic influence reached its apogee in the tenth century, when the Mozarabic element of the Leonese population was carrying the weight of that kingdom's culture. Documents of that era contain the words that modern dictionaries record, together with others (like *zavazoke* or *alhajara*) that had disappeared before the first Castilian masterpieces were recorded, or vanished in the course of the sixteenth century. The rise of Castilian to primacy over Leonese was a deadly blow to the Arabic innovations. The Spanish language turned its back on Arabic, and sought inspiration in French and Latin. The Arabic vocabulary has continued to decline, and belongs largely to the less used part of the lexicon. The names of things suffer with the change of fashion. The French tailor (Sp. *sastre*) triumphs over the Moor (Ptg. *alfaiate*); the vizier sinks into the policeman (*alguacil*), or rather 'Bow Street runner', since the modern police forces use Latin terms; the *alférez* 'horseman', who acted as Constable to Sancho II in the eleventh century, in the sixteenth had no horse but only carried the company standard for his *capitán*, and he has since given way to the *teniente*. In view of this it is surprising how much that is primary and permanent bears an Arabic name: *alcalde alcaide arroz laúd cifra cénit x* etc. It is, however, a long cry from the tenth century, when *Cite* 'my lord' (*Cid Ruy Díaz* is the last of these) gave the patronymic *Citez*, and there was even a *Mafumetez*; while Christians called themselves *Zeit diaconus, Abdalla presbyter.*

ASTURO-LEONESE

The Mozarabic dialect, cut off from literature and devoid of administrative prestige, continued in a state of arrested development, and the hegemony in Spanish lay, during the earlier centuries of the Reconquest, with Galicia and León.

The former province, which seemed the more important to the Moslem enemy, gave birth to the Galician, and ultimately the Portuguese, language—a language rich in vowels subtly nuanced, and adapted to the needs of a wistful lyric muse. In the latter was developed the Asturo-Leonese dialect—or rather dialects, since they never attained unity but were only accommodated by a series of official compromises A middle way of speech was sought which would give expression to the reunion of Spanish Christendom in a state recalling the glory of the Gothic kings; but this *koiné* could not be standardized in the absence of a vernacular chancery and literature. Latin was the language of the few men of learning—mostly Mozarabs—who compiled chronicles in León, and a popularized Latin was the language of the law.

Though the Christian revolt broke out first in the region of Gijón under Pelayo, it gathered strength in the western Cantabrian mountains. From thence, about the year 750, Alfonso I made a desert of Portugal and León as far as the Duero, and so gained a respite for the refugee colonies of Goths and Swabians in Galicia and the Asturias. The capital was established at Cangas de Onís; then at Oviedo. At Oviedo Alfonso II felt the influence of Charlemagne's prestige and victories, and possibly married a French princess and became some sort of client-king to the Emperor. These relationships have been so traversed by epic legend in later centuries that it is difficult to make positive assertions. The king's epic reputation for pusillanimity, at least, cannot be deserved, for it was Alfonso II who first seems to have dreamt of the 'empire' of the Spains. He was a *magnus rex*, that is to say, he was king of León as others were sovereigns elsewhere in the Peninsula, but he alone was hegemon and the successor of those who had ruled all Spain from Toledo. This idea grew under his successors. Alfonso III 'the Great' was again a *magnus rex*, but took upon himself the more high-sounding by-name of *imperator*, and by affecting to discover at Vizeu the tomb of the last of the Goths, he made unequivocal his claim to the hegemony of all Spain. An 'empire' of the Spains was thus vaguely adumbrated, and was associated with coronation at León until the elaborate ceremony performed for Alfonso VII in 1135. By that time, however, the seat of power had been transferred to Castile, and the Leonese pretence was gradually forgotten. This 'empire' was not incompatible with local independence. It represented a claim to speak on behalf of Spain as a whole, and is reflected in later literature by the circumstance that medieval Portuguese and Catalan chronicles restrict their scope to local affairs, leaving to Castilian the task of compiling general chronicles.

Oviedo was embellished with a metropolitan church, handsomely appointed; but it was too far north for the convenience of government when the tide of conquest and colonization swept back over León. The desert created by Alfonso I could only be held if it were effectively occupied, and the problem of the Leonese kings was to hold as much territory as they had numbers to settle. Hence there are waves of colonization across León, with intervals for recuperation. The first notable advance was achieved by Ordoño I (850–66), who occupied the northern third of this area: Tuy near the Minho, Astorga, León city, and Amaya in northern Castile. The last three fortresses controlled the great road which threads the north of the Peninsula from Roncesvalles to Santiago, south of the Cantabrian range. Settlers from all parts were summoned to occupy this area, and their colonies may be identified in village-names: *Toldaos* (Toledan Mozarabs in Galicia), *Toldanos* (by León), *Villagallegos*, *Castellanos*, *Báscones* (by Oviedo and near Amaya) and *Vascois* (on the Sil in Galicia). The occupation of northern Portugal and central León was carried out by Ordoño's successor Alfonso III (866–914), despite several grave Moorish invasions. His fortresses were Lamego, Vizeu, and even Coimbra in Portugal, Toro and Zamora to guard the line of the Duero (which he walled round with the aid of Mozarabs), Dueñas, Simancas, and Burgos (884). The last-named colony had important consequences for Spain. Immediately it allowed a rectification of the great transverse road, which was less comfortable for use running so far north as Amaya. More distantly, it assured the hegemony of Castilian. Instead of occupying the ancient Cantabria or Bardulia, a mountainous strip on both sides of the Cantabrians, backed against the Basque border, Castilian descended to the Meseta, and the tributaries of the upper Duero. Burgos became a new centre of diffusion, and acquired significance by the decisive character of its citizens and the prestige of the great Castilian epics. But in the ninth and tenth centuries, Burgos was no more than an appanage of León.

The village-names that mark displacements of population in this second movement of expansion include the usual general denominations (*Gallegos, Castellanos, Asturianos*), but also more detailed information. There were *Navianos* from Navia on the Asturo-Galician border, and *Bercianos* from the Bierzo region north-west of Astorga. At San Ciprián de Sanabria there is a linguistic islet in which unaccented final -*a* remains, but when followed by a consonant becomes -*e*-: *tú cantes, nosotros cantábemos, cases*. This change occurs regularly in Catalan, but in Spanish is restricted to the Asturian of Oviedo, and is therefore held to be proof of Oviedan colonization in San Ciprián. Mozarabic settlers brought with them their wealth, their culture, their Arabic names, and a copious vocabulary of loan-words, profoundly modifying Leonese Spanish.

Under Ordoño II the capital city became León, where he was the first of the kings to be buried (923); and it was he who first took measures to reduce the power of Castile, by seizing four Castilian counts at an interview on the Carrión and killing them at León. His son Ramiro II (931–50) carried Leonese colonies over the Duero, and occupied the Tormes basin. Ledesma, Salamanca, Los Baños and Peña Ausende were his principal fortresses in this region. The racial mixture is indicated by village-names: *Gallegos, Galleguillos, Mozarbitos, Mozárvez, Huerta de Mozarbitos, Castellanos*; and again there is a linguistic islet of Oviedans at El Payo (to the south of Ciudad Rodrigo). The component elements of the Salamancan populace remained nominally distinct as the *linajes de Salamanca*: *castellanos, mozáraves, portogaleses, toreses.* In its cathedral the Mozarabic rite continues in use.

Ramiro's aggrandisement was effected despite the overwhelming military superiority of the Caliph 'Abd al-Raḥmân III, but his kingdom was ruined by the razzias of Al-Manṣûr. Los Baños fell to the invaders in 977; León city was twice sacked (981 and 988), and in 988 the two great religious centres of León, Eslonza and Sahagún, were laid waste. The acme of disaster was reached in the destruction of the shrine of Compostela in 997, when the bells were transported to Córdoba on the backs of Christian slaves. With the great general's death, the Leonese set about repairing their misfortunes, and the city received a fresh charter in 1020. But the wounds were too deep; and the counts of Castile had profited by their relative immunity both to declare their independence, and to become serious rivals to the *magni reges*. For a period Castile was attached to Navarre, but it recovered its identity under Fernando I, now with the rank of a kingdom; and this astute monarch acquired the kingdom of León also in 1037. When he came to divide his property on his death-bed, he gave Castile to his elder son, León to his second. Rebelling against this division, Sancho II inflicted two heavy defeats on the Leonese, at Llantada and Golpejera, which left no doubt where the superiority of force lay; and though the Leonese recovered their theoretical prestige under Alfonso VI, who was their king before succeeding to his brother, yet Toledo, when it was captured, fell to the lot of Castile (1085). Alfonso VII took his title of 'emperor' in León city in 1135; but thereafter even this mark of deference to León was discontinued. The kingdoms were divided under Alfonsos VIII and IX, and the Leonese extended in a narrow wedge towards Extremadura. But the Castilians were the leading spirits in the great campaign of Las Navas de Tolosa in 1212; and in the final union of the crowns under Fernando

III and Alfonso X, the royal chancery resolutely patronized the Castilian form of Spanish.

The linguistic state of León reflects its politics. It is a language of compromise with all its neighbours: with Galicians, Castilians, and Mozarabs. The Galician influence is most marked in the west, where the diocese of Astorga serves as the basis of a western Leonese dialect. It is also predominant in the early years of the monarchy. Castilian influences strongly the counties of Liébana, Carrión and Saldaña, which constitute the eastern Leonese dialectal area, together with the great monastery of Sahagún. Through eastern Leonese Castilian forms press into central León during the eleventh and twelfth centuries; and they now occupy that whole area. Mozarabic co-operation in many important settlements brought the use of Arabic terminology to a maximum in Leonese. In the north, sheltered behind the Cantabrian mountains and more and more cut off from the imperial plans of León, the Asturian dialects continued their uninterrupted development from the common Latin base, and to this day constitute the most differentiated region of Spanish-speakers.

Leonese is marked off from Castilian by its hesitancy in dealing with the quality of the diphthongs arising from accented ĕ ŏ and the monophthong from AI AU, by its general conformity with Romance practice and with that of other Spanish dialects, and by its development (in common with Galician-Portuguese) of unvoiced consonants in weak position and of initial PL- CL- FL-. The accented ĕ ŏ are liable to retention in place-names and words of culture, the latter persisting as late as the thirteenth century: e.g. *in illo mallollo* (León 1061), Cast. *majuelo* 'new vine'. When the diphthong at last prevails, it is not impeded, as in Castilian, by a following palatal: as FŎVEU which gives *Fueyo, Los Fueyos* in the Asturias, but *Hoyo Hoyos* in Castile; HŎDIE *uuoy* Cast. *hoy* 'to-day', also *uuey*; ARRŎGIU *arruoyo* Cast. *arroyo* 'stream'. The diphthong arises by the lengthening of the vowel (*ee oo*) and by the differentiation of the parts, whereby the first element

10

becomes more closed than the second ($e̦e̦$ $o̦o̦ > ie\ uo$). The accentuation of this diphthong in western Leonese is a matter on which expert observers differ. Some hold that it may rest on the whole diphthong and on either of its parts, and especially that *ie úo* are heard as well as *ié uó*; while others maintain that the first element is always of the nature of a semi-vowel, incapable of bearing the accent. The diphthong *ie*, pronouncing the latter element yet more open, results in *ia*; *uo*, by a like dissimilation, gives *ua*, and also *ue* (with *u̯ə* as the presumptive middle stage). All these diphthongs are found in Leonese: HŎDIE *uuoy uuey* 'to-day', HŎRTOS *vortos* Cast. *huertos* 'gardens', MŎRTE *muarte* Cast. *muerte* 'death', NŎSTRU *nuastro* Cast. *nuestro* 'our', ĔST *ye ya* 'is', CASTĔLLA, *Castella Castiella Castilla*, PĔDE *pia* 'foot'. As late as the thirteenth-century *Fuero Juzgo* we have *voaltas oabras encuantra*, and the diphthong survives at Cangas de Tineo and other points in the Asturias: SŎMNU *suaño* 'dream'. Ampudia FŎNTE-PUTIDA implies *fuan(te)*. Early Castilian practice is not consistent in this respect, but it reached the final stages *ie ue* more rapidly than León.

The Latin diphthongs AI AU linger on in Leonese, which has characteristically advanced only as far as the stage *ei ou*: *karreira obtorgare* Cast. *carrera otorgar* 'road' 'authorize'. The simplification of these diphthongs is due to an impulse from the Tarraconese region, which was adopted from Aragonese by Castilian, but failed to affect León and Galicia-Portugal. In the same fashion Leonese agrees with Portuguese to retain -MB- (PALOMBA Ptg. *pomba* Leon. *palonba* Cast. *paloma* 'dove') against the impulse towards -*m*- that came from the east. These cases also show agreement between Leonese and the still more conservative Mozarabic. Leonese retains, like all Romance languages save Castilian and Gascon, Latin F-, develops -LI- and -CL- to -*ll*-, preserves initial J- Ǵ- before front vowels (as *y*-), and makes -*it*- of -CT-. In the last case there is a good opportunity to watch the intrusion of Castilian forms into Leonese territory: PACTARE Leon. etc. *peitar* Cast. *pechar* 'pay'. Forms in -*ch*- make an early conquest of eastern

Leonese, and we find *pechar* in central León at Eslonza in
1173, *Fontecha* in León city in 1136. By the next century the
forms in *-it-* had become a mark of western Leonese. Like
Aragonese, Leonese occasionally uses accented forms of ĔS
ĔST *yes ye*; and it experienced the palatalization of initial L-
which occurs sporadically in the Peninsula as a whole, but
not in Galician-Portuguese or Castilian.

In two respects Leonese innovates. Like Portuguese it has
a strong tendency to turn intervocalic -P- -T- -K- into -*b*-
-*d*- -*g*-, and the preference was lively enough to intrude into
the popularized Latin of notarial documents, where we find
CINGITUR, for instance, written CINGIDUR. The other innovation has to do with initial PL- CL- FL-, and will be dealt with
more fully when we come to discuss the formation of Galician-
Portuguese. The stage reached by medieval Leonese was [š]:
CLAUSA *xosa* 'enclosed ground for fruit trees', FLAVINU *Xainiz*.
In modern western Leonese the representative of these initial
groups is [ŝ], dental affricate, as in CLAVE *tsabe* 'key'. It
corresponds with the central Asturian (and Spanish) *llave*,
and a similar equation has occurred between central Asturian
lluna and west Asturian *tsuna*, though the source is here L-
in LUNA Sp. *luna* 'moon'.

NAVARRO-ARAGONESE DIALECTS

Navarro-Aragonese forms of Spanish were spoken in a band
which reached from the Upper Ebro to the frontiers of
Catalonia, embracing the districts of La Rioja, Navarre,
Aragón proper, Sobrarbe and Ribagorza. This region knew
no political unity until its final absorption in the Spanish
monarchy, and each part was associated politically with
people of alien speech: Navarre with the Basque provinces,
Aragón with the Catalan-speaking area. Until the sixteenth
century, however, Navarro-Aragonese was not subjected
directly to the hegemony of Castilian, and was supported by
the two chanceries of Pamplona and Zaragoza. In the early
Middle Ages its Riojan form was in use in the important

monasteries of San Millán de la Cogolla in La Rioja, and Santo Domingo de Silos in Castile. Thanks to the cultural significance of these two centres, Riojano is of great importance to the student of early Spanish and of Castilian origins.

Like Leonese, Navarro-Aragonese is a survival of the consensus of Spanish dialects which was the Visigothic platform, and which was represented quite closely in Mozarabic; it had certain north-eastern peculiarities, but generally agreed with the other dialects in their opposition to Castilian peculiarities. We may summarize them briefly. Initial F-: FILIU *fillo* Cast. *hijo*. Initial J- Ǵ- retained: *mea iermana* MEA GERMANA Cast. *mi (h)ermana*, JACTAT *geitat* Cast. *echa*. Initial L-palatalized: this occurs regularly in Aragonese, at the beginning of words and also at the beginning of syllables, e.g. *Uilla Carlli*. In modern Ribagorzano the L- palatalizes even in groups: *pllaza, dobllar*. Initial palatalization is also a feature of Catalan, so that this tendency was more declared in the north-east than in the west or south. Medial -CT- changed to -*it*-: JACTAT *geitat*, FACTU *feito* Cast. *echa, hecho*. The same change is suffered by -LT- in MULTU Arag. Leon. Ptg. *muito* Cast. *mucho* 'many'. The Castilian *ch*, however, invades Aragonese documents early, and the form *mucho* is normal in the fifteenth century. As well as *feito* Aragonese knew *feto* in the tenth century as to-day. Medial -CL- -LI- gave -*ll*- (often spelled *yl* or *yll*): FILIU *fillo* Cast. *hijo* 'son', SPĔCULU *spillu* (*Glosas Em.*) Cast. *espejo*, COLLECTURA *collitura* (*Glosas Sil.*), CONCĬLIU *conceillo* Cast. *concejo*.

Among the characteristics distinguishing Navarro-Aragonese from Leonese is the conservation of initial PL- CL- FL-, in agreement with Catalan and with Mozarabic. Aragonese and Catalan also retain -P- -T- -K- in weak position, and particularly between vowels, much more freely than do the north-western dialects. CAPUT *capot* (1081) Sp. *cabo*, *CAPĬTTIA *capeças* OSp. Ptg. *cabeças* 'heads'; TOTA VOLUNTATE *tuto bolumtate* (1062); LORICA *lorika* (1090). Such words, preserved in legal documents, may be unduly influenced by Latin tradition;

but there still exists an area lying to the north of Huesca, in Sobrarbe and across the frontier in Béarn and Bigorre, where the intervocalic unvoiced consonant persists: AQUILA *álica* Sp. *águila* 'eagle', *capeza* 'head', *marito* Sp. *marido* 'husband', *Nocito* elsewhere *Nocedo*, etc. This conservative tendency is also noted in Mozarabic.

Catalan and Navarro-Aragonese innovate by reducing -MB- to -*m*-, -ND- to -*n*-, and by simplifying the diphthongs AI AU to *e o*. The latter is a modification which has extended into Castilian also, there being early vacillation in the documents of Oña; and through Castilian it has come to be the norm in Spanish. TERTIARIU *terzero* (*Glosas Em.*), *trastorné* (*Glosas Em.*), *semdero matera* (1044); AUCTORICARE *otorekare* 'authorize' (1061). Castilian and Aragonese had completed the evolution AU *o* by the eleventh century. The vowels Ĕ ŏ, accented, give diphthongs under all conditions in Aragonese as in Leonese, and the quality of the diphthong is not determined: *ie ia, uo ua ue*. The simplification of the consonant-groups indicated is, however, a notable feature of north-eastern Spain, and has been associated with the theory of an Oscan settlement in the vicinity of Huesca, though improbably, as has already been remarked. At Ribagorza in 913 we have: '*concamiamus* nostram terram. . .in locum ubi dicitur *Intramas* Aquas' (cf. *cambiar, ambas*). This change does not appear to have taken place in La Rioja, where *mb* characterizes the language of Gonzalo de Berceo and the documents of the region; but it presses into Castile, where *concamiationem* is reported as early as 972. The assimilation of the group -ND- is more restricted. Both *nd* and *n* are found in medieval Aragonese documents: *quando quano, Galindo Galino*, SPŎNDA *espuenda* 'field by a river' Cat. *espona, illa spuenna, super illa sponna, spuanna* (S. Juan de Peña docs. 1062-85). A limited number of examples are found in Castilian and in eastern Leonese.

Navarro-Aragonese used accented as well as unaccented forms of ĔS ĔST, as did Leonese; and *ye* ET may even indicate some kind of syntactical accentuation of the conjunction.

The third person plural of the preterite borrowed *o* from the singular: Cast. *compró compraron*, Arag. *comparoron* (1062). This development is widespread in modern Leonese and Aragonese patois, but is not strongly attested by early documents. The presence of the dative pronouns *li lis*, and of the possessives *lur lures* 'their', is noteworthy in Aragonese; and in Berceo helps to confirm other pronominal nominatives in *-i*, such as *elli* Cast. *él*. There is considerable vacillation as to forms of the article in Aragonese and in Leonese: *el* concurrently with *lo, ela elos*, assimilation with *con* and *en* (*enna conna*, etc.), and in Sobrarbe *ero era*. As well as ILLE, IPSE was used sporadically in all the Spanish area as an alternative article: *super ipsa via, de ipso porto*. Thus used, however, IPSE always retains its Latin form, and is not a Romance word. An odd feature of Navarro-Aragonese is the tendency to double honorifics, especially before names of women or of clerics: *dueño dueño Cristo*.

The kingdom of Aragón rose, somewhat casually, out of a donation by Sancho the Great of Navarre. He gave the valley of the Aragón river to his bastard son Ramiro. Ramiro, however, contrived to retain his independence against Castile, and his successors gave body to the kingdom by incorporating the powerful Moslem state of Zaragoza. They were able to contribute the title and prestige of a kingdom to the counts of Barcelona in the union of Aragón with Catalonia, though the latter was the predominant partner in Catalan policy. The chancery of Zaragoza and the Aragonese Cortes and customs remained quite different from those of the other three-quarters of that state; and the language survived in official and general use until its final merger with Castilian. To the east of Aragón proper lay the two hilly counties of Sobrarbe and Ribagorza. The latter, divided into two parts by the Noguera Ribagorzana, is a land of transition from Spanish to Catalan. The westernmost limit of Catalan features is on the Cinca and Ésera, the middle line of demarcation is the Noguera Ribagorzana, and the transition is completed in the east by the time we reach the Noguera Pallaresa and the Catalan-speaking county of Pallars. This linguistic hesitation corresponds to an early political dubiety in this region, which only attached itself to the fortunes of its western neighbours in the tenth century.

At the other extreme of Navarro-Aragonese territory lay the districts of Upper and Lower La Rioja. The Upper province lies in the hills, and was closely associated with Old Castile. The Lower lay along the Ebro in the vicinity of Nájera and Logroño, and was a land of debate between Castile and Navarre. In its early history it corresponds rather to Navarre. The frontier against Castile lay on the Montes de Oca in the tenth century, which became famous in the heroic epics when the poets referred to the narrowness of the original Castile. During the eleventh and twelfth centuries the possession of this region was debated, but it was definitively incorporated with Castile in 1176, after which it suffered a rapid castilianization. What gives interest to this transitional region is the importance of its religious foundations. Albelda and Santa María de Nájera served to inspire Latin chronicles; San Millán de la Cogolla and its offshoot in Castile, Santo Domingo de Silos, provide our first vernacular documents, the *Glosas Emilianenses* in the tenth century, and the *Glosas Silenses* of the eleventh. Silos is, in fact, situated in Castile; but its traditions were Riojano, at the same time as it served to attract Castilians to visit or revere the parent monastery. San Millán was the home also of Gonzalo de Berceo, the oldest important Spanish poet to publish under his own name, whose language still bears traces of his dialect: *elli* Sp. *él*, *li* Sp. *le*, *soltóllilas* Sp. *soltóselas*. That the language of the Glosses is not Castilian may be seen from such forms as *spillu muito feito geitat aflarat aplecat ies iet uemne faca ayutorio lueco collitura adduitos* Cast. *espejo mucho hecho echa hallara allega es hombre haga ayuda luego cogedura ducho*.

THE RISE OF CASTILIAN

It was, then, amid such competitors that Castilian rose to supremacy and transformed itself into standard Spanish. Its basis is the ancient Cantabria, a district lying across the mountains near Santander, close to the Basque border. The Santander region (Asturias de Santillana, de Trasmiera), Campóo, and the northernmost part of the province of Burgos constituted ancient Castile, Bardulia or Castilla Vieja. Its long and troubled history gave a certain unity to this area. Under the Roman Republic Cantabria had been, with Asturica and the Basque country, unsubdued and sundered from the rest of Spain. It fell only to the legions of Augustus in 19 B.C. Gallæcia et Asturica and the Cantabrian region were associated with the east of the Peninsula in the Hither Spain, and so kept apart from Lusitania and Bætica, which formed the Further Spain; but under Diocletian's reorganization Cantabria was part of the conventus of Clunia, and so separated from the future Leonese and Navarro-Aragonese regions. When the Visigoths succeeded the Romans in Spain, Cantabria formed, with the Basque country, an unsubdued region, and it was there that Roderick waged his last campaign. It was not part of the Swabian kingdom of Galicia and the western Asturias. The arrival of the Moslems perpetuated the Visigothic state of affairs. Cantabria remained independent under its 'duke' Pelayo, and inflicted the first defeat on the Spanish Moors at Covadonga. The subsequent history of the Reconquest, however, based as it was on Galicia and León, tended to attach Castilla Vieja to its western neighbours. It was a Leonese king, Ordoño I, who brought these mountaineers down to the edge of the plateau by occupying the stronghold of Amaya in 860, and another, Alfonso III, who gave them Burgos in 884. Burgos on the Arlanzón occupies the centre of a river-system to the north of the Duero, and it became in time an important centre for the propagation of castilianisms over the high *meseta* east of the Pisuerga, the frontier of León. The next advance was south-eastward into the Alfoz de Lara, about

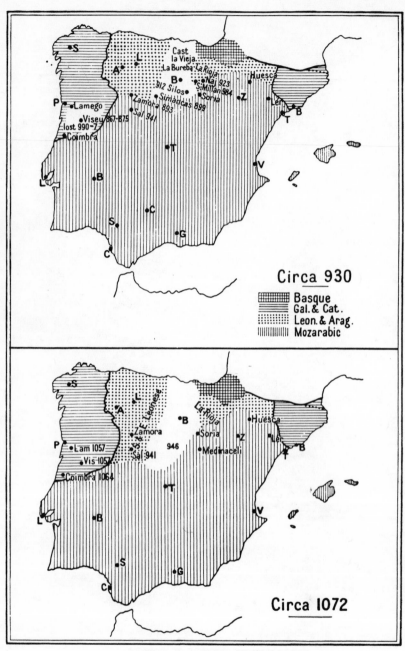

The rise of Castilian

the year 912, when the Duero became the frontier, from
Simancas to Osma. In 914 the river was crossed, and
Castilian expansion changed to a south-westerly direction.
Sepúlveda fell in 946, and this frontier became the Cea. In
the next century this frontier was crossed, and Segovia and
Ávila fell before Castilian arms. In the latter town Castile
had acquired a fragment of the ancient Lusitania. The region
had constituted an unsettled frontier (Extremadura del Duero)
for a long time, but was effectively colonized in 1088.

These successive extensions of territory are associated with
the prestige of certain monasteries. Castilla Vieja had Oña
for its cultural centre, and the documents of this monastery
are our authorities for Oldest (or Cantabrian) Castilian.
When Burgos was recovered, two new monasteries became
prominent, San Pedro de Cardeña and San Pedro de Arlanza.
They are associated with Castilian heroes and the national
gestes; the former with the Cid, the latter with Count Fernán
González and the independence of Castile. In the Alfoz de
Lara the great monastic centre was Santo Domingo de Silos,
which, however, we have seen did not pertain linguistically
to its vicinity. It was in the Alfoz de Lara that the most tragic,
and perhaps the oldest, of the epics was played out. The
linguistic supremacy of Burgos, however, was not affected by
this addition of territory, nor by the settlement of the Extremadura del Duero; and it is from Burgos that the characteristically Castilian waves of change radiated over the rest
of Spain, until Toledo was subdued by these innovations and
became the standard of correct Spanish in the eyes of
Spaniards of the Golden Age. The Castilian ascendancy
continued to increase linguistically after it had been fully
established in politics; and as this augmentation of area
occurred when the language was under the control of a
developing Spanish literature, its consideration falls within
the next chapter. For the present we are concerned only to
note the features of Castilian in its pre-literary era.

The first centre of radiation was, as we have remarked,
Castilla Vieja, and its documentation is chiefly that of the
monastery of Oña. Here we find, with certain vacilla-

tions, that Castilian had already the resolute and innovating character which it wears among Spanish dialects. The diphthong to be derived from accented Ĕ ŏ was settled in Cantabria as *ie ue*, without the alternatives existing in León and Aragón. This diphthong is not found with a palatal, apart from a single instance which may be the work of a Riojan notary (*cuejan*). The reduction of the suffix *-iello* to *-illo* (OSp. *Castiella* MSp. *Castilla*) begins to appear in this region as early as the tenth century. The diphthongs AI AU, on the other hand, still vacillate in Cantabrian Castilian, down to the twelfth century: *Tinteiro* (1017), *Emdeira* (1090), *Ferreira* (1173), but also *hera* (975). The simplification of these vowels is characteristic of Aragonese, and is carried through systematically by the *Glosas Silenses*. When Castilian begins to radiate from Burgos instead of Oña -ARIU gives only *-ero*: *karrera semdero Armentero eras fossatera*. Such forms appear normal in the tenth century. An archaic state of final unaccented vowels in Oldest Castile preserves traces of -U in the documents of Oña, and so of a declension -U -OS -*u* -*os*. This is not a peculiar sign of the Cantabrian dialect, but is seen also in the *Glosas Silenses* which belong to the Riojan patois, and is present in southern Italian and Rumanian. The *Glosas* give us *nafregatu, mintiru*, etc., but *nafregatos, elos cuerpos, aflitos, sapiendo* (from -o), though also *omiciero* HOMICIDIUM. In Cantabrian documents the -*u* continues to appear down to the thirteenth century, but without consistency: *don Peydro Martínez el Orejudu, Domingo Moçu, de lu lombo*.

The Cantabrian dialect permits the assimilation of the article with the prepositions *en* and *con*, and it shows tendencies to fix the orthography on lines somewhat different from those subsequently adopted. The letter *g* had the values [j] and [ĵ], but Cantabrian scribes tend to discriminate *g* [j] from *gg* [ĵ], fricative from affricate mediopalatal. They possessed no better means of expressing the voiceless mediopalatal affricate [ĉ] than by using the voiced sign *gg*: hence *Naggara* (*Nájera*), *bieggo* (*viejo*), *figgos* (*hijos*), and *Sanggez* (*Sánchez*), *contradiggo* (*contradicho*). The dialect used freely

two old suffixes -ĕccu and -ŏccu: *kannariekas, illa Monneka,
pedruecos, pennueco*. The former extension of these suffixes is
shown in place-names: Muñeca and variants in Palencia,
Soria, León and Oviedo; *Palomeque, Manzaneque* in Mozarabic
territory.

It was in this Cantabrian region, moreover, that the loss
of initial f- was endemic. It appears in place-names as an
aspirate *h* or silent, and was doubtless due to the specially
close association of Cantabrians and Basques. The other differentiæ from the general practice of Spanish dialects also
appeared: -cl- -li- developing to *j* (spelled *gg*), -ct- to *ch*
(spelled *gg*), loss of initial j- ǵ-, etc.

The language of Burgos was marked by the resolute completion of the few matters on which Cantabria continued to
hesitate. This was partly due to Aragonese proximity through
the neighbouring Riojano. So the diphthongs *ie ue* have
fixed their quality, and -ariu gives *-ero* alone. Medial -mb-
tends, under Aragonese influence, to *-m-*: *lomo* lombu (Leon.
lombo Cantabrian *de lu lombo*), *amos* (later *ambos* is a Latinism)
ambo 'both', *paloma* palumba 'dove', etc. The letters *j* and *g*
appear for [ĵ], as in later Spanish.

It is not possible to discover the peculiar features of south-
eastern or south-western Castilian. In the one case, the loss
of the *Leyenda de los Infantes de Lara* deprives us of our most
promising lay text, and the clergy were under the Riojan
influence of Silos. Beyond that frontier to the south, the
Poema del Cid shows a Mozarab of Medinaceli composing
in the language of Burgos, but a little uncertain as to the
right use of *ll* and *j*. The prestige of Burgos was firmly
established by the great cycles of gestes before the definitive
colonization of the south-west, where, in Ávila at least, we
should theoretically expect to have met some of the conservative marks of Lusitanian Spanish.

The change of the direction of advance in 912–14 continued in later centuries, and at length, passing through
Toledo, cut off Leonese from the south. A vast fan-wise
extension of Castilian took place at the expense of León; but

Castilian also pressed due west against its neighbour. The eastern counties of Liébana, Saldaña and Carrión, which lined the Pisuerga, had long acted with Castilian counts against the authority of their suzerains of León, and they show an early castilianization. A few years later the linguistic battle was transferred to central León. Each Castilian feature had its own original focus and its own rate of expansion, until they were all arrested by the resistance of western Leonese, supported by Galician-Portuguese. The earliest and most active were the simplification of AI AU to *e o*, and the development of -CT- through -*it*- to -*ch*- in such words as *pechar*, *lecho*, which are embedded in central Leonese by the middle of the twelfth century. The group M'N gave in Castilian -*mn*- > -*mr*- > -*mbr*-: LUMINOSU *lumbroso*, NOMINATU *nombrado*, -UMINE *firmedumbre* (the word HOMINE *hombre* ' man' does not serve as its medieval Castilian spellings are guilty of archaism in -*mn*- or -*m̃*-). Of this change east Leonese shows 86 p.c. of examples in the thirteenth century, and central Leonese only 16 p.c. The figures prove that this feature had invaded eastern León in the eleventh or twelfth century, and had become the norm at Sahagún in the thirteenth, while at the same time commencing its invasion of central León. In -ARIU- > -*ero*, in which Castilian propagates a north-eastern dialectalism, its use in León rises from 50 p.c. in the tenth century (against -*air*- and -*eir*-) to 65 p.c. in the second half of the same; in the first half of the eleventh century the figure is 85 p.c. and -*air*- has been eliminated; in the second half, 86 p.c.; and in the early twelfth century 88 p.c. In this case the whole profit of eliminating the alternative -*air*- went to -*er*-, which was supported by Castilian prestige.

For knowledge of the period covered by this chapter scholars are wholly indebted to the researches of Sr Menéndez Pidal, published in his masterly *Orígenes del español*. Texts illustrative of the dialects will be found in the brief anthology which constitutes the opening section of that work.

CHAPTER VI

STANDARD SPANISH

The year 1140, which probably witnessed the composition of the *Poema del Cid*, one of the oldest extant literary documents of Spain, is taken as apposite to mark an epoch in the history of the language. Up to that date Castilian had continued to rise from small beginnings as an unconsidered dialect spoken hard against the Basque border to a position of political and cultural hegemony over the centre and west of the Peninsula. In the century following 1140, however, Castilian continues, indeed, to meet the rivalry of Leonese and Aragonese among the Spanish dialects, and of Portuguese and Catalan in a wider area; but the contest is profoundly modified by a new impetus toward administrative and literary standardization. Replacing Latin in the chancery of Toledo, Castilian acquires more and more fixity; replacing Latin as the language of Spanish literature, Castilian becomes wealthy, supple, elevated and inclusive. It ceases to be a victorious dialect and becomes standard Spanish. Centrifugal interests set up standards for Portuguese and Catalan also, though these languages do not remain immune from the encroachment of Spanish. The weaker life of the Leonese and Aragonese dialects dwindles until they abandon their capitals to linger on in valleys and on hills remote from the foci of Spanish culture.

During the reign of Alfonso VI, in the second half of the eleventh century, various contributory influences in favour of standardization begin to operate. The capture of Toledo in 1085, the Visigothic capital and symbol of Spanish unity, is of supreme importance. This city fell, though to a king of Leonese predilections, to the Castilian nation. Alfonso took steps to give coherence to his dominions and to attach them to European traditions. He replaced the Mozarabic missal by the Roman, and the Visigothic minuscule by the Caroline. The former may be read in the pre-literary Glosses of Silos and San Millán de la Cogolla, with its characteristic broken-backed *e* and *a* so open at the top as to resemble *u*. Conservative nobles like the Cid Ruy Díaz continued to sign in the older script, but the practice of the chanceries confirmed the younger. With this overlap, we need not suppose that the change of script sufficed to obliterate a hypothetical literature of the tenth and early eleventh centuries; but it did contribute to intellectual intercourse between France and Spain. French influence thus became important for Spain simultaneously with the opening of the literary epoch, and it expressed itself in the peaceful penetration of Cluniac monks, the appointment of Frenchmen as bishops and counts in Alfonso's dominions, pilgrimages to Santiago de Compostela along the French Way, crusades like those of Barbastro and Las Navas, new standards of Latin style and popular appreciation of epic poetry. From the older script there descended one surviving mannerism. The Visigothic *z* was frequently written with a large curl for the top bar: ʒ. Further exaggerated this gave the Spanish ç, adopted by France in the sixteenth century as the French *cédille*.

FIXATION OF ORTHOGRAPHY

Literature and the chanceries demanded that some sort of uniform spelling should be adopted for the official language. Pressure in this direction is already evident in the notarial documents of the pre-literary period, in which, for instance, personal and place-names and some necessary terms presented problems of spelling for which Latin precedents were insufficient. As a result of this pressure the twelfth century already witnessed a considerable growth of uniformity in the scribal practices of Castile. The numerous experimental forms for non-Latin sounds had already begun to be reduced to a limited number of favoured forms, though these forms were not always those finally adopted in the next century (e.g. *gg*, as in *Sanggiz*, was preferred by many scribes to the *ch* ultimately adopted). In the thirteenth century Spanish spelling was regulated by the practice of the Toledan chancery, on a Castilian basis but with a notable concession to Toledo in the use of *f* where Castilian employed an aspirate *h*. The system thus adopted was almost perfectly phonetic, and with further adjustments in the sixteenth century and in the nineteenth, it has remained a true representation of the sounds of the Spanish speech. Portuguese and Catalan spelling evolved in a manner generally parallel to Spanish, though the former made greater concessions to etymological prejudices, and the latter, owing to its greater complexity of sounds, suffered more changes.

The problem set before the scribes was to find satisfactory equivalents for sounds not used by Latin. Those which the language had taken over from its parent retained their Latin representation. The alphabet, however, both exceeded the needs of Latin itself and fell short of those of Romance. Superfluous Latin letters could be given new values, until they were all taken up, and further sounds could be represented either by means of diacritical marks (as in *ç*) or by combinations. Latin presented doublets of *i* and *u* in the form of *j* and *v*. These doublets continued throughout the Middle Ages, but with an increasing tendency to make *i u* vocalic and *j v* consonantal. Late Latin had no aspirate; its *h* was conventional; it already served as the factotum of the alphabet, and had already been used in Latin to represent Greek sounds in the combinations *ph th ch rh*. This habit proved to be of great importance in Romance. Latin *y* and *z* were also equivalents for Greek sounds. The former had, however, lost its characteristic value in late Latin, and had become yet a third way of representing *i*; the latter had come to coincide with the Romance derivatives of Latin *i di*. The letters *c g* represented two values: [k g] before back vowels *a o u*, and [ŝ ĵ] before *e i*. For the value [ŝ] of *c* Visigothic offered the letter *ç*, thus setting up an antithesis between *c* [k] and *ç* [ŝ, later θ], which never became obligatory. On

11

the other hand, the double value of these letters forced the
Spanish scribes to find new ways of representing the sounds
[k g] before *e i*. German influence, as well as Greek, modified
the Latin alphabet before the Spanish scribes faced their
problem. The aspirate, which did not exist in late Latin,
made its reappearance as *h* in German words. The German *w*
corresponded with Latin *u v* but was a more tense sound;
hence the spelling *vv* or *uu*, whence the new letter *w*; but more
commonly Romance speakers imitated this labiovelar *w* by
prefixing to *u* a fricative *g*, whence *gu*. Thanks to German
also *k*, which had no acceptance in Latin, came into limited
circulation, notably in spelling Germanic names, as *Karllos*.

The new sounds which were clamouring for scribal attention were [k g] before front vowels (*e i*); the new fricative
values of *b d g*; and many palatal affricates and fricatives
[ĉ ĵ ŝ ẑ in the affricate series; š ž r̄ λ ɲ in the fricative; and
also s z]. With regard to *b d g*, the fricative and occlusive
pronunciations are closely related in the Peninsular languages, and the distinction was ignored, save in the first
instance where *v* offered a convenient way of marking the
difference: *bever* (BIBERE) *bivir* (VIVERE). This alternative
arose out of the fact that in Iberian Latin the values of *b* and
consonantal *v* were identical. For the other sounds a considerable number of possible equivalents were discovered by
experiment, and were gradually reduced to standard solutions. It was possible to set new values on superfluous Latin
letters, especially when the Romance value had evolved
from the Latin one. Thus *x* [ks] became in Spanish, Portuguese and Catalan the equivalent of [š], aided by such obvious
instances as *dixo* from DIXIT. With the evolution of Spanish
[š] to [χ] *x* has given way to *j* since the eighteenth century,
and has recovered through academical influence the value
of [ks]. The Latin value influences also Portuguese and
Catalan, where the sound [š] survives, and causes Catalan
to spell this sound not *x* but *ix*. Where aspirates existed in
Spain, *h* served to represent them; but as Castilian *h* corresponded to Toledan and Leonese *f*, *f* also served as the con-

ventional equivalent of the French and Arabic aspirates, which were also liable to remain unpronounced.

In some cases, where either the voiced or the voiceless form of a given sound existed, it was possible to use an old letter in two senses. Latin ǵ- before *e i* had the value of [ĵ], which is the voiced equivalent of voiceless [ĉ]. So we find *g* for [ĉ], e.g. *ni de nog ni de dia* (for later *noche*). More frequently the awkwardness of a double use of one sign was avoided by doubling the letter: so *Sanggiz* for *Sánchez* [ĉ]. This device of doubling was employed also in Arabic and Morisco writing, where it took the more compact form of the diacritic *tashdîd*; for instance, *b* served for Spanish *b*, but often *bb* for *p*. Doubling provided a solution for the various values of *s*. Initially and finally this letter was voiceless [s]; between vowels it might be voiced [z] or voiceless [s]. Medieval Spanish, together with Portuguese and Catalan, represented the former by *s*, the latter by *ss*, leaving the letter *z* to correspond with *ç* as voiced to voiceless. So *rosa* but *passar*. *R* had more than one value in the Peninsular languages. It is either a fricative or vibrant weakly trilled, or a tense vibrant with several trills. For the former *r* served, for the latter *rr*: *pero perro*. Initially or after *n* the *r* is always strongly trilled, and as no ambiguity arises, modern Spanish economises a letter (*rosa honra*). Medieval Spanish sometimes did the same, or continued to employ *rr* (*rrosa honrra*) or to use the capital as an additional letter of the alphabet (*Rosa honRa*). Doubling was also used in standard Spanish from the thirteenth century to represent the new palatal sounds [λ ɲ]: *Castiella sennor*. *Ñ* is merely a scribal variant of *nn*.

Combinations of letters were devised by making use of the factotum *h*, the Romance equivalents *i j y g*, the consonantal *u*, and occasionally *t* and *l*. *H* is the most useful of these letters, as it had no value in itself and could be supposed to add any shade to an existing letter. Added to *c g* an *h* confirmed them in the values [k g] before *e i*. This is the standard usage in Italian (*chérico ghetto*). It occurs in the final *-ch* of Catalan *poch*, recently abolished, and in *achesta* *strela (Auto de los Reyes Magos)*. But the same *h* might give an affricate nuance to *c* in Sp. *noche*, leading to ambiguity in Spanish, Catalan and Portuguese (Ptg. *ch* represented [ĉ] until the middle of the eighteenth century, though now [š]). *H* also served to indicate the palatalization of *l* and *n*, and as such has remained the standard of usage in Provençal and in Portuguese (*molher lenho*).

For palatalizations, however, the usefulness of some variant of *y* was apparent to our experimenters. It is a palatal semi-consonant, and it appears on rough analysis to give the palatal nuance in such words as the English *union onion senior million*, etc. The ear might fancy it detected this element either before or after its companion (since it is really simultaneous, as forming one single palatal phoneme); the tension of these consonants suggests the device of doubling; and the variants of *y* include *i j* and the Romance *g* in certain conditions. Hence there was a wide field for experimentation. The sound [λ], in addition to the *ll lh* already indicated, had the variants *yl ly yll lly, il* etc., *jl* etc., *gl gli* etc. Aragonese and Navarrese scribes tended to prefer *yl* or *yll* (*Payllas* for *Pallars*). Spanish settled on *ll* as also did Catalan. Portuguese and Provençal preferred *lh*; French *ill* (*mille fille juillet*); Italian *gli* (*figlio foglia moglie*). In Spanish documents of the eleventh and twelfth centuries we find such forms as *strela Castieilla obellgas* (Cast. *ovejas*) and even complex graphs like *igl lig*, all designed to avoid the ambiguity inherent in combined letters. Exactly the same licence of experimentation existed in respect of the palatal nasal [ɲ], for which we find *sennor senior banios vergoina kastango Compagni senigor pungno domgna*, etc. Again the Romance languages have chosen variously: Sp. *señor*, Ptg. *senhor*, Cat. *dany*, Arag.-Nav. *daynno*, Fr. *vigne*, It. *gnaffe*, etc. The palatal sibilant [š] showed similar vacillations: *Xemeniz coixu Scemeno escieret eleisco quessa eiso Kaissal*. The Peninsular languages preferred *x* or *ix*, despite the concurrence of the Latin value [ks]; Italian has chosen *sci*: *lasciare*.

The semi-vowel *u* belongs to the order of back vowels, and

so requires that a preceding *c* or *g* should have the velar quality [k g]. By losing its own peculiar pronunciation, it came to serve as a device for preserving [k g] before the front vowels *e i*, the more necessarily so since *ch* was an affricate. For [k] it was possible to make use of a superfluous letter of the Latin alphabet which was always found in company with *u*, namely *q* : *qu* is [k] before *e i* in *busqué quiero*, etc., but [kw] in OSp. Ptg. *quando*. No such resource was open in the case of [g], so that *gu* is [g] in *guerra*, but [gw] in *averiguar*. Medieval Spanish did not find embarrassing the fact that *qu gu* had two values each, but modern orthography has preferred to write [kw] always *cu*, and [gw] *gu* before back vowels, but *gü* before front ones: *cuando averigüé*.

The use of a conventional *t* to mark tension in certain palatals is characteristic of Catalan, in which [ĉ] is *tx*, [ĵ] *tj*, [ŝ] *ts*, [ẑ] *tz*, and [λ:] *tll*: Cat. *despatx mitja Prats esclavitzar batlle*. The Arabic emphatic letters *ḍ ṭ*, etc. involved a tension which Spanish indicated by prefixing to them an *l*, which, however, retained its proper value: *alcalde* Ar. *al-qáḍî*.

In the twelfth century we find Spanish spellings rapidly approaching a norm which contrasts with the licence of the eleventh-century documents of Oña. The *Auto de los Reyes Magos* shows a latinizing spirit, and limits its choice to a few main alternatives. In the *Disputa del alma y el cuerpo* one can detect only a few irregularities: *leio* (*leito* or *lecho*?), *nog* (*noche*), *festir*. The function of the Toledan chancery, therefore, was to complete a work already begun by making a final choice between the available alternatives, and giving validity to this decision in a vast number of official documents and in standard literary compilations. There was, as yet, no opposition to the phonetic principle in spelling, and no binding tradition. The result is that medieval Spanish orthography is a faithful picture of the language as it was spoken in official and cultured circles at Toledo about the year 1275. In various respects this representation became faulty towards the end of the fifteenth century, notably in the retention of *f* where an aspirate was now common in speech, and some details of the pronunciation of *b*. In Nebrija's *Gramática* (1492) and in his *Orthographia* (1517) the spelling is again made consonant with the language. Nebrija grappled also with the innate difficulty offered by combined letters for a simple sound, and proposed to indicate such by a mark of union (1492): *muchos dexar provecho*; but this suggestion was abandoned. He reaffirmed the phonetic principle, that the language should be spelled as it is pronounced; as did also the poet Herrera, who avoided the use of otiose *h* and sought to indicate hiatus and liaison between the article and a following noun or adjective.

By this time, however, the claims of tradition were stronger and the humanists had begun to insist on etymologies. Juan de Valdés (1536) allows himself to be eclectic in details. It was in the sixteenth and seventeenth centuries that changes occurred which considerably affected the pronunciation of medieval *x j g ç z s -ss-*, and as adjustment did not keep pace with the linguistic advance, Spanish orthography showed many anomalies when the Academia de la Lengua began to take official control of the language in the eighteenth century. Successive edicts have reduced the gap. *X* is officially [ks] (1815); *c g* continue to have double values, but the circumstances have been defined, and corresponding rules have been given for *z j*; *ss* has disappeared; accents indicate all deviations from certain simple rules of stress. Once again, therefore, Spanish spelling presents an accurate picture of *español correcto*, though it is necessarily conventional as an equivalent for the pronunciation of many Spaniards and Spanish-Americans. Catalan has been regularized in the present century. In Portuguese the influence of the etymologists lasted longer, especially in erudite words like *philosophia*, and the effort to standardize the spelling on a phonetic basis, connected with the name of Gonçalves Viana, may be deemed still in progress. Portuguese spelling norms have been more personal than those of the sister-languages, but in such a manuscript as the British Museum copy of the *Crónica de João I* (Add. MS. 20946) the scribe's habits are as satisfactorily phonetic as those of Alfonso X or Nebrija in Spain.

THE EXPANSION OF CASTILIAN

The later Middle Ages witnessed the completion of the process which had begun in the eleventh and twelfth centuries by which Castilian and Spanish became synonymous terms. Originally a dialect backed on the Basque border, more radical than the speech of the majority of Spanish-speakers, Castilian spread out fan-wise in a southerly and south-westerly direction until it reached the borders of Portuguese and Catalan near the middle line of the Peninsula, and then advanced southward as the sole parent of the Andalusian and American varieties. In this way Castilian cut off Leonese and Aragonese from the south, preventing their further development; and at the same time it exerted a vigorous lateral pressure which in the end has driven Aragonese off the plain of the Ebro, and Leonese out of eastern, southern and central León to take shelter in the mountains of Astorga or behind the Cantabrian range. The pressure was exerted not only by the Castilian dialect as a whole, favoured by the chanceries and the heroic songs, but by each individual castilianism. Each phenomenon has its own history of aggrandisement not identical with that of any other, but contributing to the joint result.

Of these phenomena the most outstanding is the substitution of f by h. In this respect Spanish differs from Catalan and Portuguese in the Peninsula, and from all the other Romance tongues; $f > h$ is therefore a criterion of Spanish. And yet it was not originally a practice common to all Spain, but only to Castilian. In literary documents the f is written continuously throughout the Middle Ages, and there is no vacillation until we reach manuscripts of the fourteenth century. In the next century the hesitation between f and h indicates that the actual sound was an aspirate; and the fact that h makes hiatus in the verses of Garcilaso de la Vega,

Luis de León, Ercilla and Herrera proves the continued existence of this aspirate in standard Spanish down to about the year 1580. In the succeeding generation of Lope de Vega the aspirate is weakened and lost, and is unknown to Calderón. In the Andaluz dialect, on the other hand, in Extremeño, and in such American dialects as agree with Andaluz, the survival of the aspirate is a noteworthy feature, represented in Spanish borrowings by *j* in *jándalo* 'huckster' (cf. *andaluz*), *jamelgo* FAMELICU 'starveling', *juerga* 'jollification' (cf. Cast. *huelga* 'rest, strike').

This passage of F > *h* > - has been misunderstood. Two schools of thought existed among philologists. Some laid stress on the fact that *f* is wanting in Basque (and apparently in Iberian) and in the Gascon dialects of French. They held that *f* (labiodental) was wanting in the language of the Iberian substratum, and so was not learned by the Iberians who spoke Latin. The spelling *f* of the manuscripts, under these conditions, could not represent a labiodental *f* but only some sound of an aspirate nature, which might be the bilabial aspirated fricative [φ]. Special cases would be the groups *fr- fu-* (*frente fuente*) in which either the labial sound was protected by the succeeding *r u* or has been restored by a better acquaintance with Latin. Other philologists rejected this explanation, and held that the appearance of the aspirate in Spanish was due to linguistic evolution in the fourteenth century, for which no ethnic cause should be attributed. Both explanations have been shown to repose on a misconception, namely that the evolution of Spanish was carried out uniformly over its whole area. This is not the case. The point of departure is found in the district of Castilla Vieja or Cantabria, which lies across the mountains from Santander to La Bureba, beside the Basque border. As we have no specimens of Spanish before the *Glosas Emilianenses* of the tenth century we cannot determine whether the *f* had never made a lodgment in this region, which was undoubtedly one of very late romanization. The phenomenon may or may not be Iberian, but it is certainly to be connected with the

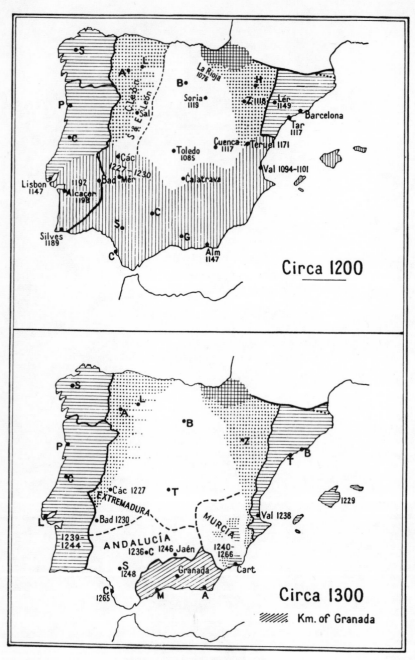

The expansion of Castilian

similar want of the labiodental as a genuine Basque sound
and is caused by the community of intercourse or origin
between Cantabrians and Basques. Place-names and the
notarial documents of Oña make it clear that the aspirate
was general in this region in the eleventh century: *Hormazuela
Hormaza Las Hormazas hayuela* (Oña 1057) *Rehoyo* (1151) (as
well as *Refoyo* 1188). The aspirate was doubtless weak, for
evidence of its suppression soon follows: *Ormatia* (1106) *Ornilla*
(1105) *Ormazola Ormaza.* Clearly, the focus of radiation
for both changes was the same, Castilla Vieja or Cantabria,
with an interval of half a century or more between them.
Very early instances are *Assur Hanniz* (Oña 944) and *Anni
Obecoz* (Covarrubias 972). In the notarial documents of
Burgos forms in *h* or - are rare even in the thirteenth century.
One of 1224 has *Forniellos* (*Hornillos*), but *Ormaza.* On the
other hand in Upper and Lower Rioja, standing closer to
the Basque border, the *ḥ* is frequent, notably in Gonzalo de
Berceo: *herropeado* (also *erropeas* in a fourteenth-century manuscript), *Henar* (*Cid: Fenares*), *hazanna, rehyertas.* The original
localization and early expansion may be studied in place-
names corresponding to the Latin SANCTU FELICE or ECCLESIA
SANCTI FELICIS. These names give three possible developments: (1) where *f* promptly became an aspirate and disappeared, the group *nt* was in favourable conditions for
survival, and one obtains the type *Santelices*; (2) where *f* persisted, the group *ntf* lost its middle occlusive and became *nf*,
which assimilated to *ff*; when the residual *f* became an
aspirate or was lost, the type is *Sahelices* (cf. *Sahagún* SANCTI
FACUNDI); (3) where the *f* survives: *San Felices, San Fiz, Safiz.*
The first type is to be found in two place-names in Vizcaya
and in the Partido de Villarcayo, to the north of Burgos.
The frontier between the second and third types occurs on
the Sella, towards the eastern end of the Asturias de Oviedo,
where we find *Cofiñal* CONFINALE. *Sahagún* and *Sahelices* stand
close together in Eastern León.

   To illustrate the further expansion of *h* and - we may take
the evidence of place-names in FONTE, as these are frequent

in Spanish toponymy. When this element is accented (*Fuen(te)*)
the association with *fuente* 'fountain, stream' is too obvious
and must have had a restraining influence on development;
but when the FONT- was treated enclitically, its etymological
value was less in evidence, and we get *Fon- Hon- On-* or *Am-*
in stricter accord with the peculiarities of the local pronunciation. Judged by this criterion there was a virtually *f*-less
region about the year 1300, extending from the Sella to
the Basque border and from Santander to Burgos (*Hontanar
Hontoria Hontamio Hontanada*, but also *Fombellida Fontecha
Fontasquesa*). South of Burgos and extending across Toledo
and La Mancha was a region of conflicting practices, with
predominant *h* or - (*Ampudia Hontangas Hontalbilla Ontígola
Oncebreros Hontanares*, but *Fontanillas Fontanar Fontalba*). On
either side the conflict affected southern León, Extremadura,
the Guadalquivir valley and Cuenca, with a predominance
of *f* (*Fonfría Fonseca Fompedrada Fontanar Fontanilla*, but *Hontillas
Hontanares Hontecillas*). Aragón, Murcia, western Extremadura, western and central León were then entirely occupied
by forms with *f*; Granada lay outside the Spanish Christian
domains. A little later we find instances of the intrusive *h*
in Juan Ruiz's *Libro de Buen Amor* (1330, 1343): *Henares
hadedura* (cf. *hado* FATU 'fate'), *herrén* FARRAGINE 'cattle-food',
hosco FUSCU 'dark-coloured'. The author was born in New
Castile, and spent his life mainly at Hita and Toledo.
Manuscripts of D. Juan Manuel (1325) show *halcón* 'falcon',
hazer FACERE 'do'. Two hundred years later the aspirate and
the elimination of the sound had gone so far as to impose
the Castilian characteristics on the whole central area of
Spanish. Old Castile from the Cantabrians to the Guadarramas lost the aspirate, and this phenomenon had invaded
the Esla valley in central León and the upper Ebro basin.
South León (with the university city of Salamanca) and New
Castile (with Toledo) continued to aspirate *h*, with decreasing
frequency in the eastern half of the area (Talavera, Madrid,
Cuenca, Albacete). The aspirate persisted, and persists to
this day, in Extremadura and Andalusia. Granada belongs

to this area of southern Spanish, but its place-names are notable for their conservatism, both in regard to f and in the treatment of vowels and diphthongs: *Farfán Las Fontanillas Funes Fornes Ferreirola Febeire Castil de Ferro.* In the bishopric of Astorga to the west of the Esla valley, in the Asturias west of the Sella, in Aragón north-east of Huesca and Monzón, the old Leonese and Aragonese f survives as also in Galicia, Portugal and Catalonia, beyond the linguistic boundaries of Spanish.

The expansion of Castilian is illustrated by several other instances in which Cantabria has imposed its will on the Spanish standard speech, as in the suffix *-illo*, the loss of initial J- ǵ- (before *e i*), the evolution of *ch* and medial *-j-* in certain cases.

The source of the suffix *-illo* is the VLat. -ĔLLU. Ĕ accented gives in Spanish *ie*, but as early as the tenth century, and perhaps from the ninth, we have cases of *-illo* in Old Castile, as *Uallilio Castillo* (Cardeña 921, copy of date 1085). In the twelfth century these forms are noticeable in the documents of Oña, the Partido de Villadiego and La Rioja (*Uozilla Asprilla Calaforilla*), but at Burgos and in the vicinity of Aguilar de Campóo *-iello* and *-illo* are equally frequent. North of Aguilar and south of Burgos (notably in Toledo) and to the west in León there is only *-iello* or the Mozarabic *-iel*. In the thirteenth century the situation is drastically changed by the adoption of *-illo* in Burgos (*Castilla Terradillos Francillos*) as the predominant form; and it is from Burgos that the innovation expands, while there is a reaction in the northern districts in favour of *-iello*. Confined to Castile in this century (it is not even found at Osma) the form in *-illo* crosses the dialect frontier in the fourteenth century, when it begins to appear at Toledo (*Johanillo* 1349) amid predominant *-iellos*. In the fifteenth century *-illo* is normal at Valladolid, Segovia and Ávila, and by the end of the period it has ousted *-iello* from literature. Some early cases of *-illo* in Aragón are not easily explained (*Guasilgu* 1055, *Fontilgas* now *Fontellas* 1083). These may be due to a suffix in -ĪCULU as a variant of -ÍCULU, and so be irrelevant to the present discussion. In common nouns -iello is used in Aragón during the thirteenth and fourteenth centuries, -illo appearing in the fifteenth: escopilla 1427, ramillya but castiellyo 1446. Closely associated with this change from -iello to -illo are certain words in -sp- as avispa 'wasp' níspero 'medlar' víspera 'eve', which displayed a diphthong in older Spanish, and also siglo 'world, century' from sieglo SAECULU.

A wider area of diffusion is found in the case of the loss of J- Ǵ-, and the reduction of C'L G'L LI to j. We meet with the change in all of Old Castile and the Asturias de Santander, in La Rioja (western portion), in eastern León as far as Sahagún, and southern León (Salamanca). This extension is attained already in the eleventh century, when the southern frontier of the phenomenon followed the crest of the Guadarramas so as to exclude Toledo, Madrid, and Medinaceli (the home of the poet of Mio Cid). In central and western León (León city, Eslonza, etc.) and in Aragón (including La Rioja, the lower part, and also the monastery of Silos, an offshoot on Castilian soil) the J- Ǵ- are preserved and C'L G'L LI take their pan-hispanic form -ll-. In the thirteenth century the Castilian practice exerts sufficient influence on the surrounding dialects to lead to vacillation. In the documents of the great monastery of Sahagún there is a notable increase throughout the century of -j- from C'L G'L LI. These groups gave first the pan-hispanic lateral palatal [λ], then the palatal fricative [j], whence a sibilant palatal fricative [ž] or affricate [ĵ]. These three related sounds coexist for the pronunciation of ll in modern Spanish, where, for instance, caballero is pronounced [kaƀaλéro] in standard Spanish, [kaƀajéro] vulgarly and in the south, and [kaƀažéro] or [kaƀajéro] on the Plate; from which it is clear that the Castilian j from the above-mentioned groups is at the end of a phonetic evolution which has the palatal fricative as its middle term. The latter was unstable, and served mainly to ease the transition. Thus at Sahagún from 1150–1274 spellings implying [λ] occur in 50 p.c. of the cases; but they drop to 10 p.c. between 1275 and 1300. At the same time those implying the palatal fricative [j] drop from 35 to 18 p.c., the whole advantage accruing to *j* [ž] or [ĵ]. The change is of the nature of a landslide, thanks to conservative habits of orthography among the notaries.

The widest initial area of a castilianism is that occupied by *ch* < CT, ULT, as in *hecho* FACTU *leche* LACTE *noche* NOCTE *mucho* MULTU. This is again a case of Castilian resoluteness in carrying through a process of change to its logical extreme. The common Spanish, and most usual Romance, solution of these groups is *i̯t*, as in the Ptg. *feito leite noite muito*. In Catalan, and to some extent in Aragonese, the semi-vowel modified the preceding full vowel, putting an end to the diphthong (Cat. *fet llet nit* but *molt*). In Castilian the semi-vowel modified the following consonant, bringing it to the same palatal position [ť], and then combining into one affricate [ĉ]. Compare Eng. *try* [tɹai] with *chi* in *China*, or the Chilean pronunciation of *t* before *r* in *otro* [óťɹo]. Already in the eleventh century the [ĉ] was normal in Castile: *manegga* 1090 *fegga* 1191, *Fregas* now *Frachela, Cadreggas*. In the twelfth century the spelling *ch* emerges supreme over the alternative experimental forms: *derechero barbecho prouecho*, etc. In the same century the pronunciation [ĉ] is indicated by documents from Toledo, Burgos, Osma, Cuenca, etc., showing that at the opening of the historical period this pronunciation covered both the Castiles. Across the southern frontier, at Medinaceli and Molina, the form in *ch* was in conflict with the Aragonese *it*: *peyte itare* but *leycho echenli* (*Fuero de Medinaceli*, 1125), *peyta feyta* but *dichos fechos* (Molina, thirteenth century). Certain words had more expansive force than others, as *fechos* and notably *mucho*, which virtually ousts the native Aragonese form from Aragonese literary documents. The invasion of León took place in two main stages, corresponding to eastern and central León. The eastern counties, accustomed to intrigue with the Castilians against their Leonese overlord, show [ĉ] well established in the eleventh century: *Fonte tega* for *Fontecha* FONTE TACTA (Sahagún

1079), *peccet* for *peche* 1096, *Frachela* 1118. *Peccet* appears at Eslonza in central León in 1173. In the capital we have *Fontecha* recorded in 1136. Though central León was conquered by this castilianism later than eastern, it is possible that the retention of *it* in notarial documents of this epoch was already an archaism, supported on the prestige of Galicia, seeing that the majority of Asturian dialects have *ch*. The *it* remains to-day only in touch with the Galician-Portuguese border, to the west of Oviedo, Cangas de Onís, Astorga, Zamora, and at Miranda del Duero, which is politically included within Portugal.

A similar range was originally occupied by another castilianism of standard Spanish, viz., sc̦ʲ > ç: FASCIA 'band' Cast. *haça haza* 'piece of cultivable land' *Hazas Hacinas*, but Ptg. *faixa faxa* Cat. *faixa* Leon. *faxa fexa* Arag. *faxa* Moz. *faša*.

CASTILE'S CASTING VOTE

In the foregoing examples we see how the self-reliant spirit of Castile imposed on the Spanish language the most logical and developed forms. Not less important is the rôle Castilian played in the acceptance or rejection of speech-habits originally restricted to one or other portion of the Peninsula. It was adoption by Castilian that made them universally valid.

Notable among these cases is the treatment of tonic ĕ ŏ and of the diphthongs AI AU. As for ĕ ŏ the Peninsular languages and dialects found themselves divided by conflicting tendencies which went back at least to the Visigothic period. To the introduction of the diphthong Tarraconensis, Gallæcia, Lusitania and the region of Granada showed a high power of resistance, radiating doubtless from their capitals Tarraco, Bracara, Emerita, Corduba and Hispalis. Thanks to this resistance Catalan does not diphthongize (except under the influence of a palatal, as in Provençal: *ull* ŏc'LU, *nit* NŏCTE owe their vowels to a simplification of *u̯ei̯*), nor Galician-Portuguese at all (*olho noite*). The other provinces are in the Spanish area, and therefore conflict with the habits

of the whole north (Leon. Arag. *uello nueite*). Castilian belongs
to this region, and exercised its influence on the history of
the diphthong in three ways: it accepted the diphthong *ie ue*
in most cases and so secured its adoption in Spanish; it
carried through the process of simplification to the logical
conclusion by eliminating the alternatives *ia ua uo*; and it
exempted from diphthongization ĕ ŏ before a palatal (*ojo
noche*). The cause of this unexpected piece of conservatism
is not precisely known. As diphthongization before a palatal
not only occurs in common Spanish and in French (*œil nuit*),
but also in Provençal and Catalan which do not otherwise
indulge in the practice, it would appear to have been the
oldest type of diphthongization. Cantabria, on the other
hand, was a land of relatively late romanization. As for the
precise value of these diphthongs, Leonese and Aragonese
vacillate between the various forms in most of their earlier
documents, and such a sound as *ua* remains to this day in
Aragonese place-names: *Lascuarres*. The pronunciation *uo* is
found in the *Auto de los Reyes Magos*, *Poema de mio Cid* and
Disputa del Alma, the three oldest documents of Spanish literature, because none of these belongs to the Castilian area of
Burgos; the first is the work of a Toledan Mozarab, the
second of a Mozarab of Medinaceli, and the third belongs
to the archaizing north (Oña).

In the case of the Latin diphthong AI, it was Catalan and
Aragonese which first carried through its monophthongiza-
tion, so that -ARIU, for instance, gave -*er(o)*. The Castilian
of the eleventh century shows the intermediate stage *ei* in
karreira, but in the twelfth these forms show a localization
in the north, and particularly in the province of Santander,
whereas in the Castilian of Burgos the vowel *e* tends to
mastery. This contrasts with the long vacillation of central
León, and the retention of *ei* to this day in western Leonese
and Galician-Portuguese. Similarly AU > *o* was a change
effected more promptly in the east of the Peninsula, but
generalized through Castilian.

Among important consonantal developments which have

been influenced by Castilian are initial L-, initial PL- CL- FL-, and medial -MB-.

Initial L- was pronounced with more tension than medial and final, and involved rather more attachment of the tongue to the roof of the mouth. By exaggerating this attachment [l:] the sound passed, in several quarters of the Peninsula, into a palatal [λ], capable of further transformation into [j] or [ŝ]. The lateral palatal was adopted in Catalan (LARGU *llarg*, LUNA *lluna*, etc.), in the Asturias (*lluna tsuna*), and sporadically in the south (Moz. *yengua* from *llengua LINGUA*); Galician and Portuguese retained the dental pronunciation (*língoa lua*). The fact that Castilian also dissented from this change caused it not to be adopted by standard Spanish.

On the other hand Castilian shared partially in the western tendency to alter the pronunciation of a voiceless initial consonant followed by *l* (PL- CL- FL-). The treatment of voiced initials of the same series is more variable, and can be left out of account here. In this case the centre of innovating activity lay in León or Galicia, while the most conservative regions lay farthest east (Catalan) or south (Mozarabic). In these regions the Latin groups survived unaltered: Cat. *pla clamar flama* PLANU CLAMARE FLAMMA, Moz. *plantain* PLANTAGINE. In Portuguese and Galician the process of change has resulted in *ch* (an affricate or a fricative palatal); in old Leonese it gave *x* [š], and in modern west Leonese it gives *ts* [ŝ]. The influence of Castilian was exerted in bringing this series of changes to a halt at an early moment of its history. The first stage must have been a pronunciation of the *l* with lingering articulation, giving *pll- cll- fll-*[1] as at present (though perhaps from other causes) in Ribagorza. Then this *ll* was aggrandized at the expense of the initial consonant, which disappeared, leaving Cast. *llano llamar llama*. Thus Castilian has deflected in standard Spanish an evolution that centres in the north-west and has there continued unchecked.

An eastern (Catalan and Aragonese) mannerism, made valid for the rest of Spain by Castilian adoption, is the simpli-

fication of -MB- to *m* in PALUMBA Sp. *paloma* 'dove', LOMBU
Sp. *lomo* 'loin'. But Castilian has not adopted the parallel
evolution of -ND- to *n* in DEMANDARE Cat. Arag. *demanar*.
Spanish retains *demandar*.

These are some of the instances in which the Castilian
dialect has imposed its will on 'correct' Spanish. Generally
it has been a bold innovator, carrying evolution to its limits.
Sometimes it has shared in the novelties of eastern or of
western Spain and given them validity for the whole country.
More rarely Castilian has opposed a change, or has even
caused a reaction against a form already part of the speech-
habits of the majority of Spanish-speakers. In each instance
it has displayed an energy and resolution similar to that
which Castilians displayed in gaining and using the Peninsular hegemony. The sum total of Castilian activities is the
peculiar cachet of Spanish among all languages descended
from Latin.

On the above, see R. Menéndez Pidal's *Orígenes del español*, *passim*.
[1] FLAMMA *llama* is the only important word to show this change in
Castilian, but FL- follows the same history as PL- CL- in Leonese and
Galician-Portuguese in a considerable number of words. Even there it
is not easy to consider FLORE OPtg. *frol* 'flower' as a 'learned' word,
and the question arises whether there are not two possibilities for Lat.
FL-, viz. *fll-* and Ptg. *fr-* Sp. *fl-*. FL- gives *l-* in *Láinez*, *Lambra*, cf. Basque
lore from FLORE.

THE LANGUAGES OF LITERATURE

The rise of a vernacular literature acted as a precipitant on
the numerous pre-literary Spanish dialects, defining with
increasing clearness the literary speech, and reducing the
others to subordinate uses. Under the conditions of the earlier
Middle Ages Galicia made more progress in wealth and culture than the harried central plains, and it contained an
important spiritual capital in the Shrine of St James. The
kings of León and of León-Castile from Alfonso VII to
Alfonso X were often nurtured in Galicia, and may have felt
an inbred sympathy for the soft Galician speech. It is certain,
at least, that they favoured the unique use of Galician in the

twelfth and thirteenth centuries for the purposes of lyrical
poetry, both courtly and traditional; and they gave expression to this preference in the *Cantigas de Santa María* of
Alfonso X for religious poetry, and the Galician-Portuguese
Cancioneiros, supposedly edited by Count Pedro de Barcelos,
for secular. The latter contained not only two strata of
courtly poems based on Provençal prosody, but also the
inimitable women's songs in parallel verses like those of the
Psalms, with their wistfully childlike accents. On the other
hand, from at least the middle of the eleventh century the
profound national sentiment of Castile gave rise to heroic
poems on the Infantes de Lara, the Castilian counts, and
Ruy Díaz the Cid. For such narrative poems Castilian was
obligatory, so that the Mozarab author of the *Poema de mio
Cid* writes in Castilian, with no more than an occasional slip
to indicate his native dialect (*Gujera* for *Cullera*, *Castejón* for
Castellón, which are instances of ultra-correction). At the
same time for courtly lyrical poetry Castilians, Sevillans, and
even an Italian adopted Galician as their medium; and there
appeared to be a specialization of dialect for literary purposes
like that of Ionic and Doric in Greece. It is not that no songs
were sung in Castilian. Indeed the evidence of later literature
suggests that a definitely Castilian manner (the *villancico*) had
already come into use, and the rhythmic chants of certain
trades and vocations must have existed then as now. But
as yet the Castilian lyric lacked official and literary encouragement.

As a result of the vast labours of Alfonso X a new department of literature was opened for the special advantage of
Castilian, namely prose. Vast histories, treatises on science
and law, books of good counsels and lastly novels appeared
to the profit of this dominant dialect. Galician, on the contrary, achieved no prose save a translation of the Castilian
Crónica Troyana of Leomarte (1373). The antithesis now
stood as Galician court lyric versus Castilian epos and prose.
The fourteenth and early fifteenth centuries saw lyrics also
fall to the share of Castilian. Firstly Juan Ruiz, in his pre-

dominantly narrative *Libro de Buen Amor* (1330, 1343), offered
samples of hill-maiden songs, songs for beggars and scholars,
hymns to the Virgin, and goliardic verses in Castilian, and
in a variety of metres and manners that showed a sturdy
independence of the Galician and Provençalizing school. The
Cancionero de Baena (1445) bears witness to the passage from
Galician to Castilian in the career of Alfonso Álvarez de
Villasandino, one of the older generation of its poets, who
commences in the Galician manner and ends in the Castilian.
A younger generation headed by Micer Francisco Imperial,
author of an important poem on the birth of Juan II (1405),
has forgotten Galician, and has passed on to a new propaganda in favour of Italian models. Similarly, whereas the
grandfather of the famous Marquis of Santillana (1398–
1458) composed his songs in Galician, the Marquis himself
has only one such experiment, all his other verses being in
Castilian. As nothing succeeded the *Cancioneiros* in Galicia,
this defection of the Castilian poets led to the complete
eclipse of the Galician dialect for literary purposes, until it
was revived as a regional literature by Rosalía de Castro,
Pondal and Curros Enríquez in the mid-nineteenth century.

In this way the use of a dual system was ended. At the
same time great strides were taken in the direction of crystal-
lizing Castilian itself. The narrative poems of the early
thirteenth century show considerable dialectal independence.
With a modicum of Castilian in common, Berceo used forms
from his transitional Riojano dialect, the *Libro de Apolonio*
is markedly Aragonese, and the short *Tres Reis d'Orient* is
near-Catalan. On the other side the *Libro de Alexandre* and
the Grail-novels (early fourteenth century), together with
the *Disputa de Elena y María*, have evident Leonese characteristics. Towards the end of the thirteenth century the
practices of the Toledan chancery begin to influence the
literary language, and they are embodied in the *Primera
Crónica General*, the *Grande e General Estoria*, the *Siete Partidas*,
and other works. These are Castilian, indeed, but no

longer the precise dialect of Burgos. The Burgalese aspirate is not admitted, the numerous contracted forms of the *Poema de mio Cid* disappear gradually, and the literary committees are preoccupied with the creation of an adequate vocabulary and polished forms of expression. The care taken by Alfonso X with the style of his works, though we cannot ascertain the details, was of the profoundest importance for the Spanish language. There came into existence an *español correcto* (to use a modern term)—Castilian with certain concessions to Leonese and many more to Latin—which appears as virtually the modern literary language in D. Juan Manuel's *Conde Lucanor* (1325) and other works. Dialectal traces are still to be found in the *Poema de Alfonso Onceno* and Clemente Sánchez de Vercial; but in diminishing numbers.

By the sixteenth century standard Spanish was firmly established. There remained only some controversy as to its interpretation. Two of the most influential law-givers were Andalusians, Nebrija for grammar in general, and Herrera for poetical diction. Juan de Valdés (1536) and 'Prete Jacopín' contested their authority, asserting the claims of polite society in Toledo to determine the Spanish standard. Both parties concurred in admiring as a practical measure of the language the style of Garcilaso de la Vega (d. 1536), and when at last the capital of the country was fixed in Madrid (1560) men of letters were drawn together and rapidly settled their differences, chiefly through the *comedia*, which served both as the theatre and as the journalism of that age.

The union of León and Castile into one medieval dominion caused Leonese first to disappear from cultural use. The history of Aragonese is generally similar, but with minor differences. Zaragoza was the capital of a kingdom which spoke a variety of Spanish, and its chancery was not bound to follow the norms of Toledo; nor was it governed by the Catalan-speaking chanceries of Barcelona, Valencia and Majorca. Latin yielded gradually to Aragonese in official documents, and Aragonese was to some extent normalized for official and literary purposes. Examples of this sort of Aragonese are to be found in the great corpus of Juan Fernández de Heredia (d. 1396), in his *Gran Crónica de los Conquiridores*, in the translations from Marco Polo, Hayton and Mandeville, and in the Vatican *Tristán de Leonís*. All these works show compromise with Castilian in greater or smaller degree (e.g. the word *mucho* is normal, with Castilian -*ch*-). Lacking the support of three-quarters of the kingdom of Aragón, Aragonese had no sufficient hinterland to develop a robust tradition of its own, and on the union of Castile and Aragón in 1479 its conventional literary dialect was obliterated in favour of Castilian. There remained to Aragonese writers an attitude of mind. The Argensolas and Gracián are more austere in matters of idiom and style than their contemporaries born to the manner of Castile; scrupulous correctness, brevity and gravity are perhaps in them signs of a language gained by self-discipline.

The use of standard Spanish passed the frontiers of the language. On the east, after the incorporation of Aragonese, it assaulted Catalan. The position of Catalan had been considerably weakened by the accession in 1412 of a Spanish dynasty. Instead of the vigorous encouragement which had been given by Jaume I, Pere el Gran, and Pere del Punyalet, the Trastamaran kings showed leaning towards their Aragonese-speaking subjects, who occupy a considerable part of the *Cancionero de Estúñiga* (1458), which represents the taste of the Neapolitan circle of Alfonso the Magnanimous. Catalan emancipated itself from Provençal thanks to the four great chronicles and Ramon Lull. Under the hands of Bernat Metge and in his *Somni* (1398) the literary dialect was firmly organized for the purposes of prose. But little use was made of this tool in the unfavourable conditions of the fifteenth century; and Catalan must be supposed already suffering a cultural decline when it felt the impact of Castilian at the end of this era, notwithstanding the individual brilliance of the Valencian poets Jordi de Sant Jordi, Auzias March, and Jaume Roig. In the sixteenth century Catalan is restricted to regional purposes; Spanish is the language of those who seek to address a wider audience. The figure who typifies this attitude is Boscán, the friend and colleague of Garcilaso de la Vega, and the joint-founder of modern Spanish prosody. He was a native of Barcelona who has deliberately preferred the language of all Spain. The sequence of antiquarian works and local histories died away in the course of the century, and in the next two Catalan was little more than a spoken dialect, supported by the peasantry, the preaching clergy, and some vulgar lyrics. It remained, however, the native tongue of Catalans, Valencians and Majorcans, and its rhythms and memories prevented a complete assimilation to Castile. In the nineteenth century an earnest attempt to solve this difficulty was made by the Castilianist school of Barcelona under Romantic impulse—by Cabanyes, Piferrer, Balaguer and Milà. They sought to express thoughts of local inspiration, and rhythms innate in them, in Castilian; but the effort was too great. On the one hand, the Castilian critics, such as Hermosilla, declined to admit the difficult rhythms of Cabanyes; on the other, the spontaneous popular lyric and local legend were necessarily falsified by transposition into an alien tongue. Compromise being unfruitful, there remained only the alternatives of submission to Castilian or the resurrection of Catalan as a literary speech. The latter line was followed. The Floral Games (1859 ff.) at Barcelona stimulated general interest, though in a conventional troubadouresque language. Jacinto Verdaguer collected genuine Catalan from the lips of peasants and poured it out in epics and lyrics of indubitable inspiration; Marian Aguiló restored the vocabulary preserved by ballads and medieval literature; Joan Maragall completed the task by forging an adequate medium for verse and prose; and Carner and López-Picó have made its rhythms subtle and its significance profound. The fact that a standard had already been reached by Metge under the old kingdom, and the abundance of national traditions, greatly facilitated the restoration. Catalan is now a language apt for poetry, artistic prose, science and journalism;

but Spanish is the language of intercourse with the rest of Spain and of appeal beyond the Catalan frontiers.

Portuguese also felt the impact of Castile. The close kinship of the two speeches, indeed, made the struggle more domestic, and of the nature of a civil war of language. Identical at first with Galician, Portuguese commenced with a rich store of courtly and popular songs in the *cancioneiros*. The work of the Toledan chancery for Castilian had an offshoot in the *Livros de Linhagens* (*c.* 1350), attributed to the same Count of Barcelos who compiled the song-books. In them the material is often of Spanish origin, but the language is the first specimen of literary Portuguese. This speech was further developed by the savoury prose of Fernão Lopes and the more academic manner of Zurara, the great fifteenth-century chroniclers. Thus Portuguese had body and tradition.

Its position as a cultural language, however, was threatened by the prestige of Castilian, and the later years of the fifteenth century and early sixteenth witnessed a severe crisis. Even the Constable Pedro of Portugal composed his works in Castilian, and Castilian was the language favoured by the court of Manuel the Fortunate (d. 1525). It occupies much space in the *Cancioneiro de Resende* (1516), which reflects the preferences of the court in lyrical poetry. It is prominent also in the farces of Gil Vicente, written between 1502 and 1536, but it is there used with a difference. Gil Vicente's Spanish is, in fact, a Spanish adapted to the norms of Lisbon, and it represents the terms on which alone Spanish could hope to supplant Portuguese in Portugal. The personal infinitive he found too useful in his own language to omit from his Spanish: *para seres loado* 'so that you be praised'. His language is full of *lusismos*, as *mor* Sp. *mayor*, *crego crigo* Sp. *clérigo*, *frecha* Sp. *flecha*, *genojos* Sp. *hinojos*, *estea* Sp. *esté*, *sentio* Sp. *sintió*, *igreja* Sp. *iglesia*. For some of these he could find justification in the dialect of León, and for others he could plead Spanish precedent, though of an earlier epoch, as for *aína cadaldia hecistes defension*, etc. In some cases he falls into ultra-correction, as *plado* Sp. *prado* (since Ptg. *branco* corresponds to Sp. *blanco*), *siendas* Sp. *sendas*, *enhadar* Sp. *enfadar*, *cierca* Sp. *cerca*, *nos* Sp. *nosotros*. He had one sibilant for *s ç* where Spanish had two, and so rhymes *romance vanse* and writes *aseche altesa sociego resar*. His vowels are not always those of standard Castilian. Thanks to Ptg. *deusa* 'goddess', he writes *diesa* Sp. *diosa*; and he can rhyme *corte* with *muerte*. Thus a modified Spanish tended to be set up in Lisbon, like the 'Inglis' of the medieval Scottish poets. Its prestige, however, varied in the poet's own lifetime. Castilian is, for him, the general tongue. He uses it for what is not specifically Portuguese, as in the *Comedia de Rubena* or the plays based on novels of chivalry (*Dom Duardos*, *Amadís de Gaula*). It is the language of serious figures: kings, angels, gods, heroes when they throw off their humble disguises, persons of biblical or allegorical importance. Portuguese is the language of his peasants, muleteers, witches, demons and comedy figures. But in his later farces Portuguese comes into its own. It is necessarily the language of 'Lusitania' and also of 'Fame' in the plays of those names, and the *Auto da Alma*, as early as 1508, is wholly Portuguese.

Vicente is the last great medieval author of Portugal. The new generation of humanists (Sá de Miranda, Ferreira, Camões, Diogo Bernardes, Barros, Agostinho da Cruz) gave an enormous impetus to the national tongue, and created the classical literature of Portugal. The *Lusíadas* (1572) were an imperishable memory. These poets, however, with the single exception of António Ferreira, versified also in the Spanish of Portugal, less far removed from that of Spain than Vicente's. They left the door open for the re-entry of Castilian as a result of the union of the crowns (1580–1640), the Castilian monopoly of the theatre, and the change of æsthetic principles implied by *gongorismo* and *conceptismo*. The early seventeenth century saw a new crisis in the use of Portuguese. Faria e Sousa expounded the *Lusíadas* in Spanish, Francisco Manuel de Melo wrote minor works in Portuguese but sought a world market for his *Historia de los movimientos, separación y guerra de Cataluña* (1645). It was in Spanish that D. João de Bragança rebelled against Spain, and in Spanish he wrote his treatise on music. But the later part of this period witnessed the dwindling of Spain's political prestige, and the sudden rise of France. To France the eyes of Portuguese thinkers turned, and Spanish seemed no longer to enjoy international currency. The mediocre poets of the eighteenth century were resolute in one thing, namely the exclusive literary use of Portuguese, and for the last time Spanish was evicted from Portugal. The talents of Bocage, followed by the more lofty inspiration of Garrett and Herculano, and finally the writers of more recent times, have found in Portuguese the only means of expressing deep and moving sentiments; though the similarity of the two languages has caused Portugal to be tolerably well informed concerning literary movements in Spain. Conspicuous in the regeneration of Portuguese has been the pervasive influence of Camões; Bocage was his disciple, Garrett his epic singer, the historians are inspired by his scenes of pathos, heroic striving and disaster. Above all it is as the 'language of Camões', as the custodian of a common tradition too valuable to be forgotten, that Portuguese unites spiritually to Portugal its great daughter-republic, Brazil.

JEWISH SPANISH

We may obtain an almost contemporary idea of what Spanish was before the great changes of its Golden Age by means of the Jewish dialects scattered over the Balkans from Constantinople to Bosnia and over the north fringe of Africa. The Jews abandoned their homeland in two principal dispersions. The first was the *diaspora* of 1492 and 1496 when they were brutally expelled from Spain by the Catholic Sovereigns and from Portugal (after a few years of feigned hospitality) by Manuel the Fortunate. The emigrants were chiefly men of the humbler classes; the rich, embarrassed by their possessions, frequently accepted the alternative of conversion, and they were so curbed by the Inquisition that their sons

lost the tradition of their fathers' worship. A third generation, however, felt curiosity as to their faith, and without
renouncing Christianity openly, they fell to intensive study
of the Pentateuch. Covertly realizing their holdings, they
took ship in small parties for free countries where they might
be at liberty to revert openly to Judaism. England was not
opened to them, and after a brief stay at Hamburg, they
negotiated an agreement with the civic authorities of Amsterdam, who longed for their capital. Thus the Jewish synagogue
was established in Amsterdam, where it became wealthy
with the rising commercial prosperity of Holland. Enabled
by Cromwell to settle in England, these Sephardic communities took part in the growing mercantile prosperity of England
and notably in the development of the East India Company's
ventures. The second dispersion has had the most important
cultural consequences, but is not of immediate linguistic
interest to us. It accompanied, and perhaps in part caused,
the mercantile prosperity of Holland and England. Jews of
this kind appreciated Spanish literature abroad; translated
directly from Spanish into Dutch and other languages some
of the main successes of the novel and drama; included poets
of high rank, like Pinto Delgado the singer of *Ester* and the
dramatist Enríquez Gómez; while out of the conflict between
Ashkenazic tradition and a rational interpretation of the Law
rose the controversial works of Uriel da Costa and the philosophy of Spinoza. The loss of Hebrew by these communities
has left their Spanish in the position of a liturgical language,
while for practical purposes they have adopted English,
Dutch or other national speeches. In Hamburg such traces
have almost died out.

The earlier dispersion is less notable culturally, but has
led to the survival of a medieval Spanish in a state of suspended
animation. The refugees fled with the miserable remains of
their property to Oran and other parts of Africa, where they
were again despoiled; and to Italy, where the House of Este
welcomed them to Ferrara, where partial toleration reigned.
This sufficed to create conditions favourable to some literary

development, as witnessed by the Ferrara Bible in Spanish
and Samuel Usque's sombre *Consolação ás tribulações de Israel*
in Portuguese. More attractive conditions were offered by
the Turkish sultans, and the migration continued eastward
to Constantinople. There they set up their printing-presses,
and the first work printed in Turkey is said to have been the
Constantinopolitan *Pentateuch* of 1547. The most considerable
was Almosnino's *Libro intitulado regimento de la vida* (1564), a
considerable achievement of scholarship. These books are
composed in almost pure pre-classical Spanish, known as
ladino to distinguish it from the *español* or *žudío* (in Bosnia
jidjó) of current speech. Connection with Spain was not at
once entirely lost. *Amadís de Gaula* was read by them, and some
new ballads (like the one on the death of the Duke of Gandia,
1496) were added to the repertoire of the *cantaderas*. The
alphabet normally employed among the Spanish Jews was
and remains that in *Raši* characters, an adapted Hebrew,
involving the use of points to indicate doubled letters, *ly* for *ll*,
initial *aleph* and vowel-glides expressly marked by *y* and *w*.
A tick above a letter sufficed to create a new symbol for a
Spanish sound unknown to Hebrew, e.g. a tick over *gimel* to
indicate both *j ǵ* [ž ĵ] and *ch* [ĉ], over *pe* for *f*, and over
beth and *daleth* for fricative *b d*. This transcription was
already in use among the Jews of Spain during the fourteenth and fifteenth centuries, but its use by Almosnino
gives an exact measure of phonetic changes suffered since his
day.

It is not to be supposed that the Spanish of Jews resident
in the Peninsula was quite uniform in itself or identical with
that of their Christian neighbours. The moral poem of Sem
Tob (1350) shows a fund of metaphor and illustration different from that of its contemporaries, thanks to his Talmudic
readings; but perhaps the most satisfactory text is the fragmentary *Coplas de Yoçef*, edited by Dr González Llubera.
There is the characteristic *el Dio* where Christians say *Dios*;
words showing a different literary tradition (*Aibto* for *Egipto*);
the Hebrew form of names (*Yoçef*, *Yishak*, etc.); archaisms

like *horro* (also in Juan Ruiz), Sp. *libre*, and a change in the form of the verse. On the other hand, even after the dispersion we hear of regional differences preserved by separate synagogues for Castile, Aragón and Portugal, and even for separate towns: *sinagogas cordubesas, lisboetas*, etc. From this it is clear that the common basis of the existing dialects is a *koiné* established since the dispersion, into which have crept new regional differences corresponding to the location of the speakers in Constantinople, Salonika, Skoplje, Monastir, Oran or Constantine. This *koiné* has absorbed the Portuguese Jews, and also others of diverse origins, as Turkish, Greek or Italian; and in so doing, it has made numerous concessions, especially in the realm of vocabulary.

The written and the spoken languages have come to vary considerably. The written tongue has almost the whole wealth of pre-classical Spanish as exemplified in the *Amadís* and *Celestina*, but the vernacular has been grievously impoverished. Thus the whole range of words *varón macho hembra niño* is possessed by the *ladino* texts but not by *žudío*. Inveterate townsmen, the Balkan Jews think of trees only as a class (*árbol*) and not of particular sorts of tree, and distinguish birds only as birds of prey (*pašaru*) or song-birds (*pašariku*); to denote species they must borrow from the surrounding languages, Turkish, Serbo-Croatian, etc. When the Spanish terms occur in ballads they are understood, but obsolete. Early travellers, however, reported that the colloquial was as correct as the language of Spain. Similarly there have been developments of the Spanish sounds. Evidently *ll* emigrated as a lateral palatal, spelt *ly*, but only *y* occurs in the colloquial, so that written *'elyịa* is pronounced *eịa* (*ella*). Cases of *yeísmo*, ancient vulgarisms, occur in the Cambridge fragment of Sem Tob, which doubtless emigrated alongside the correct *ll* and gradually took its place. In Almosnino *f* has become an aspirated *h*: *hilo hižo hallar hasta*, as distinguished from the 'silent' *h* of *hombre*, etc., which he spells *ombre, onra aber*. The colloquial is richer in sounds, as it contains the Portuguese and dialectal *f*, the old Castilian aspirate, and the modern want of aspiration: *ferir fierro forka fuir forro, huente huero huerte, avlar avla* (Sp. *habla*).

The sibilants are the Old Castilian series. The voiceless [s] is distinguished from the voiced [z] which occurs when -*s*- falls between vowels or before a voiced consonant within a word. For this distinction the *Raši* script makes use of *sin* [s] and *zayin* [z]: *Roza Firmoza mozotrus kaza* for Sp. *Rosa Hermosa nosotros casa*, but *pasar asar gu̯esu* for OSp. *passar assar huesso*. The same letters *sin* and *zayin* and pronunciations [s z] serve to distinguish OSp. *ç z*: *kavesa sinko senar amenazar vizinu siniza* for MSp. *cabeza cinco cenar amenazar vecino ceniza*. These *s z* sounds are dorsoalveolar, i.e. pronounced with the tip of the tongue on the lower teeth and a constricted passage between the back of the tongue and the alveoli; but the Spanish *s z* was cacuminal, i.e. pronounced with the tip of the tongue raised to make friction on the alveoli. This pronunciation has been lost in Jewish Spanish, but traces of it remain in frequent confusions between [s z] and [š ž], or *s z* and *x ž̌*. So we get *buškar čamuškar moška piškadu* and even *seš kantáš tenéš* for *buscar chamuscar mosca pescado seis cantáis tenéis*. The pronunciation [ẑ] also occurs for the ancient *z*: Bosnian and Constantinopolitan *ondzi dodze dodzena*, etc. for *once doce docena;* also *mandziya podzada* for *mancilla posada*, making use of the [ẑ] of the compounds of DECEM in which it is historically justified. In the same way Jewish Spanish continues the ancient distinction between *x, j ǵ* [š ž] by means of *shin* and modified *gimel* in writing, and by [š ž] in speech. Now [ž] is akin to the fricative palatal *y* [j] and to the corresponding affricate [ĵ], as in Sp. *mayo cónyuge*. So in speech the distinction runs between [š] for the ancient *x* and [ž j ĵ] for ancient *j ǵ* and *y*: x *bruša šabón lešos*; ʏ *ja jazer jerba jugo ajer ajudar lej rej*; affricate *ĵemir ĵarra ĵeneroso ĵidió ánĵel monĵe*; ᴊ *ižo* (Sp. *hijo* FILIU).

A conspicuous archaism of Jewish Spanish is the distinction drawn between occlusive and fricative *b*, a distinction maintained by medieval Castilian and even carried to the New World as late as the middle of the sixteenth century, as

Mapuche borrowings show. They discriminate *boka bien* from *vinu vela vengar*, and *barva bever* (MSp. *barba beber*). Such archaisms correspond with the language described by Nebrija in 1492, to which also belong words like *ansí ainda* (Sp. *todavía*) *arrivar* (MSp. *llegar*) *namorado konortar bevienda barragán*, etc.

In the course of their development the Jewish Spanish dialects have acquired very many peculiarities, of which we shall cite only a few which have a more general significance. They show, naturally, Judaisms. The most notable is *el Dio* for *Dios*. In the *Tragedia Josefina* (1535?) Miguel de Carvajal causes Joseph and the good characters to speak of *Dios*, but his brothers of *el Dio*. Religious motives caused the avoidance of *domingo* 'Lord's day' for the first day of the week, which is rendered prosaically by Ar. *al-aḥad* 'the first', as *alχad*. The synagogue and school contribute to the lexicon: *desmazalado* 'ill-starred' from *mazal* 'destiny' (Heb. *mazzal* 'wandering stars, planets, signs of the zodiac'), which Cervantes also used as an equivalent of *malhadado*; *malsín* 'calumniator', which Christian Spaniards used from the thirteenth century in the sense of 'mischief-maker'; *mišelikar* 'to sneak, tell tales in school, denounce', cf. Ptg. *mexericar* 'to cause strife, meddle'. The relation of these words is not certain, and the etymon may be Lat. MISCERE or Heb. *m'ṣîrâh* 'denunciation' (Yiddish *mesirá*). Care is taken to avoid inauspicious or unseemly terms by means of euphemisms, such as *blanco* 'coal' to avoid the inauspicious word 'black'; and imprecations, for the same reason, take the form of ironical blessings. Hebrew terms are used to denote moral qualities, either as more exact or more affecting than Spanish: *anáv* 'humble', *χénef* 'flatterer', *la χenoza* 'the gracious woman', *un biento* or *un gabayí* 'a proud man'. The names of men are strictly biblical; those of women are Spanish and denote gracious qualities: *Firmoza Estreya Vida Señora Palomba Grasia*. Spanish also are the surnames (*alkuñas*): as *Alkalay Kabilyo Kalderón Montiya Kavesón Perera Maestro Pinto*. Surrounding races receive cant names, such as 'Philistines' or 'Amalekites', expressive of different degrees of aversion.

The colloquial has continued to lose ground. As the language of townsmen it has been deprived of the greater part of its nature-vocabulary, for which it borrows from neighbours as circumstances demand. The bilingualism of the Jew causes these borrowings to be very numerous, and to result in crossings which are extremely complicated, while the lexicon differs between one place and the next. Thus the dragon-fly (Sp. *libélula*) is *kabayiku* among Bulgarian Jews because of the native *konče* possibly aided by the Rumanian *calul dracului* 'dragon's horse', and in Brusa the weasel (*comadreja*) is *nobiizika* 'the bride' so as to render either Turkish *gelingik* or MGk. νυμφίτσα (in Bulgaria it is called *patrona de kaza*). The precise source of a word cannot always be determined amid so many currents of borrowing: *triandáfila* 'rose' may be due to MGk. τριαντάφυλλο alone, or also indebted to Rum. *trandafir*. The word *meldar* has replaced the Sp. *leer* 'read', possibly owing to Gk. μελετᾶν 'to care for, meditate', as the manner of reading more suited to sacred texts. The word is put in the mouth of the Rabbi in the fifteenth-century *Danza de la Muerte*.

On the Adriatic coast the interests of Venice have spread a number of Italian terms among the Jews of Bosnia, and French has had a growing influence because of its international value in the Levant. The schools instituted by the Alliance Israélite have proved to be centres for the propagation of French, and the proportionate impoverishment of the Spanish element. More recently the exasperated nationalism that has been left as a dire legacy by the War has shown hostility to this minority speech. It was recognized by the Turks as a language of their empire, and the Jews as one of the peoples among many; but the succession states recognize only their own nationality and their official languages, which they decree must be the sole languages of instruction. Thus the minorities are overthrown through their children.

See the general treatment by M. L. Wagner, *Caracteres generales del judeo-español de Oriente* (Madrid, 1930). Texts in C. M. Crews, *Recherches sur le Judéo-Espagnol* (Paris, 1935).

PHONETIC DEVELOPMENT IN
THE GOLDEN AGE

Antonio de Nebrija's *Gramática de la Lengua Castellana* (1492) sums up the language at a moment of relative stability, when it had run through the gamut of its medieval changes and had not yet entered upon the important transformations effected by the sixteenth and seventeenth centuries. The date is also the point of departure of the Jewish Spanish dialects as still spoken in Salonika, Skoplje, Oran and Tangiers, which have preserved for us, in large measure, the linguistic conditions of medieval Spain. These dialects have not shared either in the ennoblement of the vocabulary and style or in the phonetic changes which were brought about by the intense life of the Spanish Golden Age. One of these changes we have already had cause to discuss. In Nebrija's *Gramática* and *Orthographia* (1517) Lat. F has finally given way to Cast. *h* in standard Spanish; it is 'la boz que comunmente succedio ala *f* latina', as well as serving in two other cases as a conventional sign. He recognizes in this *h* a guttural of the nature of Ar. Hebr. *h*, in the phrase 'nos otros la pronunciamos hiriendo en la garganta'. But while Nebrija, an Andaluz writing at Salamanca in León, aspirated his *h*, there was already a strong impetus towards its disuse in Old Castile; and this silencing invades the standard language during the course of the century, until it becomes universal about 1580. *H* prevents liaison in the verses of Fray Luis de León (Salamanca, *c.* 1578), Alonso de Ercilla (Toledo, *c.* 1578) and Herrera (Sevilla, 1582), and the latter is careful to indicate the pronunciation by his spelling; but it has rarely this effect in the poetry of Lope de Vega (Madrid, 1585 ff.).

The medieval language distinguished two values of *b d g*, a fricative and an occlusive. The fricative arose from Lat. B D G, the occlusive from Lat. P T K. An orthographic distinction was set up only in the first case, where *v* (or *u*) offered a convenient means of discriminating the two values. They were related to each other intimately, as they are in contemporary Spanish, namely, that the fricative became occlusive in absolute initial positions or after a nasal. Thus VIVERE gives *bivir*, CAPRA *cabra*, DEBET *deve*. During the course of the sixteenth century these sounds fall into a single series, invariably occlusive in strong positions, and invariably fricative in weak positions. The letters *b* and *v* continue to be used, though no longer marking a phonetic distinction; and their incidence has been regulated by the Academy more or less on etymological principles. The medieval distinction of these sounds accompanied the *conquistadores* to the New World. In southern Chile, where the conquest commenced in the second half of the sixteenth century, the Araucanian Indians distinguished the [b] from P in NAPOS *nabos* 'turnips' and *estribo* 'stirrup' from the [ƀ] of CABALLU *caballo* 'horse' and FABAS *habas* 'beans' by employing different signs: *napur irtipu* but *cahuallu* (also modern Nahuatl) *aghuas*. In that language there are only voiceless occlusives and voiced fricatives, so that the Spanish distinction between the occlusive and the fricative values becomes in Mapuche a distinction between the voiceless and the voiced. The Araucanian borrowings do not indicate the parallel distinctions for *d g*. From the fricative stage, both these sounds tended to disappear in weak positions: TEPIDU *tibio* 'warm', AUDIRE *oír* 'hear', LEGALE *leal* 'loyal'. In the fifteenth century the *d* < T in the second person plural of verbs also was attacked. As early as the third quarter of the fourteenth century the ending *-edes* had given *-ées* and *-és*, and *sodes* had given *soes*. In the fifteenth century *amáis amaes amás*, *soes sois sos*, *queréis querés*, *decís* were firmly established against the *amades sodes queredes decides* of the thirteenth. The *-d-* persisted, however, when the accent did not fall on the vowel immediately preceding, so that Cervantes, Lope de Vega, Tirso de Molina and Quevedo prefer to write *amábades haríades amásedes*. Villegas (1618) ignores this *d* also, and examples of its loss have been found as early as 1555. In the imperative -ATE -ETE -ITE, *-ade -ede -ide* ceased to offer intervocalic *d* through the early loss of final *e*, so that *d* remains in *amad quered decid*, and only disappears when this *d* becomes intervocal in *amaos* (for *amad-os*), etc.

In the modern vernaculars all intervocal *d g* are threatened with elimination, and standard Spanish has virtually accepted the innovation in the case of the group *-ado*. In such words as *prado lado amado hallado* the pronunciation [aɗo] is emphatic and rhetorical and [ao aʋ] is normal in conversation, while the standard [aᵈo], i.e. with a much relaxed fricative *d*, is of the nature of a compromise. Vulgarly *-ada -ido -ida* also lose their *d* (e.g. *ná* for *nada*) and also other inter-vocalic *d*'s disappear (e.g. *esnúo* for *desnudo*), while *g* is lost not only before *u* (*awa* for *agua*) but generally (*miaja* for *migaja*).

The medieval language was distinguished by its wealth of palatal and dental sibilants, which have been reduced in number and dispersed in space by the modern. As well as *ch*, the value of which has remained constant, medieval Spanish had *s -ss-* [ś] *-s-* [ź], *ç* [ŝ s] *z* [ẑ z], *x* [š] *j ǵ* [ĵ ž]: so *passar* [s] but *rosa casa* [z]; *çarça çebada* but *hazer*; *dixo* but *fijo hijo gente*. Two changes were carried out in the Golden Age; the first reduced these voiced and voiceless sibilants to the single order of voiceless sibilants [ś ŝ š]; the second change dispersed the voiceless sibilants [ŝ š] to the interdental and velar positions [θ χ]. A good deal of information exists as to the nature of these sounds at varying dates in the sixteenth and early seventeenth centuries—sufficient to locate the second movement in the second or third decade of the latter—but the testimony of our authors is complicated by their want of precise phonetic symbols and doubtless also by the circumstance that for a considerable time both sets of values must have run concurrently in different parts of Spain or with different classes of speakers. The evidence of archaizing modern dialects is also relevant here (Énguera, Malpartida de Plasencia, Bragança in Portugal, Jewish Spanish, American-Indian borrowings), but they, too, show evolution from the medieval position.

The medieval values of these letters may be inferred to

some extent from their etyma. When these are Latin they
indicate a probable line of development from the Latin to
the modern Spanish sound; when they are French, Germanic
or Arabic they allow of comparison with the phonetic systems
of other languages. Thus *s ss* were cacuminal, i.e. were produced (as in modern standard Spanish, but not as in Andalusian) by raising the tip of the tongue to the alveoli [ś ź].
Arabic authors transcribing Spanish place-names recognize
in this [ś] the equivalent not of their *sîn* or *ṣâd* but of *šîn* [š],
which is articulated just slightly further back in the palate
than [ś]: *Išbilîya Al-Ašbûna Šaqunda* for *Sevilla Lisboa Secunda*.
So, thanks to Arabic mediation, SAPONE gives *xabón* 'soap'.
A distinction between [ś ź] and [s z] is still maintained in the
Portuguese of Bragança. Nahuatl borrowed Sp. *señora* as
xenola, and Mapuche has *chumpiru* Sp. *sombrero*. The cacuminal
pronunciation of *s* (and of *z* where this persists) is found in
the whole tract from northern Portugal to Catalonia. In
southern Portuguese (including the standard language of
Lisbon), extreme southern Spanish, Jewish Spanish and most
of Spanish America the cacuminal has come to coincide with
the dorsoalveolar [s], which is current in French and English.
As for the distinction between the voiced and the voiceless
sound, Nebrija distinguishes *s* from *ss* between vowels in the
same way as *r* from *rr*, and recommends 'si suenan apretadas
doblar se han en medio de la palabra'. Jewish Spanish
discriminates *pasar gɥesu asar* from *Roza Firmoza mozotrus* (Sp.
nosotros) *kaza*, using *zayin* for the latter in Hebrew transcriptions. But only one *s* travelled to the New World on the
testimony of the Mapuche borrowings: *curtisia coltesia* (*cortesía*
'a hat (wherewith one shows courtesy)'), *casun* (*hacer caso* 'pay
attention'). Juan de Valdés in 1535 offers only arbitrary
rules for writing *s* and *ss*, as that he prefers *ss* in the endings
-íssimo -esso -essa, but he adds 'generalmente pongo dos eses
quando la pronunciación ha de ser espessa, y donde no lo
es pongo una sola'. To the middle of the century *-s-* and
-ss- did not rhyme together, and in 1582 the unvoicing of
the *-s-* is explicitly noted. Herrera (1582) writes *-ss-* between

vowels, whatever its origin, with the exceptions only of *peso* and *-oso*.

It is more difficult to ascertain the medieval pronunciation of *ç z*. In modern standard Spanish they have the value [θ], and in the Extremeñan dialect of Malpartida de Plasencia they are [θ ð]: *crecel* [kreθél] *jadel* [haðél] for *crecer hacer*. In Andalusia, among the Spanish Jews, in most of Spanish America, and in Portuguese and Catalan they have coincided with dorsoalveolar *s* (and *z*, where the voiced sound exists). The Latin *ċ* (before *e i*) was pronounced [k] and must have evolved to the modern Sp. [θ] along the line

	Velar	Prevelar	Palatal	Dental	Interdental
Occlusive	[k]........[c]				
Affricate		........[ĉ]........	[ŝ]........	[θ̂]?	
Fricative				[s]........	[θ]

An affricate interdental is not a stable sound, but may be supposed as the source of the Spanish interdental fricative, so as to connect the latter rather with [ŝ] than with [s]. Latin ᴛɪ also gives *ç z* (according to circumstances), and indicates a pronunciation analogous to [t], i.e. [ŝ]. In Aragonese *-ç* corresponds to Cat. *-ts* in the second person plural of verbs: *cantaç* OCat. *cantats* MCat. *canteu*. In Mozarabic Lat. sᴛ gave *ç*: *Çaragoça* Ar. *Saraqusṭa* CAESARAUGUSTA *Écija* ɪsᴛɪɢɪ, doubtless by metathesis. On the other hand *ç* corresponds to Ar. *sîn* and *ṣâd*, i.e. to [s]: *açucar* Ar. *as-sukr* 'sugar', *çaga* Ar. *sâka* 'rear', *açalá* Ar. *as-ṣalâ* 'prayer'; and *z* is the regular equivalent of Ar. *z*. Thus it would appear that *ç z* had the affricate values [ŝ ẑ] and also, whether regionally or in weak positions, the fricative values [s z]. In either case the consonants were dental, as they were not recognized as akin to the Arabic interdental *thâ*.

Between Nebrija (1492) and Minsheu (1623) another alphabet is frequently used to fix the Spanish pronunciation, viz. the Italian. We have also the verbal definitions of foreign grammarians, and correspondences with English and German. Nebrija does not define *z*, but considers *ç* 'propria de los judíos e moros', and equivalent to Heb. *samekh* [s] or to *samekh* and *tzade* [s ŝ]. Juan de Valdés (1535), writing in Italy, says that *ç* has the value of *z* (i.e. of Italian *z* [ŝ]). The Italian equation is made by Christóval de las Casas (1570), Juan de Miranda (1595), Richard Percyuall (1591, who also cited Hebrew *tzade*) and Doergank (1614); and Minsheu (1617) gives the value *ts*. Don Luis de Ávila y Zúñiga gives some German transcriptions: *Landshut* > *Lançuet*, *Zwickau* > *Çuibica*, *Unser Vater* > *Uncerfater* (*ns* giving *nts*), but also *Schäfermesser* > *Xefermecer* (where *ç* = *ss*). Oudin (1610) equates the sound with French *ç s*, Doergank (Cologne, 1614) with *ss*, Lewis Owen (1605) with *s*. It is probable that these correspond with a tenser sound than simple voiceless [s], but they do indicate the fricative value. In 1623 John Minsheu transliterates *ths*: '*çaraguelles*...*çoçobra*...*çufre*: pronounce *thsaraguelles, thsosobra, thsufre*'. This indicates a sound intermediate between the medieval dental and the modern interdental, perhaps pronounced immediately behind the tips of the teeth. *Z* resembled *ç*, save insomuch as it was voiced. The unvoicing of *z* is announced by Antonio de Torquemada (before 1574), who says of *ç z* that 'muchas personas no saben diferenciarlas', and by Miguel Sebastián (1619): 'la consonante *zeta* componen unos de las *t* y *s*, los más de las *d* y *s*; pronúnciase en el mesmo lugar que la *ç* algo más blando'. Nicolás Dávila (1631) still distinguishes the voiced from the voiceless sound. By an orthographic custom the letter *z* only was used at the end of a syllable or of a word. In the latter case, medieval Castilian required that it should be voiceless; in the former it was unvoiced before voiceless consonants, and voiced before voiced, by a principle of assimilation that still operates in the three Peninsular languages. Thus there were many cases in which *z* must have represented the voiceless consonant, as *rafez mezquino alcanz estonz pez Badajoz*. Initially, before a voiced consonant, or between vowels *z* was a voiced sibilant, which began to be unvoiced in the last quarter of the sixteenth century, and at the close of the first third of the seventeenth century was voiced only in the speech of a minority. Meanwhile both ç and z had moved forward in the mouth until from post-dental they had become almost interdental in the Castiles by 1623. It is possible that Minsheu's *ts* (1617) is due to copying from some older grammarian; and it is also possible that his *ths* may represent an affricate (or apparently compound) sound. If so, this affricate cannot long have survived.

The third pair of sibilants (*x* and *j* or *ǵ*) were palatal in medieval Spanish. The value of *x* was [š], as it has remained in Portuguese, Galician, Asturian, Aragonese and Catalan, and in the Spanish system of transcription from the Arabic. The value of *j* is open to more doubt. Its descent from Lat. J- Ǵ-, Ar. *jîm* and initial *yâ*, OFr. Prov. *j ǵ*, points to an affricate [ĵ], being the voiced consonant corresponding to voiceless *ch* [ĉ]. In weak positions, however, Ar. *jîm* may have been pronounced as a fricative [ž], and the fricative is indicated by the evolution of Lat. ʟɪ̣ c'ʟ g'ʟ through *i y* [j] to [ž]. Nebrija (1492) says the sound is peculiar to Spanish and Arabic, and not to be found in Hebrew, Greek or Latin; but Valdés holds it equivalent to Italian *gi* (1535). Testimony to the same effect is given throughout the century, while others identify the sound also with Fr. *j* which had been [ž] since the thirteenth century. In Portuguese, Catalan and Jewish Spanish the value of this pair of consonants is [š ž]. Evidence of the unvoicing of *j* occurs only towards the close of the century, as in Percyuall (1591), who indicates Andalusia as the conservative area using *zh*. Minsheu (1623) deems the sound equivalent to Lat. *gero* It. *giorno* Eng. *Geoffrey Giles* Fr. *gisant* and *sh* (*jarro* 'a pot', *sharro*) and 'in Seville and thereabout they pronounce it not so much in the teeth, but more in the throat as *cshardin csharro ozho*'. Nevertheless the unvoicing had commenced earlier in the sixteenth century, for only [š] passed to the New World in the mid-century: Nahuatl *xalo* < *jarro*, Mapuche *charu* (*kazu* is a later borrowing), Map. *ovicha ovisa ovida* < *oveja*. This stage is found in modern Asturian dialects: *xente* for *gente*. The further passage of the palatal [š] to the velar [χ] is not met with in Jewish Spanish dialects, which were

severed from the home country, but it is universal in the
Spanish of America, doubtless thanks to fresh waves of immigration. This [χ] has no equivalent in Mapuche, which
marks the velar element and ignores the fricative by using *k*
in later loan-words: *Koan < Juan*. A celebrated word launched
on Europe in 1605, *Quixote*, was accepted by Frenchmen and
Italians as including the palatal [š]: *Quichotte, Quisciotto*, but
Minsheu indicates the velar [χ] as emanating from Seville in
1623. It would appear that the early years of the seventeenth
century had witnessed a gradual retraction of the tongue
and that we have had reported to us only the end of the
process.

Consult J. D. M. Ford, *The Old Spanish Sibilants* (Harvard, 1900) and
A. M. Espinosa, *Arcaísmos dialectales* (Madrid, 1935).

THE ENNOBLEMENT OF THE LANGUAGE: LATIN INFLUENCE

Under the influence of humanism and speaking to Italian
hearers Juan de Valdés remarked that 'all men are obliged
to *illustrate and enrich* the language that is native to us and
which we imbibe at our mothers' breasts'. The sentiment
is frequently repeated by his contemporaries, who had taken
up the Italian demand for a *volgare illustre*, fit for the expression of lofty thoughts. A controversy arose, indeed, as to the
respective merits of the principal civilized tongues, but the
standard of measurement and the means of improvement
were admittedly one: the Latin language which was the
second tongue of every educated man. In this spirit Camões
says that Portuguese is virtually identical with Latin: *com
pouca corrupção é a latina*. The Latin tongue was one acquired
by art and by books, but the vernacular by common use in
speech. This circumstance made it difficult for so enlightened
a person as Queen Isabel and for Juan de Valdés to understand the need for a Castilian grammar as composed by
Nebrija, which was, as the author avers, an *Art* of Castilian.
Given these ideas, it was inevitable that the Castilian grammar should be stretched on the bed of the existing Latin

text-books, 'contraponiendo línea por línea el romance al latín', revealing in some cases the sufficiency of the vernacular, in others its want of the resources of Latin. Poets and stylists also, like Juan de Mena (in the fifteenth century) and Herrera (in the sixteenth), comparing the lexical and syntactical resources of the two languages, became aware of defects in the vernacular which could be remedied by drawing on the learned tongue for new words and moulds of speech. It was the object of those who would 'ennoble and illustrate' their native tongue to acquire for it the fullness and freedom of Latin, in so far as the genius of the vernacular permitted. The *caveat* was differently interpreted by different innovators, and even by different ages. A prudent policy of neologism was followed by Alfonso X in the thirteenth century, by the humanists of the sixteenth, and by the rationalists of the eighteenth century; bold and striking innovations were affected by the aureate poets of Juan de Mena's school, by the gongorists, and by the 'modernists' of our own day. Both classes of writers tended to add more to the written than to the spoken wealth of the language; but a detritus of their innovations sank into the bed of the vernacular, and many others remained available for the special uses of poetry and rhetoric.

The ennoblement of Romance, as a programme, is explicitly stated by the humanists, and in them has already an evidently Italianate appearance; but as a cultural necessity it became evident with the beginnings of the literature. The works of Alfonso X involved translation from the Latin of highly rhetorical writers, such as Lucan and Geoffrey of Monmouth, which threw into high relief the different resources of the languages. As an example we may cite the rendering of Lucan's *Pharsalia*, iv, 373 ff., in the *Primera Crónica General*, cap. 100:

> O prodiga rerum
> luxuries, nunquam parvo contenta paratu,
> et quæsitorum terra pelagoque ciborum
> ambitiosa fames, et lautæ gloria mensæ. . . .

O desmesura gastadora de las cosas, et que en comer not
abondas de pocas uiandas; e tu, fambre glotona, que not
cumple lo que puedes fallar por mar et por tierra; et tu
mesa deliciosa, llena de quantas cosas el comedor demanda...,

in which we note the avoidance of *pródigo, lujuria* or *lujo,
piélago, ambicioso, gloria*, which the language now possesses;
and similarly in *Ph.* iii, 297 *felix* (MSp. *feliz*) is rendered
cautiously as *cuemo princep bienandant*. These and other passages
could be cited to show how scrupulously the founder of
Spanish prose adhered to the usages established in the vernacular; but none the less, he was of necessity an innovator.
He could not but give names to things for which the vernacular had no name: '*tirano* quiere decir *señor cruel*', '*estudio*
es ayuntamiento de maestros e escolares', '*zodiaco*, que quiere
tanto decir en griego cuemo lengua que esta presto pora dar
alma a cada cosa que convenga et que seia apareiada para
rescebirla'. These words were already familiar in the Latin
of the schools, and were ripe for acceptance in the vernacular,
provided they were given a suitable form. A table of phonetic
equivalences facilitated this transfer of words.

The need for vernacular verisimilitude was felt more
strongly in the earlier period, and progressively fewer precautions had to be taken in redressing latinisms, until in our
day it is sufficient to see that the word ends in a Romance
fashion, and does not commence with an 'impure' *s;* e.g.
-ATU= -*ado*, -ABILE= -*able*, -ITATE= -*idad*, SCEPTICU= *escéptico*,
SPIRITU = *espíritu*, etc. In the thirteenth century various additional precautions were taken by neologizers. The unaccented
vowels were limited to the *a e o* of Romance: *princepe monesterio
presyon heñir* < FINGERE. Intervocalic consonants were voiced:
paladino PALATINU. Terminations were remodelled: -ICULU:
-*ejo* :: ARTICULU: *artejo*. The group -CT- was modified no
longer in a palatal but in a velar sense: ACTU *auto*, TRACTU
trauto. Notable in this era is the verbal suffix -*iguar* -IFICARE:
santiguar averiguar. In some cases these words were brought
closer to the Latin in accordance with the taste of later
neologizers: *príncipe prisión homicidio* (for *omezillo*) *verificar*. In

other instances the opportunity was presented for the fabrication of doublets, leaving the more concrete sense to the older word: *artejo* 'knuckle' *artículo* 'article', *santiguar* 'to bless or cross oneself' *santificar* 'to hallow', *heñir* 'to knead' *fingir* 'to pretend', *auto* 'a playlet, performance, writ' *acto* 'an act, act of a play', etc. Particularly notable was the influence of the Church, where the habitual public use of the two languages involved the perpetual comparison of certain important terms. *Auto* is within this category by virtue of the medieval performance of plays in churches (the strictly vernacular form should have been *echo). So SAECULU has not given *sejo but *sieglo siglo*, DIABOLU not *jablo but *diablo*, FIDE *fe* and FESTA *fiesta* retain their *f* which is lost in the exclamation *a la he* 'i'faith' and the lay term INFESTU *enhiesto* 'steep'. It was the Church which retained the use of the nominative DEUS *Dios*, for which Spanish Jews preferred the normal accusative *El Dio*; and to the Church must be ascribed *cruz mártir vírgen sacerdote espíritu*, etc. The administration was responsible for a lesser share of latinisms, such as *treudo* (later *tributo*) *justicia censo precio homicidio notario*, as well as for maintaining archaic forms in place-names like *Córdoba Mérida Segovia* (not *Segueva) *Cértigos Gállego*.

The fifteenth century witnessed a considerable influx of new latinisms. The *Divina Commedia* of Dante and the Latin works of Boccaccio and Petrarca, together with numerous translations from Classical authors either directly or through the French, created a demand for a type of Spanish not merely more worthy of its Latin source, but even more on a par with the *illustre volgare* of Italy. At the same time, there was still wanting the sense of measure and simplicity of the true humanists. The experiments conducted by the Marquis of Santillana, Villena, Juan de Mena and their well-wishers are characterized by more boldness than discretion, and much that they have proposed has been rejected, e.g. Villena's *presuposición* 'preamble'. The diction of this age resembles the 'aureate' style of Lydgate in its striving after an artificial dignity, together with vernacular lapses. The suffixes -*al* and -*ífico* rise into favour at this time: *humanal divinal mundanal poetal marçial triunfal magnífico*. The trisyllabic ending is used for its dignity, contrary to Hispanic tradition: *gállico itálico délphico ínclito*; and a free use is made of -*ción*: *destruyçión restituyçión defunçión*. Santillana, the most prudent of the group, apologizes for his novelties by attaching the more familiar term: '*familiar* e servidor', 'andan e *concurren*', 'cenizas e *defunçiones*', *difícil inquisiçión* e trabajosa pesquisa', 'mensajero o *embaxador*', and even '*sçiençia de poesía* e gaya sçiençia'. By recurring to the Latin he creates doublets; e.g. beside CIBU *cebo* 'fodder', he proposes '*çibo* del alma', which the language has not admitted. His principal novelty of syntax is his attempt to hold back the verb to the close of the sentence. In Juan de Mena there is a systematic attempt to acquire all the resources of Latin style by a single effort. He was so far successful that Nebrija was able to draw from him Spanish examples of most of the traditional figures of speech: including the reprehensible ones, like the caco-syntheton *A la moderna bolviendo me rueda* for *bolviendo me a la rueda moderna*. For this measure of success in capturing Latin resources, Nebrija deems that Mena deserves the title of '*the* poet' among Castilians, as Vergil among the Romans. In vocabulary his intemperate neologisms stand out in sharp contrast with the humble medieval vernacular with which they are mixed, so that even those which have later been adopted by the language appear strange in the *Laberinto*: for instance

> Toda la otra vezina *planura*
> estaua çercada de *nítido* muro,
> assi *trasparente*, *clarífico*, puro,
> que mármol de Paro pareçe en *albura*;
> tanto que el *viso* de la criatura,
> por la *diafana claror* de los cantos,
> pudiera traer *objetos* atantos
> quantos çelaua so sí la *clausura*.

In this period there was a considerable reduction in the gap between the Latin and the Spanish forms. Unaccented *i* and *u*

appear, and even the 'impure' *s* (*spiritu sçiençia*); unvoiced
consonants remain between vowels; trisyllabic endings are
encouraged. Lat. -GN- gives *-n-* in DIGNU *dino*, x gives *s* in
esaminar, and Lat. -PT- -CT- give *-t-* in *cativo objeto*; which are
equivalences allowed during the whole Golden Age and not
questioned until the establishment of the Academy. In some
cases this has led to duplicates or to the retention of the older
spelling for a more serviceable form: *auto acto fruto fructífero
luto luctuoso*.

The sixteenth century—an age of great physical and
mental activity for Spain—subjected the language to many
varying stresses. The connection with Italy was drawn close
by the conquests of the Great Captain in Naples and by the
international policy of Charles V. Castile thus entered on
a relationship which had, in the Middle Ages, been peculiar
to Aragón. The Italian literature of Ariosto, Bembo, Tasso,
Castiglione and Machiavelli, with its layman's outlook and
sense of decorum, superseded as a model the medievalism
of the *trecento*. The Italian humanists and Erasmus popularized in Spain the notion of Nature's perfection, and of
popular speech, proverbs, etc., as the spontaneous products
of Nature; while at the same time they established a new
canon of graceful perfection in the use of Latin. The character
of the 'gentleman' or *cortesano*, involving an apparently
effortless perfection in all the arts of life, prescribed the ideal
simplex munditiis for language also, while elaborating forms
of courteous address and intercourse to make up the so-called
estilo cortesano. A powerful thrust towards the raciest and
most widely intelligible terms and syntax was delivered by
the prose of Sta. Teresa and the verse of S. Juan de la Cruz,
who eschewed all forms of affectation as conducive to false-
hood and sin. On the other hand, there was a more conscious
determination to raise Spanish to an intellectual rank com-
mensurate with its vast power in the world, to challenge the
supremacy of Italian in art, and to acquire from Latin whatever additional resources the language required. An earnest
attention to style in Herrera becomes in the age of Góngora

an obsession with style, and leads to extravagances in the Baroque era curiously similar to those of Juan de Mena.

Nebrija's *Gramática* (1492) sums up the medieval achievement as a basis for further advance. He explicitly asserts the connection between language and empire. In the *Celestina* (?1499) we see a racy language heard in the streets jostling with the new courtly and humanistic manner of the protagonists. But the thrilling events of the first third of the century did not allow of sophistication, and the numerous reports from the New World are normally colloquial in their diction. In the poems of Garcilaso de la Vega (published in 1543), in Boscán's *Cortesano* (1534) and in Juan de Valdés' *Diálogo de la Lengua* (1535) we find the first manner of this century. They eschew invention; and propose only to select out of the existing language the noblest and sincerest expressions. They are not afraid of colloquialisms (e.g. *ganar por la mano* 'to anticipate or get the better of anyone'); and Valdés makes a cult of proverbs, which he uses as the standard of reference for purism. Garcilaso praises Boscán in that he 'avoided affectation without falling into harshness; his style is pure and employs courtly terms (*términos muy cortesanos*) allowed by good judges, neither novel nor apparently unused by the people'. In the same spirit, Valdés applies the criterion of his Toledan upbringing to prefer *enemistad* to *omezillo*, *subir* to *puyar*, un *cotal* to *quillotro*, *fácil* to *raez* or *rece*, *triste* to *lóbrego* (which has since been reintroduced as peculiarly suited to poetry); and at the same time he censures as Andalusian many of the idioms offered by Nebrija. Yet a cautious policy of innovation was made necessary by the existence of new ideas. Valdés recommends the adoption of *paradoja tiranizar idiota ortografía ambición e(x)cepción objeto decoro* and others; and while Nebrija knows of no morphological superlative, Garcilaso (1536) has 'ilustre y *hermosísima* María'. Luis de León (1583) is of this way of thinking, adding that purity of language consists in a sense of rhythm, weight and proportion.

The attempt of the greatest of the mystics to avoid all

affectation, including that measure of artifice which is implied by the humanistic scrutiny of words, transferred the emphasis on the language to its traditional content. Colloquialisms like *naide* for *nadie*, *anque* for *aunque*, *relisión* for *religión*, appear in Santa Teresa, who also (a feminine trait) makes full use of the affective diminutives offered by Spanish, allows the verb a predominant rôle in the sentence, and practises ellipsis with the freedom of actual speech. The need for precise psychological distinctions in matters of religious experience causes her to enrich the language with subtle distinctions, as between *contento* and *gusto*, often in the form of oxymora: *gozosa pena*, *borrachez divina*, etc. The prestige acquired by her writings in the raciest Castilian may have helped to spread the phonetic preferences of Castilian, despite the opposition of the earlier Toledan writers, notably in the matter of silencing the *h*.

Meanwhile, in the south, at Sevilla, Fernando de Herrera adopted a more formal attitude to the language. That he proposed to repeat in Spain the literary triumphs of Italy made his content less important to him than his manner. The thought belonged to the Petrarchan tradition, but the style had still to be created in Spain. His policy was therefore to discover in Latin or Italian such additional words and forms as Spanish could be induced to absorb; it was the policy of a neologizer, limited by a wish for actual rather than spectacular success. The lyrics of Garcilaso gave him the highest measure of achievement in artistic Castilian, and his famous *Comento* was planned to display Garcilaso's merits, correct some blemishes, and point out where further ennoblement was possible. *Tamaño* 'so great', for instance, he considers vulgar, though it has survived his criticism. He favours new adjectives in *-oso*, the doubling of epithets, and their careful choice. In his latinisms he keeps in mind those which have already found a lodgment in Italian. The result is a language quite removed from the colloquial, which it systematically eschews, discreetly latinized, rich in adjectives and nouns of quality, which have mostly been adopted for poetical rather than for general use. Such are those complained of by Barahona de Soto:

Esplendores, celajes, rigoroso,
selvaje, llama, líquido, candores,
vagueza, faz, purpúrea, Cintia, ardores,
otra vez esplendores, caluroso,

though the complaint is, in some cases, against the undue frequency of a common word.

In Herrera the equilibrium between Latin and Spanish tilts slightly towards Latin. The great writers who cultivated the drama and the novel in Madrid—Cervantes, Lope de Vega, Tirso de Molina, Alarcón—drew inspiration from all sides, being as racy as Castile and as erudite as the Sevillan according to their mood and subject. Appealing to the widest possible public, they demanded a language not ignoble, but also not liable to be misunderstood. But to Góngora, at Córdoba, popular appeal was antipathetic. He stressed the importance of art, and of artifice in language, and he took up more defiantly the experiments of Herrera, wresting from Latin its last secrets. Thus arose the *culta latiniparla* which Quevedo burlesqued, but could not avoid practising. New vocables arose like (according to Quevedo)

Fulgores, arrogar, joven, presiente,
candor, construye, métrica harmonía;

which recall those attributed to Herrera, and have generally been adopted at least by the language of poetry. More novel was the attempt to construe clauses in the Latin manner. Sufficient resources of declension and conjugation remained in Spanish to·allow the adjective to be separated from the noun without ambiguity to the eye, though perplexing for the ear, and the verb to be removed from its subject by intervening parentheses, subordinate clauses and absolute constructions. There is no difficulty in recognizing the groups *pasos perdidos, peregrino errante, cuantos versos* in

Pasos de un peregrino son errante
cuantos me dictó versos dulce musa:
en soledad confusa
perdidos unos, otros inspirados,

though the association of *versos inspirados* is perhaps less evident. The reader's suspension of mind as he looks forward or backward for the reference of the words introduces into Spanish verse a more complex music than that of Garcilaso or Lope de Vega. Thirdly, the new style sought to convert the ordinary stuff of poetry into metaphor, by the systematic use of terms in their transferred senses, while achieving extraordinary effects by unusually happy metaphors or similes. The Duke of Béjar's hunting spears are 'spruce walls with diamond battlements', i.e. wooden shafts tipped with steel. Later the same spear is called 'the ash'. In this way a vocabulary of transposed terms arises which afflicts the prose and poetry of the seventeenth century, subordinating the sense, where there is any, to a perpetual juggle of dead metaphors. *Nieve* 'snow' and *plata* 'silver' signify not these things, but 'white'; *cristal* takes the place of *agua* 'water', *tálamo* that of *casamiento* and *matrimonio*, a blood-stained stream is *espumoso coral*, a bird is a 'feathered flower' or 'wingèd nosegay'.

The consequences for speech and style of the alternative æsthetic of the seventeenth century are not far different. Properly speaking the 'conceptist' should make it his business to squeeze out the utmost refinements of style by way of associating ideas and ordering the phrase, but leaving untouched the grammar and vocabulary. He aimed at *agudeza*, not *culteranismo*. He cultivated the 'conceit' which was, according to Gracián, a 'beautiful correlation between two cognizable extremes, expressed by an act of the understanding', and the latter he identified with 'the decorum of the words'. Novelty in the latter was reached through a certain amount of re-definition of words apparently familiar, by means of unusual contexts, antitheses, etymological precision and puns. This toying with language was by no means new, and had indeed marked the whole Golden Age. Lope de Vega, who is rarely gongoristic, is often a conceptist before the word arose; and Castiglione, no mean judge, deemed the court-lyrics of Garcilaso's youth too subtle for translation into Italian. What is new in Quevedo and Gracián is the insistence on the 'conceit', seeking in the warping of the ideas, or at least the language, a sole, or at least a main, literary virtue. Strange 'conceits' could not be carried out without the occasional use of strange language or figures, and thus the frontiers of gongorism and conceptism are blurred. Góngora, as a great wit, used many a 'conceit', and Quevedo's verse is scarcely less gongoristic than Calderón's. Between the two movements, the language appropriated once again all the figures and devices allowed by the textbooks of classical rhetoric—oxymoron, antithesis, meiosis, paronomasia, etc.—and suffered from cultural indigestion.

The eighteenth century worked off much of the surfeit, proclaiming the rights of reason and *buen gusto*. To this end the younger Moratín wrote his *Derrota de los pedantes* and Forner his *Exequias de la lengua castellana*. Simplicity, in the Horatian sense, was proclaimed the criterion of language; the style of Luis de León was revived so far as his descendants at Salamanca were capable; and a resolute resistance was offered to neologism. The new Latin formations which appeared at this time were generally in the debt of France, as those of the previous period had been in the debt of Italy. They are utilitarian, and tend to be abstractions, often with a cosmopolitan air: *el Ser Supremo* (as a serious rival to *Dios*), *infundamentabilidad incontestabilidad coacción radiación superficialidad*. The repression of fancy was excessive, and the language became infertile; but at least the eighteenth century came nearer than any other to endowing Spain with a prose style capable of all uses.

Romantic authors launched few interesting innovations into language, though their general attitude was favourable to novelty. Their immediate successors devoted themselves to stereotyping the epithet and enforcing binary rhythm. Words of international circulation found a lodgment in Spanish as elsewhere: *teléfono telégrafo cine radio cazatorpedero krausismo*, etc. But there was no policy of innovation until the closing years of last century, when the 'Modernist' writers (chiefly of American origin at first) sought for proof of genius in novelty and the exotic. Only a residue of their effort has any permanent significance for the language, and we are still too close to discriminate. The dactylic rhythm was again exalted, and trisyllabic endings were obtained by borrowing from Greek (real or imaginary), as in Darío's address to Verlaine:

Padre y maestro mágico *liróforo* celeste.

Latin served in

Ínclitas razas *ubérrimas*, sangre de Hispania fecunda,

though *ínclito* was not new, but only inserted in a novel rhythm. New doctrines and doctrinaires were recruited by the suffixes *-ismo -ista*, as *rubeniano rubenianismo rubendarismo modernista*. Typical terms are *psiquis biforme homérida panida dionisiaco áulico*. Insistence on shades of colour (as with the gongorists) and on musical terms are typical of this increment of the language. Native words also, fallen into desuetude or of rare or local occurrence, are revived, especially if they have some technical nuance, as in Azorín's

aquí están los *tundidores, perchadores, cargadores, arcadores perailes*; allá, en la otra, los *correcheros, guarnicioneros, boteros, chicarreros*.

At its best, the new manner implies a refusal to employ trite phrases, even at the risk of being bizarre, and it implies close attention to the music of the phrase. The language has become more cosmopolitan, but also richer, subtler, more athletic and more graceful.

Consult the article in *España* (Madrid, 1925), and R. Menéndez Pidal's 'El lenguaje del siglo XVI', *Cruz y Raya* (Madrid, 1933). Toro Gisbert's *Nuevos derroteros del idioma* (Paris, 1918) is polemical, but contains interesting *obiter dicta* on terms launched by various 'Modernists'.

VARIOUS CHANGES IN MORPHOLOGY, SYNTAX AND LOAN-WORDS AFTER 1140

(a) MEDIEVAL PERIOD

In the medieval period, as we have seen, the lines are marked out by the great prose compilations of Alfonso the Sage, the plenitude of Juan Ruiz, and the 'aureate' manner of Juan de Mena, who, with his contemporaries, shows both a striving towards a new humanism and the bankruptcy of medieval methods. Literature begins in the thirteenth century to be something written, and therefore something open to grammatical scrutiny as never before. Unrestricted spoken development treats each expression as a unit, and gives each such unit the form most convenient for speech. In this way the language of the *Poema de mio Cid* shows many syncretions of the types *con ellos' cojo* (*ellos se*), *coio' Salon aiuso* (*cojóse*), *cabadelant*, *hyáuengaluon*, *nimbla* (*ni me la*), etc., while admitting *nuef* beside *nueve*, *rees* as the plural of *rey*, etc. The language of the thirteenth century proceeded to iron out these incongruities, which are rather visual than phonetic. It restored the final -*e* to many words which ended in a consonant in the singular, using the analogy of the plural: so *cort cortes* gave *corte*, *noch noches* gave *noche*, and similarly *siete nueve* quite displaced *siet nuef*, and *rey ley* took plurals *reyes leyes*. Only a limited number of consonants were left as finals: *l r n s z x d*. The nett result of these modifications was to arrest a tendency which would have left Spanish an iambic language like French or Catalan rather than trochaic like Italian, by weakening final vowels. A particular case of colloquial syncretions was presented by the enclitic pronouns attached to verbs, which, having no stress accent of their own, are liable to be absorbed by the neighbouring word. The restoration of full forms to enclitic pronouns can be watched in the *Primera Crónica General*. The first and second persons were first restored from *m t* to *me te*, while the third still lingered as *l*. During the whole medieval period these pronouns were regarded as leaning on the preceding word, which was not necessarily a verb, as in *Cid*: *quandol vieron, muchol tengo por torpe*, but they are also strongly attracted by the verb; in Spanish of the Golden and Modern Periods these pronouns are regarded as supported by the verb only.

The Spanish noun is simple and stable with respect to number, but allows of alteration with regard to gender, which has no self-evident basis in ideas. In particular, there was room for an extension of the suffix *-a* where it was convenient to indicate sex, so that medieval *la señor la yffant* have come to be modern *la señora la infanta*. Medieval Spanish possessed (especially in Riojan) a pronominal nominative case exemplified in *qui elli otri nadi(e)*, which has since disappeared. But the chief area of liveliness was the verbal conjugation, towards the rationalization of which more effort has been expended in Spanish than in Italian or French. The number of irregular verbs was reduced, or they were passed into regular categories. Thus *exir* (pret. *ixe*) appears in the *Cid*, but not in Juan Ruiz who has preferred *salir*, and knows only the noun *exido* 'common land, land at the outgoing of a town' (MSp. *ejido*). The past participle was another point of attack, and the twelfth-century *Auto de los Reyes Magos*, in proposing *veído* from *ver*, has gone beyond even modern usage (*visto*, but *proveer proveído*). Very few 'strong' past participles survive, e.g. *dicho hecho visto puesto*. In the regular or 'weak' conjugations the *Cid* shows that the form of the participle in *-udo* (corresponding to verbs in *-er*) is already menaced by rival forms in *-ido*: *vençudo vençido metudo metido*. Juan Ruiz still has *entendudo sabudo*; but at the end of the fifteenth century Nebrija admits only *-ido* beside the *-ado* of verbs in *-ar*: *amado leído oído*. The termination *-udo* and the relics of former 'strong' participles have become adjectives: *velludo barbudo bienquisto provisto*. The preterite tense has shown more resistance. In 'weak' or regular verbs the terminations have a definite semantic value inasmuch as they represent the idea of past time which the stem alone no longer indicates, and only some minor analogical changes took place, as 2 Pl.

hablasteis from *hablastes* through the influence of *habláis habléis*. In the 'strong' verbs the preterite stem was preserved by familiarity, since only the most common verbs have been able to resist assimilation to regular conjugations. Characteristic of ballad syntax is a periphrastic preterite in *fué a*, as *tal respuesta le fué a dar* 'such was the reply he gave him', which may be compared with Cat. *vaig anar* 'I have gone, I went'. The form proved ephemeral.

Care was taken to restore some of the damage wrought to the conjugation by phonetic change. In such a series as *amo amas ama* and most of the verbal forms the presence of a vowel before the personal ending made *toviés toviesses toviés* and *pudier pudieres pudier* appear anomalous. In these cases the loss of final *-e* after *s r* remained normal in nouns and persisted during the fourteenth century for verbs; but at the close of the fifteenth Nebrija records only *amasse dixiere*, etc. He still has the apocopated *amardes leyerdes oirdes* in the second person of the plural, and S. Juan de la Cruz has *pastores los que fuerdes*. The loss of final *-e* is still notable in Juan Ruiz, not only in the two subjunctive tenses, but generally: *diz plaz yaz faz fiz mantién pud pus quier trax val*, etc. for which Nebrija has *tiene dize*, etc. On the other hand, final *-e* is frequent in the *Poema de mio Cid*, so that the conflict between phonetic tendency and the analogy of the paradigm lasted throughout the medieval period. The thirteenth century knew *fallare* (or *fallar*) and *fallaro* as 1 S. to *fallares fallar(e)*, etc. The former was due to Latin perfect subjunctive in -RIM, the latter to the future perfect indicative in -RO, and the two Latin tenses were identical in the rest of the persons. The ending *-ro* is unknown to Per Abbat who copied the *Poema de mio Cid* in 1307. Another set of anomalies existed in the imperfect indicative of second and third conjugation verbs which ran *tenía tenies tenie teniemos teniedes tenien*. The reason for this change of vowel is obscure, and it conflicts with the imperfect of the first conjugation which preserves the *a* throughout: *amava amavas amava*, etc. Even in the *Cid* alternative analogical forms appear: 3 S. *auya*, 3 Pl. *fazian*; on the other hand diplomas also record a 1 S. in *e*: *auie proponie*. In Juan Ruiz forms in *e* and *a* exist in evident conflict, but the former go out of polite usage during the fourteenth century, though they are still found as vulgarisms as late as in the sixteenth-century farces.

Broadly speaking, then, the activity of the medieval period with regard to the verbal paradigm was such as to reduce anomalies, and to leave to the Golden Age a simple and precise notation to indicate both person and tense. At the same time the verb was not stripped of any of its essential forms.

In the sphere of vocabulary no less activity is discernible. The steady enrichment of the idiom by fresh borrowings from its Latin source has already been discussed. Apart from Latin, the principal influence exerted on medieval Spanish is that of French. It was an epoch of undisputed French hegemony in Europe. Many words entered the language through being borne by pilgrims along the Pilgrims' Way to Compostela or by the minstrels who entertained the pilgrims. Cluniac monks reorganized conventual discipline; Norman crusaders and soldiers in the French and English service saw fighting in the Peninsula, and carried with them the seeds of innovations in chivalry, good society, organization, arts and industries, commerce and cookery. A mark of age in a loan-word of this class is the use of *j ǵ* to represent a French *j ǵ*: *jardín monje paje sergente*. The French aspirate *h* was to be encountered in Germanic words passed on by the French to Spain, and it resulted in Sp. *f* or *h*, and was also occasionally ignored: 'Tristram's harp' was the *farpa de don Tristán*, but also *arpa, fonta* Fr. *honte* Ger. *haunitha* 'shame', *una fardida lança* Fr. *hardie* 'a bold lance', the latter both to be found in the *Cid*. The pilgrims are specifically to be credited with the Galician *cizallas* 'clippers' and *baleo* 'mat', the occurrence of which in Compostela bears witness to the denser agglomeration of strangers in that shrine. The organization of the Church brought *fraile* (Provençal) *monje chantre* and (in Berceo) *enclín* 'bow' *baylía* 'subordinate office'. Chivalrous terms appear in the *Cid* and elsewhere as *batalla* 'line of battle' *coraje homenaje usaje mensaje mensajero* (compare the native *portero*) *ardiment doncel garzón linaje palafrén gañán*. According to Fernão Lopes it was the Earl of Cambridge's expedition to Portugal in 1381 which caused *avanguarda* and *retaguarda*, both gallicisms, to replace *delantero* and *zaga*. Organization and society employed the terms *chancillería sumiller ugier paje doncel dama*; literature introduced *troba trobar trobador* (of society verse-making) *balada son* 'tune' *jayán* 'monstrous fellow' Fr. *géant*. The industries and commerce adopted terms like *cofre chapitel chimenea jaula* (Fr. *geôle*) *cordel mercante bajel virar manjar anís*. Not all of these terms have survived: *fonta* has yielded to the more general term *vergüenza*; *fontaina sojornar maletía habillado*, current in the fifteenth century, have yielded to *fuente demorar enfermedad vestido*. Through French penetrated a few northern words connected with seafaring, of which the most important were the points of the compass: *norte sur este oeste*. The general directions are given by the Latin *septentrión mediodía oriente* or *levante occidente* or *poniente*.

One notes, in the last place, the circulation of some common particles in the medieval period which either perished with it or did not survive the Golden Age. Thus UBI gave *o*, which was the homonym of AUT *o*; and UNDE gave *onde* 'whence'. Poetry retains *do* (DE UBI), but prose has given *donde* (DE UNDE) the sense 'where', and created *adonde* 'whither' *de donde* 'whence'. *Otrosí* 'also' has yielded to *también*; *ca* to *que* and *porque*; *alguandre* 'somewhere' *otri* 'someone else' have disappeared for centuries; *cras* and *otro día* have yielded to *mañana* in the sense of 'morrow', and *mane* to *mañana* in the sense of 'morning'; while the attempts to use *om(n)e* as an indefinite pronoun like Fr. *on* and to develop the partitive (*dellos dezien* 'some of them said') have been checked. *Ansí* and *agora* linger into the Golden Age and then yield to *así ahora*; *tornar a hacer* 'to do again' yields to *volver a hacer*, *catar* 'look' to *mirar*, *cuidar* 'think' to *pensar*, etc.

(b) The Golden Age

The curiosity of foreigners, which Nebrija had anticipated, was attracted by the empire to the language. Exiled Jews, as at Bordeaux or Amsterdam, helped to satisfy this interest, and Spanish masterpieces were rendered into French by Des Essarts or into English by Mabbe and Shelton. Spanish did not attain the circulation of French or Italian, but it did become one of the languages in which an author might address the world, for which cause Melo employed it rather than Portuguese in his history of the Catalan rebellion. Shakespeare, who does not appear to have known Spanish, presents Italianate sketches of Spaniards in 'Don Adriano de Armado, a fantastical Spaniard', and the contrasted Don Pedro and Don John of *Much Ado about Nothing*. Spanish began to be taught as part of a gentleman's education, and conversation-grammars or 'arts' were composed, such as those of Percivall and Minsheu in England and Oudin in France, which have great importance as contemporary witnesses to Spanish phonetic changes. Under these circumstances Spain re-exported the names of American plants and animals and of the essential possessions and grades of Indian society, so that words like *canoe cacique barbecue quinine puma*, etc. have an international range. *Quixotry* is a tribute by English to the genius of Cervantes; *colonel* we pronounce with the *r* of Sp. *coronel* as a sort of witness to the efficiency of the Spanish infantry *tercios*; *picaro* and *picaroon* represent one aspect of Spanish life, at the opposite pole from *grandee*; *pundonor* is connected with the Spanish code of honour; *inquisition* and *inquisitor* are latinisms which received a new lease of life from Spain, connected with the *autos-da-fé* (the form is Portuguese, Sp. *de fe*). *Desenvoltura* 'ease and dignity of manner' gives It. *disinvoltura*, Sp. *desembuelto* gives Fr. *desinvolte*; Sp. *esforzado* 'brave' attaches that meaning to Castiglione's *sforzato* (It. 'violent'), Sp. *sosiego* 'calm deportment' becomes Filippo Sassetti's *sussiego*; Sp. *grandioso* (a derivative of OSp. *grandía* = MSp. *grandeza*) spreads, perhaps via Italy, to France, England and Germany. Some words express contemporary admiration for the dignity and gravity of the Spanish *caballero*; but more frequently the loan-words express contemporary (and especially French) fear or dislike, either by their low origin (*pícaro matamoros* Fr. *matamore* 'swashbuckler') or through semantic depreciation (*bravo* in the sense of 'bully', *bizarre* from 'gallant' to 'freakish').

The early part of the period marks a national preoccupation with behaviour, *cortesanía*. Much of the wit of Spanish plays turns on the inability of the boor and the lackey to appreciate courtly refinements of speech. Forms of address are important. Between men and women they take the form of a perpetual courtship; between man and man they consist of giving or exacting respect. It is doubtful whether courtesy or self-esteem is the more effective lever: the starveling squire in *Lazarillo de Tormes* lays down the terms in which he is to be addressed. When a tradesman used the formula *Mantenga Dios a vuestra merced* he retorted *Vos, don villano ruín, por qué no sois bien criado?* and explained to Lazarillo that superiors should be addressed *Beso las manos de vuestra merced* or *Bésoos, señor, las manos* (the latter only from a gentleman). The second personal pronoun suffers rapid changes in this period. The former era left *tú* and *vos*. *Vos*, the plural of dignity, was more formal, *tú* was intimate and also poetical. To change from *tú* to *vos* implied an access of formality, of stiffness, and therefore was suited to angry or insulting language: among the Spanish-Jews *vos* is an insult, but to a Spanish beggar *tú* is so informal as to convey a slight. In Spanish America these forms in *tú* and *vos* have developed into a state of confusion which will be described in the next chapter. Above them there developed new forms of courtesy involving an abstract substantive and the third person of the verb. Most of these were based on *vuestra merced*, abbreviated *v.m.*, which took such forms as *vuesarcé vuesasté ucé océ usted*. Of all these forms the modern period has selected *usted*, which, however, is simply a second personal pronoun, without a definite connotation of respect. It is not, in contemporary Spanish, a mark of courtesy. In the Cortes, for instance, deferential address requires *Vuestra Señoría* (which is rather an Italian than a Spanish formula in the Golden Age, and may be abbreviated *Usía*). In Chile *usted* is familiar, *vos* either insulting or condescending, *usía* (pronounced *su señoría*) formal, and respect tends to employ titles: *el patrón*, *la señora, el señor ministro*. Forms in *vos(otros)* are, however, in poetry and oratory the plurals of *tú*, which retains its archaic value in the higher literary style.

In this period was fixed the construction known as the 'personal *a*'. As early as the *Cid* it was optional to indicate an animate object of the verb by prefixing the preposition *a*, otherwise the sign of the dative (indirect object). Thus we find both *veremos vuestra mugier* and *veran a sus esposas a don Elvira e a doña Sol*. The distinction between the direct and indirect objects is often tenuous, and depends on the construction of the verb one happens to use, as 'to address anyone', 'to speak to anyone', which are identical in meaning though different in case. One may note, however, that for the purposes of a particular verb the direct object (the 'patient' in Basque) is deemed inert, but the indirect object (the dative, or 'recipient' in Basque) reacts at least to the extent of receiving. There is no logical difficulty in supposing animate beings and particularly persons as inert in any given circumstances, such as 'the man beat the child'; but there is a considerable psychological difficulty, since it is impossible to visualize living beings without reactions; the child, for instance, will certainly react in some way (by shrinking, crying, kicking, etc.) to a beating. Consequently several languages, like the whole Slavonic group, make a grammatical distinction between the animate and the inanimate accusative cases. They do so by means of declensional suffixes; but in Spanish and Rumanian the distinction is made by preposition, in Spanish by *a* and in Rumanian by *p(r)e* Lat. PRAE. The animate or personal object is not deemed inert with respect to the verbal idea, but the recipient or person interested or affected by the action. This usage becomes absolute in the Golden Age. Classes of persons, of course, are not living qua class: one says, therefore, *busco un médico* 'I am looking for a doctor', i.e. any member of the profession. On the other hand a town may be considered as the sum of its inhabitants, so that one says *quiero visitar a Toledo* 'I want to visit Toledo'. As we have seen the direct and indirect constructions are to some extent interchangeable, so that *a* may be prefixed to neuter objects for reasons of grammatical convenience: *el invierno sigue al otoño* 'winter follows autumn'; or it may be omitted from a personal object for the same reason: *antepongo el Ariosto al Tasso* 'I prefer Ariosto to Tasso'. In both these cases possible ambiguities are avoided by relaxing the rigour of the construction. The preposition and its omission serve to personalize or depersonalize objects: *llamar a la muerte* 'to summon Death', *la escuela de la guerra forma los grandes capitanes* 'the school of war forms great captains (as a class)'. The use of this construction has been deemed a mark of Spanish realism; we may accept the word provided that we do not regard either the Middle Ages, when the usage was still fluid, or the modern period, when it is petrified, as less realistic than the Golden Age in which it came to fruition.

With regard to the verb, the Golden Age showed itself highly conservative. It maintained the metathesis of *-dl-* to *-ld-* in the 2 Pl. imperative followed by a 3rd personal pronoun (*dalde* for *dadle*) and the assimilation *-ll-* from *-rl-* in the infinitive (*dalle* for *darle*). St John of the Cross has the archaic, and doubtless colloquial, apocope of *e* in *fuerdes* for *fuéredes*; and the language as a whole still recognized as a compound the future and conditional tenses, inserting between the infinitive and the auxiliary personal pronouns: *daros he*, where modern Spanish uses *os daré*. As early as the *Cid* we find both *direvos* and *dezirvos he*. The most striking innovation in the paradigm was the disuse of *-ra* in the indicative sense. HABUERAM *hubiera* is, by its origin, a pluperfect indicative, and has in Spanish a pluperfect or preterite sense in *salto diera de la cama que parece gavilán* 'he leapt from bed like a sparrow-hawk', in which *diera = dió*. But the use of HABUERAM in both the protasis and apodosis of hypothetical sentences caused *hubiera* to acquire also the value of a conditional (*habría*) and of a pluperfect or imperfect subjunctive (HABUISSEM *hubiese*). The indicative use occurs freely in the Medieval Period, and in the Modern Period it is also admitted (especially as a pluperfect) by men of letters, and notably by those of Galician birth. In Galician and in Portuguese *-ra* has its historic value of pluperfect indicative. In the Golden Age of Spanish, however, this indicative sense suffered eclipse. The verbal auxiliaries were developed. *Haber* was limited to service as an auxiliary or an impersonal verb, so that the medieval *tres hijuelos había el rey* 'the king had three sons' became impossible. As a true auxiliary *haber* takes an invariable participle, which no longer agrees with the direct object as in medieval Spanish. Medieval usage was to some extent fluid, as the *Cid* has both *la lança a quebrada* 'he has broken his lance' and *dexado a heredades* 'he has left his inheritance'. In the thirteenth and fourteenth centuries agreement with the direct object becomes more general; but in the Golden Age this concord ceases. At the same time new semi-auxiliaries developed, such as *tener llevar*, etc., with which there is concord of participle and direct object. As HABERE is a transitive verb, ESSE is the more logical auxiliary for use with intransitives, and so we have the medieval *es nacido, es muerto* (transformed in the Golden Age to *ha muerto, ha nacido*); while at the same time the distinction between *ser* and *estar* became sharper through the restriction of the freer medieval practices, and fresh equivalents were developed from *quedar resultar*, etc.

Among conservative indications outside the verb one notes the use of *quien* as both singular and plural (*amigos a quien llamo* 'friends whom I summon'), the greater wealth of demonstratives (*aqueste aquese estotro esotro*), and the persistence of such words as *ansí agora mesmo escuro do vido vía (veía)*, etc.

In its relations with foreigners the Spanish of this epoch

shows a much diminished dependence on French. Constant wars in France caused French words to enter the language through soldiers' slang: *trinchea* (now *trinchera*) *marchar sorpresa alojar rindibú* (Tirso), together with some other immigrants: *tusón gage jarrete claraboya*, etc. On the other hand, the Italian influence was of the highest importance and influenced art, commerce and war. In a general way the Italian of the humanists served as a precedent for the latinisms of Herrera and others; Valdés proposed to take over from Italy *facilitar fantasía cómodo incómodo entretener discurrir discurso servitud novela pedante asasinar* as well as other terms which have not been adopted. Direct indebtedness appears in Garcilaso's *selvatiquez* 'savagery' and Herrera's *vagueza* It. *vaghezza* 'charm, beauty'; but confessed italianisms belong rather to the technicalities of war, commerce and the arts. In commerce the Genoese bankers had such a prestige that *genovés* means 'banker, usurer' since the Middle Ages; and in this line we have *banco banca millón estafar* 'swindle' *tráfico*. Soldiers, sailors and travellers brought back many terms like *bisoño* 'recruit' *infantería escopeta* 'musket' *parapeto*, together with others that were less needed: *centinela* for *vela* 'sentinel', *emboscada* for *celada*, *foso* for *cava*. Among useful naval terms are *piloto proa fragata galeaza góndola brújula* 'compass'. Torres Naharro mingled Italian and Spanish to amuse his polyglot audience in Rome, and another soldier, Cervantes, cultivates italianisms (*aquistar fracasar testa*), but is little touched by French. The technical terms of architecture, music, painting, sculpture and literature are Italian in Spain as in the rest of the world: *fachada friso grotesco pianoforte claroscuro esdrújulo terceto soneto novela pedante*, etc.

Apart from its Latin sisters, Spanish of that age had important creditors only in the New World, where a large vocabulary of Arawak, Nahuatl, Quechua and Guaraní words was, and still is being, absorbed into the current language. It will be more convenient to discuss these when treating of the Spanish of America. A few Far Eastern words also filtered into Spanish, as *champán* 'sampan' and *té* 'tea' from China (Fukienese; the Mandarin *cha* appears in Portuguese), and *prao* from Malaya. Holland supplied *holanda* 'holland', but also several nautical terms came from England: *estribor* 'starboard', *babor* 'larboard, back-board'. From Germany there was also an import-trade of soldiers' slang: *sacanete* Ger. *Landsknecht* 'lansquenet', *trinquis* 'drink' (verb *trincar*).

(c) THE MODERN PERIOD

The modern period may be more succinctly discussed as many of its features have been implicitly considered in the previous sections. It opens with the sentiment of exhaustion left in the best minds by the failure of the later Hapsburgs. The linguistic habits of the seventeenth century were not indeed forgotten. They persisted in the theatre and elsewhere to express a much depleted content of thought. The best minds of the age, however, found such expression to be at variance with the circumstances of intellectual life, and they waged war against gongorism as a force which corrupts the language. We find the attitude of censure in Feijóo, Forner, Luján, Cadalso, and the two Moratíns. Their criticism is directed not only against the words but also against the things to be expressed; on the one hand they ridicule the inflated diction of poetasters, on the other they call attention to the philosophic and cultural achievements of Europe. Europe, in that age, was essentially France, its brightest luminary: and French becomes paramount among the foreign influences which have moulded modern Spanish. Not only the leaders of the Age of Reason, but the principal Romantics in the early nineteenth century, and the principal Modernists at its close, brought from French sources their novelties of doctrine and language. The eighteenth century borrowed social terms: *etiqueta sortú laqué (lacayo) petimetre burgués equipaje*; and it favoured an abstract vocabulary: *Ser Supremo* for *Dios, infundamentabilidad superficialidad infalibilidad*, which, though drawn from Latin or native sources, bear witness to the influence of the 'philosophes'. Cadalso has

jefe de obra 'masterpiece'; and *remarcable* appears in the eighteenth century in Spain, whence it has disappeared only to
reappear in Buenos Aires. During almost the entire period
there has been a strong opposition offered to gallicisms,
which has succeeded in removing several while delaying
recognition of others. The successive editions of the Academy's
dictionary fall short of the vocabulary of even refined speakers
by several thousands of common expressions, not all of
which are used with a sense of their strangeness, e.g. *buro-
cracia* and *silueta* first appear in 1914. This resistance has been
strengthened by the campaigns for purism in American
Spanish, and especially by the Venezuelan Baralt's pillory,
Diccionario de galicismos. On the other hand, the prestige
of French culture has stood higher in some American republics than in Spain, and a considerable half-absorbed
vocabulary is to be found on the Plate and elsewhere. As
the continued unity of the language demands not only correctness, but compromise, it is to be expected that some of
these American gallicisms will ultimately receive official
sanction in Spain. In the meanwhile a lively, but perishable,
lexicon serves social life, politics, fashion, etc., which are all
departments deep in the debt of France.

A mark of the gallicisms of the modern epoch is the failure
of the equation between the French and the Spanish *j.*
The former remains [ž], the latter has passed to [χ]. The
nearest equivalents possessed by modern Spanish for the
French sound are *ch* [ĉ] and *s* [ś]. Thus we get *charretera*
Fr. *jarretière* 'garter', *pichón* Fr. *pigeon* 'pigeon', *bisutería* Fr.
bijouterie 'jewelry'.

The decline of Italy is marked in the loan-words of the
modern period, and also the rise of Anglo-Saxon prestige.
In the latter case, the lexicon is largely unauthorized and
perishable. It deals with forms of sport, social life in its
expensive aspects, and industrial practices: *club fiveclock* (tea
at 6 p.m.) *futbol(ista) récord repórter espiche mitin túnel vagón
tranvía* (with *-way* hispanized) *biftec rosbif.* Some of these
terms appear in Spain by virtue of their previous appearance

in French. The conflict of the languages is more marked in Mexico and the Plate region, and I propose to discuss these elements more fully in the next chapter.

THE SOUTHERN DIALECTS AND ANDALUZ

The history of Spanish bears witness to the paramount importance of the two Castiles both as innovators and as conservators, but a very great influence has been exerted by the cities of the Guadalquivir valley upon the colloquial speech in Spain and Spanish America. The most important of these cities is Sevilla. Pedro the Cruel used Sevilla as his capital during the greater part of his reign, following a practice which had been growing among his predecessors. The city was recommended by its wealth and beauty, and by its proximity to the debated frontier of Granada. Under the Trastamaran dynasty this importance remained with the Andalusian capital. It was from Sevilla that Juan I organized his war against Portugal in 1383 and the years following, and from the Guadalquivir both Juan II and the Catholic Monarchs conducted their campaigns against Granada. Sevilla and Córdoba again figured prominently in the suppression of the Morisco rising of 1568–70, and it was to Sevilla that the victorious fleet returned from Lepanto. Sevilla was the centre of colonial administration and trade, and the effectual capital of the ultramarine empire. It enjoyed a vigorous literary life, and saw the rise and most of the masterpieces of the Spanish school of painting before Velázquez. It continues to be an influential centre for art, music and literature, while it has acquired some other claims for popularity as the capital of bullfighting and native sportsmanship and the seat of the gypsy convention. It enjoys from these sources a reputation for swagger that makes conventional Andalusian the tongue of all jolly roysterers.

The south of Spain forms, in consequence, an area of resistance to Castilian novelties, and a focus whence southern innovations irradiate. Its extent is not easy to define, because of the suspicion which must still wrap the concept of *andaluz*; for, on the one hand, the region has not yet been systematically investigated, and on the other, stage conventions and popular opinion have included in this dialect the greater number of vulgarisms common to all Spain. Its differential features are, in strict accuracy, still unknown. We may take, however, two criteria which will serve roughly to fix the boundaries of these southern varieties of Spanish. The one criterion is negative: the persistence of aspirate *h*; the other positive: the diffusion of two varieties of *s*. The persistence of the aspirate is not peculiar to southern Spanish, as it occurs also in eastern Asturian dialects; but in either case it is a symptom of resistance to a change focussed on Old Castile. Unlike the Asturian dialects those of southern Spain are not variants of the common tradition of Spanish Romance, but of its particular Castilian variety, from which they differ partly by the slowness with which certain changes have been effected. Hence the criterion of the aspirate, though not singularly Andalusian or southern, has value as a means of delimiting vaguely the line of conflict between the two varieties of Castilian-Spanish.

The silencing of the aspirate took place earlier on the east of the Castilian domain than in its centre and west. Descending along the Aragonese border by Cuenca to Albacete, silent and aspirate *h* were already concurrent in the sixteenth century; but in the centre, at Toledo and at Ciudad Real, on the middle sections of the Tagus and Guadiana, only the aspirate was heard until the closing years of the century. Another area of dispute was centred on Salamanca in southern León. Since the sixteenth century these regions have silenced their *h*; but the aspirate continues to be heard in all Extremadura, Andalusia and Granada. To the east of these provinces lies that of Murcia, which has had a somewhat chequered history. Conquered and occupied by James I of Aragón-Catalonia for a brief period between 1263 and 1266 owing to a revolt of Moslems against

Castile, Murcia, though returned to Castile, did not cease to be an objective of Aragonese policy. In respect of the transformation of Lat. f, Murcian has a history linked with that of the Aragonese and Valencian frontier dialects, viz. that *f* passed directly into silence, without an intervening aspirate. The southern dialects are thus *extremeño, andaluz* and *murciano*.

Varieties of *s* form a precise means of determining the limits within this area of Andalusian dialects. To the layman they seem characterized by the reduction of the sibilants *s ç z* to a single sound, which is normally [s] —*seseo*—but occasionally [θ] —*ceceo*. Recent investigations show that this account is not strictly accurate. The prime cause of the two confusions was a change in the value assigned to *s*, which is cacuminal in Castile, in all the north, in Extremadura and Murcia, but coronal on the Andalusian border. The cacuminal *s* is produced by raising the tongue-tip to a point behind the alveoli, with a concavity in its upper surface; the coronal *s* is that produced by raising the point of the tongue against the meeting-place of the upper teeth and gums, with less concavity. The cacuminal *s* differs from the coronal *s* in the direction of the palatal sibilant *x* [š], and for this reason Gil Vicente represents his Mooress in the *Cortes de Júpiter* (1519) as making her *esses* into *exxes*. Coronal *s* coincides with [ŝ] in every respect save only that the one is a fricative, the other an affricate. When, therefore, *ç z* had attained the stage [ŝ] they were liable to fall into coronal *s* on losing their affrication. This has actually occurred within a territory less extensive than that of coronal *s*, which is itself less extended than the political area of Andalusia. The Castilian *s* covers all the central Meseta, and descends its broken edge, the Sierra Morena, until it meets the plain of the Guadalquivir. This line between hill and plain corresponds roughly with the frontier of coronal *s*. The *seseo* lies within this frontier, and is wanting in the province of Jaén, where *s* and *ç* are successfully distinguished, as also in part of the province of Huelva. It occurs outside these limits in a linguistic islet near Cartagena, perhaps thanks to shipmen in part, and on the frontier near Badajoz, in a district long disputed between Spain and Portugal. As the *seseo* is the older sound it is deemed the more correct, and so is predominant in Sevilla, where the *ceceo* is frequent among the vulgar. But we actually find that the greater part of Andalusia prefers the *ceceo*—the entire coast-line from Huelva, via Cádiz, Gibraltar and Málaga, to Almería, the country round Sevilla, most of Granada, and islets at Guadix, Baza and near Cartagena. It is perhaps to be attributed to local Morisco peculiarities in pronouncing Ar. *sîn*. The area agrees somewhat imperfectly with a second value given to *s*, a predorsal *s* with the tongue-tip on the lower teeth. This *s* is, according to present information, the *s* of almost all Spanish America. As these changes run concentrically round Sevilla, where the less cultured are addicted to the provincial *ceceo*, we may take them as examples of the diffusive power of this centre. Firstly, the coronal pronunciation of *s*; secondly and in dependence on the first, *seseo*; third and fourthly, *ceceo* and the predorsal value of *s*, with the co-operation of Granada in the former case. We note that from Sevilla *seseo* and predorsal *s* spread over Spanish America, to which the conquerors had taken cacuminal *s* only; and if Minsheu means by his spellings *czh* for *j* that the velar [χ] spread from Sevilla against the older [š], it is the less remarkable that Castile and Spanish America should have effected the same change, in apparent independence of each other.

Consciousness of the existence of *andaluz* is shown by the hostility of the Castilians Valdés (1536) and 'Prete Jacopín' to the authority of the Andalusians Nebrija (1492) and Herrera (1580), but the first explicit indication is given in 1570 for both *ceceo* and *seseo* at Sevilla by Arias Montano, and the Granadine Núñez Muley (1567) is an evident *ceceante* (he writes *çuzedió neçeçidad vaçallos*, etc. for *sucedió necesidad vasallos*). How much earlier we can go is doubtful. The lisp attributed by Ayala to Pedro the Cruel was doubtless a personal defect of this otherwise typical Andalusian king. The dialect cannot go back directly to the Mozarabic of the region, since it has evidently been brought from New and Old Castile by the Christian settlers and agrees with Castilian in all its points of divergence from Mozarabic. But there may have been from the first some commingling of indigenous speech-habits with Castilian, such as might produce the opposition to cacuminal *s*. The playwrights of Lope de Vega's school established the hegemony of Madrid in standard Spanish, and it was at Madrid that even an Andalusian like Góngora sought to propagate his innovations. Since 1600, therefore, there has been no 'correct' Andalusian, and the dialect has gathered to itself all current vulgarisms and has even affected a gypsy jargon, that of the *cantes flamencos*, on the ground that it is the language of wit (*el lenguaje de la gracia*).

Ceceo and *seseo* are terms applicable to the pronunciation of *s ç z* at the beginning of syllables, which includes in Spanish cases where they occur between vowels. At the end of the syllable these consonants are normally aspirated, and the aspirate may take on the characteristics of a following consonant, either partially or entirely. Thus *mismo* may become *mihmo* or *miṃmo* (where ṃ represents an unvoiced *m*, as a reminder of the voiceless *h*), and *usted* may go so far as to become *uté*. When an *s* occurs within the breath-group at the end of a word and between vowels, it may be treated intervocally or as final of the syllable: in the former case it remains, forming liaison with the following vowel (*lo sojoj* or *lo zojoj* are conventional representations of the intervocal *seseo* and *ceceo* in *los ojos*, with final aspirate); in the latter, and more usual, case it is aspirated, and may not even prevent synaloepha (*lo jamigo, vamo jayá, e jeso* for *los amigos, vamos allá, es eso*, and *tú entrará en, mientra en*). This *h* is represented conventionally by *j*, but is not the velar vibrant [χ] but the true aspirate [h]. The same aspirate, also represented in modern times by *j* though Herrera used *h*, is found as the descendant of Lat. F, both initially and medially, as well as in those cases where Castilian-Spanish has retained *f* (i.e. before *r* and *u*, and in many learned words). This aspirate is found in some words contributed by the dialect to standard Spanish, as *juerga* 'jollification' alongside *huelga* 'rest, strike' from *holgar folgar* FOLLICARE, and *jamelgo* 'sorry nag', FAMELICU *famélico* 'hungry', *jaca haca* 'nag, pony'. The aspirate may be misplaced in words that had no F originally, as in the loan-word *jándalo* 'huckster', which is merely the regional name. These two circumstances give the aspirate an important rôle in *andaluz*, a rôle that is somewhat unsettled and liable to change. A further main characteristic is *yeísmo*, i.e. the pronunciation of *ll* as *y* or the derivatives of *y* (which are [ž] and [ĵ]): *cabayero* and its variants for *caballero*. *Yeísmo* is not universal in the province (it is not used in parts of the Huelva district), and it is not at all restricted to Andalusia and the south. On the contrary it occurs everywhere in vulgar Spanish, is normal in Spanish America, and existed in the past history of most of the Peninsula. A stage of *yeísmo* is implied in the passage of -CL- -LI- to [ž] in Old Castilian *ojo fijo hijo* OCULU FILIU. In the case of LL Old Castilian must have retained the pronunciation as a lengthened [l:] during the period in which CL LI had become [λ]. Thus the Andalusian *yeísmo* is merely a change in keeping with the general tendency of the Spanish language. It appears that the poet of the *Cid*, a Mozarab of Medinaceli, had not mastered the *yeísmo* of twelfth-century Castilian when he was betrayed into spelling *Cullera* as *Gujera* and *Castellón* as *Castejón*. Mozarabic had *y* for *ll* representing initial L- in *yengua* LINGUA. The passage from *ll* to *y* is found outside the Peninsula, and notably in French: *fille* is pronounced [fiy:], and *Bastille* is an ultra-correction for *Bastie*.

Other features of *andaluz* are also common to all vulgar Spanish, and are due to the interchange of certain sounds and the tendency to lose others. Among the more notable equations are *bue* = *hue* = *güe* and *bu* = *gu*, together with $l = r = n = d$; the principal losses are intervocalic *d g r*. Thanks to the first equation we find *güeno* for *bueno* 'good', *güevo* or *buevo* for *huevo* 'egg', *güérfano* for *huérfano* 'orphan', *güey* for *buey* 'ox', as well as *abuja* for *aguja* 'needle', *guñuelo* for *buñuelo* 'bun', etc. The profit goes mostly to *g* and this *g* may then be applied analogically where no justification exists in the standard sounds: e.g. *huele* 'it smells' gives *güele*, and hence *goler* for the infinitive *oler*. The second set of equivalences causes a number of interchanges between *l r n d*. In this series the *r* is not the vibrant of standard Spanish, but a relaxed fricative as in English [ɹ], and the four sounds are thus all dental fricatives with the same point of articulation. So we find *l* for *r d* in *picaldía alvertío perfilia jacel* for *picardía advertido perfidia hacer*; *r* for *l* in *artura gorpe er tar* for *altura golpe el tal*; *r* for *d* in *seguiriya soleares* for *seguidilla soledades*; *n* for *r* in *mejón* for *mejor*. A special case is that of *l* combined with an occlusive or fricative initially, which passes to *r* as in Leonese and Portuguese: *branco prata* for *blanco plata*. The disappearance of fricatives between vowels is illustrated for *g* by *miaja* for *migaja* 'crumb'; for *d* by *soleares esnúo* for *soledades desnudo*; for *r* by *paeres* for *paredes* and *paese* for *parece*. Final *-d -r* normally disappear, when not converted to other sounds, and initial *d-* is also liable to be lost either by confusion between the prefixes *des- es-* as in *esnúo*, or as a result of syntactical phonetics where an initial *d* may fall between vowels, as *ice eja* for *dice deja*. This is especially probable for *e* as the remains of *de*. On the other hand *d-* may be intruded into *dir dentrar* for *ir entrar*. These substitutions occur in all vulgar Spanish, and are not peculiar to Andalusian varieties. They are as frequently to be encountered in Madrid.

Not much is known as to the peculiarities of *andaluz* vocabulary. It contains what may be archaisms due to the survival of words imported by the original settlers, and the probability is increased when we find the same word in Aragonese or Asturo-Leonese: *babero* 'bib' (in Aragonese 'pinafore'), *ansias* for *náuseas*, *fiemo* (cf. Cat. *fem*) for *estiércol*, *dengún* for *ningún*, etc. There is no marked correspondence with Arabic reported from Andalusia, but a notable feature of some forms of the dialect is their indebtedness to Romany.

The Spanish gypsies were tolerated by the Church authorities who, if we may judge by Calderón, have considered want of religion remediable but difference of religion perilous. On the other hand their irregular life and reputation for theft led the civil powers to class them with malefactors. For their own purposes it was convenient to substitute in essentially Spanish sentences Romany words for certain special terms. On the other hand their freedom, tribal habits and knowledge of horses attracted admiration, which their conflict with authority made romantic. They receive the attentions of amateurs (*aficionados*), who cultivate the gypsy pose more thoroughly than the Romanies. The gypsy songs (*cantes flamencos*) are not the inventions of Romanies or relics of a tribal tradition; they are basically Spanish, and the Romanies are executants. They include a number of common words from Romany (*caló*), as *parné* 'money' *gachí* 'girl' *abelar* or *abillar* 'have' *chai* 'girl' *penar* 'tell' *plaloró* 'brother' *querelar* 'make', etc.; but songs˙which attempt a thoroughgoing Romany are often later than more Spanish versions, and betray the hand of the non-Romany *aficionado*.

The *andaluz* dialect has a considerable literature and theatre, including collections of popular songs and traditions, regional novels and essays of an Andalusian tint like those of 'Fernán Caballero' and Estébanez Calderón, while the Quintero brothers in their dramas are held to be the best representatives of the wit of the region. Specimens of *murciano* are offered by Vicente Medina's *Aires murcianos* (1899) and of *extremeño* by J. M. Gabriel y Galán's *Extremeñas* (1902). These contain the elements we have already noted as 'Andalusian', though they distinguish the sibilants as in Castilian. *Extremeño* possesses a marked aspiration for *f h*, and employs *i u* for *e o* as finals; while modifying variously medial unaccented vowels as *andaluz* also does. The region is sparsely populated for various reasons: it was much thinned by the emigration to America, it depends much on live-stock which require space, and parts are malarious. In consequence, the province is one of retarded development, and the language also shows remarkable archaisms. To the north of Cáceres in Plasencia, Coria and Garrovillas, the medieval distinction between voiced *z* and voiceless *ç* remains perceptible. Each sound had evolved to the interdental position without coalescing into one, and the distinction is represented as between *c* or *z* [θ] and *d* [ð]: *jadel idil podu adeite* for *hacer decir pozo aceite*, OSp. *hazer dezir pozo azeite*. By virtue of *ceceo* this *d* appears for OSp. voiced *-s-*: *Pladencia codah* for *Plasencia cosas*. *Extremeño* is in other respects a dialect of transition between *andaluz* and the patois of southern León.

On *andaluz* consult T. Navarro Tomás, A. M. Espinosa (hijo) y L. Rodríguez-Castellano, 'La frontera del andaluz', *Rev. Fil. Esp.* xx, A. Castro, 'El habla andaluza' in *Lengua, Enseñanza y Literatura* (Madrid, 1924), and the admirable article by H. Schuchardt, 'Die Cantes flamencos', *Zeitschrift für rom. Phil.* v. See also A. M. Espinosa (hijo), *Arcaísmos dialectales* (Madrid, 1935).

ARAGONESE AND ASTURO-LEONESE

It remains for me to mention the fact of the continued existence of the ancient dialects of Spanish Romance in a thin arc from the Galician frontier to the Catalan. They are an essential source for knowledge of medieval Leonese and Aragonese, and their archaic forms constitute for Spanish a sort of contemporary antiquity. It is possible to hear and use language long lost in the evolution of the standard speech. Moreover, as their point of cleavage from Castilian-Spanish goes back to Spanish Romance itself, they have more distinguishing marks, and maintain them more consistently, than dialects of recent growth like *andaluz*. Their minor internal differences of usage are also numerous, so that in comparison with them the rest of the Spanish-speaking area seems homogeneous and scarcely differentiated. Reasons of this kind have attracted to them, and especially to Leonese, the interested attention of several distinguished researchers. For our purpose, which is historical, the place in exposition of Aragonese and Leonese has been earlier in the book, where we discussed the conflict of dialects which ended in the supremacy of Castilian. At this point a brief summary may suffice.

The area of the non-Castilian Spanish dialects has been modified since the Middle Ages by the steady expansive pressure of Castilian. Expanding fanwise to the south, Castilian severed the ancient link constituted by Mozarabic between Leonese and Aragonese. Its north-eastward thrust widened the northern gap, as almost all the Basque border is occupied by the standard language. On the Spanish side Basque merges abruptly into Castilian-Spanish, whereas on the north it shades off more easily into Gascon *parlers* of French. Driving east and west Castilian has occupied the great towns and all the level country—the environs of León and Salamanca, and the upper Ebro Valley. The dialects have retreated into or across the hills, to places remote from Madrid where communications are difficult and society simple and traditional. West Leonese lies about the Montañas de León and has the backing of Galician, towards which it effects the transition from Spanish; the Asturian (*bable*) dialects lie in the confined valleys behind the Cantabrian range; and the shy survivals of Aragonese lurk in the valleys leading to the Pyrenees.

As in medieval times, Asturo-Leonese and Aragonese agree to differ from Castilian in certain broad respects. They extract diphthongs from Ĕ ŏ even before a palatal: Arag. *viengo tiengo*, NOCTE Leon. *nueite* Arag. *nueite nuet*, FOLIA Leon. Arag. *fueya*, where Spanish has *vengo tengo noche hoja*. They make use of *y* between vowels to prevent a crasis: *seyer*, Sp. *ser*. Among the consonants the most important are initial F and J ǵ, together with medial -C'L- -G'L- -LI- -CT- -uLT-. In Castilian-Spanish F has become silent. The dialects preserve either their native *f* (in western León, Asturias de Oviedo and Aragón) or the primitive innovation *h*: FOLIA *fueya*. The aspirate occupies the eastern Asturian region, of which Santander is the capital. The Montaña, as it is called, is more accessible from the central Meseta. Initial J was early lost in Castilian but was preserved in Leonese and Aragonese, where it had the value of [ž ĵ] according to circumstances. Both Leonese and Aragonese have unvoiced this palatal, doubtless in the course of the sixteenth century: Asturo-Leonese has unvoiced the fricative [ž] and so gets *x* [š] in *xineru xelar* Sp. *enero helar* JANUARIU GELARE, while Aragonese has unvoiced the affricate [ĵ] and so gets *ch* [ĉ] in *chinebro chirmán* Sp. *enebro hermano* JUNIPERU GERMANU. These changes affect all *j*'s: Asturo-Leonese *xente xudíu* Arag. *choben* Sp. *gente judío joven*. The medial groups -c'L- -LI- give *ll* or *y* in both dialects: Leon. *muyer* Arag. *mullé* Sp. *mujer*, Leon. *oreya* Arag. *agulla* Sp. *oreja aguja* from MULIERE AURICULA ACUCULA. Medial -CT- gives in each dialect -*it*-, which may be further reduced to *t* in Aragonese: FACTU Leon. Arag. *feito* (Arag. *feit fet feto*) Sp. *hecho*; and the same conclusion is reached in Leon. Arag. *muito* Sp. *mucho* MULTU. They agree also in using accented forms of the verb 'to be', leading to diphthongs in *yes ye yera*, etc., and in using -*oron* as 3 Pl. preterite, on the analogy of the 3 S. -*ó*.

A few traits are peculiarly Aragonese. As to vowels this dialect shows readiness to discard final -*e* and does so invariably in adverbs in -*ment*; it tends also to discard -*o*: *breu* (Sp. *breve*) *finalment estan* (Sp. *estando*). As a result of this change the plural sign *s* is directly attached to a consonant, as *biens* Sp. *bienes*, and the verb has *tiens tenez* (from *tenets*) for Sp. *tienes tenéis*. As final -*r* is not pronounced we have *mullé mullés lugá lugás* for *mujer(es) lugar(es)*. As for the consonants, apart from the *ch*- in *choben* and its likes, the leading peculiarity of Aragonese is its conservation of PL- CL-: *¿cómo te clamas?* 'what is your name?' In the eastern end of the area, in Ribagorza, there is a strong tendency to palatalize *l* when it occurs either singly or in combination at the head of the syllable, thus giving not only *pll- cll-* but also *bll-*. There is a characteristically Aragonese use of gender, a tendency to convert adjectives in -*e* into -*o* -*a*, to express sex: *tristo* -*a*, *cualo cuala*, *grando* -*a*. The pronouns contain several novelties: the disjunctive is *yo tú* not *mí ti*; *le(s)* dative is distinguished consistently from *lo(s)*; there is a masculine article in *lo* and locally *o*, and a 3 Pl. possessive in *lur(es)*. The archaic pronominal adverbs *y en* still survive. The verb tends to form its gerunds and past participles from the preterite stem rather than the present: *supiendo supido* from *saber*. By compensation, Aragonese makes many efforts to regularize irregular verbs: *sabiese dase decié facié* for *supiese diese dije hice* from *saber dar decir hacer*. In most of these particulars and in its vocabulary Aragonese marks the transition from Castilian to Catalan. A special interest attaches to the district of Ribagorza, in which the transition actually takes place, as the local speech is ambiguously either Spanish or Catalan. At Énguera in Valencia an archaic dialect still preserves the medieval distinction between voiced and voiceless sibilants *s ç z* as [θ ð s z]; and near Viella in the Vall d'Aran we have the only fragment of a French dialect on Spanish soil.

The Asturo-Leonese dialects are in a better state of conservation than the Aragonese, and they show more variety. There are three main divisions. In the east, the Montaña de Santander is the source of the local idioms in Pereda's famous novels. They give him racy words to amplify his Spanish, but he does not seem to have esteemed the dialect as such. In this region the aspirate stands for F. The central region, the Asturias de Oviedo, provides the typical *bable* of dialect authors. Apart from the features already cited as held in common with Aragonese, we find that initial L- palatalizes (*lluna llana llamber llingua*), -ORIU becomes -*oiru* (*retortoiru cobertoira*), final -*o* becomes -*u*, the preposition *con* is assimilated to the article (*cola piedra* or *cuna piedra* for *con la*, *con una*), DEDIT-ILLI is *dio-lle dioye dioi*, -*ra* forms are still pluperfect indicative, and -*in* is a favourite suffix (*vecín sobrín molín*). Near Oviedo, as a local peculiarity, -*as* -*an* become -*es* -*en*, as *casa cases canta canten*. Western Leonese accentuates the common Asturian features with a greater admixture of forms approximating to Galician. The most important of these are the retention of the diphthongs *ei ou*, as in *cantey matey caldeiro cousa pouca cantou*. Similarly *muito* as in Galician, *feito*. There is considerable variation in the treatment of CL-

PL- FL-. In medieval times these gave already [š] in *Xainiz xosa*. WLeon. solutions are [ĉ] as in Galician (*cheiro chombo chanicu* from FLAGRU PLUMBU PLANU) and [ŝ] as in *tsabe* CLAVE. The *ts*- may also arise from palatalized initial L- in *tsuna tseite* for *luna leche*, where central Asturian has *ll*. These forms co-exist with invaders from Castilian which establish themselves first in single words that are commonly used, such as FLAMMA *llama* in S. Ciprián de Sanabria and *llena*, while they also give rise to inconsistencies like CLAVES *chaves* but *ez llaves* Sp. *las llaves*. The Leonese dialects enjoy a popular literature of folk-tales and songs which some attempt has been made to erect into a regional art-form; but for such purposes the most important variety has been the *sayagués* which was the conventional rustic dialect of the classical Spanish stage. Juan del Encina imitated for the delectation of the Duke of Alba the dialect of the peasants in the neighbourhood òf Salamanca and Alba de Tormes, which is properly termed *charruno*; an incorrect identification with Sayago, near Zamora, gave it the misnomer *sayagués*. At Miranda on the Duero, a town in Portugal which was once a portion of the Astorgan bishopric, an extreme dialect of Leonese is spoken on Portuguese soil.

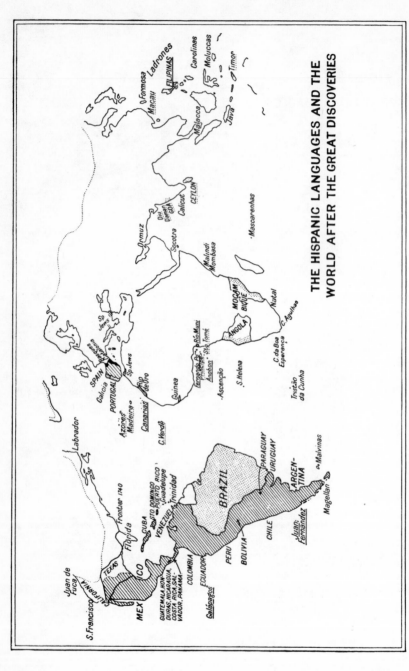

THE HISPANIC LANGUAGES AND THE
WORLD AFTER THE GREAT DISCOVERIES

[Note how closely the distribution of Spanish and Portuguese corresponds with the outline
of the world as known before 1740]

CHAPTER VII

THE EXTENSION OF SPANISH TO SPANISH AMERICA

The extension of Spanish overseas is the legacy of Spain's great age of discovery and conquest, and its distribution follows the contours of the world as known before the rise of the second British Empire. Roughly speaking, the year of Anson's circumnavigation of South America (1740) may serve to mark the conclusion of the expansive efforts of the sailors, conquerors and missionaries who carried the language over so vast a portion of the globe. The treaty of Tordesillas (1494) reserved for the Portuguese the African littoral and the southern coasts of Asia, where factories and a fringe of coast-line were in their possession; to the Portuguese also it gave a segment of the Brazilian coast which lay a little to the west of the sailing route round Africa, and which has since been aggrandized to cover the sub-continent of Brazil. The remainder of the world was the legitimate *conquista* of Castile, and covered not only the Americas, but also the Pacific Ocean. Spain was established in the Philippines, Portugal at Macau, and the Moluccas were debated territory. The initial stages of discovery and conquest were rapid. In 1492 Columbus sighted the New World and established the first Spanish fort. In twenty years Cuba and Hispaniola were firmly occupied, a factory had been set up at Darién, the isthmus of Panama crossed, and the Pacific discovered. In the next decades Magellan circumnavigated the globe and set up the Castilian banners in the Far East, while Cortés and Pizarro overthrew the barbaric empires of Moctezuma and Atahuallpa. The coasts, populous centres and great rivers were rapidly occupied or at least traversed, but the work of internal colonization was slow until, in the nineteenth century, it was speeded up by the stimulus of independence, the influx of capital and the call for European immigrants. Up to the year adopted as typifying the maximum expansion of the Spanish tongue (1740), penetration into the interior was the work primarily of Catholic missionaries, such as the Jesuits of Paraguay or Fray Junípero Serra of California, whose desire it was, in other than religious matters, to build up communities of the natives by preserving their customs, language and economy. In this way Spanish came to cover an enormous extent of territory—from north of the Río Grande to the Horn, and including the Philippine Islands— as the language of administration, of the organized Church and (owing to the failure of the Maya-Aztek and Incaic civilizations) of culture; but at the same time millions of Mexicans, Central Americans, Peruvians and Guaranies continued, and continue, to employ in their market-places their historic tongues, and to practise their ancient customs, both socially and, with some slight modifications, in their religious ordinances. The northward political frontier is now fixed by the limits of Mexico and Lower California, but beyond that boundary Spanish dialects are spoken in the south-western states of the United States, and the place-names are Spanish within a parabolic curve that descends from San Juan de Fuca Strait to Florida, including notably southern California, Arizona, New Mexico and Texas.

Thanks to this vast territorial expansion which makes them unique among neo-Latin tongues and comparable only to English and Russian, Spanish and Portuguese have stored experience which is of the highest value to students of language. Just as the language of a minute portion of Italy has been taught to Germans, Celts, Ligurians, Etruscans, Iberians and Berbers, so what was once the dialect of Burgos has been acquired by Azteks, Mixteks, Zapoteks, Aimarás, Quechuas, Araucanians, Guaranies and Tagalogs. The problem of ethnic substrata arises in each case, but with the difference that speech-habits which are merely conjectured for Celts or Iberians, can be precisely known for Azteks or Quechuas, Both Latin and Spanish have been diffused over vast areas but the circumstances of the Spanish diffusion are recorded in chronicles, lists of emigrants, and missionary circulars. There have been forces in operation, and there still are, which tend to make Spanish no longer one speech but a family of languages in America, similar to the Romance family: isolation, illiteracy, novel surroundings, the pressure of other languages. But there are other factors which forge again the broken links: education, pride in a common literature, more and more rapid communications. Doubtless some of these introduce considerations that are foreign to the history of Latin in its decomposition, and not all the conclusions valid for the Spanish of America can be adopted by the Romance philologist. But the scientific student of language will not debate in the abstract problems of the extension and evolution of language which can be settled, with Spanish-American evidence, on a basis of fact.

Apart from the theoretical interest of the Spanish of America, there is its strong social and historical appeal. In it is recorded a traffic with an enormous variety of tribes and nations of whom the ancient world knew nothing, and from it has filtered into European tongues such knowledge as we possess of their implements, houses, customs, organizations and beliefs. It stores up, too, the experience of exploiters and colonists who struggled against unprecedented difficulties and on a gigantic scale of achievement. It possesses great variety in itself, and has entered into a remarkable series of compromises with speakers of other tongues. It has expanded and modified the Spanish of Spain, and has even, in recent times, altered its prose rhythms; but it has also resisted the process of change, being resolved to maintain its Spanish identity.

On the Spanish of America see principally R. J. Cuervo, *Apuntaciones críticas sobre el lenguaje bogotano* (Paris, 1914), M. de Toro, *L'Évolution de la langue espagnole en Argentine* (Paris, s.a.), R. Lenz, 'Beiträge zur Kenntnis des Amerikanospanischen', *Zeits. für rom. Phil.* xvii, M. L. Wagner, 'Amerikanisch-spanisch und Vulgärlatein', *Zeits. für rom. Phil.* xl, R. Grossmann, *Das ausländische Sprachgut im Spanischen des Río de la Plata* (Hamburg, 1926), E. F. Tiscornia, *La lengua de Martín Fierro* (Buenos Aires,

1930), C. C. Marden, *The Phonology of the Spanish Dialect of Mexico City* (Baltimore, 1896), A. M. Espinosa's studies of New Mexican Spanish in various publications, P. Henríquez Ureña's essays in *Rev. Fil. Esp.* xvii and elsewhere, A. Alonso, *El problema de la lengua en América* (Madrid, 1935). For the native tongues consult P. Rivet's article in Meillet et Cohen, *Les Langues du Monde* (Paris, 1924), and G. Friederici, *Hilfswörterbuch für den Amerikanisten* (Halle, 1926).

THE ABORIGINAL LANGUAGES

Man arrived in the New World at a comparatively recent date, when some of the great primitive inventions had been made, but before the discovery of the wheel or the domestication of animals. This may have been about 10,000 B.C. His high cheekbones and other physical characteristics argue for kinship with the Mongolian race, doubtless using the Aleutian bridge and descending the mountainous spine of the two Americas; and this derivation is supported by some myths of migration, and by the evidence of diffusion of archaic utensils. There may also have been infiltrations from Polynesia, which, at Easter Island, approaches within a thousand miles of the South American shore. There is a widely distributed archaic culture, essentially the same north and south of the isthmus of Panama, but the semi-civilizations of the Mayas and Azteks in the one continent and of the Incas in the other are independent of each other, though each unique and unrivalled in its own sphere.

In disconcerting contrast with this uniformity and youthfulness of the aboriginal cultures is the linguistic diversity of the Americas. In Eurasia and Africa great languagefamilies like the Indo-European, Semitic, Sino-Thibetan and Bantu cover the greater portion of the land, and everywhere great national and international tongues have been fashioned and spread. All such movements in the New World have been feeble and restricted, and 123 speech-families, apparently each independent of the others, have been calculated for the two Americas: 26 north of the Río Grande, 20 in Central America and 77 in the southern continent. Against this

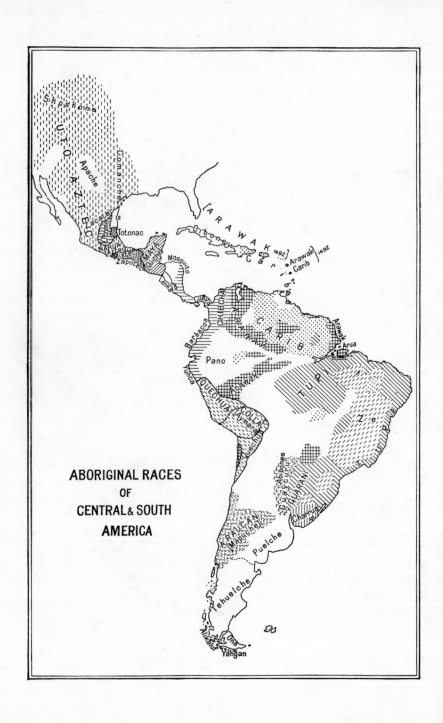

ABORIGINAL RACES
OF
CENTRAL & SOUTH
AMERICA

diversity there has been but little reaction. The Mayas were the only begetters of such civilization as existed in North America, but their language, Quiche, remained purely local. The Tolteks and Azteks who succeeded in establishing a loose warlike confederation in central Mexico were content to employ any one of four recognized languages: Nahuatl, Mixtek, Zapotek, and Hia-Hiu or Otomí. These tongues still divide the market-places. In the south the Peruvian monarchs insisted on Quechua as part of the curriculum for vassal princes, with the result that its official use extended along the spine of the Andes from Quito to Tucumán. Its influence on the Spanish of America is thus widely exerted, but it did not oust or subdue the local languages, and even in Bolivia had to share the ground with the Aimará language of the Colla tribes. As for the *koiné* which arose from the Tupi-Guaraní speech-group, the Lingoa Geral, it was the work of missionaries after the conquest.

The causes of this diversity included, no doubt, political weakness and scarcity of population. Exaggerated estimates of the destruction committed by the Spaniards in the Greater Antilles, and of the pomp of Moctezuma and Atahuallpa, have tended to conceal the fact that the two continents were vast, empty spaces. If we assume that the repressive action of the conquerors was sufficient to counteract the natural rate of increase (and the assumption is probably unjust), if we add the figures adduced for the Antilles and make a liberal allowance for the ruin of the Prairie Indians in the United States and Canada, it would still be doubtful whether the pre-Columban population of the two continents exceeded that of modern France. The greater number were concentrated in Mexico and Guatemala on the one side, and in the Bolivian plateau and Peruvian valleys on the other, amounting to almost half the total number. Here the want of hand-writing and of education based on literature left mainly unchecked the tendency to local variation. The Incas proceeded in the direction of writing no further than their celebrated *quipus*, or knotted strings which might serve as numerical mnemonics for a narrative; the Mayas had stone hieroglyphs, which have been deciphered in so far as they indicate dates; and the Azteks used highly ambiguous hieroglyphs in the form of an almost incomprehensible rebus. There was no absolute want of spoken literature. In Mexico the melancholy genius of King Nezahualcoyotl gave rise to lyrics in which J. J. Pesado has sought inspiration in more recent times; the Peruvian sun-cult inspired noble hymns, and there is a corpus of proverbs by the Inca Pachacutec. But all this amounts to less than we find in the empires of the Old World at the dawn of historic time.

These languages have been important for the development of American Spanish either because of their date of discovery or their importance in administration. The first voyage of Columbus brought him into contact with the gentle Arawaks only, with the result that the names for the principal American novelties are of Arawak origin. The headquarters of this family of languages was probably a region to the north of the Amazon, between the Japura and the Negro. A considerable body is found to the south of the great river on the upper course of the Madeira and Ucayali, which may be due to the advance of a wedge of Katukinas up the Amazon valley. An offshoot has crossed the Bolivian Desaguadero into northern Chile; another body migrated northwards across the plains of the Orinoco, and thence by sea to the Greater Antilles. It was this last fragment of the Arawak nation which the Spaniards first met, and which supplied the first American loan-words. In the second voyage Columbus saw his first Carib. They were cannibals, fierce warriors and bold sailors, and their search for Arawak brides gave rise to a curious symbiosis of the two speeches, the one for men, the other for women. Originally concentrated on the Xingú, about 10° South, they formed a secondary mass on the Negro from which they radiated fanwise into the Guyanas, Orinoco basin and Lesser Antilles.

In his fourth voyage Columbus encountered the complex linguistic conditions of Honduras. Here every village had its own speech which the explorer declared to be as unlike those of the others as Arabic to Spanish. Such languages could not contribute much that was serviceable to the invaders, who borrowed freely again only when they encountered the high culture and simplified linguistic conditions of central Mexico. Here the semi-civilization of the Azteks offered many new objects which had not been known in the Antilles, and the circumstance that Mexico belongs to a distinct floral and faunal region caused the Spaniards to learn here many new names of animals and plants. Four principal languages were employed in the market-places of the plateau: Nahuatl, Zapotek, Mixtek, and Hia-Hiu. Each has contributed to Spanish vocabulary, but none so much as Nahuatl, the language of the Azteks. The language and the nation were immigrants from the north. The Shoshon Indians of Montana and Idaho, the Pueblos of Colorado, the Tolteks and Azteks of Mexico and offshoots in Guatemala indicate the line followed by the Uto-Azteks in their march towards the great Mayan focus of civilization. It was from Mexico that the conquest of Yucatan and Guatemala was effected, with the consequence that borrowed names for objects common to the whole region are of Mexican origin.

The first stage in the reduction of the southern continent, apart from Balboa's unquiet colony at Darién, was the overthrow of the great Inca empire by Pizarro. By this time it was not necessary to learn new names for many objects peculiar to America, but there were novelties in the flora, fauna and administration of Peru which called for fresh contributions to Spanish vocabulary. At the same time the administrative prestige of Quechua enabled these loan-words to remain valid over a vast extent of territory. Most Southern American borrowings are thus Quechua, even beyond the frontiers of that tongue; and, in fact, Spanish conquerors and missionaries helped to give it a wider diffusion than it had under the Incas, as they also diffused Arawak and Carib words with such rapidity that they were later reported as indigenous in many different parts. Associated with Quechua is Aimará. The name was originally that of a Quechua tribe living on the border of the Colla nation, and was wrongly given to the latter. The language served perhaps more speakers than Quechua in Inca times and is now predominant among the Indians of Bolivia.

Other South American language-families have made less notable contributions to the speech of the colonists. In Colombia a few words were picked up from the Chibchas who had attained to some degree of civilization; and in Chile the long war against the Araucanian Indians brought into prominence their language, Mapuche. This contact has been made the more interesting to philologists by the fact that the language itself has been described with unusual competence and its relations with that of the invaders scientifically investigated by Lenz. Its rôle, however, is strictly supplementary to Quechua. In the east, between the Paraguay and Paraná Rivers, we find the primitive mass of the Tupi-Guaraní people, the 'Phœnicians' of America. They supply the language of the Paraguayan markets and the vocabulary of the great river flats. Offshoots from this stock penetrated partly along the Paraguay and Tupí into the basin of the Amazon, partly along the Brazilian coast, where they left many settlers, so as to advance up the Amazon from its mouth. In so doing the invading waves flowed round the block of Ze tribes established on middle ground between the S. Francisco and Xingú around the Araguaya and Tocantins, tributaries of the Amazon. These northerly extensions, known by the name of Tupí, have contributed the greater number of Indian words required by Brazilian Portuguese, which have to be further borrowed by Spanish when the topic is Brazil, and their general agreement formed the basis for the Lingoa Geral formed and fomented by Portuguese missionaries to serve as the *koiné* of the Amazon basin. In the extreme south of the continent Alakaluf, Choni and Yahgan offer no special interest for the hispanist, though the general linguist may take notice of them on account of their remarkably primitive development.

It is not possible, as we have seen, to speak of American

languages save in a geographical sense; but there are American phenomena of language which tend to repeat themselves in different speech-groups. Older philologists divided languages into polysynthetic, incorporating, agglutinative and isolating. These terms are not valid for the classification of languages; examples of them all occur in the two Americas. The number of polysynthetic languages, however, is notably high, that is, of languages which include with the verbal element most or many of the other parts that go to make up the discourse, with the result that words do not exist as units but only in combinations. An extreme example is the Esquimaux: *Takusariartorumagaluarnerpâ?* 'Do you think he really intends to go and bother about that?' composed of significant-elements rather than words. One cannot say, for instance, *iartor-* by itself, but only (with the aid of a prop) *iartorpoq* 'he is going to'. In Nahuatl we have the standard instance of an incorporating language, in which not only pronouns but also noun-objects are included in the verb: *ka* 'eat', *ni-k-ka* 'I eat it', *ni-naka-ka* 'I eat meat' (*nakatl* 'meat'), *nipetlaĉiwa* 'I make mats' (*petlatl* 'mat' Sp. *petate*). Quechua has many agglutinative peculiarities; in forming the plural, for instance, it makes use of suffixes which are semi-independent with regard to the noun they modify. The Hia-Hiu tongue of the Otomí Indians in Mexico is a surprising example of an isolating language, as unlike all its neighbours and as inexplicable as Basque is in Europe. Among all this vast number of linguistic experiments we find oddities like the presence of a fourth person in connection with Mapuche verbs and its device of pro-verbs, the failure of Quechua to achieve the notion of a plural as 'more than one', etc. Not one of all these speech peculiarities has passed into the Spanish of America. Far from conserving their own mental habits while adopting a new vocabulary, the American Mestizos have abandoned their ancient speech-habits but passed on a number of words needed to describe new things and customs. There is not even any syntactical influence of any of these tongues on Spanish, apart from the dubious instance of the Quechua suffix -*y* in the Argentine district of Tucumán. In the language of the nursery, where the nurses are Indian women, one hears in Tucumán such words as *mamay* (*mamitay*) for *mamá mía* (*mamita mía*) in which the suffix indicates in Quechua the possessive 'my'. The words, however, have no general range outside the nursery, and within it they may be rather terms of endearment (cf. our *dearie* for *dear*) than of possession. No indigenous sounds have passed over to Spanish, such as the Nahuatl lateral click *tl* or the emphatic Quechua *cc*; and at most the phonetic influence has not gone farther than to exercise an option where the evolution of Spanish offered a choice. The influence of the American substrata, in short, has done no more than provide the names for exotic things, not all of which have a wide circulation, and many of which stand liable to replacement by newer European terms.

On the other side it should not be forgotten that the impact of Spanish upon these languages has been tremendous. A large European vocabulary has had to be adopted for things unseen theretofore in America: *caballo señora jarro sombrero* and other everyday terms. These are, in the Indian tongues, irreplaceable necessities. Spanish has commingled the languages, carrying the Arawak *canoa* and the Quechua *quinina* or *quina* into all the American languages as well as over the rest of the world. It has forced some languages to acquire new sounds, as *r* in the Nahuatl of New Mexico, where only *l* is indigenous. So the old loan-word *señora* gave *xenola*, but the later *manera* remains as *manera*. There has been interference with the intimate structure of the language, by which verbs, nouns, adjectives, particles and phrases are used as though they were true Nahuatl stems: *ti-desear-oa* 'you wish', *oqui-formar-oque* 'they transformed him', *tehua ti*pobre 'thou art poor'.[1] Above all, Spanish has eclipsed the prestige

---

[1] Some idea of this interference may be obtained from F. Boaz's article, 'Spanish elements in modern Nahuatl' in *Todd Memorial Volumes*, i, Columbia Univ. Press, 1930. Borrowings include:

Sounds unknown to Nahuatl: *r ñ* (*libro compañero pobre*, but older loan-words *xenola xalo* for *señora jarro*).

Vocabulary: Terms of relationship (*tiò sobrinò hermanò papà mamà familia*, etc.),

of every aboriginal language and dialect, not one of which serves any more to express an elevated or commanding idea. 'The state of Quechua', says J. J. von Tschudi, 'is so ruinous on account of the many strange words it has incorporated, on account of its mixture with other Indian tongues, and on account of its advanced stage of phonetic decomposition (due to Spanish), that if it be not immediately recovered by scholars, it has only a black outlook before it.'

AMERICAN INDIAN LOAN-WORDS IN SPANISH

The interpreter of Christopher Columbus, Lucayo, was a native of Guanahani in the Bahamas, and thus an Arawak. His language was that of peaceable communities who traded in their long canoes, without interruption, among the Bahama Islands and along the shores of Cuba (save the extreme west) and Hispaniola, until in the vicinity of Martinique they gave way to the warlike Caribs. Their country formed part of a natural floral and faunal region which included the northern coast of South America, but was quite distinct from Mexico, and in consequence the new objects encountered by the early settlers received, in the main, Arawak names, eked out by Carib and the language of the Cueva Indians in Tierra Firme. The principal lenders were the Tayno tribe in Haiti, who were thoughtlessly exterminated as a result of the colonists' exactions. They perished too soon to experience

of religion (*dios santo ángelis cristiano misa campana alma*, etc.), political organization (*rey reina pueblo carcel preso justicia* and even *compañero amigo*), society (*haciendero rico pobre asesino lazarino*), ranching (*hacienda rancho corral puerta cuarto letrero*), horse (*cahuayo jáquima cordel*), weights and measures, money and numerals (*semana peso secientos*), clothing (*vestido pantalón*), implements (*acoha* for *aguja, cuchillo machete máquina xalo* for *jarro*), games, food (*pan*), animals (*cahuayo león gallo pato*), plants (*arroz membrillo*).

Adjectives: *bueno flaco flojo mal mayor pobre primero solo tonto*, etc.

Verbs: *admirar cantar desear estar formar lograr mandar negar pasar sentir vestir*, etc.

Particles: including almost all the common ones in Spanish.

Suffixes: tsitsi*quito* 'the youngest one', quahui*tero* 'woodchopper'.

Together with an unlimited facility for treating Spanish words as though they were genuine Nahuatl stems.

the influence on their speech of Nahuatl and Quechua, but our early authorities sometimes confuse Arawak with Carib, so that it is best to group all Caribbean loan-words together. The earliest among them, recorded by Nebrija, is *canoa*, a Carib word already adopted by the Arawaks, and meaning a 'dug-out'. It makes its first appearances in forms that suggest dialectal variation, and proportionately guarantee the faithfulness of the borrowers: *canoa canaoa canaua canahua canagua*, etc. The word scattered immediately over both continents, from the Chapote-Utah Indians in the north to the Fuegians in the south, and is discussed by Marcoy (1869) once as if Quechua and once as Chontaquiran. Modified by a few planks, the more perfect canoe was called the *piragua* 'pettiauger', which is probably Carib of Tierra Firme, but may be Arawak. The bark canoe is known to Brazilians as *ubá*, a Tupí term. The simple polity of the natives yielded the word *cacique* 'chief of a tribe', which later displaced in Peru the Quechua *curaca*, and has yielded the Spanish derivative *caciquismo* 'political bossism'. Indian corn, the staple food of all New World communities, received the Arawak name *maíz*, derivative *maizal*, without taking into account the prior interest of the Mayas in that article. Within thirty years Pigafetta is found reporting it as an indigenous word from Brazil; and in Peru, thanks to the Spanish conquerors, *maíz* displaced the Quechua *zara*. The Arawak hut erected on the ground, *bohío* (also *boío boyo bochio buhio buío bujío buhiyo buihio boa*), was accepted as suitable for all native hutments; a round hut was named by the Arawak *caney*. *Huracán* 'hurricane' is a Caribbean word, probably taken from the Arawaks of the Antilles, and so are *sabana* 'savannah', *ceiba* 'cotton-tree', *maguey* 'agave americana', *henequén* 'agave thread' (unless this comes from Yucatan), *guacamayo* 'parrot', *nigua* 'jigger flea', *batata* 'sweet potato', *barbacoa* 'barbecue', *iguana, tabaco*. The spread of these words was gradual. While Nebrija accepted *canoa*, Las Casas tells us that *ají* (Guinea pepper), *cazabí* (manioc bread) and *yuca* (manioc), though current in the islands, were unknown to Spain about 1512.

Among these words there intruded a few of Oriental origin, brought to America by the sailors and there given a new attachment: *azagaya* (Arabic and Medieval Spanish), *almadia* (Arabic and Portuguese) 'boat, canoe', *prao* (Polynesian), *ñame* or *iñame* 'yam' (from Africa), *anta* or *danta* (Ar. *lamṭ*) meaning some sort of antelope in Zurara, but applied to the tapir (*tigres tantas*, also *vaca* and *vaca montés*) and also to the elk, moose or wapiti. Orellana, the discoverer of the Amazon, saw a *vaca danta*, which was either a tapir or a manatee. The word *tapir* is Tupi-Guaraní (*tapiruçu tapireté tapihire*). These words became lodged in the Antilles and are often included among the primitive americanisms of Spanish. Together with those borrowed from Arawak and Carib they form the most assuredly established group of loan-words.

The conquest of Mexico occurred when this primitive insular vocabulary was already established in Spanish use. New words were required, however, to name the plants and animals unknown to the islands: the *tomate* 'tomato' (Nah. *tomatl*), *aguacate* 'alligator-pear', *cacahuete* 'pea-nut', *camote* for the insular *batata* 'sweet potato' (also *camote apicho* Quechua *apichu*), *hule* 'rubber', *nopal* 'prickly pear', etc., together with the *ocelote*, the *zopilote* 'vulture' (Nah. *tzopilotl*), *sinsonte* 'mocking-bird', and *quetzale*. New foodstuffs included in this region *cacao* 'cocoa' (Nah. *cacahuatl*), *chocolate* and the *jícara* (*xícara*, Nah. *xicalli*) from which it is drunk, *tamale* 'maize cake', *mezcal* a spirituous liquor, etc. The better known word *pulque* (whence *pulquería*) is of uncertain origin and probably insular. The higher civilization of the Mexican plateau gave to Spanish a number of cultural terms, among which the most striking is *teocalli*, the name of the stepped pyramid temples where human sacrifices took place. Mexico was a great centre for commerce, whence the interest of such a loan-word as *tiangue* 'market-place' with its derivative *india tianguera* 'Indian market woman', and the associated *tameme* 'porter'. The large floating gardens on the central lakes were called *chinampas*, and the name was extended to the pile-villages found among them. The Indian barrack (*galpón*,

Nah. *calpulli*, in Nicaragua *galpon*), the native mat (*petate*, Nah. *petlatl*), the pestle and grindstone for Indian corn (*metlapil*, *metate*), were also first named in this region; and in *nagual* we have a rare instance of indebtedness in the intellectual sphere. Based on Nah. *naualli* 'witch', *nauallotl* 'the black art', the word names a man's dæmon or other self, through the proper control of which he is enabled to carry out feats of sorcery; whence German *Nagualismus*, to denote the superstition which connects the souls of men with certain beasts.

It is a tribute to the genius of Garcilaso de la Vega el Inca that Spain and the world have felt such keen interest in the social and political organization of ancient Peru. Without attaining the command of mathematics, architecture, hieroglyphic writing or other arts which was reached by the Mayas and Azteks of Central America, the Inca despotism was free from the most revolting barbarities, especially from wholesale human sacrifice; and in other respects it was capable of presentation as a sort of primitive utopia, in which private property was rendered unnecessary through the wisdom of a paternal government. Such is the brilliant picture offered, in good faith at least, in Garcilaso's *Comentarios Reales*, and reproduced with reluctant reservations by Prescott. The system centred on the *Inca* or *Inga* (adj. *incásico*) and his *coya* 'queen'. The royal family descended from and worshipped the Sun, in whose honour were dedicated the vestal virgins called *mamacona* (the word is merely the plural 'women'). The traditions of the state were guarded by the sages or poets called *amautas*, and great posting-roads carried the Inca's orders from stage to stage (*tambo*) by his messengers (*chasqui*). The free people were organized in tribes (*ayllo*) under *curacas*, though this word is only used technically and yields in general use to the insular *cacique*. Military colonies (*mitimaes*) were employed to hold down and civilize subdued lands; those of the ruling class were worked by serfs (*yana-conas*). The characteristic Peruvian burial mound has given archæology the word *huaca*; and *chacra chácara charca*, etc.

serve to denote a cultivated place or a farm. Apart from this special vocabulary, Quechua has served to name the more important novelties in South American flora and fauna. The language had much intercourse with the so-called Aimará of the Colla tribes in Bolivia, and their respective shares in offering loan-words cannot be clearly distinguished (*chinchilla* is attributed specifically to Aimará). The official speech of the Inca empire was valid as far north as the Presidency of Quito, whence access was obtained into the inner parts of Colombia; and on the south it extended into the Atacama desert so as to reach the Araucanian tribes of Chile. In a south-easterly direction Quechua served as a second language for the inhabitants of north-western Argentina, at Tucumán, Salta, Jujuy, etc.; and these were among the earliest settlements in that republic. Hence the pervasive influence of Quechua words among those which Spanish owes to aboriginal tongues. They are at least universal in South America, while their Tupi-Guaraní rivals are strictly local. Hence the *pampa* is named from Quechua as much as the *puna* (Andean desert plateau) or the *pongo* (Andean river gorge); and the calabash (*mate*) from which Paraguay tea is drunk (Guar. *caá*) is used for the drink itself (*mate* or *yerba mate*). Quechua had the further advantage over its rival of the rivers that it contained little in its phonetics unsuited to Spanish taste. Among the principal animals named from this language are the *cóndor puma llama alpaca vicuña viscacha*, and among plants the invaluable *quina* and *coca*. It has supplied also the most general term for a native woman (*china*), a pet name for the baby (*guagua*), the name for jerked beef (*charqui*), and that for a native song (*yaraví*), as well as *guano* and *guaso* (the Chilean peon or *roto*).

The Tupi-Guaraní language occupied the great river-basins of South America where it has acquired an intertribal value. It has served to name the beasts and plants of Brazil, and has exerted an immense influence on Brazilian Portuguese. In the Spanish-speaking area, it is still the normal language of Paraguay, where the first settlements were made

244 THE EXTENSION OF SPANISH

by Cabeza de Vaca, Irala and others. These were frankly polygamous, and a large mixed population arose familiar with both tongues. It was from Asunción that Garay descended in 1580 to found Buenos Aires, and so to occupy eastern Argentina for Spain. The Charrúa Indians of this region, however, were intractable, and a truceless war ended in their entire destruction. The Araucanian tribes bestrode the Andes to the west. In this way the principal loan-words adopted in Argentina, like those of the river states, are of Guaraní origin, though they take precedence after Quechua terms. They serve to name animals (*aí capibara coati tamanduá tucano paca ñandú tapir* or *tapireté jaguar* or *yaguareté agutí urubú* 'vulture', *urutaú* a bird of night, *quincayú*, etc.) or plants (*mandioca tapioca ipecacuana ananas caá* 'Paraguay tea' *curare*). *Bagual* 'untamed horse', and *catinga* 'Brazilian scrub' complete the list of common words.

Other American languages have offered little to Spanish which has found general acceptance. Some specialized words have been adopted from the Chibchas of Colombia, and the Mapuche tongue of the Araucanian Indians has furnished a few supplementary terms, such as *gaucho* 'cowboy', *poncho* 'cloak-blanket', *maloca* or *malón* 'Indian raid'. The language does, of course, serve to name such articles in southern Chile as have not received names from Arawak, Nahuatl, Quechua or Guaraní.

The above are a selection of the most generally acceptable words of Indian origin. How many are to be deemed 'Spanish' is a question that cannot be answered so long as Spanish dictionaries record admittedly so much less than even the Spanish of Spain. The Spanish of America undoubtedly makes use of more than are current in Europe, seeing it has more cause to name the objects peculiar to itself; but even in America there are considerable differences of usage which menace the continued existence of many such words. Arawak, Quechua and Nahuatl were propagated, along with the Lingoa Geral, by missionaries beyond the historic frontiers of these languages, making all their rivals strictly local; but Mexico, Peru and the Plate region employ many terms from the local Indian tongues which might not be understood elsewhere. The vulture, for instance, is *zopilote* in Mexico, *zamuro* in Venezuela, *urubú* on the Plate, but *gallinazo* (regularly derived from *gallo, gallina*) in Colombia, and it is doubtful whether any of these can compete with Sp. *buitre* for general utility. Similarly *maíz* contends with Quechua *zara* and Tupi-Guaraní *abatí, canoa* with Tupí *ubá, bohío* with *oca*, etc. Anchored to things, such names perish with the thing, and are incapable of increase. Thus the word *tambo* or *tambillo* is used in the Argentine Republic for a dairy, but only one of a primitive sort; electric dairies have gone back to European sources for *lechería*. The growth of a town population unfamiliar with animals and plants threatens to restrict severely the circulation of their names, while favouring substitution where common forms are available.

On the other hand, the number and accuracy of these borrowings is remarkable. It is true that we have early complaints that the native tongues are misrepresented. There is a wide difference between *Ahuilzapan* and *Orizaba*; and the *Collas* have been miscalled by the name of a Quechua tribe, the *Aimará*. Words have undoubtedly been hispanized in their structure and by means of suffixes; but they nowhere become monstrously perverse like the English (and North American) *wigwam mugwump chipmunk*, etc., so as to leave their originals beyond possibility of identification. For this we have to thank several circumstances of the colonizing effort of Spain. Royal patronage caused governors like Fernández de Oviedo accurately to investigate the resources of their governments, and scholars like Peter Martyr to record the facts with all the philological science of the day. Missionaries like Las Casas learned and practised native languages to convert and protect the Indian tribes, and were not slow to offer linguistic as well as other criticisms of the civil officials. Soldiers, coming to fight and settle without their wives, mated with Indian women in open polygamy and produced bilingual descendants, most notably in Portuguese territory; and while the supremacy of the whites was maintained, especially after the coming of European women, there was no colour bar comparable to that in English-speaking areas. Above all, in Spanish and Portuguese America as distinct from Canada and the United States, the Indian survived, and still speaks his ancestral languages in large communities where there is no more than an official recognition of Spanish and Portuguese.

AMERICAN INDIAN EVIDENCE FOR THE EVOLUTION OF SPANISH

An important service which is rendered to philology by the contact of Spanish with the various American languages is that of dating certain linguistic changes by comparative tests. It is clear that when the Spaniards entered Chile in the second third of the sixteenth century they still possessed an occlusive *b* derived from Lat. P. The Araucanian Indians possessed occlusives only of the voiceless series, and so rendered this occlusive by *p*, while the fricative *b* they rendered by the fricatives *f*, [φ] (bilabial voiceless fricative), *hu ghu* [w]: *napur capra etipu* or *irtipu* for *nabos cabra estribo*, but *huaca aghuas llahuy cahuallu* for *vaca habas llave caballo*. The latter is confirmed by the Nahuatl *cahuayo*. Similarly it is evident that the *s* brought by the conquerors was cacuminal, as in Castile, not dorsal as in Andalusia: Nah. *xenola* for *señora*, Map. *chumpiru* for *sombrero* and *chiñura* for *señora*. Both [š] and [ĉ] are palatals. On the other hand, *ç* and *z* were already identical before the conquest of Peru, and *x* and *j* *g* had coalesced into *x* [š]: Nah. *xalo* for *jarro*. The passage of this *x* [š] to the modern *j* [χ] is seen in comparing Nah. *xalo* with the later loan-word *jáquima*. In Mapuche the former sound is rendered by a palatal *ch* [ĉ] as the nearest equivalent, the latter by a velar *k*: *ovicha* (also *ovisa ovida*) for *oveja*, *achur* for *ajos*, *chalma* for *enjalma* 'packsaddle', but *Koan* for *Juan*. Already in Nebrija's time *f* had become an aspirate with a tendency to disappear: Map. *aghuas* or *ahuas* for *habas* FABAS. It remained only when supported by *u* or *r*; and in Spanish America, as in Andalusia, the aspirate has generally persisted.

AMERICAN VARIATIONS ON STANDARD SPANISH

There is a perceptible difference between Spanish as spoken by a Spanish-American and that spoken by a European, just as there is with us always a consciousness of the difference between our English and that of the United States: but there is the same difficulty in defining this difference. It is more deeply rooted in popular sentiment than in scientific fact. The music-hall artist has less difficulty in reproducing the 'American accent', whether of North or of South America, than the philologist has in proving that the alleged 'accent' really exists. Two favourite assumptions of the popular mind have no right to exist: the notion of uniformity in America, and the comparison with the standard language in Europe. Standard Spanish (*español correcto*) is admittedly the language of a minority even in Spain—an influential, educated minority, speaking with intentional accuracy. The same persons speaking colloquially already diverge from the prescribed standard (e.g. by reducing -*ado* to -*ao* or -*au*, or omitting final -*d*), and they may even adopt vulgarisms for comic or sociable effects (e.g. the common *¿pa qué?* for *¿para qué?*). Even at that they use a language from which somewhat more than half their fellow-countrymen dissent. Apart from those whose native idiom is Leonese, Aragonese or Galician, there are the seven or eight millions who speak Castilian in its Southern forms. The pronunciation of *c z* as *s* and of *ll* as *y* is that of the majority of persons in the Spanish Peninsula, and the former is allowed to be correct by force of numbers. When, therefore, Spanish spoken by an American is compared with Spanish as a whole, it is found to be in constant agreement with the practices of the Peninsula. Compared with this measure of agreement, which amounts almost to identity if we allow vulgarisms to enter into the count, the want of uniformity in America itself becomes the more evident. The Peruvian or Colombian stands closer to Spanish, and even to *español correcto*, than the Argentine or Chilean; the language of the latter varies considerably with his status and his intention at the moment. When he seeks to address a wide audience he adopts, at least in writing, a language scarcely distinguishable from the standard. There is, perhaps, this difference: *español correcto* is the actual spoken tongue of a select minority of European Spaniards, but it cannot be used by a Spanish-American without a sense of diverging from the colloquial. It is for him an acquired idiom; and for that reason, no doubt, the great preceptors of Spanish idiom have been Spanish-Americans: Bello, Baralt, Caro, Cuervo.

It is not just, either, to estimate Spanish-American by its differences from that of Spain. The Spanish language is greater than the language of Spain; every word and phrase used by the Spanish-American comes to him by birthright and is therefore part of the Spanish of America. The imperfections and exclusiveness of the dictionaries, which represent mainly the usage of men of letters in Europe, have given an impression that the Spanish language is very much poorer than it really is. They lack thousands of words of good pedigree current in Spanish America; but they also lack thousands in Spain. The 'language of Cervantes' belongs as much to the American as to the Spaniard; upon it as a foundation each has built up the modern language, generally on the same plan, and all the legitimate varieties of this speech are Spanish. As, however, we have already considered the evolution of the modern tongue with special reference to Europe, we shall look at the American variants for the sake of their divergence, but always with the proviso that such an examination is partial.

'Spanish-American' is not the name of a dialect or language, nor even of a group of dialects or languages; but it is an abstract term covering miscellaneous tendencies exemplified in America, in a few of which there is general agreement in all parts of the Continent, and also, to some extent, in Spain. Characteristic of these are the *seseo* and *yeísmo* already referred to, which are almost universal in America as well as widespread in Spain. But the term also covers tendencies which have slight expansion in the Americas, such as borrowings from local Indian tongues or the special jargon of the Buenos Aires docks, *lunfardo*, or of Chilean peons. All these tendencies, however, fall within a strictly defined space: they are all forms of the Castilian pattern of Spanish, and do not show the more fundamental divergence of Leonese, the Asturian dialects or Aragonese. The presence of Peninsular dialectalisms is rarely indicated: such as a preference for the Catalan and Aragonese *pesebre* 'manger' over the Castilian *belén* 'Bethlehem' for the representation of the Nativity, or the Galician *saraviado* for Castilian *pintado* 'gaily-coloured' (of birds). The numerous Basque and Galician immigrants of the eighteenth and nineteenth centuries have not implanted their languages at all, but have gone to strengthen the demand for a Castilian *koiné*. Furthermore, the Castilian basis is more modern than that which serves for Jewish Spanish in the Balkans and Africa. The conquerors already brought with them some of the great sixteenth-century sound-shifts. As we have seen ç z have become one sound, which has generally given the modern s, and x and j have come together as x [š]. The first poetry written in the New World still followed medieval formulas, and knew nothing of Italian prosody; but the Spanish colonies felt the whole force of the great literary age of Spain, to which they contributed many of the glories. In common with its mother-tongue it has experienced enrichment of vocabulary and phrase, where Balkan-Spanish knows only impoverishment. And just as words and works crossed the Atlantic, so did speech-tendencies, particularly those which originated in southern Spain. The cacuminal s of the conquerors has become the dorsoalveolar current in America and Andalusia;

their *ll* has passed generally into *y*; *x* has been thrust back in the mouth from palatal [š] to velar [χ], with a preference for the spelling *j*, which Bello made unique in Chile while Spain still allows *g* before *e i*; and the Academy's reintroduction of the Latin value for *x* [ks] has passed on to America, and gives rise to confusion where *x* had still survived in the orthography, e.g. *México*, Sp. *Méjico*. It is within these strict limits of a relatively modern stage of standard Spanish that all American variations occur.

A tempting hypothesis is that which would attribute the American variations to the influence of the Indian substratum or substrata. Knowledge of these languages is so rare among Romance philologists that one evident crux of the substratum-theory is not always realized, namely that the American Indian languages have nothing in common and so do not provide the fairly uniform substratum which might account for the fairly uniform features of American varieties of Spanish. We should expect wide divergences, where only slight ones are found. We should also expect to see reproduced some of the native habits of thought: some incorporation, some development of agglutinative suffixes, some peculiar phonemes. Actually nothing of the kind occurs; all variations are such as the Spanish language spontaneously offers of itself. The invariable penultimate accent of Quechua may have aided in producing the sing-song accent of Andine Spanish, but only because it agrees with the normally penultimate accent of Spanish. The oxytone vowels of Tupi-Guaraní (*yaguareté tamanduá urutaú*, etc.) resemble the accent already adopted from Arabic in the suffix -*i*. It is possible that this Guaraní habit is recognizable in the Argentine fondness for accenting certain enclitics (*vamonós digaló*), but only because such enclitics bear a secondary accent in Spanish itself, and the conversion to principal had already taken place sporadically, especially in verse. In supplying the names of things (especially animals and plants), the Indian tongues have affected Spanish only in the same manner, though in a more intense degree, as they have affected French, English or German; and such loans are accepted only on the borrower's terms. A word like *mbaracayá* 'ocelot', with its un-Spanish initial *mb-*, reported for Argentina, should be accounted a foreign term existing on sufferance; and the same is doubtless true of a great part of the unfamiliar Indian vocabulary. This element is in full retreat and cannot now look for reinforcements.

There has been no want of experiments in mixing Spanish with American languages. A hybrid jargon was required by Spanish captains of Aztek or Zapotek troops, and consisted of Spanish into which were thrust, as occasion required, native key-words; by these and the intonation the speaker conveyed his intention, but his grammatical framework (used for his own satisfaction as a speaker) remained Spanish. It was a mere substitution of terms, and essentially unstable. The intruding indianisms could not pass on to the general speech of Spanish residents in Mexico, and were removed wherever the Spanish term had been learned by the natives. Of this nature are the hybrid Spanish-Quechua phrases used by Lugones or Rojas to indicate half-Indian communities in the western Pampa: Dios *yaya*, Dios *churi* 'God the Father, God the Son', a mere substitution for Dios *padre*, Dios *hijo*.

The classical investigation of this point was that of Lenz, who studied the language of the peons (*huasos, guasos*) of southern Chile together with the Mapuche language of the Araucanian Indians. It is the only case in which a complete knowledge of the two languages has gone together with philological skill. Lenz held, as a result of his investigation, that the substratum theory was proved for south Chile, in the sense that the speech of the *huasos* was Spanish modified by Mapuche; but later students have not accepted this interpretation of his results. The Mapuche vowels are *a e i o u* and *ɯ*. The last-named, an unrounded *u*, does not pass into the language of the *huasos*, nor still less into general Chilean; and from the others all that results is vacillation as to the value of narrow vowels, such as occurs spontaneously also in Spain. Among the consonants there is a high palatal *t* [ť] which resembles the *tr* in 'try'. It occurs in the Chilean pronunciation of words like *otro*; but the cause is not that alleged by Lenz. In contrast with the standard tense vibrant *r rr* of Spanish, there is throughout all America a sporadic relaxed fricative [ɹ ɹ], like the English *r*, in which the tip of the tongue reaches up to the high palate. This palatal relaxed fricative palatalizes the preceding *t*, from New Mexico downwards, and also in Spanish Navarre, La Rioja and elsewhere. A voiceless labial fricative [φ] exists in Mapuche, in Chilean Spanish, but also very widely in all Andalusian and American variants of the language; it should not be attributed to an Araucanian substratum. There is a lateral palatal *ll* in Mapuche and in the districts of Llanquinhué and Chiloé, whereas central Chile uses *y*. Here the local speech-habit may have had force enough to retain in use a Spanish sound which was liable to undergo change. The same subaltern rôle may have been played by Quechua in preserving *ll* in the Peruvian highlands; but at Atotonilco in Mexico *ll* has survived where the native tongue has no such sound, but only a lengthened *l* (as in Italian) and a click *tl*. The original list of Mapuche loan-words in Chilean Spanish included many that were Quechua in origin and international in range; Lenz's revised list is still long, but contains few words whose patent of nationalization is clear.

The comparison between the Mapuche language of the Araucanian Indians and the Spanish of their descendants, the *huasos* of southern Chile, is not valid as a basis for describing Chilean Spanish. The latter is necessarily the language of the capital, and even, in a special degree, of educated society in Santiago and Valparaíso, whereas the dialect of the *huasos* may be no more than a stage in the process of acquiring Chilean Spanish. The same difficulty has beset other investigations into popular variants of Spanish in America, such as the dialect of Mexico City or the language of Argentine *gaucho* poetry. The language of the populace offers the greatest degree of divergence from *español correcto*, indeed, but that is not uniquely an American phenomenon.

An investigation of Madrid dialects based on the language of the southern wards or on the playlets of Don Ricardo de la Vega would show equally wide divergences from the standard language, and in most instances there would be striking coincidences of idiom. Various dictionaries of 'Argentinisms', 'Cubanisms', etc., bring to light an array of archaisms, vulgarisms, new words or new senses, and foreign words (Indian or French or English), of which few are strictly local, and most would be rejected with distaste by educated speakers and still more so by writers. They are parts of a fluid and unstable vocabulary which has still to be standardized; but where standardization has been attempted on American soil, its pattern is scarcely different from that of *español correcto*. The various Spanish American countries can only agree on a basis of their common inheritance, the language of Spain, under the ægis of a common literary tradition; variants from the model must be scrutinized, and allowed only when justified by necessity or some forgotten tradition. It was in this sense that the Colombian classicists laboured: Miguel Antonio Caro as head of the school, and Rufino José Cuervo as its mouthpiece. Even the advent of 'Modernism', a movement which took novelty for a virtue, left Colombian Spanish strictly 'correct' in the work of Silva and Valencia. Similarly Montalvo in Ecuador provided patterns of Spanish more 'correct' than that of Spain; and in Chile Bello's famous grammar is a powerful instrument for disciplining speech. In fifty years, it is recorded, this text-book has stamped out in Chile the misuse of the familiar second person which some Argentine writers hold to be ineradicable from their tongue. There are thus powerful tendencies which favour the reunification of the whole Spanish language on its old European basis. Communications between Europe and America, and still more between different parts of America, are becoming ever more speedy. Airways and the motor-car will complete the work of the steamship and train by eradicating local obstacles to mutual comprehension; and a transigent attitude on the part

of the Spanish Academy, by offering a ready acknowledg-
ment of established usages, may suffice to knit up again the
ravelled sleeve of the language. Undoubtedly the various
'Argentinisms', 'Chilenisms', etc. offer the possibilities of
change should they be adopted as standards of the language.
Either, therefore, Spanish will emerge as one language,
richer and more varied than it is yet admitted to be, or a
series of national landslides will break up its cohesion. What
will not occur is that process of gentle and unperceived drift
away from the common inheritance which is presumed, in
theory, to have been the history of Romance.

The claims of nationalism have already been raised, notably
in the Argentine. American things require American names;
American ideas require American moulds. Attempts to express this sense of nationality in writing have, however, not
given an American, but rather a technical, language. This
is true of Gregorio Gutiérrez's famous poem on the cultivation
of maize in the valley of Antioquía, which requires a glossary
even for a Colombian. The famous verse of Guido Spano:

> ¡ Llora, llora, *urutaú*,
> en las ramas del *yatay*;
> ya no existe el Paraguay,
> donde nací como tú!
> ¡ Llora, llora, *urutaú*!

is an example of technical indianism, appropriate to a Paraguayan maiden lamenting the ruin of her country *en idioma
guaraní*. José Hernández's *Martín Fierro*, the most celebrated
of the *gaucho* poems, uses a language deliberately plebeian,
the appeal of which is based on its contrast with the language
of readers in the capital. It could not serve as the foundation of an Argentine national speech, not merely because it
would have to be artificially acquired by most educated
Argentines, but also because it is bound up with the peculiar
circumstances of cowboy life on the great Pampas, which has
already vanished in its traditional form. The claims of
Argentine Spanish were first raised by the distinguished
statesman Domingo Faustino Sarmiento during his exile in

Chile. He came into conflict there with Bello's reforms, characterized by their respect for the traditional inheritance, though Bello himself had provided excellent models of a poetry true to American experience. Sarmiento, devoid of any formal education but possessed of a racy intelligence, insisted that new experience required new language; and in this he was supported by the thinker Alberdi. The proposition was evidently true. It was developed by J. M. Gutiérrez, whose studies in Argentine literary history led to the belief in an Argentine language. But of what did this language consist? An attempt at definition was made by Lucien Abeille in 1900, calling attention to divergences from the Castilian standard. His book, instead of codifying the *idioma nacional*, produced a violent reaction. The divergences from Castilian were also lapses in taste, and Buenos Aires was horrified to find itself identified with the jargon of its docks. Critics were not slow to point out Abeille's ignorance both of good Argentine and of linguistic science; Paul Groussac and Ernesto Quesada preached a return to standard Spanish as a national duty. The present tendency is thus strongly in favour of reunion, and may triumph. The Argentine abroad is, however, conscious of a gap between his speech-habits and those which are proposed to him as patterns; he is wont to apologize for his pronunciation or idiom, and if he stays away for years, he has an uneasy feeling that a tide of new colloquialisms has overflowed the language he knew. The state of Spanish in the Argentine is fluid.

On the surface all the Spanish of America is characterized by its andalusianism. The *seseo* and *yeísmo*, the persistence of *h* as a weak aspirate (though written *j*) and the aspiration or disappearance of *s* at the end of syllables, are features so convincing that 'the Spanish ear may confuse a Spanish-American with a native of Extremadura or an Andalusian, but not with an Asturian, Castilian or Aragonese', and 'the conversation of educated persons in Spanish America is, in its salient aspects, a cultured Andalusian, mixed with an occasional vulgarism'. How does this arise? The cause must be sought in the epoch of first settlement, since the later immigration from northern Spain (Basque and Galician in the main) has not imposed northern varieties of Spanish on the American republics: the immigrants have been assimilated to the language of their new abode. The conquest was carried out from southern Spain. Cortés and Pizarro were from Extremadura; Sevilla was the sole centre of colonial administration and trade; the sailors of Columbus' ships were recruited from Palos, etc. Various efforts have been made to determine statistically the provenance of the settlers. Those based on chronicles and chronicle-poems give a high percentage of Andalusians and Extremeñans. Barros Arana stated that almost all the sixteenth and seventeenth-century colonists of Chile were Extremeñans; but Thayer Ojeda reduced the Andalusian percentage to 35, as against 40 from the Castiles and León. Even adding Middle Spain to the South, there would only be a superiority of 1.6 p.c. For the Argentine, Miguel de Toro gives 60 Andalusians and 20 Extremeñans among the primitive nucleus of 124 settlers in the Plate region. On the other hand, elaborate computations by Henríquez Ureña on the basis of sailing-lists allow only the smallest margin of superiority to southern Spain, even when the borders of the latter are advanced far to the north. Of colonists addicted to the *seseo* there would be an actual minority in America. It is not certain whether the count should be one of heads or of influential persons. The habits of outstanding men are liable to be admired and reproduced, especially in circumstances that favour personal display of heroism. The Conquest was a warlike achievement, and in war men cultivate a swagger in language as in walk. The use of pieces of nautical slang (*amarrar* 'to tie', from 'to moor', *flete* 'horse', etc.) are not attributable to the number of sailor-colonists, but to slang adopted by landsmen who had had cause to admire sailors. A 'rough and ready' pose among the settlers doubtless accounts for the vulgarisms current in American Spanish.

Whatever be the true interpretation of these early statistics,

nothing is gained by denying the self-evident similarity between American-Spanish and the language of Andalusia;
but this similarity is crossed by other lines of demarcation.
There is a vast difference between the language of American
highlands—the Mexican plateau, Bogotá and Popayán, Quito,
the plateaux of Bolivia and Peru—and that of the lowlands—
Chile, Argentina, Uruguay, the Mexican coast, etc. It is in
the latter that American 'andalusianism' is most pronounced, in accumulated details of conflict with Castilian.
A climatic theory has been suggested to explain this division,
but, though attractive, it is incapable of proof. The high
ground in the Tropics reproduced conditions more congenial
to European settlers, and especially to those already habituated
to the Castilian Meseta; but we have no data to suggest that
colonists showed regional preferences in the New World. It
was the high ground also that was first occupied by the conquerors, and from thence ran out the tentacles of government.
Further these regions include some of the most important
Indian masses, including some 4,500,000 in Mexico and
3,500,000 in Peru and Bolivia, whereas the Charrúas of the
Plate were exterminated and the Araucanians of Chile driven
south by incessant wars. The presence of alien masses made
Spanish aristocratic and governmental, whereas that of the
Argentine and Chile adopted democratic norms. In Colombia
isolation has produced some tight aristocratic nuclei, which
probably account for the hold of classical Spanish on that
region; and Mexico City and Lima undoubtedly transmitted
the influence of the Spanish capital during the whole colonial
epoch, while the Chilean *pueblos* and Argentine ranches lay
on the periphery of culture. Thus very varied influences have
been at work to ensure that the Spanish of America, within
its indubitable andalusianism, conforms to no single pattern.

DETAILS OF THE SPANISH OF AMERICA

The following are among the peculiarities which have been reported with regard to the Spanish of America. They are neither exclusively nor universally American:

Phonetics and Phonology. The two leading characteristics of American Spanish are *seseo* and *yeísmo*. By *seseo* we mean the confusion of *ç z s* into one sound [s]. It occurs universally in America, with the exception, perhaps, of some Indians in Peru who generalize the pronunciation [θ]. In southern Spain the *seseo* is general, but it runs parallel with the opposite fault, the lisp or *ceceo*. *Yeísmo*, the pronunciation of *ll* as *y*, is not quite so widely spread in America. The district of Atotonilco in Mexico conserves the original sound, which is also found on the high plateau in Colombia, in Peru, in northern and southern Chile, and in the Argentine province of Corrientes. In some cases the existence in Quechua and Mapuche of *ll* may have helped to preserve the Spanish sound. It was undoubtedly brought to America by the conquerors as their normal pronunciation, but was probably accompanied by *y*, which is reported as early as Mozarabic times, and has to be assumed as a stage of the development of C'L LI > OCast. *j* [ž]. This further stage has been reached in the Argentine, where *ll* has passed to *y* (province of Cuyo, Córdoba, etc.), and thence to [ž ĵ] (Buenos Aires and generally). As the final state corresponds to the Italian *g* it may be represented conventionally as transforming *Calle Cuyo* into *Cage Cugio*. The result of these two changes is to reduce four Spanish sounds represented by five letters (*c z s*; *ll y*) to two in America, and thus to make a permanent rift between speech and spelling. Hence come many orthographical errors by ultracorrection, such as '*Popallán*' for *Popayán*, '*Guallaquil*' (in old documents) for *Guayaquil*, and even '*enzallando*' for *ensayando*.

The *s* brought to America was undoubtedly a cacuminal voiceless sibilant [ś], which is attested by Nahuatl and Mapuche borrowings at each end of the area (Nah. *xenola*

Sp. *señora*, Map. *chumpiru* Sp. *sombrero*). This consonant was readily confused, even by Spanish speakers, with kindred palatals, and notably with *j* [ž]. Hence Sp. *tijeras* and *tiseras* 'scissors' Lat. TONSORIA (FERRAMENTA); and this process is carried further in the vulgarisms found in America of the type *frijoles* for *frisoles* 'kidney-beans'. Conversely, there are cases of *s* for *j*, as *relós* (as well as *reló*) for *reloj* 'watch', *almofrés* for *almofrej* 'mattress-bag'. But the *s* now reported as normal in America, as in Andalusia, is the dorsoalveolar *s* pronounced with the tip of the tongue resting on the lower teeth and not raised toward the palate; and it is this lowering of the tip which makes possible the fusion of *s* with *c z*, for which also the tip of the tongue rests near the lower teeth. At the end of a syllable final *-s* passes very commonly to a weak aspirate *h*, which becomes slightly voiced before a voiced consonant, and may finally disappear. It is represented conventionally by *h* or *j*: *no maj, ma (más), vamoh a quejar, loh enamorao* (*los enamorados*), Chilean *le tréyamoh papah, señorita* (*le traíamos papas* 'we should like to bring you potatoes'). The retention of *-s* characterizes the Spanish of the American plateaux in Mexico, Colombia and Peru, whereas it has become an aspirate on the coasts of these countries and in Chile and the Argentine. When it disappears, it is not even represented by hiatus in *está escribiendo* (for *estás*), and leads to contractions like Chilean *ontá mi tío* (*donde está mi tío*) 'at my uncle's house'. In this connection we note instances of confusion wrought by the reintroduction of the value [ks] for *x*, for words containing this Latin value of *x* have been misconstrued as if it were the vernacular *x* [š], the source of the modern *j*: hence *plejo* 'plexus', *ortodojo* 'orthodox', *jilología* 'xylology'.

The Latin F had been universally replaced by Cast. *h* (aspirated) at the time of the Conquest, as witnessed by Nebrija's grammar. This aspirate has remained a characteristic of American Spanish as of Andalusian, whereas *español correcto* has lost the sound. It is conventionally represented by *j*, but is not a rasped velar [χ]. Hence *jarto* Sp. *harto*

FARTU 'stuffed, sufficient', *jijo* Sp. *hijo* FILIU 'son'. But this aspirate occurs even in connection with *r* and *u* (as in *ojrecer ajuera* for *ofrecer afuera*), and where there was never an F (*jirme* for *irme*), and where the word is a recent latinism in Spanish (*jácil* for *fácil*).

Certain interchanges and omissions of consonants also occur very generally in America, southern Spain and among speakers of the lower classes in Madrid. The equation *bue* = [we] *hue* = *güe* gives *buevo* = *güevo* = *huevo* 'egg', *güele* = *huele* 'it smells', whence *goler* 'to smell' for *oler*. The consonants *l r d* belong to the dento-alveolar region, and are vulgarly interchanged: *repué* for *después*, *ran* for *dan*, *rise* for *dice*, *eturio* for *estudio*, *culandrero* for *curandero* 'quack', *candilato* for *candidato*, *ardil* for *ardid* 'stratagem', etc. Between vowels -*d*- -*g*- -*r*- tend to be lost: *ehpeasa* for *despedaza* 'smashes', *hería* for *herida* 'wound', *miaja* for *migaja* 'crumb', *pa* for *para* and *pal* for *para el*, *pasque* or *paez que* for *parece que* 'it seems', *señá* for *señora*; and final -*r* is lost in *señó*, etc. Initial *d*- is sometimes lost by confusion of the prefixes *des*- and *es*-, sometimes through its occurring within the breath-group between vowels: *ehpeasa* for *despedaza*, *etráh* for *detrás* 'behind', and *ilaten* for *dilaten*. A characteristic case for its loss through syntax is *sombrero e paja* for *sombrero de paja* 'straw hat'.

In respect of accentuation the reduction of vowels in hiatus is characteristic of Spanish in America, and no more than a prolongation of a general Romance tendency: *páis bául atáud* for *país baúl ataúd* 'country' 'box' 'coffin'. There is vulgarly (and even in academic Spanish) some hesitation as to the accentuation of Greek words in -*ia* -*ia*, as *academia*, and learned words form false trisyllabic endings, as *méndigo intérvalo* for *mendigo intervalo*. The accentuation of enclitics is notable in the Spanish of the Argentine: *vamonós, dijolé*.

Morphology and Syntax. The declension of nouns is so simple in Spanish that few errors are possible. Double plurals occur vulgarly: *pieses* for *pies* 'feet', *ajises* for *ajíes* 'peppers'; or are applied to words incapable of a plural: *tomo mis onces* 'I am taking my eleven o'clock (refection')', *exclusives* and *inclusives* (adverbs). The ideas underlying grammatical gender are confused, and American Spanish has taken advantage of variation of gender to create useful new words: from *cabra* 'nanny-goat' it has made *cabro* Sp. *cabrón*, from *oveja* 'sheep' *ovejo* Sp. *carnero*, from *testigo reo* 'witness' 'criminal' *testiga rea*, from *tigre tigra* (which is also Old Spanish), *serviciala*, *seglara*, etc. The feminine suggests smaller size or rounder shape, though these notions may lead to contradictory results. The *lora* is not only rounder, but bigger, than the *loro*. *La maunifica* for *el Magnificat* is a popular development in Bogotá.

The pronouns have suffered some modification. Owing to *me*, *nos* frequently becomes *mos* and *nosotros mosotros*. In New Mexico a further confusion gives rise to *lohotroh*, as *la casa de lohotroh* 'our house'. The reflexive *se* tends to become an impersonal pronoun (*cuando se es poeta* for *uno es*), and to be used in place of the other reflexives; while the dative *le* is made use of for vague reference in *le dice adiós a las garzas que pasan* (for *les*) 'he says adieu to the passing herons'. The relative adjective *cuyo* tends to disappear, partly under French influence. Pronouns of courtesy have suffered considerable changes. The apologetic avoidance of the first person leads to some absurdities such as that of the senator mentioned by Cuervo who said in his oration *el infrascrito dice* 'the undersigned (!) says'. The familiar second person *tú* has been lost and *vos* is the nominative singular, but the accusative and dative are *te*; the plural, even familiarly, is *ustedes*. In the verb the singular -*as* -*es* -*es* and -*a* -*e* (imperative) have been confused with the plurals -*ás* -*és* (alternatives for -*áis* -*éis*) -*ís* and -*á* (for -*ad*) -*é* -*í*. Thus we get *Dios te bendecirá y serán felices* 'God will bless you (fam. sing.) and you (fam. plur.) will be happy', *ofrecerles un porvenir a vos y a tu hijo* 'offer you and your son a future', *váyanse* 'get out' (to dogs), etc., *sentáte* 'sit down'. This confusion is believed ineradicable in the Argentine, but has been cleared up in Chile by fifty years' use of Bello's grammar. In Uruguay, thanks to the proximity of Brazil, there is a tendency to consider *usted* too familiar, and to substitute a noun, e.g. *el señor doctor viene* 'you come'. Among other curious uses of the pronoun is the misplaced verbal plural sign in *hágamen* for *háganme*, *siéntensen* for *siéntense*; the order *me se, te se*, for *se me, se te*; *lo que* used as a temporal conjunction, and *lo* before a personal name in the sense of 'at the house of'.

The verb presents numerous irregularities. Of the verbs which develop diphthongs under the accent (*forzar fuerzo*) some may be left with monophthongs (*yo no forzo a nadie*), others show diphthongs; the passage from *-y-* to *-ig-* in Sp. *caiga* is extended to *haiga leiga* (*lea*) *huiga creiga*, etc. The preterite *amasteis* becomes *amaisteis* thanks to *amáis*, and *andar* gives *andáramos* for *anduviéramos*. The synthetic future tense is attacked by the periphrasis of the immediate future, and in the Argentine there is a tendency to treat this as a national shibboleth (like the pronunciation [j] of *ll*). So *daré* is threatened by *voy a dar*; and at the same time *va a llover* tends to be replaced in Bogotá by *va y llueve*, while in the continuous present there is a curious pleonastic use of *ir* in *voy ir cogiendo* = *voy cogiendo* 'I am gathering'. The subjunctive mood is unstable. The future in *-re* gives way to a present indicative or subjunctive according to circumstances in colloquial Spanish, but has left traces of itself in wrong uses of *-se* like *si ella obedeciese al entusiasmo que hoy domina la nación, no hay duda que decretará la República* 'if the Republic obeys the enthusiasm now dominating the nation, it will undoubtedly decree. . .'. The past subjunctive *-se* is less used than its rival *-ra*. The imperative is conjugated on the model *ama amá* or only *amá*; and the gerund develops, probably thanks to French, false participial uses: *la ley concediendo* (for *que concede*), *la tienda está bajando la plaza* (*debajo de la plaza*). In equipping impersonal verbs with plurals (*hubieron temores de guerra* 'there were fears of war') vulgar Spanish has 'construed according to the sense' in the same fashion as standard English, with its 'there is, there are'. In *hubimos muchos heridos* 'there were many of us wounded', this impersonal *hubieron* has been crossed by the personal *tuvimos* or rather by *estuvimos*.

Under French influence there is a strong tendency to ask questions by means of the formula *es. . . que*, which allows the question to keep the affirmative order, and to use the same device for making emphatic assertions: *fué en el siglo XV que se descubrió América = descubrióse América en el siglo XV*. When introducing a sentence, *es que* means 'the fact is that' (*ello es que*); confused with *diz que* 'it is said that', this results in *i que*, introducing an anecdote. Strange ellipses have given rise to *yo fuí fué mar* or *lo soy es Pérez* or *lo hablaba era usted* 'what I was like was the sea' 'as for me I am Pérez' 'what we were discussing was you'.

Various particles have developed original uses in the New World: *cada nada recién hasta entre donde. Cada nada* means 'every trifle', whence *hasta cada rato* 'in a little time'; *él no viene nada* Fr. *il ne vient point. Recién* is found as an adverb in Spanish in *recién casados* 'newly wed', standing before an adjective or participle, but otherwise *recientemente* is required. Not so in America, where phrases like *recién que llegó* 'as soon as he arrived' correspond with Sp. *apenas, no bien. Hasta* implies the negative in *hasta ayer comencé a trabajar* 'I did not begin work until yesterday'; and *entre más* has the sense of *mientras más* in *entre más bebe más sed le da* 'the more he drinks the thirstier he gets'. *Donde* in Chile has the sense of 'at the house of' in *donde mi tío* 'at my uncle's'; with *está* it gives *ontá*, with a past tense *ontava*.

Vocabulary. By far the most important and constant differences between the speech of a Spaniard and a Spanish-American occur in the realm of vocabulary. The latter is compelled to name things which are outside the European's experience or which differ in some particular. For this task he makes use of the large vocabulary of native Indian terms which have been partially digested by the language as a whole. These have already been discussed; but they are by no means the only source of new terms. Not infrequently some slight similarity caused the colonists to give a Spanish name to a new bird or plant, with the result that *gallinaza gorrión jilguero níspero piña ciruela madroño* and other terms have quite different meanings in Spain and in America. In this way the wintry season, which is not only cold but rainy in Europe, gives the name for the rainy season (*invierno*), even if this occur in summer. Diminutives have offered a way of multiplying names, with the result that the stock of affective diminutives has been seriously depleted in America.

There is only the slightest dialectal trace in American Spanish, apart from dialects of Castilian such as Extremeñan and Andalusian. There are, however, numerous archaisms: *entrar a* (MSp. *en*), *es muerto, es nacido* (MSp. *ha muerto, nacido*), *truje* (MSp. *traje*), *vido* (MSp. *vió*), *pararse* 'get up' (MSp. *levantarse*) as in *párese y camine* which is a plain contradiction in Europe, *dende* as well as *desde, topar* (*encontrar*), *mercar, duce* (*dulce*), *recordar* 'awake'. With *entierro* 'treasure' (MSp. 'burial') we have not only an archaic survival of the days before banking, when treasure was regularly buried, but also a reminiscence of the customs of the conquest, of which *desecho desecha* 'track' is another. On meeting a promising track the explorers must frequently have said *echemos por aquí* 'let's take this one', and when it petered out they would use the verb *desechar*. Thanks to *caminos pasos atajos* the noun became in Colombia *desecho*; but also *desecha* on account of *senda vereda trocha*. As settlers were carried by long sea-voyages, they picked up the slang of sailors: whence *amarrar* 'tie' in *amarrar una corbata* (properly 'moor'), *flete* 'horse', *caramanchel* 'hut' ('hatchway'), *trincar* 'to pin anyone down' 'seize', *vientos* 'strings connecting a kite with its cord' ('guys, braces'), etc. Ruts are *canjilones*, as resembling the crinkles of the sixteenth-century ruffs. The special concern of the colonists with cattle-raising has given rise to complex colour-spectra, varying in different parts of America, and serving to distinguish primarily horses, but also cows: *cisne moro*, etc.

There has been necessarily much independent semantic development, and the formation of new words. *Irreverencia* is the model serving to give *irrespeto*; *una contradicción, un contrasentido* causes *una contracaridad* 'an uncharitable act'; *sangriligero sangripesado* are a new pair signifying 'agreeable' 'disagreeable'. The transference of *páramo* from the Castilian Meseta to the Andine plateaux is natural. The latter are accursed with snow and rain, so that *páramo* acquires the sense 'drizzle' (*llovizna*), whence *paramar* 'to drizzle' and *emparamarse* 'to chitter with cold' (*arrecirse*). The volcano not only belches out fire but overturns everything, whence *volcar > desvolcanarse*; *temperar* acquires easily the sense of to enjoy a change of air (*mudar aires*); *olear* 'to use (holy) oil' means in Spain 'to administer the supreme unction', in America 'to baptize', while *santolio* is 'extreme unction'. In the case of *barranca* and its congeners, what is a ravine to one looking down is a cliff to one looking up, as it was in Cervantes' *despeñar a uno de una barranca* 'to throw someone down from a cliff' (MSp. *en una barranca* 'into a gully'). *Montaña* and *monte* refer not only to the hills, but also the scrub on them; in Chile the mountain is *cerro*.

The application of *niño niña ña* to grown up persons is an extension of the language of the nursery by faithful retainers. As the distinction between *c s* has been lost *cocinar* 'to cook' has been created to avoid the homonymy *cocer* 'cook' *coser* 'sew', *ceba* 'fodder' against *cebo* 'fodder' *sebo* 'tallow', *cacería* 'chase' against *caza* 'hunt' *casa* 'house'. Admirable metaphors have been drawn from novel circumstances: as *echar pólvora en gallinazos* 'to waste effort', *a la pampa* 'in the open air', *ver gatos ensillados* 'to see stars', *achicar a uno* 'to kill anyone' (to make him cower into a small space and then to despatch him), *machetear* 'to persevere' by hacking one's way through obstacles with a bowie-knife (Sp. *porfiar*). Popular etymology gives *vagamundo* as well as *vagabundo* (common also in Spain), and *arremueco* beside *arrumaco* 'caress' (*mueca* 'grimace'). *Comendante* comes from *comandante* and *comendar*. The prefixes *des-* and *es-* are liable to confusion in all vulgar Spanish; the suffixes *-ear* and *-ecer* are used without discrimination (*florear florecer*), and *-ear* merges into *-iar* by the same process of phonetic reduction which makes *pior* out of *peor*.

The influence of 'Modernism'. The basic principle of R. J.

Cuervo's *Apuntaciones sobre el lenguaje bogotano*, which remains
our best general introduction to American variants of Spanish,
was a conservative one: he would admit what was justified
either by reliable tradition or by imminent need, but he
sought to eliminate useless and slovenly departures from the
common Spanish inheritance. This was the position maintained by the great literary preceptor Miguel A. Caro, who
was pleased to think of Bogotá as 'the Athens of America',
the seat of classical elegance. The 'Modernists' (members of
a movement that had its apogee between 1896–1916), and
to some extent their successors, have considered innovation
a virtue: they seek novelty not from need, but as a mark of
refinement. Possessed of a really great poet in Rubén Darío
and of other lesser lights, the 'Modernists' could not but exercise an influence on the language in a sense opposed to that
of Cuervo. The colloquial language, however, they have probably left unaffected; and little change has occurred in prose
apart from that small fragment which claims to be artistic.
Most of their influence has fallen on the language of poetry,
which they have substantially altered, for the better in most
respects. The long straggling sentence has been broken up;
attention has been called to rhythm even in prose, and to
trisyllabic rhythms long neglected by verse; the wearily
paired adjectives of classicism have departed. Preaching
'the rare' as a virtue, they employed a vocabulary drenched
with exotic words, pseudo-Greek via Paris or pseudo-oriental,
sometimes without any etymological sense. Hence *bulbul
ronronear bandó palimpsesto* (= *literatura*!). The trisyllabic ending
again appeared peculiarly poetical to Darío as to the contemporaries of Góngora:

que *púberes canéforas* te ofrenden el acanto;

and pseudo-Greek suffixes gave an easy crop of '-ists' and
'-isms': *verleniano* 'in the manner of Verlaine', *poeniano* 'in
Poe's style', *murillesco, prerrafaelista, neoyorkino, hamlético*. The
last word exemplifies the artificial and literary basis of this
vocabulary, and the last but one the fact that little trouble

was taken over words which no one expected to survive the immediate occasion. This vocabulary has to be sifted, and not much will remain. Those with the best prospects are refurbished archaisms taken from Old Spanish. The exotic, indeed, was at once challenged by the doctrine of 'Americanism' which demands that American literature and language should fit the facts of American life. To do so it will eschew the exotic, and it will probably draw fewer cheques on the moribund Indian bank than on the circulating currency of racy colloquialisms, which have not been sufficiently explored since Santa Teresa. Though it is clear that the present literary tendencies favour change, the career of the 'Modernist' movement suggests that the change will come very slowly in the body of the language; and in the same way the slang of the cosmopolitan centres, though effervescent, will leave few permanent deposits, especially since it does not enjoy the prestige and fixity of literature.

THE NORTHERN FRONTIER

The political frontier of Spanish-speaking America runs along the Río Grande, between Texas and Mexico, but the colonial empire reached vaguely out to the north and the linguistic frontier lies beyond the political. Florida was discovered before Mexico, and for ten years Álvar Núñez Cabeza de Vaca worked his way painfully through the coast of the Mexican Gulf, discovering the great Mississippi, until he fell in with Cortés' frontier garrisons and learned the news of Moctezuma's fall. A complication of nationality in this region arose out of the French occupation of Louisiana, which has left a legacy of French language and literature to New Orleans and its hinterland. North and north-west of the Mexican boundary expeditions were drawn by the lure of the 'seven cities of Cíbola', imperfectly realized by the villages of the Pueblo Indians. Lower California was early discovered and named from an island in the novel of *Amadís de Gaula*, the Colorado river was ascended a short distance by Coronado in 1540; Juan de Oñate made a settlement in New Mexico in 1598, but his colony was obliterated by a terrible Indian revolt in 1680 and had to be repeopled in 1692. Devoted missionaries, of whom the most illustrious was Fray Junípero Serra, established stations in California, and they left behind them the mission style of architecture in the south-west, a tradition balancing the colonial style of the east. Thanks to these influences the nomenclature of the whole south-west is predominantly Spanish: *California, Nevada, Colorado, New Mexico, Texas, Florida* among States; *Sierra Nevada, San Juan, Sangre de Cristo, Sacramento, San Andreas,* etc. among mountain ranges; the words *mesa* and *canyon; Sacramento, San Joaquin, Colorado, Brazos, Nueces,* etc. among rivers; *San Francisco, Los Angeles, Sacramento, San Diego, Monterey, Palo Alto, Albuquerque, Amarillo, San Angelo,* etc. among towns. The travels of shipmen carried Spanish names for capes, bays, straits, etc. much further north, especially along the west coast where the *San Juan de Fuca* strait separates Washington from Vancouver and *Juan Pérez* Sound is not far short of Alaska. It is not to be supposed that these names indicate effective occupation; the greater part of the territory was attached to the empire in little more than name, and a scanty fringe of colonists in the south-west held the ground behind a still scantier fringe of mission stations. Consequently the territories fell easily to the expanding United States, when Napoleon had led the way by his Louisiana sale of 1803. Florida was transferred in 1819; Texas, nominally an independent republic, was acquired in 1845; the possession of New Mexico was the bone of contention in the war of 1845–48; Utah, Nevada, Arizona and California were carried by the gold rush of 1849–50.

The official language of all this region is now English, but tradition has handed down the use of Spanish, particularly in New Mexico. The peculiarities of this region offer a double interest: they display the delayed action of Spanish evolution since they lay so far from the heart of the Mexican viceroyalty, and they exemplify in an intense degree the conflict of the two great American languages, English and Spanish, which occurs also with less violence elsewhere. The material and political predominance of the United States affects the colloquial vocabulary of Mexico City and Buenos Aires, where, however, it is treated as a foreign element and rejected or circumscribed. In New Mexico it pervades and decomposes the local Spanish.

New Mexican lies within the Uto-Aztek Indian region, and has the same aboriginal vocabulary as Mexican Spanish both in this respect and with regard to the numerous archaisms and vulgarisms of a plebeian speech uncontrolled by literature. Thus one may enumerate such typical words or pronunciations as: *agora ansí ansina naiden anque pus comigo escrebir mesmo dende quese (que es de) escuro traidrá lamber entensión vide (ví) vía (veía) muncho tráir (traer) páis eclise indino esaito (exacto) cáusula (cápsula)*, etc. *Seseo* is universal, but *yeísmo* varies. In Mexico City and on the coast *ll* has the value of *y*; at Atotonilco it is *ll* and at Puebla [ž]. In New Mexico it has the value of [ž] or [ĵ] when initial, as in *lluvia* [ĵubi̯a or žubi̯a], but medially it may disappear, as *allá ayá aá á*. We know that the settlers brought with them [š] as the pronunciation of *x j ǵ*, and developed this sound into [χ]; the latter circulated out from the viceregal city and reached New Mexico. It provoked everywhere a parallel evolution of Nahuatl [š] to [χ], but this took place more slowly, and in northern New Mexico not at all. So there Nah. *xocotl* 'bunchosia' gives still *šocoque* as against Mex. *jocote*. Similarly Nahuatl has no *r*, but has been compelled to learn this sound from Spanish and uses it in later borrowings: it possesses *l*, *ll* in the sense of a lengthened *l* [l:], and *tl* which is a sort of click. The laterals offered no support for Spanish *ll* [λ], and at first Nah. *l* did duty also for Sp. *r rr*: *xenola xalo* for *señora jarro*, *Malinche* for *Marina*. There is still some uncertainty as to the values of *l r* in native minds: *carsetín* for *calcetín*.

The conflict with invading English in New Mexico has been studied in a suggestive fashion. Of special dialectal forms totalling 1400, about 1000 are Spanish, 300 English,

75 Nahuatl, and 10 local Indian. The Spanish forms are met with elsewhere, and so prominence is given to the unusually heavy English element. As there is no literature other than ballads and a folk-song or two, it is not possible to point to a reaction against this vocabulary or to draw a distinction between those words which have been assimilated and those which remain foreign. The situation is that any English expression may be adapted to the speaker's use by simple devices of pronunciation. The English accent is free to occupy any syllable and tends to come early in the word; it is also significant as indicating the root idea. In Spanish borrowings the accentuation is Spanish in character, not important for meaning, and frequently drawn towards the end of the word by elevating a secondary into a primary accent: *fíremàn* gives *fayamán*, *hóld òn* gives *jolón* 'insult', *hígh-tòned* becomes *jaitón*. The use of a Spanish suffix occasionally eases the transition: *shooter* gives *šutiador*, *switchman* becomes *suichero*. The English vowels have been simplified: *ī* is *ai*, *ŭ* is *a o*, neutral *e* is *a*: *fayamán* 'fireman', *flaya* 'flier', *lonchi* 'lunch', *jamachi* 'how much', *šarape* 'shut up!' *guasa* 'washer'. An *e* precedes 'impure' *s* (*escrepa* 'scraper') and follows consonants not used finally in Spanish (*estail* 'style', *esmarte* 'smart', *šope* 'shop', *cute* 'coat'—after palatals comes *i*, as *lonchi* 'lunch'). *W* is *gu*: *Guayomén Güile* (Wyoming, Willie).

The consonant system of English requires less modification to serve for New Mexican Spanish. Though [š] is not found in Spanish words, its survival in Nahuatl loan-words makes it available to render English *sh*: *šope* 'shop'. A sense of the equivalence of *f* and *h j* [χ] leads to such duplicate renderings as *ful jul* 'fool', *telefón telejón* 'telephone' (Sp. *teléfono*). As fricative *r* interchanges with *d* in the colloquial, so 'how do you do' becomes *jarirú*, 'goodbye' *gurbái* and 'drink' *rinque*. English *ǧ* is rendered by the corresponding voiceless palatal affricate [ĉ]: *Chochis* 'George'. Unfamiliar consonant-groups are simplified (*parna* 'partner', *cuara* 'quarter', *sangüichi* 'sandwich'), and the final *-er* represented as a vowel *-a*.

The loans greatly exceed what is either useful or necessary, and their difference from the native Spanish stock indubitably disintegrates the idiom. *Jamachi* 'how much', *jaló* 'hello' (on the telephone), *guerop* or *guirape* 'get up', *fone felo* or *jone jelo* 'funny fellow', are disreputable members of a vocabulary which includes the whole range of English names, adopted without translation, and numerous common nouns that occur frequently: *saiguoque* 'side-walk', *bisnes* 'business', *puši* 'push', *laya* 'liar', *besbol* 'base-ball', *šotegón* 'shot-gun', *rapa* 'wrapper'. The English, of course, is that of the United States, and many of the loans are taken from slang: *broquis* 'broke', *šante* 'shanty', *guiangue* 'gang', *nicle* 'nickel', *cranque* 'cranky'. The freedom with which such words take Spanish suffixes, whether adjectival or verbal, is a sign of their intimate penetration: *cuitiar* 'to quit', *fuliar* 'to fool', *šutiador* 'shooter'. Such treatment implies a permanent lodgment in vocabulary.

COSMOPOLIS

On the southern frontier there occurs another area of conflict between world-languages, though the situation is in many respects different from that of New Mexico. The Plate Region is in intimate contact with Europe by reason of its great ports and its copious immigration. Representatives of all nations flock to Buenos Aires to make up the future Argentina, and they bring with them their own languages. The problem of nation-building is acute, and consequently that of language-building. These are growing pains, not, as in New Mexico, the throes of dissolution. We have seen that several of the founders of this republic united to demand an *idioma nacional argentino*, though the demand proved premature. To erect colloquial peculiarities into national standards—the pronunciation [ĵ] of *ll*, the misuse of *vos*, or the future *voy a decir*—is to call attention to vulgarisms that are not peculiarly Argentine, and also to impoverish the language by blurring useful distinctions. The Indian element offers no satisfactory basis for such a development. To exalt the Guaraní word against the Quechua is to lose the power of communicating with other Spanish Americans, and perhaps with other Argentines; but the Quechua vocabulary is in no sense national. Besides, all this vocabulary is static, and must diminish before the advance of material prosperity in the great towns. These towns already use forms which are not current in Córdoba, Tucumán and the inland cities, with their more traditional mode of life. Thus there exist differences in the Spanish of Argentina which have not yet been investigated to the full.

Apart from the *idioma nacional*, however, there remains a sense of the insufficient resources of Spanish for the expression of Argentine experience. As originally voiced by Sarmiento and Alberdi, this complaint no doubt showed ignorance of the resources available in the mother-tongue, which are much greater than any Spanish-speaker, whether European or American, is aware. Still it is not possible to deny that French has fuller and more precise expressions for society and culture at the present day than has Spanish, nor that Englishmen are more versed in sport and the arts of comfort, nor that North Americans enjoy a vastly superior material development. For these reasons words are borrowed in Spain itself from French, English, German and other languages, and are slowly naturalized; in the Plate Region there is a much greater readiness to adopt neologisms of this sort, and less trouble is taken to see whether the existing funds suffice. Constant touch with foreigners—with merchants and financiers, with teachers and intellectuals, with immigrants—leads to a constant linguistic ferment in this most cosmopolitan region of America.

One may remark, in the first instance, that the proximity of Brazil has not greatly affected the language of the Plate. Its influence is felt chiefly in Uruguay, which was for a period part of the empire of Brazil; but it is slight. The variant *brasilero* for Sp. *brasileño* (Ptg. *brasileiro*), *saudade* for Sp. *añoranza* (Cat. *anyorança*), and some terms used in prohibited trades, together with a tendency to use periphrases like *el señor doctor* for *usted*, are the total contribution from this quarter; though a mixed language exists precariously as a stage in the acquisition of Spanish by Brazilians, and it is sometimes parodied in comic papers of Montevideo.

Apart from these neighbours, the principal foreign elements found in the Plate region are English and Americans, French, Italians, Germans and Poles. The last-named exert no linguistic influence, and the Germans little. There remain for discussion English, French and Italian. The English are mainly associated with the financial and technical interests of the country: they have offered loans, built railroads, despatched machinery, helped to develop the meat industry, etc. For these ends a relatively small number of immigrants suffice, about ·5 p.c. of the whole, who keep themselves pretty much to themselves, speaking English to each other but Spanish in business. They have an organized club-life, and are indifferent to linguistic or cultural proselytizing. The North American exaggerates these qualities. He is a more recent investor, using up his surplus of war-gold. He has less desire to settle, but monopolizes the motor and cinematographic industries, and is the day's embodiment of material greatness. The Germans are engaged in business and commerce, and assimilate rapidly to the body of the nation, of which they constitute about 1 p.c. The French are also financiers and town-dwellers, but they supply many individuals to the professional services. Their hold on the Argentine began with Louis Napoleon's *coup d'état*, when many middle-class Liberals fled overseas and became the instructors of the Argentine youth. They held up the model of French culture and language, instilled in their pupils a desire to finish their education by a visit to Paris, established French booksellers on the Plate (Ollendorff, Garnier, etc.), and made French the necessary intermediary between any European achievement and Spanish-America. A striking evidence of this power is the circumstance that, though the Argentine army was reorganized by Germans, the terms employed were French: *abatís conscripto* (Sp. *quinto*) *edecán reclutar*. Amounting to some

2·5 p.c. of the whole body, the French element exerts a disproportionate influence through its intellectual propaganda. The Italians are of a humbler class. They total over 2,000,000, or 25 p.c. of the whole, and, apart from sellers of lottery tickets and dock-labourers, they are wont to move out on to the land, where they struggle to scrape together enough from the soil to enable them to return to a life of village prosperity in Italy. They have nothing cultural to offer, and their influence on the language is exiguous. The Italian loan-words are those terms of music, architecture, painting and sculpture which have entered all European vocabularies, together with the military and financial words adopted by Spain in the sixteenth century.

The huge number of the Italian immigrants demands some attention for the mixed Italo-Spanish dialect known as *cocoliche*. At first blush this looks like the marriage of two languages that would lead to the birth of a third; but in fact *cocoliche* contains no threat against the purity of Spanish. The jargon is frequently parodied in the popular press, and a specimen 'poem' opens as follows:

> Amico Dun vieco Panchos:
> Usté, per yenar papiel,
> han hechos in gran pastel
> que nun lo come ne il canchos, etc.

The immigrant arrives completely illiterate and without any knowledge of Spanish. Spanish he must learn if he is to eat bread, and he learns it wholly by ear, misunderstanding what he hears and keeping up his prejudices for some Italian forms in a quite haphazard fashion. For instance, in the above example, having no -*s* plural, he tacks -*s* on at random to singulars; having no [χ] he substitutes [k] in *vieco*; he fails to recognize the true unaccented *o*, and he keeps a grip on his Italian particles, *per il ne*, etc. He frequently borrows verbal endings from his own tongue and uses Italian where it will pass muster, e.g. *dovia* for *debía*. But his language is in a state of flux, and he will go on augmenting the Spanish element during the whole of his stay, while the precise mixture is purely personal and is not a means of communicating with other members of his class. His children, if he stay so long, will learn accurately colloquial Argentine, and will endeavour to correct their parent. *Cocoliche*, in short, is merely Spanish imperfectly learned.

The French influence is very powerful in intellectual spheres. The newspapers multiply new political and social terms, and the jargon of the Quartier Latin and Montparnasse serves to name literary and artistic novelties. These terms force their way in even when satisfactory Spanish equivalents exist. One has *apostolado* (in the political sense) *arrivista campaña* (Sp. *campo*) *clientela control etapa malentendido* (Fr. *mal entendu*) *sindicato tirada vitrallas*, etc., with adjectives of the same class like *banal alienado* (Sp. *enajenado*) *fatigante parsimonioso remarcable* (used in Spain in the eighteenth century); verbs are *admitir* (in the sense of *conceder*) *hesitar nulificar*, and prepositional phrases *excepción hecha de* (Sp. *prescindiendo de*) *lejos de* (Sp. *en vez de*). The formal relations of society are on the Parisian plan: *matiné supé té-dansant suaré* (Fr. *soirée*) *parvenú*. Fashionable shopping, and especially everything that adorns the woman of elegance, is French: *georgette reps, dernier cri, Maison Clothilde*. Intercepting the language of modern science, French has sent on to the Plate *antisepsia* for *antisepsis, panslavismo* for *paneslavismo*, and *psichiatría* for Sp. *psiquiatría*.

The English vocabulary is almost entirely one of nouns. Only one verb is common, *linchar*, which is fortunately not from England. Club-life, sport and commercial organization are the principal sources of supply: *club clubman* (for *socio*) *jockey highlife el flirteo fiveoclock* (fashionable tea) and *Palace Hotel* (in the English order), together with *futbol boxeo* and *lockout selfmademan pioneer snob repórter bluff* (and *bluffman*), etc. An odd reduplication has occurred in respect of horseracing, which is an old sport of the Argentine plebs and also a costly entertainment imported from Europe. The former (*carreras criollas o del país*) take place on *el día de reunión* in a *cancha*, and *apuestas* are made; the signal to start is given by the *abanderado*, and the *corredores* urge their horses up to the *lazo de llegada o raya*. But the fashionable race in the big town takes place at *el meeting*, amid *el betting*, in the *hipódromo*; the signal is given by *el starter*, and *los jockeys* make for *el winning-post o la meta*. The more general terms are French, the technicalities English.

The whole of this vocabulary is insecure, and particularly when it descends to details and takes on strange phonetic shapes. It consists of neologisms and foreign words (*neologismos y extranjerismos*). A neologism is one which has been adapted to Spanish norms; the others remain evidently foreign. The neologism is thus the word more likely to pass unnoticed in discourse and to survive; against the un-naturalized foreign expression the national conscience revolts. Adaptation is an intelligent process and especially frequent in cultural loan-words, which are of French origin, as we have seen; French words, conversely, admit readily of adaptation to Spanish by their common Latin origin. English words neither agree with Spanish principles, nor do they occur in spheres where permanence is assumed or even desired; all but a few remain foreigners, and are menaced with expulsion. A very keen linguistic sense exists among the Argentines as among all persons of Spanish descent. Without defining what is Spanish, they are quick to note what is foreign. This quick resentment is seen in the nicknames of foreign nations: all are *gringos*, but especially the Italians; the Spaniards are *godos*, the French *franchutes* or *gabachos*, the English *yónis*. If a word is to be definitely admitted it must be reshaped, and sometimes translation takes place before this occurs: *durmiente* railway 'sleeper', *estrella* cinema 'star'. The strange word is humorously misrepresented (*sietemetógrado* for *cinematógrafo*), and it is excluded from the literary pages of the newspaper. The sporting pages are written in the outlandish jargon which disfigures them everywhere, as

> El *referee* al finalizar el primer *half-time* concedió a los húngaros un *penalty-kick*. Inmediatamente se produjo un *clinch*, siguió un *upper-cut*, luego un *hook* de derecha...la

lucha prosiguió en *out-fighting*. . . un hombre de fuerte *punch*.

These examples from among those given by Grossmann give point to his remark that while not a single neologism or foreign word was found by him on the editorial page of *La Nación* in a count of 2500 lines, 240 neologisms and 500 foreign words occurred in an equal number of lines under the rubric 'Futbal y boxeo'. Under a surface agitation of incessant experiment, the essential language changes with almost geological slowness; and despite every temptation to differ, the language of the Argentine does not abandon its traditions, but even becomes increasingly Spanish. It has become a national principle to preserve this patrimony.

CHAPTER VIII

PORTUGUESE

Camões entitled his national epos 'The Lusitanians' and reckoned among the first events of national history the resistance of Viriathus to the legions; but there can be no doubt that the kingdom and the language descended from the north. The south and centre of Portugal, as far as the Douro, was occupied by a Mozarabic dialect, which owned for its centres the Roman capital of Mérida and the Moslem seat of Badajoz. Roman Lusitania extended so far into Spain as to include Ávila. This dialect was eminently conservative; no innovations are reported as originating in the south-west. The tonic vowels ě ŏ remained simple vowels (*Mérida* EMĚRITA *Caçela* CASTELLA), and proparoxytones appear to have been unusually tolerated. In these respects Badajoz and the Algarve resembled the conservative parts of Granada. Between vowels -*n*- was preserved in *Odiana* ANAS *Fontanas Al-Ašbûna* (Fr. *Lisbonne* Eng. *Lisbon* OSp. *Lisbona*); and intervocalic -*l*- remained in *Mértola* MYRTILIS *Ròliça* and probably *Baselgas* BASILICAS. *Caçela* shows the Mozarabic evolution of -ST- to *ç* as in *Çaragoça* (*Zaragoza*) and *Écija*; and Moz. -*a* for -E appears in *Lisboa Mértola*. Mozarabic names appear in documents, as *Cidi Adaredici, Zidi presbyter, Torsario Daviz, Arias Salamoniz*. From the Douro southwards the linguistic and political frontiers do not now precisely correspond, but the more pronounced differences are due to former lines of demarcation (e.g. the Portuguese spoken at Olivenza in the Badajoz region); there is no shading off from Portuguese into Spanish such as occurs north of the river. Central and south Portugal have thus been overrun by the northern dialects, which they resembled in their conservatism (extreme

---

The principal works of reference are mentioned in the note at the end of Chapter I.

even among Mozarabic dialects), but with which they agreed in no innovation.

The Gallæco-Portuguese massif in the north-west is one of the best defined subdivisions of the Iberian Peninsula. The narrow fringe of the Cantabrian mountains splays out at its western end, and the highest line bends round in a south-westerly and southerly curve along the Montes de León to the knot of Peña Trevinca, backed by a second line formed of the Sierras de Picos, Caurel and Queija. Spurs run down from these ranges into Portugal, where they occupy the province of Traz-os-Montes and the eastern half of Entre-Douro-e-Minho. Hills maintaining the original east-west direction of the Cantabrians run down to the sea in fingers, between which lie the Galician *rías* and their small plains; while there are two inland river-depressions, that of the upper Minho which has Lugo for its capital, and that of the Sar and Santiago de Compostela. The consequence of this mountain formation is that Galicia cannot be approached from the central Meseta or the Portuguese coastal belt save over parallel ranges of mountains. The region is thrown inward on its own centre; and at the same time its *rías* and river-valleys make it capable of sustaining a considerable population. Administrative frontiers have not coincided with these natural bastions, but tend to adopt the lines of bounding rivers. The Douro serves admirably as a frontier against central Portugal, since from the falls to the sea it runs rather through a trench than a valley. Against Spain a number of ecclesiastical and other frontiers have adopted at various moments of history the line of the Esla, which runs approximately parallel to the Montes de León. Both banks of this river, however, belong geographically and culturally to the Spanish Meseta, which extends at least to the Orbigo. Indeed the mountains themselves serve less for a barrier than as an area of transition to the Galician region which lies behind them. To a considerable extent Galicia is the product of the Minho river. Though bordering on the sea, the region is not mercantile like the lower Tagus basin; it lacks the proper hinterland,

and there is a want of unity between the centres of population, each established in a depression between ranges of hills.

Racial and political divisions have emphasized the semi-independence of the region. A frontier which goes back to remote times is that between the Astures and the Cantabri in the Asturias, and farther south the Astures held the Astur River (Esla) against the Vaccæi. Behind the Astures of western León lay other tribes, of whom the most influential were the *Gallæci*. The name bears a superficial resemblance to that of the *Galatæ*, a Celtic people, but this is less evident in Strabo's spelling *Kallaïkoi*. Similarly the *Arotrebæ* resemble superficially the Celtic *Atrebates*, but this also may be misleading. We only know that there were *Celtici* living about the promontory of Nerium, between Coruña and Finisterre, and that Celtic names were given to fortresses and settlements in Galicia and Portugal with considerable profusion. There is no evidence sufficient to show a Celtic predominance in the north-west, and nothing definite is known concerning the circumjacent tribes. As the force of the 'Iberian' invasion, presumed to have come from Africa, appears to have expended itself on the central Meseta, it is likely that the Iberian quota in Galicia was unusually small. The tribes have been assigned to the 'Ligurian' stock, which is perhaps meaningless, and only amounts to calling them non-Iberian.

In historical times, we find Galicia, North Portugal and Western León forming an administrative block in the Roman Empire, and assigned to Hither Spain (under Augustus) or kept separate as a diocese. Under the Visigoths this line of division remained to separate the arch-diocese of Bracara (Braga) from those of Carthaginensis, Tarraconensis and Lusitania. The diocese of Astorga, the eastern bulwark of the Galician province, covers approximately the area of Western Leonese, and included originally the Leonese-speaking city of Miranda do Douro, now within the Portuguese border. At this time the thrust of the Visigothic invasion concentrated in Galicia their enemies, the west Germanic Swabians (*Suevi*), who were subdued only in the sixth century. Early in the eighth the Visigothic monarchy itself was annihilated by Țâriq and Mûşâ. The remnants of the nation fled northward to hide in the valleys of the Cantabrian mountains and the Pyrenees, in barren regions that offered little prospect of establishing new states. In the Galician river-basins, however, there were means of maintaining considerable numbers of men, who would be almost perfectly screened from invasion. Here Alfonso I organized his Christian kingdom, and even overran and laid waste the plains of León, before the Christians were forced again to concentrate behind the mountains. Indications of this period of Germanic settlement are to be found in the Germanic place-names, such as *Godos Gude Aldegode Valgode Goda Gudín Gudiña Godón* or *Sabín Sabrigo Jabaríz Saboy Sabegode*, which denote Gothic or Swabian nationality, or in names based on that of some prominent chief. That the process of settlement occupied time is evidenced by the changes of syntax and vocabulary: the Latin genitive in *Vilagude* as against the Romance *de* of *Casal de Goda*, the diminutives in *-iño* and augmentatives in *-aço*, or the Arabic *alde-* 'village'.

The tenth century saw the balance of power transferred to the plains of León, but Galicia continued to make the most rapid reconquests in the valley of the Mondego. Here Alfonso III's campaigns had to be fought afresh in the eleventh century by Fernando I, who established the Mozarabic count Sisnando in Coimbra (1064). Alfonso VI divided the whole region between Raymund and Henry of Burgundy, and thus commenced the separation of Portugal from Galicia. Henry's son, Afonso, contrived to wrest the title of king from Alfonso VII in 1143; but his claim would have had little substance had he not seized the great Mozarabic city of Lisbon with the aid of a crusading army in 1147. This feat brought Portugal into veritable being, since it imprinted a wholly new direction on its policies. Its future was to be controlled not by the massif from which the conquerors had come, but from the amphitheatre of the lower Tagus, facing the ocean and cultivating the friendship and commerce of oceanic neighbours. It was an orientation which Galicia could not share, and despite community of history and language a split occurred, which has converted the Minho from a medial line into a frontier. The land between Minho and Douro remained with Portugal, though standing close to Galicia in dialect and interests. The Portuguese monarchs did not immediately use Lisbon as their capital, but resided at Coimbra or Leiria by preference until the Moslem menace had been driven farther south. Portugal reached its full extent in 1250. In the disturbances caused by the failure of the legitimate Burgundian line in 1383, the paramount importance of Lisbon emerged as the guarantor of Portuguese independence; and the monarchs of the house of Aviz resided normally in the city or its near neighbourhood (Cintra). The various stages of the Christian advance are marked by dialectal differences in Portuguese.

GALLÆCO-PORTUGUESE AND SPANISH

In their earliest stages Galician and Portuguese were one language of a markedly Ibero-Romance character. The resemblance between them and Spanish leaps to the eye as they are written, especially if allowance is made for mere orthographic variants such as Ptg. *lh nh* for Gal. Sp. *ll ñ*. As spoken the resemblance is less in evidence, but an attentive listener will soon become aware that the languages employ the same general phonetic pattern. The rhythm is trochaic, owing to the conservation in both languages of final vowels, and the elimination of unaccented penultimate vowels. Portuguese preserves rather more finals than Spanish, e.g. -*e* after *d* in *parede verdade estae* for *estade*, as also in the brief -*ĕ* often heard after infinitives (as also, to some extent, in Leonese Spanish). The language is also rather more tolerant than Spanish of trisyllabic endings: Ptg. *dúvida dívida bébado* Sp. *duda deuda beodo* 'doubt, debt, drunk'. In the vowel-series Portuguese and Spanish have none of the mixed group so characteristic of French (y œ ø), though stress alters quality as well as tension in Portuguese vowels, but only tension in Spanish. The rich series of nasal vowels in Portuguese is of comparatively recent growth; and at all events they are not akin to French nasals, which require a considerable depression of the uvula. Among the consonants, we find in both Spanish and Portuguese the peculiar transition from occlusive *b d g* to fricatives; and these are, in the same fashion, frequently due to voicing of intervocalic -P- -T- -K-. As this process was of western origin in the Peninsula, it has been carried through rather more systematically in Portuguese, e.g. Ptg. *liberdade* Sp. *libertad*. Both languages employ the same strongly vibrant *rr*, which is wont to develop before or after it, especially in Portuguese, a fugitive vowel. Ptg. *preto perto* 'black' 'near' are barely distinguishable [pᵉrétṳ pérᵉtṳ], owing to the same causes as give in OSp. *perlado* beside *prelado*. In morphology, Portuguese has, like Spanish, lost all trace of the two-case system which operated in OFr. Both languages form plurals in -(*e*)*s* and have eliminated neuter plurals in -A. Comparison is by MAGIS, not PLUS. In the verbal paradigm both languages have eliminated the conjugation in -ĔRE, identifying it with -ĒRE; and both favour -*ir* at the expense of -*er*, though Portuguese does so less than Spanish: Ptg. *dizer* Sp. *decir* DICĔRE. They have kept -*ra*, the ancient ending of the pluperfect indicative, though Spanish employs it only as a conditional or an imperfect subjunctive. The future perfect indicative and perfect subjunctive have united to give a future subjunctive, Ptg. -*r* Sp. -*re*. There has been in both an immense simplification of past tenses and past participles, which very generally conform to the present stem; and they have favoured, in common, a multiplicity of auxiliaries. Here Portuguese has gone further than Spanish by making *ter* (Sp. *tener*) its usual auxiliary, and restricting *haver* to impersonal uses (save in the literary style). Both tongues use the Latin inceptive suffix -ĔSCERE to form new verbs from nouns, without necessarily an inceptive sense. In the matter of vocabulary, both Portuguese and Spanish have made the same choice of alternative Latin expressions (*querer quedar calar falar* = Sp. *hablar chegar* = Sp. *llegar dexar* = Sp. *dejar*); they show the same iberisms, but rather fewer in Portuguese; the same celticisms and germanisms; and substantially the same arabisms. In the last respect, Portuguese, like Old Leonese in Spanish, has retained words which have been lost to Castilian-Spanish: *alfageme* 'barber' *alfaiate* 'tailor' *leilão* (Arabic?) 'auction'.

The appearance of similarity to Spanish is thus very strong when we compare the literary languages, but it increases when we compare Portuguese with the Spanish *koiné*. A few of the apparent differences are due to the historical development of Galician and Portuguese, but the great majority are due to the peculiar features of Castilian among medieval Spanish dialects and to the sound-shifts which occurred in the sixteenth century. In most of its features Portuguese agrees with Leonese or Mozarabic Spanish against Castilian, and as these are archaic stages through which the Castilian changes have passed, it follows that Portuguese has the air of an archaic Spanish. Its conservatism is shown in the fact that the vowels ĕ ŏ do not result in diphthongs under any circumstances; they become [ɛ] [ɔ], and differ in timbre from the [e] [o] resulting from ē ō. There are thus seven tonic vowels in Portuguese as in Catalan, and only five in Castilian (apart from shades of variation); but to the Castilian series we should also attribute the diphthongs *ie ue*, to make up the Peninsular seven. They are indivisible diphthongs, distinct from others whose pronunciation is optional (e.g. *suave* or *su-ave*). In the Spanish-speaking area certain Mozarabic dialects also failed to produce diphthongs from ĕ ŏ, especially those of Granada and Lusitania; in León, too, the process was slow and hesitant. The exact correspondence of Lat. ĕ ŏ Ptg. [ɛ] [ɔ] is disturbed by the principle of metaphony, according to which final *-a -os -as* opens a previous accented *e o* in nouns, and *-e* does the same in verbs; but *-o* closes a previous accented *e o*: *óvo óvos* 'egg(s)' *óva óvas* 'fishes' egg(s)', *môrto mórtos mórta mórtas* 'dead', *dêvo dêva déve* from *dever* 'owe'. Metaphony gives rise to complex develop-

ments in Portuguese, but the principle, at least, is not exclusive to that tongue. At Mieres and Lena, in the central
section of the Asturian dialects, we find *bubu bobos boba bobas*
and *guetu gata* 'cat (tom and tabby)', *diniru timpu puirtu*,
showing the power of final [u] to close a preceding accented
e o. Thus, although metaphony and the absence of the diphthongs *ie ue* are circumstances which plainly distinguish
Portuguese from literary Spanish, they fail to draw a sharp
line between Portuguese and the whole of Spanish. The connection with regional or discarded Spanish forms is still more
evident in the *ei ou* which result in Portuguese from AI AU,
and are pronounced in NPtg. [ei̯ ou̯], in SPtg. [ɐi̯ ọ], when
the latter is not dissimilated to *oi*: ALTARIU CAUSA SALTU
JANUARIU IBAIKA AURU *outeiro cousa coisa souto janeiro veiga ouro
oiro*, Sp. *otero cosa soto enero vega oro*. As Mozarabic Spanish
had *ai ei au ou*, and Leonese normally *ei ou*, the Gallæco-
Portuguese form is clearly related to a pan-Iberian evolution.

It is in the system of consonants that the greatest apparent
difference between Spanish and Gallæco-Portuguese lies. We
must first, however, deduct all those sound-shifts which have
occurred within the history of literary Spanish, and restore
to -*ss*- -*s*- *ç z x j* their older values of [ś ź ŝ ẑ š ž]. These were
formerly their values in Portuguese, and as for [ś ź] it still
persists in the Bragança region distinct from *ç z* [s z]; but
otherwise Portuguese has reduced -*ss*- *ç* to [s] and -*s*- *z* to [z],
while *x j* remain [š ž]. The former simplification characterizes parts of Andalusia and most of Spanish America. We
must restore also to Spanish, for purposes of comparison with
Portuguese, all the innovations peculiar to Castilian, the
change of F to *h*, loss of initial J ǵ, the evolution of -CT- to *ch*
and MULTU to *mucho*, and of -C'L- -LI- to *j*: Ptg. *forno filho
feito janeiro olho molher muito* are forms exactly parallel to
Leonese, Mozarabic, Aragonese and even Catalan derivatives of FURNU FILIU FACTU JANUARIU OCULU MULIERE MULTU.
Portuguese differs from Spanish in evolving -LL- -NN- to
l n: *cavalo dano* Sp. *caballo daño* Cat. *cavall dany* CABALLU

DAMNU > DANNU. But this merely indicates that the passage of *ll nn* to [λ ɲ] was perceptibly later than that of LL C'L, NI GN, and that, by archaism, Portuguese has not accompanied the other Peninsular languages. That the change from dental to palatal pronunciation was relatively late was already clear from certain cases in Spanish where *ll nn* arose from assimilation of alveolars (*echallo* from *echarlo, conno* from *con lo*), since these imply originally [l: n:]. One cannot exclude the possibility that they may still have been tense alveolars, with a long and large application of the tongue to the alveoli, and not palatals, in the poetry of Gonzalo de Berceo and his contemporaries. With regard to *ch*, its present SPtg. pronunciation [š] dates only from the eighteenth century; previously, as in NPtg. Gal. Sp. Cat., it was [ĉ], for which cause Chinese *ĉa* gave Ptg. *cha* 'tea'.

The oldest of the three principal criteria which distinguish Galæco-Portuguese from Spanish belongs, at least in its initial stages, to a period when the Peninsular unity was still maintained, i.e. before the opening of the eighth century. It is that which has come to oppose Ptg. *ch* to Sp. *ll* < PL- CL- FL-: Ptg. *chorar chover cheio chão chaga chegar, chamar chave chousa, chama,* Sp. *llorar llover lleno llano llaga llegar, llamar llave llosa, llama* FLAMMA. This development did not take place in the Mozarabic dialects of the centre and south, nor in the Navarro-Aragonese of the east. The part affected was the north-west of the Peninsula only, and within that region the Leonese variety of Spanish was associated with Galæco-Portuguese in giving a palatal fricative *x* [š]. The different groups have different expansive powers, and indeed the passage of FL- to *ll-* is supported only by *llama* in Spanish (and, within the word, by *hallar* *FAFLARE AFFLARE), and scarcely amounts to establishing a rule. FLAMMULA (a personal name) gave *Llambla* and *Lambra,* but FLAVINU *Laín,* FLACCIDU *lacio,* which show a development from FL- to *l*; and there are numerous cases of initial *fl-* which can hardly all be due to erudite influence: *flaco flanco flecha fleje flojo flor flujo.* These show a wave of change which lost impetus as it attained Castilian territory.

Portuguese has a fuller series of FL- > *ch*-: FLAGRARE *cheirar*
FLAMMULA *Chámoa* FLORE OPtg. *chor* *FLORUTU *chorudo*, etc.,
together with numerous cases where the three groups have
been preserved by dissimilation of the *l* to *r*: PLATEA *praça*
PLANTA OPtg. *pranta* and *chanta* CLAMARE OPtg. *cramar* and
chamar FLORE OPtg. *frol* and *chor* MPtg. *flor*. These words
seem less likely to be due to Latin influence than to offer
an alternative possibility for the treatment of the three groups.
The value of *ch* in modern Portuguese is [š], but this pronunciation is first mentioned in 1671, and in 1739 is still treated
as peculiar to Lisbon. The older pronunciation was [č], an
affricate palatal, as in northern Portuguese and Galician. In
medieval Leonese *Xainiz xosa* (FLAVINU + ICI, CLAUSA) indicate
[š], a fricative palatal, as normal. In modern west Leonese
the representative of these groups is *ts* [ŝ], an affricate dental,
which also stands for the *ll*- derived from L-: *tsabe tseiti* CLAVE
LACTE, Sp. *llave leche*, Ptg. *chave leite*.

It is evident, from the foregoing examples, that the north-
west of the Peninsula was an area of active experimentation in respect of these initial groups, both in León and in
Galicia-Portugal, while Castile lay where the waves of innovation died down. Commencing under conditions of Peninsular
unity, the development had already reached its extreme
limits before the opening of the twelfth century: *chamam*
occurs in the first Portuguese document (1192); CLAUSA *xosa*
is misspelt *flausa* and *plosa* in 1034 and 1084, and *x* [š] appears
in *Xainiz* (1101, 1171) *xosa* (1123). The first steps were the
lengthening and then the palatalization of the *l* after the
initial *p c f*. This occurs in modern Ribagorzan, as a modern
development; and perhaps Berceo's *Hllantada* preserves a
dim memory of an initial consonant. These presumed groups
pll- cll- fll- gave Sp. *ll*- through the aggrandisement of the
lateral palatal at the expense of the initial consonants. It is
unlikely that the western dialects passed through the stage
ll-, since this was the result of palatalizing initial L- in Leon.
lloco lliueram (908) *llauore* (1082), and that does not pass farther
to *x*. Mod. WLeon. *ts* for both PL- CL- FL- and L- is there-

fore a definitely modern confusion. The basis of the western experiments is thus probably *pll- cll- fll-*, and the stages may have included delateralization of the [λ] so as to give *y*, as in literary Italian *piano chiamare fiamma*; restricting the space between the back of the tongue and the middle palate so as to convert this *y* into a palatal fricative (cf. at Somana, Italy, *pšan pšega pšanta* PL-) or palatal affricate (cf. at Bellinzona, Italy, *pĉü* PLUS); and so by aggrandisement of the [š] or [ĉ] (cf. at Genoa, *ĉau ĉan* CLAVE PLANU, *šu* FLORE) to give OLeon. *x* Gal. Ptg. *ch*. If this explanation be correct, it would appear that Galician Leonese and Castilian developed together as far as *pll-*, etc., when Castilian diverged to *ll-*; and Galician developed with Leonese through *py-*, etc. to *pĉ-* or *pš-*, after which they reached their separate conclusions: *ch* and *x*. Modern standard Portuguese has lost the affricate element of *ch* in the pronunciation [š]; but modern west Leonese has developed the palatal affricate [ĉ]—doubtless concurrent with *x*—into a dental affricate [ŝ]. The final triumph of *ll* in literary Spanish is due to the rise to hegemony of Castilian among the Spanish dialects, eclipsing the earlier prestige of Galician and Leonese. A vigorous linguistic condition in the west led to innovations characteristic of that area, but not yet to a loss of interdialectal contact in the Peninsula, between the eighth and the tenth centuries.

The loss of *-l-* and *-n-* between vowels severed the connection between the Ibero-Romance languages in the course of the tenth century, by introducing a clear-cut line of demarcation. The former can be dated with much assurance by comparing *artigulo paadulibus auellanales* (883) *portugalense mollinarum* (907) with *Fáfia* FAFILA *Fiiz* FELICE (995) *Váásco* (1092) *O Castro* for *lo* (1161). The loss of *-l-* occurred in the course of the tenth century; its mechanism is more conjectural. The suggested cause is that the *l* may have been construed in the same syllable as the preceding vowel (*Fáfil-a* for *Fáfi-la*), and then have taken on the velar timbre [ł] which resembles *u*, before being completely assimilated to the vowel. However this be, the *l* has not contributed a velar timbre to that vowel as it does when indubitably final of syllable (as in SALTU *salto*, whence *souto*).

The loss of -*n*- was doubtless contemporary with that of -*l*- in so far as the nasal consonant was converted into a nasalization of the preceding vowel. In 907 we have *resona*, but in 1092 *padroadigo* *PATRONATICU *eenúú* IN UNU *particoens* PARTITIONES. Up to the sixteenth century the vowels nasalized are frequently written double (*maão* MANU), as also those left in hiatus by the loss of -*l*-, though the usage is not rigid, and the nasal sign is placed on any constituent element and frequently on the last (*maaõ*). These spellings suggest that for a while after the loss of the consonants, such vowels were recognizably longer than others, while not more than the latter portion may have had a nasal quality [maãu̯]. Essentially the whole process is one of denasalization. First, the nasal consonant was replaced by a nasal resonance in the vowel; then, in certain cases the nasal resonance itself disappeared. This occurred especially in the combinations *e-o e-a o-a* MPtg. .*veio* *VENIUT *veia* VENA *Lisboa* OLISIPONE *boa* BONA; but the nasal quality persisted to the sixteenth century (*boõa*, etc.). In other cases the nasal vowels survive either as simple vowels or as diphthongs, indicated either by ˜ or by *m n* (since all nasals final of syllables are vocalized): LANA *lã* BENE *bem* FINE *fim* BONU *bom* COMMUNE *comum* CANES *cães* ORPHANU *órfão* PARTITIONES *partições*.

The combined effect of these two consonantal losses has been to give Portuguese and Galician their notably vocalic character, distinct from the equipoise of Spanish, and the consonantal nature of Catalan. The loss of *l* between vowels spread to the definite article and enclitic pronouns: *o a os as*, which, with other vocalic particles, cause Portuguese words to be joined through vowels, always ready to enter into liaison with others which may happen to be at the end of one word or beginning of the next. The indefinite article is also vocalic *um* [ũ] but *uma*. An order of nasal vowels and diphthongs has arisen beside the buccal vowels, and both exist in tonic and atonic series (in which the vowels *a e o* are reduced to relaxed sounds [ɐ ə i u]). Thus we have complex vowel liaisons in Portuguese (*se o eu ouvisse, tenho visto uma ave* with sequences *e-o-eu-ou* and *o-ũa-a*), and the possibility of the subtlest cadences in verse. The language has come to seem intrinsically lyrical, just as the balanced and sonorous Castilian seems intrinsically oratorical and Catalan nervous and concise. As the languages differ, so too the literary achievements of the three peoples are not interchangeable, particularly in respect of poetry. Attempts by Portuguese and Catalans to write poetry in Castilian have been numerous and sustained, but they have reached their true stature only in their own idioms, so subtly different in texture from Spanish.

Notwithstanding the circumstance that the characteristics of Galician-Portuguese thus date from the tenth century, the *l n* occasionally appear in popular lyrics until the sixteenth century. Thus we find in the fourteenth-century *Cancioneiros*: *sedia la fremosa seu sirgo torcendo*; *eu al rio me vou banhar*; *louçana*; *levad' amigo! que dormides as manhanas frias!*; and in Gil Vicente: *vi venir serrana gentil, graciosa*; *donde vindes, filha branca e colorida*; *um amigo que eu havia mançanas d'ouro m'envia*. Nearly six centuries seem to have been required before the resistance of conservative rustics was entirely conquered.

We should mention here also, among the primitive characteristics of the Galician-Portuguese language, the syntactical device known as the 'personal' infinitive. Where it is desirable to indicate person with an infinitive, as when there has been a change of person between the principal verb and the dependent infinitive, or where there has been no indication otherwise of any person, Spanish adds a personal pronoun in the nominative case (*a ser yo tal* 'were I such'), but Galician-Portuguese adds personal terminations to the infinitive, and, as it were, conjugates the infinitive (1 - 2 *es* 3 - 4 *mos* 5 *des* 6 *em*). This device dates from the period of Gallæco-Portuguese unity and is frequent in the *Cancioneiros* and in Alfonso X's *Cantigas de Santa María*: e.g. *ben per está a os reis de amaren Santa Maria* 'it is well for kings to love St Mary'.

THE DIVERGENCE OF PORTUGUESE
FROM GALICIAN

Thanks to the innovations we have mentioned, but still more to the resolute consummation of Spanish evolution by Castilian and the superiority exercised by this speech over Leonese, Galician-Portuguese takes the field as a separate language by the commencement of the eleventh century. Political events of the same era confirmed its independence. The reigns of Fernando I, Sancho II and Alfonso VI witnessed the shift of the political centre eastwards to Castile, and the last-named, after confirming Castilian supremacy by making the capture of Toledo a Castilian triumph, gave a beginning to Galician localism and Portuguese independence by appointing two Burgundian brothers, Raymund and Henry, counts of Galicia and Portugal respectively, each as the husband of one of his daughters. Portugal was the less promising of the two fiefs—a fragment lying between the Minho and Mondego, open to the full fury of Moorish war; but perhaps by reason of its peril, it aspired most vigorously to independence. The struggle to avoid admission of dependence on Castile occupied the lives of Henry of Burgundy, his wife Teresa, and his son Afonso Henríquez. The third of the line wrested the title of king from Alfonso VII in 1143, but he earned it by the capture of Lisbon, one of the great Mozarabic capitals—in 1147. With this triumph the centre of Portuguese power began to shift southward, and away from Galicia. The Minho as a frontier became gradually more significant; and particularly after the commercial prosperity of Lisbon began to give a maritime outlook to Portuguese policy—e.g. friendship with England and Flanders, the nearest maritime neighbours—quite distinct from the landward interests of Galicia. The earlier kings of the Burgundian house frequently resided north of the Tagus, but the reigns of the last two (Pedro I and Fernando) witnessed the rapid economic development of Lisbon. This development had its counterpart in the language, where a rift became apparent between

20

Galician and Portuguese about the year 1350, more or less; after 1383 the struggle against Juan I of Castile, who claimed the Portuguese crown for his wife, Fernando's heiress, the military triumphs of the patriotic house of Aviz, its oceanic adventures ending in the voyage of Vasco da Gama, and a vigorous prose literature, all caused Portuguese to develop in a peculiarly national sense, while at the same time Galician entered into a provincial decadence. About the middle of the fourteenth century, therefore, both speeches entered their middle period of development, characterized by the dissolution of their old unity, and leading up to the humanistic settlement of the sixteenth century.

The old united language we meet in documents of various sorts, but chiefly in the form of a conventional language for use in the courtly lyric. The contributors to this poetry are not merely Galicians or Portuguese, but also Leonese, Castilians, Andalusian Castilians, and even one Italian; and its patrons Alfonso X of Castile as well as Diniz of Portugal. No doubt songs were sung in Castilian also—by sentinels, harvesters, pilgrims and other persons who were engaged in communal activities. It would be absurd to suppose Castile lyrically dumb, and given over to the epos and prose. But it is also undeniable that the Galician lyric enjoyed higher repute, courtly patronage, and alone was preserved in writing. A token thereof is the fact that the poets' names are known, from the primitive *Palla* 'Straw' at Alfonso VII's court to Count Pedro de Barcelos, the reputed collector of the Galician-Portuguese *Cancioneiros* and reputed author of the prose *Livros de Linhagens*. The *Cancioneiros* contain the secular lyric, amatory or satirical; the songs of Alfonso X's *Cantigas de Santa María* are their pious counterpart. Alfonso X, the father of Castilian prose, is the most prolific poet in Galician-Portuguese and the leading patron; his contemporary Diniz, founder of Portugal's agricultural prosperity, comes second in inspiration and patronage. The sweetest poetical inspiration is supplied by Galician singers, such as Airas Nunes of Compostela and Martin Codax of Vigo, when they use the simple love-songs in parallel couplets (the *cossantes*, as Mr Bell calls them) considered suitable for the love-songs of women. In them we have the native fountain of song and, no doubt, the unconfessed reason for Galician lyrical prestige; but the greater number of the surviving lyrics have been pressed into forms borrowed from Provençal troubadours, and it is on their triumphs of artifice that both Alfonso X and Diniz claim to base their repute.

The unity of Galician and Portuguese did not, even in this conventional language, amount to identity. For certain Romance sounds, after the age of experiment closed, different solutions were adopted. For the palatal nasal and lateral consonants Galician, like Castilian, chose *ll nn* (later *ñ*), but Portuguese writers preferred the Provençal *lh nh*. To indicate a nasal vowel, apart from a superposed *til* (˜), Galician preferred *n*, Portuguese *m*; but the *Cancioneiros* frequently employ *n* in poems by Portuguese poets (e.g. in an early lyric: *como vivo en gran cuidado*). An orthographic *h* served also to add a palatal element to *m* in *mha senhor* 'my lady', *mh'a mentido* 'he has lied to me'. In morphology, the 3 S. preterite of 'strong' verbs in Galician ends in -*o* (*fezo quiso disso tevo poso*) as in Spanish, but in Portuguese in -*e* (*fez(e) quis(e) diss(e) teve pos*). The poems of King Diniz are found to employ Portuguese forms always unless there is metrical reason to prefer the Galician; he has thus 55 cases of *fez* to 3 of *fezo*, 24 *quis* 2 *quiso*, 11 *disse* or *diss' o disso*, 1 *teve o tevo*, 7 *pos o poso*. The 'weak' verbs of the conjugation in -*ir* form their 3 S. preterite, Gal. -*eo* Ptg. *iu*: Gal. *ouueo* Ptg. *ouviu*. One finds also the opposition Gal. *oydes diamos* Ptg. *ouvís demos*. Characteristic of Galician is the dative second-personal pronoun *che*. It appears in Portuguese in the prose of a law by Afonso III (*estas son as palavras per que a demanda he contestada per negaçon: non ch'o deuo, non ch'o conhosco*, where the formula of refusal may show legal archaism), and once in 1262 (*chu = ch'o*). King Diniz uses only *te*.

After the compilation of the *Cancioneiros* in Portugal, this lyrical Galician continued in vogue until the beginning of the fifteenth century at the court of Castile, where it gave way at last to Castilian. The change was covered by the lifetime of Alfonso Álvarez de Villasandino, the last of the troubadours, and Juan Alfonso de Baena, editor of the *Cancionero de Baena* (1445). The Marquis of Santillana has one Galician song; his grandfather was a noteworthy poet in this idiom. In prose the division between Galician and Portuguese was not impeded by literary convention, and we find on the Portuguese side the *Livros de Linhagens, Livro da Montaria, Leal Conselheiro, Demanda do Santo Graal* and the great chronicles of Fernão Lopes and Zurara, forming a growing mass of differences in the late fourteenth and the fifteenth centuries from Galician works like the *Crónica Troyana* and *Crónica general de* 1404 (partly Castilian). The last-named has *moy(to) froyto çibdade gãando régeo* (MGal. *rejo) igllesia* (MGal. *ilesia) obispo* (a castilianism), *-s* in *Roys Gomes Peres, -eu* in *saeu departeu oyeu, -o* in *fezo teuo disso*, and *che*, for Ptg. *mui(to) fruito cidade gado rijo igreja bispo Roiz Ruiz Gomez Perez saíu departiu ouviu fez teve disse te.* Such differences are slight, but they show that Portuguese and Galician had, by the fifteenth century, finally separated.

MODERN PORTUGUESE

The years between 1500 and 1550 witnessed, in Portugal as in Spain, the transition from the linguistic conditions of the Middle Ages to those of the adult and imperial tongue. They were years of the intensest physical and mental activity. The patient explorations undertaken by Henry the Navigator southward along the African coast came within sight of their reward when Bartolomeu Diaz rounded the Cape of Storms in 1488, and were crowned by the arrival of Gama in Calicut in 1498. In the next fifteen years a dominion was established in the Indian Ocean by Almeida and the great Albuquerque, held by the tenure of key-positions at Ormuz, Diu, Goa, Cochin and Malacca. In a general way the African coasts formed part of this scheme, in so far as they might be needed by the armadas in transit. Beyond the Straits of Malacca, Macau was a door into China from the south, Japan was reached by St Francis Xavier and Mendes Pinto, but Ternate, Amboina, Java and the Spice archipelago proved to be the dazzling source of Portuguese wealth. The intoxication of success afflicted the homeland, but at first stirred up aspiring minds to every form of excellence. Gil Vicente, the keenest observer of the time, was not slow to speak of the *fumos da Índia*, and to complain of the impoverishment of the countryside as the court and capital grew richer. Towards the close of the sixteenth century, the Portuguese thalassocracy was challenged by the Dutch, who had conceived the idea of sailing to the Spice Islands south of the monsoon belt. The struggle lasted with them and the English throughout the first half of the seventeenth century, while Portugal was unequally yoked with Spain, and ended by England's succession to Bombay and the Indian trade. Portugal was left in possession of most of those factories which she had held in strength to support her armadas, and her vague African claims lay dormant until they expanded into the colonies of Angola and Moçambique during the nineteenth-century scramble for Africa.

The discovery of the land of the Holy Cross, called Brazil from the brazil-wood found there, was a by-product of the Indian voyages, whether accidental or deliberate. From the date of Cabral's voyage in 1500 and throughout the century the colony attracted little attention. It grew steadily, however, and showed its mettle by expelling the Dutch from Pernambuco in 1654. From that time Brazil began to compensate Portugal for the loss of India, and its importance has grown on a series of booms—mahogany, sugar, diamonds, rubber, coffee. In 1808, when Junot occupied Lisbon, the Portuguese royal family fled to the huge colony, honouring it with the status of kingdom. Both João VI and Pedro II proved reluctant to return to the less wealthy motherland, and Brazil became an empire (1822) before following at last the example of other American states and becoming a republic (1882).

The directions and dates of the Portuguese expansions have had the effect of limiting their importance for the history of the language. The earliest achievements lay in the old world, with the plants and animals of which civilization had long been familiar, at least in a distant fashion. Gama met in Calicut a Moor from Morocco; the Portuguese traders displaced their hereditary foes who spoke Arabic; the elephant, paraded through Rome at the orders of Manuel the Fortunate, was a monster new to the eyes of Europeans, but with a very old name. The Asiatic contribution to Portuguese is thus of restricted interest: *cha* and *chavena* 'tea' and 'tea-cup' we see the language borrowing directly from Mandarin Chinese (*ĉa, ĉa wan*), *azagaia* 'assegai' was borrowed afresh from Arabic to describe weapons used by African tribes, and *inhame* 'yam' is another witness to these voyages; *samorim naire sabaio* are names of Indian rulers or officers, of only local import. For many of the essentials of the new commerce—*cravo* 'clove' *pimenta* 'pepper' *especiarias* 'spices' *marfim* 'ivory'—there were already well-established names. On the other side the slow development of Brazil led to a marked Spanish priority in naming the plants, animals and institutions of the New World. Arawak, Carib, Nahuatl and Quechua names were applied to those objects which excited curiosity in Europe, and the Tupí languages of Brazil served only to supplement their rivals. The Tupi-Guaraní contribution is of great importance for the vocabulary of Brazilian Portuguese, where *oca uba catinga*, etc. are more exactly apposite than any other terms; but the Portuguese of Europe is satisfied practically with the terms which Spanish also has borrowed: *jaguar capibara aï mandioca tapioca*, etc.

The intellectual activities of the period between 1500 and 1550 were connected with the humanistic renaissance and the creation of that literature which culminated in Camões (*Lusíadas* 1572, *Rimas* 1595). The general nature of this influence has been indicated when we considered the development of Spanish in the same epoch. In place of the French and Provençal borrowings of the medieval period (French: *achatar* 'buy' *dayan* 'dean' *Denis Diniz mester* 'necessary' *rua* 'street' *jardim* 'garden', etc.; Provençal: *assaz* 'enough' *freire* 'friar' *manjar* 'eat, meal' *trobar* 'compose verses', etc.) Italian suddenly rose to importance as the source of those artistic, military and commercial terms in Portuguese which were also borrowed by Spanish, as we have already noted. Under the Braganzas, as under the Spanish Bourbons, the stream of gallicisms commenced afresh, borne along on a vast literature of translations of pachydermatous style and idiom.

As in Spanish, this epoch witnessed a renovation of the Latin element in vocabulary, and 'etymological' orthography was pushed further in Portugal. In Portugal initial *sc- sp-* (*sciencia spirto*) are frequently found in texts of this period, and the 'Greek' *ph th ch* come down to the twentieth century, having only been eradicated by quite recent reforms. Latin neologisms were introduced with caution, and a hostile critic was able to discover no more than 118 in Camões. The model achievements of Portuguese prose and poetry were made while those who sought to enrich the language professed a creed of classic sobriety. After the death of Camões, which corresponded with the fall of the Portuguese state, gongoristic extravagances poured in from Spain; but they were identified with the foreign language, as the period was one in which Portuguese writers forsook Portuguese. With the inevitable reaction, in the eighteenth century, the simpler manner of *circa* 1550–80 was again exalted to high repute, all the more so as the leading poet, Bocage, deliberately modelled his verses and himself on Camões. Portuguese is, to a unique extent, the language of one inspired man.

At the opening of the Renaissance period, the great line of medieval chronicles had come to an end, and those of Fernão Lopes were engrossed with care by the Manueline scribes. The best manuscripts of this author, therefore, show the extent of literary ground conquered by Portuguese and the development of the language and its orthography on the threshold of the Golden Age. Garcia de Rezende's *Cancioneiro* (1516), with its wholly medieval outlook, is a faithful mirror of the court. King Manuel the Fortunate, intent on the Spanish alliance and on a policy of intermarriages, marks the zenith of a castilianizing epoch, which threatened to reduce Portuguese to the status of a dialect. The Castilian hegemony is felt in the earlier poems of Gil Vicente, whose dramatic activity lasts from 1502–36, over some of the years most fruitful in linguistic change: in his earlier works the serious characters speak in Castilian—a Castilian of Portuguese character; in the later they employ Portuguese. Castilian is the language he employs for all his ballads, or for dramatizing literary material drawn from Castile or from his general reading. In his language, as in his technique, Gil Vicente remains medieval. He is the last to be inspired by the wistful *cossantes*; after him popular improvisations take on the new quatrain form which lasts to this day. He is singularly sensitive to the different varieties of Portuguese: he distinguishes carefully between peasant and townsman, Christian and Jew, negro and gypsy. The peasants employ the archaizing dialect of Beira province, with *er* 'now, also', *semos* for *somos*, *dixe* for *disse*, *aito* for *auto*, *som* for *sou* 'I am', *quige fige* for *quis fiz*, *catar* for *mirar*, *casuso* 'up here', *omagem* for *imagem*, 2nd person plurals in *-ade(s)* *-ede(s)* *-ide(s)* for *-ae(s)*, etc. (which are employed by personages of standing). Characteristic of the plebs also are their archaic interjections (*bofá, aramá, samicas, dá ó demo*), and the vulgar forms of personal names. The Jews favour *oi* for *ou* (*doitor coisa moiros poica*); Greek goddesses lisp in what João de Barros calls *o çeçear çigano de Sevilha*; the negro speaks Guinea-Portuguese (*a mi falla Guiné*) with ruinous morphology and syntax; and the Moorish witch puts *x* for *s*. His younger contemporary, Sá de Miranda, looks forward to a new era of Italianate and humanistic poetry, though his best work is in traditional metres. He vindicated, however, the literary worth of Portuguese, though also cultivating Castilian. António Ferreira, the celebrated author of *A Castro* (1567), is the only poet of high rank who consistently refused to toy with Castilian. His verses bring us to the full development of the language in Camões, Diogo Bernárdez, Agostinho da Cruz, and their compeers in verse, with Barros, Castanheda, Couto and others in prose. A description of this stage is given by Duarte Núnez do Lião in his *Orthographia da lingoa portuguesa* (1576) and his *Origem da lingoa portuguesa* (1st ed. 1606, but composed before 1601). Among post-classical authors perhaps the most interesting from the stylistic point of view is Francisco Manuel de Melo, a convinced *conceptista* and one of the best prose-writers in either Spanish or Portuguese; he represents, however, a tendency which was not carried further by the contemporaries of Bocage. Bocage brings with him afresh the influence of France, which has increased with Romanticism (Almeida Garrett, Herculano), Realism (Eça de Queiroz), Parnassianism, Symbolism and other modern literary schools.

The changes carried out in the epoch under review affect vocabulary, the sounds and forms of the language, and the combination of words in sentences. Some of the consequences to vocabulary of the new experiences of that age have been indicated. To them we must add instances of the wear and tear of the language: words which have disappeared, as FINIRE *fĩir fiir*, replaced by *acabar*, *catar*, *mãer maer* MANERE, replaced by *fincar*; words which are dialectal only, as RADERE *raer rer*, BASILICAS *Baselgas*; and words which remain part of the standard tongue, though much transformed, as FENESTRA *fẽestra feestra freesta fresta* 'sky-light'.

The equation *ou = oi* is older than the Golden Age, and still exercises its influence on spoken Portuguese. *Ou* arises from Latin AU (*cousa pouca* CAUSA PAUCA) and AL+consonant (*souto outro outeiro* SALTU ALTERU ALTARIU); *oi* from metathesis in -ORIU (*Doiro coiro* DURIU CORIU), or from palatalization of -CT- (*noite* NOCTE). But by dissimilation *ou* gives *oi* (*coisa ouro oiro* AURU), and conversely -ORIU -URIU -*oiro* -*ouro* (*Douro*). Half-learned words with -CT- give *ut*, as in Spanish; *auto doutor* (later still, *t* preceded by an open vowel: *dòtór* spelled *doctor*). Hence also in primitive words like *noite* we have the alternative *noute*. Usage varies. Generally speaking, the literary forms employ *ou* but the colloquial is *oi*; the *Rua d'Ouro* in Lisbon is normally pronounced [d'oịru]. But while *coisa* is normal, *oitro* exists only in the vulgar speech of the Saloios, near Lisbon, and Gil Vicente gives *doitor poica*, etc., to his Jews, doubtless as inveterate townsmen of low social grade. The *ou* is a diphthong in Galicia and northern Portugal [oụ], but in Lisbon and standard Portuguese it is a vowel [ọ], as in Spanish.

The medieval language is characterized by the numerous instances of vowels in hiatus. The disappearance of -*l*- or -*n*- left in contact vowels which did not at once coalesce, and the same was true of other lost consonants: POPULU *poboo* MPtg. *povo*, GENERALE *geeral* MPtg. *geral*, MEDIETATE *meatade* MPtg. *metade*, TENERE *tẽer* MPtg. *têr*, PERSONA *pessõa* MPtg. *pessoa*. Even in the *Cancioneiros*, representing the language of the thirteenth and early fourteenth centuries, these vowels were not always held apart; so that we meet *fe ben seer* as monosyllables alongside the normal hiatus-vowels of *creede loor seer rijir veer doo tẽedes*, etc. The orthographic tradition doubtless survived the hiatus, and was maintained by the consciousness of length (as in modern Galician) and open quality. Thus Brit. Mus. Add. MS. 20946 of Fernão López, which dates from the end of the fifteenth century, regularly maintains the two letters where the vowel has arisen from hiatus, e.g. *beesta* and *beesteiro* 'arbalist(er)' is not confused with *besta* BESTIA 'animal'. In the *Cancioneiro de Rezende* (1516) *moor fee beems* are monosyllables, *alguum* a dissyllable, *geeraçam* a trisyllable. In Alvaro do Couto de Vasconcellos's copy of Fernão Lopes, executed in 1538, duplication of vowels occurs without cause (e.g. *Braaguaa* for *Bragaa* BRACARA), showing that the copyist is not aware of any valid distinction of length. The same is true of original authors of the same date. These longer vowels tend also to be pronounced open, and resist the tendency to obscure unaccented vowels.

This pronunciation, indicated by a grave accent, is still current in a number of words: *pàdeiro* 'baker' Sp. *panadero*, *càveira* 'skull' Sp. *calavera* CALVARIA, *gèração* Sp. *generación*, *crèdor* 'creditor', *Càmões*, *Bèsteiros*, *Rèzende*, *còrado* Sp. *colorado*. The contractions were accompanied by denasalization, by which OPtg. *vĩir viinr* became *vir*, *tẽer* became *ter*, *boõa bõa* became *boa*, etc. In the case of *éo éa*, Gil Vicente still maintained the medieval forms *alheo meo*, and Núnez do Lião protests in 1576 that these alone are correct; but Camões normally employs the modern forms *-eio -eia* (*arreceio rodeio alheio freio cheio*), though allowing himself the licence of the older forms in rhymes, e.g. for the latinisms *Cyterea Dea* he admits *arrecea*, for *Amalthea rodea*.

The ending *-ã* represents -ANA, but MPtg. *-ão* is the result of several earlier suffixes, as well as its etymological -ANU: LANA *lãa lã* 'wool', ROMANU *Romão*. -ONE gave OPtg. *-om*: RATIONE *razom* 'reason', for which *razaom* begins to appear as early as the fourteenth century. Scribal tradition maintained *-om* in Brit. Mus. Add. MS. 20946 (Fernão Lopes), for which the Torre do Tômbo MS. has regularly *-ão*. King Duarte's *Leal Conselheiro* (1428–38) has *irmaão* GERMANU, and *carvom* CARBONE; but his *orfom* ORPHANU shows that this *-om* and *-ão* were not different to the ear. -ONU *-om*, as in BONU *boom bom* was a perceptibly different sound from -ONE *-om*, doubtless less open; and it has persisted to this day. The 3 Pl. of verbs also gave -UNT *-om*, which has the same history as -ONE *-om*. The suffix -ITUDINE appears in OPtg. *-idũe*, but already in the oldest texts had been assimilated to -ONE in the forms *-õe -õ*: MULTITUDINE *multidõe multidõ multidom*, and it accompanied -ONE when the latter was assimilated to -ANU *-ão* in the course of the fifteenth century. Finally, -ANE first appears as *-ã -am*, CANE *cã can cam* 'dog' PANE *pã pam* 'bread', and in the fourteenth century is distinguished from the *-ãa* of -ANA and the *-ão* of -ANU; but in the latter part of that century it fell in with the latter: *cão pão*. In the plural the original distinctions continue to be observed: *lã lãs*; *irmão irmãos*; *coração corações*, *certidão certidões*, *pão pães*; *bom bons*; *jejum* *jejuns; bem bens.* The *Cancioneiro de Rezende* shows *-om* and *-ão* rhyming together in the instances above mentioned, so that the former was by 1516 at most a dialectalism and a scribal tradition.

As in Spanish, this period saw considerable progress in the evolution of the sibilants, though Portuguese did not transfer the voiced sibilants to the unvoiced order. Portuguese possessed, when the sixteenth century commenced, seven sibilants: *s-*, (*-ss-*), *-s-*, *ç z, x, j ǵ, ch,* pronounced [ś ź s z š ž ĉ]. *Ç z* had originally the value of affricates [ŝ ẑ], but as early as 1277 *susesores = successores* appears in the Algarve, and *synqy = cinque* in Lisbon (1296). The Arabic transcription *sîn* proves that the sounds were not affricates in weak positions; but rather dorsoalveolar [s z]. *S* is still distinguished from *ç z* in dialects of Tras-os-Montes and Entre-Douro-e-Minho; it is there cacuminal, as in Spanish, i.e. pronounced by raising the tip of the tongue to the roof of the mouth, so that the place of greatest contraction of the buccal cavity corresponds to the tongue-tip, not the forepart of its back. This [ś ź] was easily confused with [š ž], both by Mozarabs (*ximio xarope enxofre* SULPHUR), and by northerners (OPtg. *xe xi* SIBI OPtg. *pugi quigi* POSUI QUAESI OPtg. *prijom* MPtg. *prisão*). It is evident that [ś ź] were the sounds attributed to *ss s* at King Manuel's court, since Gil Vicente makes the *Moura Taes* (1519) turn all her *esses* into *exxes.* The same fact shows that the dorsal pronunciation of *ss s* was then identified with Algarve and the south, and in fact was continuous with the dorsal *s* of Andalusian Spanish. The adoption of this vulgarism by Lisbon led to its acceptance as the standard pronunciation. No difference was perceived between *s* and *ç* by the Lisbon-born (1671) D. Luis Caetano de Lima (*Orthographia,* 1736) nor by C. A. du Bruillar in 1700; but it was noted for Bragança in 1739. *X j* still possess their ancient values of [š ž], though the latter has quite lost the affricate [ĵ]. *Ch* was an affricate [ĉ] in standard Portuguese until the eighteenth century (*c.* 1739), when it passed to [š], and so became identified with *x* [š]. It seems probable, therefore, that for

Camões the sibilants were still [ś ź s z š ž ĉ], though the southern values for s were gaining ground.

In conjugation and declension changes were taking place between 1500 and 1550 which led to the modern forms employed by Camões. The 3 Pl. -UNT had already become -ão. The 2 Pl. -TIS -TE remained -des -de until the middle of the fifteenth century. King Duarte's *Leal Conselheiro* (1428–28) has *podedes diredes achades notade consiirade façades parade* but also *dizee filhay louvees queiraes ponhaaes avisaae*. The chanceries continued to employ forms in d (*façades* 1462, *sabede* 1483), and Gil Vicente attributes them to plebeian characters, while those of standing employ such words as *passeae andae esperae*. Forms in -*des* still occur in Portuguese, either when following a nasal (*vindes tendes*) or another consonant (*pôrdes puderdes*) or in the conjugation of monosyllabic verbs (*ide ides credes vede*). The past participle in -*udo* lasted into the fifteenth century, when it gave way to -*ido*, and it was made to agree with the object in number and gender until well on in the sixteenth century. *Teúdo manteúdo conteúdo temudo* remain, but without participial value. The present participle -*nte* appears as late as 1563, when Garcia da Orta says *estante em Goa*, and then yields to the gerund -*ndo* (*estando em Goa*). Miscellaneous differences between medieval and modern conjugation are: the loss of 1 S. preterite -*i* (*pugi puge quige* MGal. *pujen quijen* MPtg. *pus quis*); analogical substitution of *fizeste ardo sinto quereria* for *fezeste arço senço querria*; in the verbs 'to be', *sou seja esteja* for *som sam sia esté*; the restricted use of *haver* save in impersonal senses. Barros in his early romance *Clarimundo* (1520) could still write *como todas estas cousas houverão fim*.

Numerous minor changes affected nouns and minor parts of speech. Adjectives in -*ês* -*nte* -*or*, frequently referring to persons, continued to be used as both masculine and feminine in the Golden Age of Portuguese; and those ending in unaccented -*ez* -*es* added a further -*es* in the plural: *ourivezes* MPtg. *ourives*. The medieval language possessed an atonic series of possessive pronouns (as *mha, ta, sa irmãa*), which was lost before the language reached its maturity; and both then and in the Golden Age it was possible to prefix *aqu-* to *este ese*, as well as in *aquele*.

GALEGO

On the break up of Galician-Portuguese towards the middle of the fourteenth century, the Galician dialect (*galego*) entered upon its separate provincial career. From about 1350 to 1500 the language remained that of official documents drawn up in the province, highly conservative in its general conditions, but increasingly exposed to Castilian intrusion. *Galego* remained the conventional language of the courtly lyric not only in Galicia, but also in Castile to about the year 1400, and it was employed in the redaction of a few prose works, of which the most important was a translation of the Castilian *Crónica Troyana*. They were not numerous enough to constitute a prose literature. The prestige of Castilian meanwhile was growing both as an official tongue, and as the language of a wider culture. Castilian forms invaded Galicia. In a document drawn up at Santa María de Monferro on the 12th October, 1501, we find such castilianisms as *uno lo lamamento* (*llamamiento*) *fijos nyetos camino año*. The language sank to the status of a mere dialect which, in the sixteenth, seventeenth and eighteenth centuries, was rarely deemed suitable for legal documents, and possessed no literature. It continued to serve, in more or less corrupt forms, for family and general intercourse in the province; but it was held inappropriate for serious employment, as may be illustrated by a modern practice at Fereiros in Orense, where sermons and even private prayers are made only in Spanish. Attached to the orbit of Spain, Galician lacked the cultural acquisitions of Portuguese in its Golden Age, but received, somewhat passively, the words added to Spanish, particularly the names for new things, e.g. the italianisms *centinela escopeta piloto* and the americanisms *chocolate petate cacique tabaco furacán tomate canoa*. Qualitative improvements

had less cause to be adopted in dialects which had resigned
their pretension to culture. A flood of castilianisms entered
them, displacing quite adequate native words: *llano* for *chao*
'plain', *conejo* for *coello* 'rabbit', *güeco* for *oco* 'hollow', *güeso*
for *oso* 'bone', *cual* for *cal* 'which', *ostede* for *vostede* 'you', etc.
It is characteristic of these loans that they are needless, and
in some cases vulgar (*güeso güeco* Sp. *hueso hueco* in correct
speech). The invasion still persists. Railways have drawn
the province closer to Madrid, and increased the demand for
a language of more than local usefulness. The large towns—
Vigo, Coruña, Santiago, Lugo—are centres for castilianization, apart from small groups devoted to the cult of the local
tongue; and education is in Spanish. Galicians look for a
career in literature or politics at the capital or emigrate in
search of livelihood to the Argentine Republic. Several distinguished Spanish writers have been of Galician origin:
Dona Rosalía de Castro, Countess Pardo Bazán, D. Ramón
del Valle-Inclán. They have even exerted a provincial influence on the standard language, e.g. the re-employment of
-*ra* forms of the verb in an indicative sense, or of *aquillotrar*
'change'. On the other side, not merely Castilian words,
but Castilian pronunciation penetrates Galicia, notably the
interdental pronunciation of *z*.

In the eighteenth century there were the beginnings of a
revived interest in Galician. It was an age of antiquarian
investigation. Father Sarmiento made a glossary of words
heard in the district of Pontevedra. A poetical contest was
held in 1708 in *galego*, and the vicar of Fruime published
various dialect poems in his works (1778-81). The source
of strength was the practice of poetical improvisation by
women, which had apparently descended unchecked from
the most early times. A difference of form has been effected;
whereas the ancient *cossantes* were in couplets, the modern
improvisations are characteristically in quatrains. However, not merely octosyllabic quatrains have been employed
in the popular poetry of modern Galicia, but various other
metres: triplets and hendecasyllables with ternary rhythm

have been the most influential. In addition to the attachment of the peasantry to their maternal language, therefore, Galician enjoyed the support of a considerable body of spontaneous poetry—sometimes sly, at others pathetic, of varying æsthetic values but always intimate. It was on the basis of this poetry that the Galician literary revival of the nineteenth century took place, partly under the influence of federal theories as to the Spanish state and the influence of the Catalan Renaissance. A poetess of spontaneous felicity—Rosalía de Castro—wrote with a freshness of style that contrasted with the academic formalism of her contemporaries in Madrid. Eduardo Pondal exploited local inspiration in some happy verses, and Curros Enríquez attempted to use the local language and technique on themes of general human concern. *Galego* poetry still continues; an academy protects regional studies; and there have been serious attempts at creating a prose literature.

The area lacks complete unity in modern as in ancient times, and one of the obstacles to a Galician revival is dialectal particularism within *galego*. Provincials speak of four dialects, corresponding with Coruña, Lugo, Orense and Pontevedra. The forms, however, are much more interwoven than such an account supposes, but at least these names indicate centres of irradiation for certain forms. Thus the opposition of *chan* to *chao* (PLANU) is mainly one between Pontevedra province and those of Coruña and Lugo, but shows exceptions on either side; *tu* is a disjunctive pronoun in Lugo and much of Orense, against *ti* in Coruña and Pontevedra; a 3 Pl. preterite -*ano* is chiefly heard in the northerly parts of Coruña; analogical forms *faguer figuen tanguer* for *facer fijen tanger* pertain chiefly to Orense; and the interdental *z* radiates outward chiefly from Pontevedra.

The system of sounds employed by Galician is, when compared with Portuguese, notably archaic, apart from a tendency to break up under Castilian pressure. The latter is exerted both by speech and by orthography. In the former respect the Castilian [θ], as we have seen, tends to be attached to *ç z*. In the latter, the fact that the *til* is not used in Castilian with vowels, causes Galician nasal vowels to be indicated by unmodified vowels or by *n*. This influences pronunciation in two directions: either the Galician vowel is denasalized, or the nasal element may be reconsonantized. Hence Gal. *homes virges quintás patrós negús irmao(s) chao(s)* Ptg. *homens virgens quintans patrões nenhuns irmão(s) chão(s)* and Gal. *gando monllo painzo* Ptg. *gado molho* but *painço*. The Galician *l* is not velar before another consonant, as in Portuguese, but tends to acquire a nasal resonance. In plurals it is often restored from the singular, partly by Castilian influence: Gal. *iguás crimináz papés aqués fusís mos azús* (by assimilation from older plurals in *-aes -áas*, etc.) or *catedrals vals vales mortales papeles aqueles fusiles moles azuls*.

Galician vowels which result from contraction of vowels left in contact by loss of *-l- -n-* are still longer and more open in quality than uncontracted vowels, though the memory of this process is not preserved in all cases. This difference of quantity is no longer felt in Portuguese, where only the qualitative distinction remains in certain words. Similarly, though the final vowels are much relaxed in *galego*, they do not completely lose their timbre as in Portuguese. To Ptg. *ui* corresponds Gal. *oi* in *moito coito froita coitelo* Ptg. *muito cuito fruita cuitelo*. In the consonant-system, Galician belongs to an area which includes Spanish in two important respects: *b v* are identical [b], as in northern Portuguese also, but not in standard Portuguese; the sibilants have been brought to a single voiceless order. The former affects not only Spanish, but also the greater part of the Catalan domain; the latter extends beyond Spanish into Valencian. Thus *z > c* in *decer facer viciño*, and *s* represents both the older *-ss-* (*paso*) and *-s-* (*casa*). Indications of the cacuminal pronunciation of *s* [ś] are those cases in which it passes to a palatal as in NASU *najo* 'nose' *registir* 'resist' *quijen* QUAESI, etc. This *j* is pronounced as a voiceless palatal affricate and so equivalent to *ch* [ĉ], but there are cases in which it has been identified with the fricative *x* [š]; and in some localities the voiced

21

pronunciation remains (as at Fereiros: *cruzes jardĩs janeiro jolho*). The passage of -ST- to -*ch*- is characteristic of Galician, ancient and modern, though it was also known in the oldest Portuguese: FECISTI *fijeche figueche* QUAESISTI *quijeche*. Thus the 2 S. preterite is in Galician -*che*, but Pl. -*stes*. A local and relatively modern change in Galician is one which converts initial *g* (before *a o u*) into an aspirate [h], which is frequently, but not correctly, identified with Sp. *j* [χ].

The Galician verbal system includes the personal infinitive characteristic of the whole Galician-Portuguese group, and also metaphony of the tonic vowels. In the way of personal endings, Galician still has traces of -*d*- in the 2 Pl., uses -*ch*- for -*st*- in the preterite (2 S. and occasionally 2 Pl.), and nasalizes the final vowel of 1 S. preterite as either -*in* (OPtg. Gal. -*i*) or -*en*. Thus for tenses formed from the present stem the personal endings are - *s* - *mos* (*d*)*es n*, and for the preterite *en* (*i in*) *che* (*ches ste stes*) - *mos stedes* (*chedes*) *ron* (*no*). The accentuation of the 1, 2 Pl. imperfect indicative and subjunctive is as in Latin (*cantabámos falasémos*, etc.) and not withdrawn to the first syllable of the suffix as in Spanish and Portuguese (Ptg. *cantábamos falásemos*). The 2 Pl. imperative has various forms: *amade amá amai amaide*. OGal. verbs in -*ir* formed their 3 S. preterite in -*eo*, Ptg. -*iu*. Strong verbs show many analogical forms in Galician which are not to be found in Portuguese owing to the activity of speakers unchecked by instruction. DICERE gives, for instance, *dicir decir dicer decer*, and FACERE *facer far fayer faguer*, with preterite *fijen figuen*. In the imperfect indicative *ir* has *iba ia iña*, and the preterite is *fum fuche* (*foche*) *foi*, etc. Pronouns and other small words of frequent occurrence show many forms that differ from Portuguese, as Gal. *unha duos* (as well as *dous*) *ise il miño* (as well as *meu*) *mia miña ña cal alguén ul dulo*, etc., Ptg. *uma dous ese ele meu minha qual alguem* and Sp. *en donde está él, de donde viene él*. Very notable in MGal. is the dative *che* (Sp. Ptg. *te*), because of its wide use as a dative of vague interest, to give vivacity to the conversation by continually bringing into it the auditor as an interested party: *s'un rayo*

che fende de súpeto a barca 'if a thunderbolt suddenly smashes
the boat'. The accusative is *te*, but *che* occasionally occurs.

On Galician consult V. García de Diego, *Elementos de gramática histórica
gallega* (Burgos, 1909).

PORTUGUESE DIALECTS

A sense of the difference between the archaizing northern
dialects and the standard language of the Portuguese capital
appears at the beginning of the sixteenth century in the plays
of Gil Vicente, whose peasants use the colloquialisms of Beira
province, and receives expression from the first Portuguese
grammarian, Fernão de Oliveira, author of a *Grammatica da
linguagem portuguesa* (1536), from João de Barros in 1540,
and from Duarte Núnez do Lião in works composed in the
last quarter of the century. These three authors quote peculiarities of the *minhoto* dialect: the use of *b* for *v*, the retention
of the ancient *-om*, and the insertion of *y* to prevent liaison
when two *aa* come together: they cite *fizerom amarom taballiom
cidadom, bida bos bossa, ay alma, ay agua,* for *fizeram amarão
tabalião cidadão, vida vos vossa, a alma, a agua.* These features
are held by the northern dialects in common with Galician,
and represent the gradual transition from that tongue—as
the parent language—to the Portuguese of Lisbon. They
have occupied their present ground continuously from the
early days of the Reconquest, when the Douro was established
as the frontier against Islam, with the result that there is
greater local diversity between village and village in this
region than elsewhere in Portugal, and there is a blurring of
the linguistic frontier against Spain. At Miranda, on Portuguese soil, Leonese is spoken in a form almost Portuguese,
and in compensation, Portuguese is spoken at Ermisinde;
while there are curious transitional dialects used at Riodonor
(twin villages, the one Spanish and the other Portuguese),
at Guadramil and at Sendim. In the south the frontier is
not transgressed save at Olivenza, near Badajoz, where
Portuguese still holds to an older political frontier that lay

to the east of the existing line. Thanks to the autonomy of each commune within this area it is only possible to describe the northern dialects *grosso modo*. For a more exact treatment it would be necessary to trace the area occupied by each several phenomenon, noting its centre of diffusion, its frontiers and islets of resistance at certain points.

Speaking generally, then, there exist in northern Portugal, between the Douro and Minho, many local speeches which are transitional between Galician and Portuguese. They fall into two main divisions: those of Tras-os-Montes and those of Entre-Douro-e-Minho. The former lead eastward to Leonese dialects of Spanish. The latter are commonly called *minhotos*, from the colloquial name for the province (*Minho*); but it is convenient to keep this term for the dialects spoken on the Minho itself (on its higher or lower course), by way of distinction from those employed on the Douro (similarly divided into higher and lower). To cover the whole area a latinism, *dialectos interamnenses* (subdialects: *minhoto—alto e baixo* and *duriense—alto e baixo*), is employed, to march with the *dialectos trasmontanos* (of which the frontier varieties are the *dialectos raianos*). Crossing the frontier, as the Reconquest first did, into the hilly inland province of Beira, we meet with *beirão*, a dialect in the course of which the northern peculiarities are shed and those of the south acquired. Estremadura, Alemtejo and Algarve form the southern area, which is that of the standard tongue. Towards the extreme south this southern Portuguese acquires distinctive features, due to instances where the local habit of speech has developed beyond the point attained by the capital.

The bilabial pronunciation of *v* as *b*, normal in Galicia, extends over the whole northern and central area—Entre-Douro-e-Minho, Tras-os-Montes and Beira. It connects Portuguese with one of the most characteristic speech-habits of the Peninsula, from which Lisbon and southern Portugal dissents, in company with some Catalan dialects. Similar in extension is the pronunciation of *ch* as an affricate [ĉ], for which Lisbon and the south has employed a fricative [š] since about 1700. The ancient distinction between *s* [ś] and *ç* [s] is maintained along the frontiers of Entre-Douro-e-Minho and Tras-os-Montes and in parts of Beira; but at other places in these provinces the distinction has been lost, as it has in literary Portuguese and throughout the south. The conservation of the old -ONE- -*om* takes place on the Lower Minho and Douro, and also in a fraction of Beira contiguous to this region. The termination is sometimes attributed to words where it has no historic justification, as CANE *cõu* Ptg. *cão*. In the Minho district also we find characteristic developments of purely local range, such as the denasalization of final -*m* (*birge foro* Ptg. *virgem foram* 'virgin, they were'), the change of *l*+consonant into *ur* (*aurma siurba úrtemo* Ptg. *alma silva último* 'soul, wood, last'), and the diphthongs formed from *ê ô* in contact with a labial (*piêra tiêmpo puôco fuônte* Ptg. *pêra tempo pouco fonte* 'pear, time, little, fountain'). Lisbon shows some local characteristics, such as the occasional use of an *r-grasseyé* [R] as used in French, and the value [ɐ̯i̯] for *ei*, with the corresponding nasal diphthong. Characteristic of the southern dialects (*alemtejano, algarvio*) is the tendency to reduce diphthongs to single vowels, viz. *eu* to *ê* and *ou* to *ô*. The latter is the accepted practice in standard Portuguese wherever *ou* is not respelled *oi* (or so pronounced contrary to the orthography): *cousa* is pronounced [kóze]. The southern dialects, however, have not merely *côsa*, but also *Dês, morrê-lhe* Ptg. *Deus, morreu-lhe* 'God, died to him'. These peculiarities ascend through Beira to portions of Tras-os-Montes. Similarly the diphthong *ei*, at Moncorvo in Tras-os-Montes, in Lower Beira and throughout the south, becomes the monophthong *ê* (*madêra* Ptg. *madeira*); in the north it is pronounced [ɛi̯], but in Lisbon [ɐ̯i̯]. In some cases *ai* may be reduced to *a* in the south, as *vas* for *vais*. Both *u* and *o* are sounds which, in the south, change their basis of articulation to some extent, the latter becoming *ö* in the diphthong *öu* for *ou*.

The rich store of archaic or obsolete expressions which have survived in the dialects to the north of the Douro makes *minhoto* and *trasmontano* unrivalled reservoirs of pure Portuguese upon which the literary tongue may draw.

This section and all that follow are based on J. Leite de Vasconcellos, *Esquisse d'une dialectologie portugaise* (Paris, 1901).

INSULAR PORTUGUESE

Madeira and the Azores (Ptg. *açor* 'hawk') appear on the Catalan map of 1351, based on the previous voyages of Arab and Christian merchants, and were occupied by the Portuguese in the first half of the fifteenth century. Concerning Madeira a romantic legend is told of the runaway lovers Robert Machin and Anne d'Arfet, said to have been driven out of their course from England to France by a storm which threw them up on the uninhabited Madeira. Effective settlement was undertaken by a certain João Gonçálvez *o Zarco* ('the blue-eyed'), despatched by Prince Henry the Navigator in 1420 from the Algarve, after having already touched at Porto-Santo in 1418. The occupation of the Azores was somewhat later, 1432–57, by Gonçalo Cabral. This also was an incident in the vast scheme of African exploration directed by Henry from his naval academy at Sagres, in Algarve.

The Portuguese here spoken is, like the Spanish of the Canaries, essentially European, and moreover reproduces the principal features of the southern dialects. The simplification of diphthongs and the occurrence of modified forms of *o u* are signs of its immediate parentage in Portugal. In the islands *ô* becomes *u* in *flur amur* Ptg. *flor amor* 'flower, love'. The Azores simplify *-ão* to *-ã* (*mã* for *mão* 'hand'), and in Madeira *cousa* is pronounced with a special diphthong approximating to *a* (*coasa*), and the quality of the *lh* is such as to resemble the *l* of Portuguese.

CHAPTER IX

THE PORTUGUESE LANGUAGE OVERSEAS

IN AFRICA

Portuguese seamen entered the Senegal River in the year 1445. The event aroused the keenest excitement in Portugal, as it seemed to justify the dream of attaining powerful alliances behind the back of the Moslems of Morocco. It was recorded in Gomes de Zurara's *Conquista da Guiné*, and even when other explorations had eclipsed its fame, and the political hope had proved empty, it was from the Guinea coast that barbaric wealth was drawn and Guinea slaves appeared in the streets of Lisbon. They formed, in fact, by the opening of the sixteenth century a recognized comic type. Gil Vicente's *Fragoa d'Amor* (1525) introduces a negro *falando Guiné* or *língua do preto* for the amusement of King Manuel's court, both in Portuguese and Spanish. Though to some extent conventional this language of the negro has some of the features of the extant Guinea-Portuguese: the negro drops the -*s* of the plural in nouns (*por quatro día*), confuses the persons of the verb (*das* for *dais*), employs a possessive pronoun for personal (*boso* for *vos*), fails to pronounce *lh* (*abêia oio*), dissolves clusters involving *l r*, simplifies the diphthong *ou* in the southern fashion (*matô* for *matou*), and is vanquished by gender (*bosso roupa*), etc. Actually Portuguese of this kind—insular Portuguese, with certain grammatical and phonetic modifications—is to be found in S. Tomé, Principe and Annobom (where it is called the *fá d'Ambú = fala d'Anobom*) in the Gulf of Guinea, and in Portuguese settlements on the coast. Formerly it existed in Saint Helena also, one more among the naval stations on the road to India. Portuguese is also spoken in the Cape Verde Islands.

The situation of the language in the great colonies of Angola and Moçambique is quite different. Under the old naval system these coasts were held but slightly, and the hinterland has been occupied only since the end of the nineteenth century. The Portuguese there used is official. The natives speak their own dialects, which tend to be much affected by official Portuguese. The reverse influence is slight. On the east African coast the language has a certain currency as far north as Zanzibar.

INDO-PORTUGUESE

The main strength of the Portuguese thalassocracy in the sixteenth century lay on the western fringe of the Indian subcontinent. The capital was Goa. It was held for Portugal not merely by European troops and settlers, but also by the class of Eurasians deliberately multiplied by the policy of the great Afonso de Albuquerque. Thanks to them the use of Portuguese has, in various places, outlasted the empire, so as still to be talked under French or English rulers. The sites chosen for occupation were those which provided ready defence against superior land powers, with an especial preference for islands (as Diu, Goa, Bombay, Ceylon), and nowhere did the language penetrate into the hinterland. At Goa and in Ceylon Portuguese has been used in local forms for a considerable body of religious literature. Diu and Daman are the most northerly of the line of old Portuguese factories. Next follows the region of the *dialecto norteiro* or *dos norteiros*, spoken at Bombay, Salsette, Bassein, etc., in the region ceded to England as part of Catharine of Braganza's dowry. To the south of Bombay we find the mid-point of the coast-line occupied by the Portuguese possession of Goa; on the Malabar coast the language is used by the Christians of Mangalor, Cananor and Cochin in English territory, and Mahé in French India; at Pondicherry (French possession), Tranquebar, Cuddalore and Karikal, Portuguese is spoken by Christians on the Coromandel coast. The island of Ceylon was first encountered by the Portuguese in 1503, but its subjugation did not take place until towards the end of the century. Many of its natives became Christians and adopted the Portuguese tongue. About the middle of the following century the Dutch dispossessed the Portuguese, and strove also to eradicate the language, which was so well established that even the native ruler spoke it 'excellently well'. Finally, the English replaced the Dutch at the close of the eighteenth century, bringing with them the vast political and commercial prestige of our tongue; but Portuguese continues in use among certain classes, and supports a literature of hymns and devotional books.

The discussion of Indo-Portuguese forms belongs rather to the student of mixed (or 'Creole') languages than to our present purpose. One or two peculiarities alone need be mentioned. They are, in the first place, a prolongation of southern Portuguese dialects, and agree most intimately with the insular Portuguese of the Azores and Madeira. The diphthongs are either reduced to simple vowels or pronounced with an enfeebled semivowel (*azête ôtro pôco feĭto*). As the occupation of Goa dates from the sixteenth century, the pronunciation of *ch* brought by the settlers was the affricate [ĉ], which is still in use. *L* tends to become *lh* in the *dialecto norteiro* as in Madeira, and the plural of *oficial* is *oficials* (Ptg. *oficiais*), which may be compared with the Azorean *azul azules*. *Lh* becomes *y* in Ceylon (*oyá foya* Ptg. *olhar folha* 'look, leaf'); *r* ceases to be a vibrant, and at the end of words disappears; and *j* has here and there (as in Ceylon) the affricate pronunciation of an English *j* [ĵ].

To these characteristics we must add, particularly in morphology and syntax, usages that are specifically Creole. The concords of gender and number are not maintained in conversation, the one indication being deemed sufficient for all the components of an expression (*bonito orta* 'pretty garden', *três animal* 'three animals'). Reduplicated plurals occur, showing an attempt at simplification of the plural idea (*Norteiro: fi-fi=filhos* 'sons'; Diu: *cão-cão* 'dogs'). The rules for the collocation of personal pronouns with reference to the verb are, as in Brazil, misapplied, and in Ceylon prepositions are made to follow their noun through Dravidian influence. The verbal paradigm is altered, generally in an analytic sense (e.g. preference for the perfect tense over the preterite; or with *já* 'already'). A phonetic habit that occurs throughout this area is the loss of all final vowels: *dinheir, minh filh, ru, navi = dinheiro, meu filho* (*minh < minho* cf. *minha*), *rua, navio,* 'money, my son, street, ship'.

MACAU AND MALAYA

Macau, situated at the mouth of the Si-Kiang, was occupied in 1557, and is still a Portuguese possession. The language there spoken has interesting analogies with that used in India and Ceylon, such as the simplification of *ei ou* to *ê ô*, the affricate pronunciation of *ch j* [ĉ ĵ], save when the latter becomes *z* (*jardim* but *greza = igreja* 'church'), the loss of vibration in the *r*. Adjectives retain invariably the masculine form, and reduplicated plurals are frequent (*porco-porco* 'pigs', *nhônhônha* and *nhônha-nhônha* as plural of *nhôna* (*senhora*) 'young girl'. Past time is indicated with the help of an adverb (*eu já vesti*). Portuguese is spoken in Java, with Malayan admixture, at Malacca (conquered by Albuquerque in 1511) in the *dialecto malaqueiro* and by some Malaccan settlers in Singapore, and in the island of Timor. In the last case there is no Creole dialect properly speaking, but owing to contact with Macau there is some use of *crioulo macaísta* among those who have recently arrived from China and servant-girls who have come from the interior. It represents for them an intermediate stage in the acquisition of correct Portuguese.

BRAZILIAN PORTUGUESE (BRASILEIRO)

The development of Portuguese in Brazil presents some features in common with the Creole dialects of the Middle and Far East, in addition to peculiarly American elements; but it differs from them by its cultural claims as the native expression of so vast a society. The demand for a national language arises in Brazil from the same sense of well-being, politically, socially and economically, which has given cause for the Argentine claim to an *idioma nacional argentino*. Brazilian authors are conscious of the gap that lies between the spontaneous and the literary expression of their thoughts. Authors complain, in perfect Portuguese, of the difficulty they find in expressing their ideas in a mould that does not serve for polite conversation. 'Our grammar' (says Professor J. Ribeiro, *A língua nacional*, São Paulo, 1921) 'cannot be exactly that of the Portuguese. Regional differences demand a difference of style and method. The fact is that when we correct our language, we risk mutilating the ideas and feelings that are our personal contribution. It is not our language that we correct; it is our spirits that we subject to an inexplicable servitude.' To bridge the gap numerous grammars and treatises on style are issued, which seek to define the literary usage; but as the authority for the latter is that of classical Portuguese literature, formalized and standardized, the idiom is neither Portuguese proper (which is continually recreated from the vernacular), nor Brazilian, but a third tongue called by Mário de Alencar *o idioma da seita gramatical*. Such a situation is not satisfactory; but its remedy is not easy. Various persons have been provoked into tempestuous onslaughts on the language of Portuguese writers, individually or collectively; but these attacks can hardly be sustained without compromising the usages of good society in Brazil. More numerous than the points of difference are those of contact: *a língua portuguesa será eternamente a língua do Brasil*. It is manifestly absurd, for instance, to banish the *Lusíadas* from Brazilian schools, as one patriot suggests, merely because Camões does not happen to devote to the discovery of Brazil more than a couplet. The maintenance of Luso-Brazilian linguistic unity is a necessary condition of its international importance; so that the situation calls for a certain amount of concession on either side. Portuguese must accept as 'correct' certain syntactical and phonetic features which strike them as provincial or unidiomatic; and Brazilians must continue to reject alterations which break down the scaffolding of the language. This solution, in its essentials, is already adopted by responsible stylists, and the greater concession required from Brazilians is generally made.

The question of the *língua nacional* or *dialecto luso-brasileiro* refers mainly to the use made of the European heritage; but the most obvious basis for such a language is the new experience offered by America, and which leads to *nativismo* or *indianismo* in literature. To express this experience Brazilian has drawn on the Indian languages, and chiefly on Tupi-Guaraní. These additions to the lexicon have been made available for Portugal also, in so far as Portuguese writers may have cause to mention Brazilian beasts or plants or scenery. The difference in this respect between the two speeches consists in the much greater frequency of such words in Brazilian. Owing to the relatively late occupation of Brazil many American words are part of the common European stock of americanisms, learned in the Antilles, Mexico or Peru by Spanish discoverers, and passed by them into Portuguese. In such cases, there may also exist in Brazilian a Tupí loan-word of more exact local significance. Thus beside *canoa* we find Tupí *iga* and *ubá*; in the place of *bohío* 'hut' we find Tupí *oca*; alongside *maíz*, current in Portugal, we find Tupí and Brazilian *ubatim*. In other cases, where the object named was first encountered in Tupi-Guaraní territory, its name has equal currency in Spanish (through the Plate region) and in Portuguese-Brazilian: e.g. *banana, curare, mandioca, tapioca* and the animals *jaguar, tapir, aï, tucão*. The classes of words borrowed are chiefly the names of things, and especially of animals and plants peculiar to the country. Of such a nature are *capibara coatí manatí* (Tupí?) *piranha tamanduá yacaré* and *cajú cajoeira ipecacuanha*. Features of Brazilian scenery often require special names: *sertão* 'unoccupied land, interior' is of European provenience, but *catinga* 'the thin white scrub of the Brazilian Campos', *capão* (Sp. *capón* in Plate countries) 'forest-clumps in the Campos', *capoeira* 'partially cleared land partially overgrown', *igapó* 'forest tracts liable to be flooded by the rivers of North Brazil', are necessary local terms. The life of the natives is relatively little noticed by these loan-words, since it had little to offer that could compare with the civilizations of Mexico and Peru. *Tupan* stands for a vague supernatural 'God, lightning'; *tapuya* 'non-Tupí' serves to denote an 'enemy'; *sarbacana* is a 'blowpipe', *tembetá* 'lip-plug', *tucapú* a kind of shirt, together with the words for hut and canoe already cited.

In the use made of its European inheritance Brazilian literature shows considerable diversity. Impeccable academic Portuguese, or Portuguese with only involuntary brazilianisms, is characteristic of many of the best authors. A regional Portuguese appears in the works of José de Alencar, author of *Iracema*, *O Guaraní* and other 'nativist' novels, standing at the head of the emancipated literature of his country. His speech employs the Brazilian order of pronouns, the affirmative form of questions, copious indianisms, but maintains the grammatical framework unimpaired. The *Poemas bravios* of the popular bard Catulo Cearense are typical of the attempt to write in the *idioma brasileiro*, based on the vernacular and local forms. These forms, however, include many vulgarisms which would not be part even of the colloquial idiom of educated persons, represented more exactly by the regionalism of Alencar. To reach academic Portuguese it is admitted that the educated Brazilian must submit his manner of speech to a further formal test. There occurs, therefore, in Brazil the same oscillation between extremes both in writing and in speech as we have already seen in the Spanish of America; and in the same fashion we must give specific attention to those matters in which the former colony departs most from the parent tongue without affirming that these points of contrast are universal or even deemed reputable in educated circles.

The parallel established between the Spanish and Portuguese of America extends also to the general description of their disagreement with the European tongues. Apart from the Indian vocabulary already mentioned—the Tupi-Guaraní character of which is shared by the Spanish of Paraguay and the Plate—Brazilian differs from Portuguese usage in respect of archaisms, independent evolution, vulgarisms, dialectalisms, and creolisms. It is based on Portuguese of the south, approaching closely to insular Portuguese, and there are phonetic and morphological changes which connect it with the creole dialects of the African coast. Over the vast subcontinent we do not expect to find a completely uniform tongue, but the regional differences do not offer the rich dialectal diversity of northern Portugal. Those dialects go back to the romanization of the Peninsula and conditions moulding the primitive Reconquest; but Brazilian ascends only to the Portuguese of King Manuel's court and time, which is far enough to allow of words and sounds since rendered archaic in Europe, but not to permit of deep dialectal fissures. Brazil also, like Spanish America, was liable to constant increments of Portuguese influence during the whole colonial period.

The vowel-system of Portuguese as spoken in Brazil is readily distinguished by the greater clarity of atonics, which, as in Galicia, do not lose their timbre [e o]. An archaic feature is the retention of the [ɛ] in the diphthong *ei* and the nasal diphthong *em*. In Lisbon this element has passed into an obscure *a* [ɐ], but the Brazilian usage is corroborated by the northern dialects. The denasalization of a final accented nasal diphthong also occurs in northern Portugal, and leads in Brazil to pronunciations like *capitá fazia vivia* for *capitão fazião vivião*. Final accented *a* tends, conversely, to become a nasal diphthong (*papãi̯ mamãi̯ = papá mamá*), and final *ê* (sometimes due to loss of *-s*) becomes an oral diphthong (*fêi trêi francei = fêz três francês*). Marks of southern provenience are the simple vowels which arise from the diphthongs *ou ei eu*, and the feebleness of the *yod* in *ai*: *pôco andô madêra cuiê = pouco andou madeira colheu* and *caįxa* (with much relaxed *i̯*). The *yod* of terminations tends to be lost (*consciênça matera negoço palaço = consciência matéria negócio palácio*). In hiatus also vowels are reduced (*mió* from *melhor*), and a relaxed *a* [ɐ] is heard frequently before initial *l r* or between consonants in an initial group (*arrespirar alembrar falô Caláudio* = *respirar lembrar flôr Cláudio*). The above spellings are imitative, and are not used save to indicate colloquial forms. The standard orthography ignores the actual pronunciation, or else causes it to conform to the spelling.

The Brazilian *s* differs somewhat in timbre from the Portuguese, being described as less palatal. No distinction is made between *s* and *ç* nor between *z* and the voiced sound corresponding to *s*. In this respect Brazilian shows its kinship with southern and standard Portuguese, but it does not transform *s* and its congeners into [š ž] at the end of a syllable before a consonant. At the end of a word, where Portuguese uses only the voiceless [š], Brazilian speech frequently drops the *s* (*cinco dia, trez ano, nós tudo, uns negoço* for *dias, anos, tôdos, negócios*, etc.) or replaces it with *i̯* (*trei fei* = *três fêz*). This loss of -*s* affects the plural of nouns and adjectives since the plural sign is added to one member only of the group (*duas galinha* 'two hens'). In the verb the second person singular loses its final -*s* in this fashion, and the third plural is denasalized; while a combination of both processes may bring the first plural to the same form. Thus *come* may be *comes, comem, comemos: nós tudo fazia* = *nós tôdos faziamos*. We meet also fuller forms of 1 Pl. like *nós havemo de andá* = *nós havemos de andar* 'we must go'; and the termination of the first conjugation in 3 Pl. may be the archaic -*om* in *dero* = *derom* = *deram*. Parallel with this loss of -*s* is the frequent loss of final -*r*, which particularly affects the infinitive, together with the interchange of *l r* which leads sometimes to the disappearance of -*l* also. Thus *salvado lealdade* become *sarvado léardade* (with the open pronunciation of atonic *e* usual in Brazil), and *mel fel* become *mê fé*; while conversely *animal* gives *animar*. Loss of -*r* is exemplified in the infinitives *andá sê tá* = *andar sêr estar*, in the future subjunctive *quizé* = *quizer*, and in *muié doutó mió faló* = *molher doutor melhor flor*. *R* disappears from groups in *sempe dento* = *sempre dentro*. The metathesis of *er re* is current as in all vulgar Portuguese and Spanish: *perzidente* = *presidente*. The lateral palatal *lh* is imperfectly conserved. It has passed to *l* (as in Madeira) in the pronunciation of some speakers (*aleio* for *alheio*, failure to distinguish *cavaleiro* from the castilianism *cavalheiro*), but normally *lh* has become *y*: *muié cuié véio oio paréia = molher colher velho olho parelha*. This development is found in European Portuguese only at Olivenza, on Spanish soil, where it may be due to the influence of Spanish vernaculars; but it takes place in most of the creole dialects, commencing with the Cape Verde Islands. The delateralization of *lh* occurred, no doubt, spontaneously in each region. Medial -*d*- may be lost: *tou = tôdo*. The deformation of Portuguese pronunciation is essentially vulgar in Brazil, and even when one or other of the above-mentioned sounds occurs in a person's speech, he feels bound to restore the standard pronunciation in reading poetry or making a speech.

There are some notable differences between colloquial Brazilian syntax and Portuguese, and they ascend into literature with authors of regionalist tendencies. What chiefly arouses remark is the failure to observe the traditional Portuguese order in grouping pronouns with the verb. In Portuguese, as in old Spanish, the personal pronouns of the unaccented order (*me te se*, etc.) are enclitics, with a strong tendency to gravitate towards the first accented word of the clause. They cannot, therefore, head a clause (*tenho-o* 'I have it', *não-me lembro* 'I do not remember', *assim se exprime* 'he expresses himself thus', *o homem que-me viu* 'the man who saw me'), but they do not rest on a noun (*o vizinho deu-lhe uma maçã* 'the neighbour gave him an apple'), nor on a coordinating conjunction like *e mas porem contudo todavia*. In Brazilian, as in modern Spanish, the pronouns are either enclitic or proclitic, and attached to the verb only. They thus frequently head the sentence (*me disse* 'he said to me'), intervene between the noun-subject and the verb (*a pobrezinha se cansou* 'the poor thing grew weary'), or follow the verb even when a preceding particle makes enclisis possible (*não lembro-me* 'I do not remember'). There is even a tendency to avoid these unaccented pronouns by using the disjunctive series (*vi éle, encontrei éla = vi-o, encontrei-a* 'I saw him, met her'). There is a tendency in Brazil, also, to ask questions in the affirmative form (*Qual das bonecas tu amas?* 'Which doll do you like?' *Quando eu hei-de ter uma rôla?* 'When am I to have a dove?'). The imperative is used negatively as well as positively (*não faz isto* 'don't do this'), and there is a noteworthy extension of the use of the personal infinitive to serve for subordinate verbs which differ in person from the principal— a case in which Portuguese uses finite subordinate clauses. Thus 'he brought this for me to see' is *trouxe isto para mim ver* (Ptg. *para eu ver*), 'he made them all sit down' is *fez todos sentarem*. The association of prepositions with certain verbs differs from Portuguese practice, frequently through archaism: *olvidar de tudo, subir num galho, parecer com, passar uma lição no filho* (Ptg. *dar uma lição ao filho*).

In respect of vocabulary colloquial Brazilian shows many peculiarities. Among the particles we find *ansim* for *assim* (cf. OSp. *ansi ansina*, current in America), the dialectal *munto* for *muito, di si* for *de se, inté* for *até*, the use of *a* for *para* and the vulgar contractions *prá pró prú = para a, para o. Gintem* appears for *vintem* (a coin), *passo* for *pássaro* 'bird', and special senses are attached to common words like *doce* 'sugar' Ptg. *açúcar, queimada* 'ground cleared by burning for planting', *montaria* 'canoe', *sítio* 'place for agriculture', *manteiga* 'oil', etc. Sometimes Brazilian has made a choice between alternatives different from that made in Portugal: 'train' Braz. *trem* (cf. Sp. *tren*) Ptg. *combóio*. In minute respects the two countries exert different preferences: Braz. *minha senhora* Ptg. *minha molher* 'my wife', Braz. *descarrilhou* Ptg. *descarrilou* 'ran off the rails', Braz. *uma casa mobiliada* Ptg. *mobilada* 'a furnished house'. Somewhat remarkable is the effusion of diminutives in Brazilian, doubtless due to the same cause (native nurses) as leads to the perpetuation of nursery terms in American forms of Spanish: *sinhàzinha* (from *sinhá = senhora*), *merunhanha* 'light drizzle', or (with a gerund) *dormindinho* 'sleeping lightly'.

22

APPENDIX

PHONETICS AND PHONOLOGY

The foregoing discussion has involved the use of phonetic symbols and of certain phonological conclusions. Peninsular phonetics should be studied in T. Navarro Tomás, *Manual de pronunciación española* (Madrid) and the general scheme published in *Revista de Filología*, ii, A. R. Gonçalves Viana, *Portugais* (Leipzig, 1903), and J. Arteaga Pereira et P. Barnils, *Textes catalans avec leur transcription phonétique* (Barcelona, 1915). A. R. Gonçalves Viana compared the three languages in *Romania*, xii. The outlines of the phonology of the three Romance languages are found in the works noted in the first chapter. However, for the purpose of immediate reference, I give a tabular account of these two aspects of Peninsular philology.

I. Phonetics

(Ċ ġ mean c g before a front vowel, e i; k means occlusive c)

Vowels

A.　Sp. *a* is medial in timbre, but becomes slightly velarized in contact with *u l*. Ptg. Cat. accented *a* is more open than the Spanish, and is considerably velarized in contact with *u l* [ɑ]. Spanish unaccented vowels retain their timbre and merely decrease the tension of utterance. Ptg. unaccented *a* becomes [ɐ], as *a* in Eng. *above*. Cat. unaccented *a e* are pronounced [ɐ] before the accented syllable.

E.　Sp. *e* is medial in timbre. It is more open in a closed syllable or in contact with *j ġ rr* and more closed in an open syllable or one closed by *n* or *s*. Ptg. *é* Cat. *è* are more open than Sp. *e* and have the value [ɛ]; Ptg. *ê ê* Cat. *é* are more closed [e̩]. Ptg. unaccented *e* is much relaxed [ə]. Cat. unaccented *a e* are pronounced [ə] after the accented syllable.

I.　Sp. Ptg. Cat. *i*. The sound varies according to circumstances but retains its timbre.

O.　As for *e*. Sp. [o] Ptg. Cat. [ɔ o̩]. Unaccented Ptg. Cat. *o* becomes [u].

U.　Sp. Ptg. Cat. *u*. Varies, as for *i*. It is sometimes whispered as an unaccented final in Ptg. [ɯ] is found in some varieties of Chilean pronunciation. It resembles [u], but without rounding of the lips.

Semi-vowels and semi-consonants. These are principally *i u* in combination
with a more open vowel. When that vowel comes first, the diphthong
is described as decreasing, and the *i u* as semi-vocalic [i̯ u̯]; in the
reverse case, the diphthong is said to be increasing and the *i u*
semi-consonantal [j w]. The distinction is useful in philology, since
the former lead to vocalic, the latter to consonantal changes.

For sake of brevity, any element akin to semi-vocalic or semi-
consonantal *i* is called *yod*.

Nasal vowels. In Ptg. *a e i o u* are pronounced [ẽ ẽ ĩ õ ũ] beneath the
sign ~ or before *m n* in the same syllable. The *m n* has then no consonantal value, but the *m* indicates a labial semi-vowel [u̯].

Consonants

Nasal consonants take the point of articulation of the following consonant. In all three languages there is regressive assimilation, by which
the first of two consonants may be voiced or unvoiced to agree with the
second, e.g. Sp. *rasgar*, with [z]. In Cat. absolute finals are unvoiced.

Occlusives. Voiceless [p t k] Sp. Ptg. Cat. *p t c qu* (before *e i*). [kw] Sp. *cu*
Ptg. Cat. *qu* (with diacritic before *e i*). Voiced [b d g] Sp. Ptg.
Cat. *b d g gu* (before *e i*). [gw] Sp. Ptg. Cat. *gu* (with a diacritic
before *e i*). Sp. Cat. Gal. NPtg. *v=b*. These occlusives become fricatives [ƀ đ g] in weak positions, i.e. when not initial nor preceded
by *m n* (or *l* for *d*). The two sounds are so related that substitution of the fricative for the occlusive does not denaturalize the
pronunciation. In Catalan the occlusive occurs more frequently
than in Sp. Ptg., for instance in the group *bl*.

Peninsular occlusives differ from English ones in the absence of
any aspiration with *p t k*, or any unvoicing of *b d g*.

Fricatives [ƀ đ g]. Labiodental [f] Sp. Ptg. Cat. *f*. [v] SPtg. Catalan
dialectal *v*. Bilabial [φ] occurs in some varieties of Chilean Spanish;
it corresponds to a *p* without closure of the lips. Interdental [θ ð]
Sp. *c z*, and *z* before voiced consonant. At Malpartida de Plasencia
c z are two distinct sounds, the one voiceless, the other voiced; but
in Spanish they are both voiceless.

The *sibilant fricatives* are complex. *s z* are alveolar. Their varieties
are the cacuminal [ṡ ż], pronounced with the tip of the tongue
rising to the roof of the mouth; the coronal [ṡ ż], and the dorsoalveolar [s z], pronounced with the tip of the tongue resting on the
lower teeth, and point of articulation between the forepart of the
back of the tongue and the alveoli. Sp. *s* is [ṡ]. The coronal pronunciation occurs in Andalusia (see p. 218), and the dorsoalveolar [s]
in southern Andalusia and America. In Sp. [z] occurs only through
the influence of a following consonant. Cat. *s* is [ṡ], but before a
voiced consonant or between vowels [ż]. Cat. *ss*, used between
vowels, is [ṡ]. Cat. *z* is [ż]. But [s ż] also occur. Cat. *ç=ss s*.
At Bragança, in Portugal, *ss s* are [ṡ ż], but *ç z* are [s z]. In standard

Ptg. *s -ss- ç* are [s], *-s-* (between vowels) *z* are [z]. Before a consonant Ptg. *s z* palatalize to [š ž] according as the consonant is voiceless or voiced, and when absolute finals *s z* are both [š]. This palatalization does not occur in Brazilian-Portuguese. [š ž] are palatals, OSp. *x j ĝ*, Ptg. *x j ĝ*, Cat. *(i)x j ĝ*. Ptg. *ch* is [š].

Palatal [j] Sp. Ptg. Cat. *y i* (consonantal or semi-consonantal). Velar [w] Sp. *hu-*, Sp. Ptg. Cat. *u* (semi-consonantal). Velar [χ] voiceless and vibrant, Sp. *j ĝ*. Laryngeal [h] is the Andalusian and American pronunciation of *h* Lat. ғ, and also results from *s* at the end of a syllable. The latter may be slightly voiced [н].

Affricates. These are treated by some phoneticians as compounds of an occlusive (generally represented by *t*) and a sibilant fricative. The alveolar affricates [ŝ ẑ] occur in Cat. *ts dz* and western Leonese *tsabe tsobu.* The palatal affricates [č j] are Cat. *ch tx* and *tj (i)g*, Sp. *ch* [č], Gal. NPtg. *ch* [č]. It was the general pronunciation of Ptg. *ch* until the eighteenth century. *Tr* in Chilean *otro* [óṭɹo], with palatal *t* and fricative *r*, closely resembles the affricate [č]. Sp. init. *y* and after *l n* is [j].

Laterals. Sp. Ptg. Cat. *l* is [l], but in Ptg. Cat. it is velarized at the end of a syllable [ł]. In Spanish it is then only slightly modified in a velar sense. The *l* may be interdental, dental or alveolar, according to the following consonant in Spanish. The palatal [λ] is Sp. Cat. *ll* Ptg. *lh.*

Vibrants. Sp. Ptg. Cat. *r* has one vibration [r]; but initially, or after *n* or *s*, or when written *rr* it is a multiple vibrant [r̄]. Finally it is relaxed, and disappears in Catalan and in Andalusia. The relaxed fricative pronunciation occurs in Chile, both simple [ɹ] and compound [ɹ], and this resembles English *r*. The French *r-grasseyé* [ʀ] is sometimes heard in Lisbon. In correct Spanish *r* assimilates a preceding *s* in the form of an additional vibration.

Nasals. Bilabial [m]. Labiodental (before *f*) [ɱ]. Dental and alveolar [n]. Palatal [ɲ] Sp. *ñ* Ptg. *nh* Cat. *ny.* Velar [ŋ]. In Sp. Cat. the nasals take the position of articulation of the following consonant. In Ptg. they are consonants only initially or between vowels. Otherwise *m* indicates a nasal diphthong, and *n* a nasal simple vowel.

II. Phonology

Latin	Rom-ance	Spanish dialects	Sp.	Ptg.	Cat.	Examples
TONIC VOWELS						
AE Ĕ	ę	e ia a ie	ie	ę	ę	Moz. *ben Alporchel Gudiel Cazalla šaḥamialla.* Leon. *siellas Peni-alla ya.* Arag. *tene kien.* Sp. *viene tierra viento cielo,* but *lecho* (before a palatal). Ptg. *vem terra vento céu leito.* Cat. *vé terra vent cel,* but *llit* (before a palatal)
ŏ	ǫ	o uo ua ue	ue	ǫ	ǫ	Moz. *bono noḥte Ferreirola welyo porco puerco.* Leon. *tuorto vortos duano puablo Quoencha poesta Valbuena.* Arag. *malluolo Uosca Fuanti Lascuarre Pueio Aragüés.* Sp. *bueno luego majuelo puente,* but *ojo noche* (before a palatal). Ptg. *bom logo forte noite olho.* Cat. *bó lloc fort,* but *nit ull* (before a palatal)
OE Ē Ĭ	ẹ	e	e	ẹ	ẹ	Sp. Ptg. *mesa verde vez ameno.* Cat. *mesa vert*
ō Ŭ	ọ	o	o	ọ	ọ	Sp. Ptg. *sol monte lodo.* Cat. *sol mont llot*
A	a	a	a	a	a	Sp. Ptg. *andar.* Cat. *anar*
Ī	i	i	i	i	i	Sp. Ptg. *cinco.* Cat. *cinc*
Ū	u	u	u	u	u	Sp. *luna.* Ptg. *lua.* Cat. *lluna*
Palatalizations						
AI (ARIU ASI A + C > ai) AGINE	ai	ai ei e ain ein en	e en	ei agem	e atge	Moz. *baika atarey pandair yanair carreyra Ferreira plantayn bega.* Leon. *baica ueika ueca ferrajne ferreynes ferrenes molineiras.* Arag. *terzero uerdateros Veila peitet Reimon Remon.* Sp. *vega ataré pandero llantén herrero pechar.* Ptg. *veiga feito beijo cavaleiro,* but *chantagem.* Cat. *vega fet bes ferrer,* but *ferratge*
E + yod						Sp. *tibio vidrio cirio.* Ptg. *tibio vidro círio.* Cat. *tebi vidre ciri*
O + yod						Sp. *lluvia rubio sucio.* Ptg. *chuva ruivo sujo.* Cat. *pluja roig*

Latin	Rom-ance	Spanish dialects	Sp.	Ptg.	Cat.	Examples
TONIC VOWELS (*continued*)						
ORIU		oiro	uero	oiro	uri	Leon. *terituria cobertoira Doyro*
URIU		uero		ouro		*Boisone Bueso* Sp. *cuero Duero agüero cobertera.* Ptg. *coiro Douro agouro agoiro.* Cat. *auguri*
Ē + Ĭ						Sp. *hice vino.* Ptg. *fiz vim.* Cat. *fiu*
Velarizations						
AU	au	au ou o	o	ou oi	o	Moz. *lauša.* Leon. *sauto souto*
AL + cons.	al	au ou o	o	ou al	o al	*ouro xosa.* Sp. *losa cosa soto*
		al	al			*salto oro.* Ptg. *lousa cousa souto salto ouro oiro.* Cat. *cosa altre*
A + U		ou o u	u	ou		OSp. *sope ove.* MSp. *supe hube.* Ptg. *soube ouve*
Hiatus						
Ẹ Ọ			i u			Sp. *mío mía judío tua sua.* Ptg. *meu minha judeu judia teu tua*
ATONIC VOWELS (*other than final*)						
A	a	a	a	a	a	Sp. Ptg. Cat. *amar*
Ĭ Ē Ĕ AE	e	e	e	e	e	Sp. Ptg. Cat. *mesura*
Ī	i	i	i	i	i	Sp. Ptg. Cat. *mirar*
Ŭ Ō Ŏ	o	o	o	o	o	Sp. *orgullo.* Ptg. *orgulho.* Cat. *orgull*
AU	au	au ou o	o	ou	o	Moz. *Laujar Mourqât.* Leon. *auteiro otero auctorigare obtorigare.* Sp. *otero otorgar posar.* Ptg. *outeiro outorgar pousar.* Cat. *posar otorgar*
Ū	u	u	u	u	u	Sp. Ptg. Cat. *mudar*
FINAL VOWELS						
A	a	a	a	a	a	Sp. Ptg. Cat. *mesa*
I E AE	e	e -	e -	e -	-	Sp. *pared ved ven sol mar cortés paz noche rey hace nueve Lope* (OSp. *nog faz nuef Lop*). Ptg. *parede vem sol mar noite rei faze nove.* Cat. *nou ben set rei ve sol mar*
O	o	o -	o	o	- }	Moz. *pandair yenair Gudiel bono.*
U	u	u o -	o	o	- }	Sp. *bueno enero Gudillo.* Ptg. *bom (bõo) janeiro castelo.* Cat. *bo ou.* Glos. Sil. *kematu aflitos*

Latin	Rom-ance	Spanish dialects	Sp.	Ptg.	Cat.	Examples
VOWEL OF SUPPORT					e	Cat. *pare pere*
INTERTONICS						Sp. *huérfano limpio duda deuda yerno sesenta castigar tilde pró-logo.* Ptg. *órfão dúvida dívida genro sessenta til.* Cat. *orfe dubte gendre títol prólec*

CONSONANTS

(Strong position is at beginning of word or of syllable after another consonant; weak position is between vowels or between a vowel and *r l*)

	Latin	Rom-ance	Spanish dialects	Sp.	Ptg.	Cat.	Examples
L							
Initial	l	ll y l š	l	l	ll		Moz. *lauša Laujar yengua.* Ast. *lluna tsuna.* Sp. *luna losa lengua.* Ptg. *lua lousa lingoa.* Cat. *lluna llengua*
Strong	l	l	l	l	l		Sp. *hablar.* Ptg. *falar.* Cat. *faula*
Weak	l	l	l	-	l		Sp. *cielo salir.* Cat. *cel.* Ptg. *céu sair*
Final	l	l	l	ł	ł		Sp. Ptg. Cat. *mal*
Doubled	ll	ll y ž -l	ll -l	l	ll		Sp. *caballo* [kaβáλo -jo -žo] *mil.* Ptg. *cavalo mil.* Cat. *cavall mill*
N							
Strong	n	n	n	n	n		Sp. Ptg. Cat. *ni*
Weak	n	n	n	-	n		Sp. *lana mano.* Ptg. *lã mão ter vir.* Cat. *tenir*
Final	n	n	n	m	-		Sp. *bien.* Ptg. *bem.* Cat. *bé mà vé orfe* (*bens*, etc.)
Doubled	nn	ñ -n	ñ -n	n	ny		Sp. *año paño.* Ptg. *ano pano.* Cat. *any pany*
M							
Strong Weak	m	m	m	m	m		Sp. *cama llama.* Ptg. *cama chama.* Cat. *om flama*
Double	mm						
Final	m	n	n	m	m		Sp. *harén.* Ptg. *harem.* Cat. *Guillem*
R							
Str. Double	r rr	(r)r	(r)r	(r)r	(r)r		Sp. Ptg. *rosa garra.* Cat. *rosa esquerra*
Weak	r	r	r	r	r		Sp. Ptg. Cat. *pero*
Final	r	r -	r	r	-(r)		Sp. *mujer.* Ptg. *molher.* Cat. *mulle(r).* Arag. *mullé mullés*

Latin	Rom-ance	Spanish dialects	Sp.	Ptg.	Cat.	Examples
CONSONANTS (continued)						
S						
Strong	s	s	s	s	s	Sp. *soy.* Ptg. *sou.* Cat. *soc*
'Impure'	is	es	es	es	es	Sp. *estoy.* Ptg. *estou.* Cat. *estic*
Weak	[z]	s [z]	s	s [z]	s [z] -	Sp. Ptg. Cat. *rosa* (OSp. Ptg. Cat. [z]; MSp. [s]) (Cat. *veíble*)
Final	s	s h -	s	s [š]	s	Sp. *más.* Andal. *mihmo ma'.* Ptg. *mais.* Cat. *més*
Doubled	ss	ss	s	ss	ss	OSp. Ptg. Cat. *passar.* MSp. *pasar*
P T C [k]						
Strong	p t c	p t c	p t c	p t c	p t c	Sp. *pasar tener castigar queso* (*qu*=[k] before *e, i*). Ptg. *passar ter castigar queijo.* Cat. *passar tenir casa quiet*
Weak	b d g	p t c b d g	b d g	b d g	p t c b d g	Moz. *boyâṭa merkatal.* Arag. *marito capeza cocote.* Leon. *baséliga tidulare La Sagra.* Sp. *mercado marido cabo cogote conde* (OSp. [b d g]; MSp. [b d g]). Ptg. *caber saiba cada lago liberdade.* Cat. *llibertat comte vegada naba*
Final	t c	-	-	-	-	Sp. *ama sí aquí.* Ptg. *ama sim aquí.* Cat. *ama si açí així*
Doubled	p t c	p t c	p t c	p t c	p t c	Sp. Ptg. Cat. *copa.* Sp. *hasta.* Ptg. *até.* Sp. *pequeño.* Ptg. *pequeno.* Cat. *petit.* Sp. Ptg. Cat. *vaca*
B D G						
Strong	b d g	b d g	b d g	b d g	b d g	Sp. *buey dar gozo.* Ptg. *boi dar gozo.* Cat. *bou donar goig*
Weak [b d g]	b	b v u	b v u	b v u	b v u	Sp. *cabo beber cautivo.* Ptg. *bébedo beudo cavalo.* Cat. *haver heure beure cavall faula paor*
	d	d -	d -	d -	- u	Sp. *nudo nido frío.* Ptg. *desnudo ninho nú.* Cat. *cru veure*
	g	g	g	g	g	Sp. *negro llaga jugo migaja.* Andal. *miaja.* Ptg. *negro chaga.* Cat. *negre plaga*
Final	d				u	Cat. *peu creu*

Latin	Rom-ance	Spanish dialects	Sp.	Ptg.	Cat.	Examples
CONSONANTS (continued)						
F						
Strong	f	f h	h - fr fu	!		f	Moz. Leon. Arag. *fillo.* Andal. *jamelgo.* Extrem. *jechu.* Cast. *hijo hecho frente fuente.* Ptg. *feito filho.* Cat. *fet fill*
Weak		v -	v -	v		f v	Moz. *prouectura.* Sp. *provecho dehesa.* Ptg. *proveito deveza.* Cat. *profit provecte*
V=B						
Final					u		Cat. *breu*
W						
German		g	g	g	gu	g	Sp. *ganar guerra.* Ptg. *ganhar guerra.* Cat. *guany guerra*
Arabic		w	gu	gu o		gu	Sp. Ptg. Cat. *guad-.* Ptg. *Odiana*
H						
Latin	-	-	-	-	-		Orthographic in Sp. *haber.* Ptg. *haver.* Cat. *heure*
German⎱		- h f	- h f	- f		-	Sp. *arpa farpa fardido fonta*
Arabic⎰		- h f	- h f	- f		- f	*yelmo Alhambra.* Ptg. *farpa Alfama forro alfageme.* OCat. *alforro*
Ć						
Strong	c	c [s]	c [θ]	c [s]		c [s]	Sp. Ptg. *cinco.* Cat. *cinc*
Weak	z	z [s]	c [θ] ⟨z	z [z]		z [z]	Sp. *hizo diciembre.* Ptg. *feze dezembro vizinho.* Cat. *desembre vei*
Final		z [s]	z [θ]	z [š]		u	Sp. *paz diez.* Ptg. *paz dez.* Cat. *pau deu*
J Ǵ DĮ						
Strong	j ǵ	j g y x	j g -	j g		j g	Moz. *Junqueira yenair.* Leon. *Yeluira Junco.* Astur. *xente.* Gal. *xente*, etc. Sp. *enero hermano junco jornal Elvira gente* (from *yente* with *ye* from Ĕ). Ptg. *janeiro irmão junco jornal gente* (with original *g*) *junho.* Cat. *gener germà gent junc jorn joc*
Weak		- y				t j	Sp. *rey saeta vaina reina treinta peor.* Ptg. *rei rainha trinta peior.* Cat. *rei trinta veina pitjor*

Latin	Romance	Spanish dialects	Sp.	Ptg.	Cat.	Examples

CONSONANTS (continued)

Consonantal Groups

PL CL FL
Initial — pl cl fl — {pl cl fl / pll, etc. / x ts ch / y} — ll / ll l — ch — pl cl fl

PL: Moz. *plantain plâna.* Ribagorza *pllorar pllaza.* Arag. *plorar.* Leon. *xano.* Sp. *chopo* (western loan-word). Sp. *llorar llantén llano* but *placer.* Ptg. *chão chantagem* but *prazer.* Cat. *pla plantatge*
CL: Rib. *cllaro.* Arag. *claro.* Leon. *xamado xosa.* Astur. *tsabe.* Sp. *llamar llave* but *clavo claro.* Ptg. *chamar chave* but *cravar cravo.* Cat. *clamar*
FL: Rib. *fllama.* Arag. *flama.* Leon. *Xainiz.* Sp. *llama hallar Llambla* but *Lambra Laínez lacio* and *flor flaco flojo.* Ptg. *chama achar Chaves cheiro* but OPtg. *frol* MPtg. *flor frouxo.* Cat. *flama*

After *m n* / Medial — — — ch / ll — ch / ch — {pl / cl / fl}

Sp. *ancho hinchar henchir.* Ptg. *encher.* Cat. *omplir.* Sp. *resollar allegar.* Ptg. *achegar.* Cat. *aplegar*

BL GL
Initial — bl — bl — bl — br — bl

Sp. *blando blanco.* Ptg. *brando branco.* Cat. *blanc*

— gl — gl l — gl l — gr — gl

Sp. *landre lirón latir* but *gloria.* OPtg. *grolia*

Weak — bl — bll bl — ll — br — ul

Rib. *dobllar.* Sp. *trillar chillar* but *hablar.* Ptg. *obrigado* but *falar.* Cat. *faula*

TL CL GL — tl cl gl — ll y — j — lh — ll

Moz. *welyo.* Leon. Arag. *uello viello.* Sp. *ojo oreja conejo viejo hinojo teja reja* but *siglo.* Ptg. *olho relha rolha serralha velho governalho coalha abelha.* Cat. *ull abella rella*

QU — qu c — — cu c — qu c — qu c

Sp. *cuando cuarenta cuajar ca catorce quedo quien.* Ptg. *quando quarenta quedo quem.* Cat. *quan quiet catorze*

Latin	Rom-ance	Spanish dialects	Sp.	Ptg.	Cat.	Examples
ONSONANTS (continued)						
CT ULT	ct lt	ct χt ht it	ch	it	it lt	Moz. *noχte truḥta laḥtairuela leiterola.* Arag. *feito peito muito mucho.* Leon. *confaita leito feichu muito.* Sp. *noche trucha lecho pechar mucho ocho lechuga hecho.* Ptg. *feito leito leite muito.* Cat. *fet nit llit vuit* but *molt*
X CS PS ULS			x > j s	ix is	(i)x s ls	Sp. *dejar mejilla cojo seis fresno caja pujar soso.* Ptg. *deixar eixo frouxo coixa seis puxar ensôsso.* Cat. *cuixa sis caixa pols*
Initial			s	s	s	Sp. *salterio.* Orthographic *ps = s*
SĊ		ç	ç	sç x	ç ix	Sp. *ciencia centella mecer peces.* Ptg. *sciência mexer peixes.* Cat. *centella peixes pèixer.*
ST		ç	z			Moz. Sp. *Zaragoza Écija mozárabe*
Yod	bį		bi	bi	ig	Sp. *rubio.* Cat. *roig*
	apį		ep	aib		Sp. *sepa quepa.* Ptg. *saiba caiba*
	cį tį		z > [θ]	ç	- ss	Sp. *razón pozo pereza.* Ptg. *razão juizo Galiza.* Cat. *raó perea menassa*
	after cons.		ç > z	ç	ç	Sp. *fuerza verguenza cazar tercero.* Ptg. *força caçar terceiro.* Cat. *força calça tercer*
	dį gį		y -	i	j tj ig	Sp. *rayo poyo correa.* Ptg. *raio meio corrêia.* Cat. *raig mig puig major corretja*
	after cons.		ç			OSp. *orçuelo berça goço.* MSp. *z [θ]*
	lį	li ll y	j	lh	ll	Moz. Leon. Arag. *fillo muller.* Sp. *hija mujer ijada paja majuelo hoja mejor.* Ptg. *filho folha melhor palha molher.* Cat. *fil muller*
	mnį nį ndį		ñ	nh	ny	Sp. *caloña señor.* Ptg. *senhor Espanha aranha vergonha.* Cat. *senyor vergonya*
	arį	air eir er	er	eir	er	See under vowels, above
	erį	eir er				Sp. *madera.* Ptg. *madeira*
	orį	oir	uer	oir our	ur(i)	See under vowels, above

Latin	Rom-ance	Spanish dialects	Sp.	Ptg.	Cat.	Examples
CONSONANTS (continued)						
Yod	asi̯		es	eij	es	Sp. *besar beso.* Ptg. *beijar.* Cat. *bes*
	ssi̯	x	x>j	ix	(i)x	Sp. *bajar rojo.* Ptg. *baixar roxo.* Cat. *baixar*
	sci̯ } sti̯	x	ç	x	x	Moz. *faša.* Leon. Arag. *faxa.* Ptg. *faixa enxada.* Cat. *axada faixa.* Sp. *hacinas haza azada mozo.* OSp. *uço*
NĠ	ng		nz ñ	ng nh	nz ny	Sp. *uncir reñir lueñe.* Ptg. *renhida longe.* Cat. *senzill renyir*
MB ND	mb nd	mb m nd	n m nd	mb nd	m n	Leon. *palomba lombo.* Arag. *paloma lomo demanar.* Sp. *paloma lomo demandar andar.* Ptg. *pomba lombo demandar andar.* Cat. *coloma llom demanar anar ona*
MN	mn	ñ	ñ	n	ny	Sp. *daño dueño otoño.* Ptg. *dano outono.* Cat. *dany*
GN	gn	ñ	ñ	nh	ny	Sp. *tamaño leña.* Ptg. *tamanho lenha conhecer.* Cat. *leny*
NGL	ngl	ñ	ñ	nh	ngl	Sp. *uña.* OSp. *seños.* MSp. *sendos.* Ptg. *unha senhos sendos.* Cat. *ungla sengles*
NF	ff		ff nf	ff nf	nf	OSp. OPtg. *iffante.* MSp. MPtg. *infante*
NS	s		s	s	s	Sp. Ptg. Cat. *mes mesa.* Cat. *Anfos*
TR DR GR Weak			dr gr r	dr gr ir	dr gr i	Sp. *padre negro entero pereza cadera.* Ptg. *padre negro enteiro cadeira.* Cat. *pare Pere pedra enter cadera*
RS	ss	ss	s	ss	ss	Sp. *oso suso coso tieso quiés* (popular). Ptg. *pêssego travessia almoço.* Cat. *dos bossa mossegar colors* (pron. *s*)

SOME ROMANCE GROUPS

Examples

ml mr and Sp. *mr* ⟨*mn*	Sp. *hombre hembra hombro cohom-bro rambla semblar.* Ptg. *homem femea cogombro ombro semblagem.* Cat. *om femella cambra semblar*
nr ñr lr	Sp. *tierno viernes tendrá pondré* (OSp. *porné verrá) prenda saldré valdré.* Ptg. *tenro terei prenda sairei valerei.* Cat. *tendre gendre pondré saldré*
rl sl sn nl	In infinitive: OSp. *rogalle.* MSp. *rogar-le.* Ptg. *enviâ-lo.* In finite verb: Sp. *vámonos.* Ptg. *procuramo-lo.* Preposi-tions: Leon. OCast. *eno cono pelo.* Ptg. *no pelo.* Ptg. *todolos*
nm	Sp. Ptg. *alma*
tl dl tn dn	Sp. *tilde espalda cabildo rienda candado.* OSp. and classical Sp. *dalde dandos.* MSp. *dadle dadnos.* Cat. *títol espatlla motlle*
bd	Leon. *dulda belda.* Sp. *deudo.* Ptg. *beudo bébado*
dg	Leon. *julgar -algo.* Sp. *juzgar -azgo*
çt çd	OSp. *aztor.* Sp. *azor amistad rezar.* Ptg. *amizade rezar praço*
str	Popular Sp. *nueso.* Ptg. *nosso*
Epenthesis	Sp. *manzana ponzoña comenzar mensajero mancilla monzón ren-glón.* OSp. *alguandre -mientre*

INDICES

I. *RERUM*

II. NOMINUM

III. *VERBORUM*

(a) *Spanish, Portuguese and Catalan*

350 INDICES

24

(b) Basque

[a. See also under h]
-a 23, 24
a(h)ate 19
aita 18, 20, 23, 24, 32
aitzinean 25
ala 25
alaba 28
andi 30
andre 18, 32
antzar 19
ap(h)ezpiku 19
ar- 25
ara 26, 28, 39
aragi 32
ardit 34
ardum 32
arima 19
artu 23
asto 19
asturu 19
atxeter 19

b- 23, 28
ba, bai 23, 25, 28
bage 18, 23, 30
bai 26
baizikan 32
bake 19
banintz 23
barka(tzen) 32
bat(zu) 25
bederatzi 25
bei 34
belaterra 32
bere, bere, burua 25
berri 17, 26, 30, 34
berrogei 18, 25
besta 19
bezela 32
bi, biga 25
bigarren 25
bizar 34
borondate 19, 32
boronte 19
bortz, bost 25

d- 20, 22
da 20, 23, 28
dabe 22
ditue 22

doa 21
dot 22
draukat 30
du, dut 20, 22

[e. See also under h]
e- 23
edin 32
edo 25
egin 30, 32
egon 32
egun 32
e(h)un 25
ek(h)arri 17, 18, 22, 36
eman 30, 32
erda, erdera 28
erori, -ko, -tzen 23, 32
errege 17, 19, 32, 36
erreinu 32
esker 17
eskola 19
eta 24, 25
et(h)orri 17, 30, 32, 36
etxe 15, 17, 26, 34
euki, eduki 22, 32
ez 23, 25, 32
ezker 17, 34, 65
ezta 23

g- 22
gabe=bage
gaitz 32
gana 23
gara 28
gari 32
-garren 25
gaur 32
gauza 19
gisuarri 34
gorputz 19
gorri 26
gu 22, 25, 30, 32
gure 23, 24, 32
gurutz 19

[No aspirate in Spanish Basque]
h- 22
hamabi 25
hamaika 25
hamar 25

han 25
hari 17
hartz 18
haur 17
hemen 25
herri 15, 17
hi 25
hirur 18
hirurogei 18
hogei 18, 25

[i. See also under h]
i- 23, 28
ibaiko 34
ibiltze 23
-ik 28
ik(h)usi, -ko, ik(h)usten 17, 23, 36
ildu 28
ioan, joan 22, 30
iri, ili 17, 18, 26, 28, 29, 39
ixker 17
izan 23
izen 32
izoki 18

jaun, jaungoikoa 32
jon 22

-k 22, 24, 28
kanto(in) 34
-ke 23
-ki 22
kide 28
-ko 23, 25

-la, -lako 23, 28
lau(r) 25
laurogei 18, 25
lege 19
len(engo) 25
libra(tu) 32
liburu 19
lur 32

maitatu, maitatzen 20
mediku 19
mezpera 18
mila 25
miriku 19

n- 22; -n- 22; -n 23, 28
ña, na 22
naba 9, 33
nekarren, see ek(h)arri
ni 23, 25
nioan, see ioan
nor 25, 30

[o. See also under h]
ogi 32
-oi 26, 28
on 25, 30
opus 19
ori 25
ork(h)atz 18
ortzi 32
otz 26, 28, 30

pake 19
pizar 34

-ra 18, 28

saldi 35
santifikatu 32
sarna 34
sei 25
seme 19

-t 22
ta 25
-te 22, 23
tentazio 32
toi 28
-tu 23
txakur 34
-tze 23

ur 17, 28, 32
utzi 32

z-, -z-, -z 22, 29
zaldi 19, 35
zamari 19
zati 34
zaudena 23, 32
zazpi 25
zekor 34
zen 25
zentsu 19
zer 25
zeru, zeruetan 19, 23
  32
zor 32
zordun 32
zortzi 25
zu 22, 25, 30
zugur 34
zure 32